MEDICAL SPEECH PATHOLOGY

Robert M. Miller, PhD
Chief,
Audiology and Speech Pathology Service
Seattle VA Medical Center
Seattle, Washington

Michael E. Groher, PhD
Assistant Chief
Audiology/Speech Pathology Service
New York VA Medical Center
New York, New York

AN ASPEN PUBLICATION®
Aspen Publishers, Inc.
Rockville, Maryland
1990

Library of Congress Cataloging-in-Publication Data

Miller, Robert M. (Robert Michael), 1946- .
Medical speech pathology/Robert M. Miller, Michael E. Groher.
p. cm.
"An Aspen publication."
Includes bibliographical references.
ISBN: 0-8342-0112-7
1. Speech therapy. I. Groher, Michael E. II. Title.
[DNLM: 1. Speech Disorders--diagnosis. 2. Speech Disorders--rehabilitation.
3. Speech Pathology--organization & administration. WM 475 M649m]
RC423.M555   1990   616.85'5--dc20   DNLM/DLC
for Library of Congress
89-17787
CIP

The authors have made every effort to ensure the accuracy of the information herein, particularly with regard to drug selection and dose. However, appropriate information sources should be consulted, especially for new or unfamiliar drugs or procedures. It is the responsibility of every practitioner to evaluate the appropriateness of a particular opinion in the context of actual clinical situations and with due consideration to new developments. Authors, editors, and the publisher cannot be held responsible for any typographical or other errors found in this book.

Editorial Services: Ruth Bloom

Library of Congress Catalog Card Number: 89-17787
ISBN: 0-8342-0112-7

Printed in the United States of America

1 2 3 4 5

To Nance and Leslie,
and Andrew, Lindsey, Logan, Casey,
and Grant . . . for your sacrifices
and patience.

To our parents
for their lifelong love and support.

Table of Contents

Preface

We grew up not more than six blocks apart, and while he (Bob) consistently claims, and I (Michael) categorically deny, that he made a living from hitting left-handers (me) in our hometown Little League, I have almost forgiven him enough to combine on this book some 30 years later. And even though we attended the same secondary schools, university, and post-master's training program, our career decisions that ended in employment within the Department of Veterans Affairs medical system were made independently without mutual consultation. This fortunate coincidence of circumstance has given us an admittedly biased N of 2 in sharing an analysis of our perspectives of speech/language pathologists entering and ultimately surviving in a medical community that seemingly has just begun to understand the need for, and impact of, our services. Our hope is that similar experience will not cast a negative bias, but will be compensated in the adage that "two heads are better than one," allowing the provision of a more comprehensive and detailed discussion than either of us alone could accomplish.

Our intention is to provide the reader with not only a basic orientation to the practice of speech/language pathology in a medical setting, but to provide by detailed example some new perspectives in meeting the diagnostic and treatment challenges that are particular to the medical environment. Our philosophy of practice comes from three sources: (1) what we have learned about politics and peaceful coexistence in the medical world and its perception of the role of speech/language pathology as a specialty, (2) what we have learned that has allowed us to compete in a setting that we were not fully trained to enter, and (3) how we have come to adapt our academic training and combine it with some practical applications of medicine. It is an effort to define more clearly and, in some cases, to expand our roles in the hope of becoming more useful and therefore more recognized participants in the treatment of hospitalized patients. This task will require that we explore how our unique talents can be utilized more fully.

We were not motivated to provide a reorganization of well-known facts concerning the anatomy and physiology of communication, its pathology, or details of treatment. Rather we emphasize the application of this knowledge in solving problems seen most often in medical settings. In a sense it is an attempt to present the art within the art form. Hopefully it will be viewed as a departure from our over-reliance on prescriptive diagnostic and treatment approaches. The loss of flexibility that accompanies such approaches only serves to alienate our profession from the mainstream of hospital practice that adapts to the patient's current, not textbook, needs. The style and content are departures from the usual professional text. While we may sound pedantic (read "narrow") at times, we recognize and welcome the fact that we do not have all of the answers. Our expectation is that experienced clinicians will challenge points of philosophy and expressed opinions. If the book serves to stimulate such discussion, requiring you to reflect on your own practice and preconceptions, then we have achieved part of our goal.

We have written this book with the deliberate intention of providing a solid framework of reference for not only beginning clinicians who may choose to practice in a medical setting, but for advanced clinicians who might need to solidify their own perspectives and who might be willing to assume new ones. Hopefully they will share it in their teaching of new interns. It is our intent to involve beginning students early in their training, attract those who may be considering employment in a medical environment, and attempt to give them early guidance and direction that we wish had been given to us prior to beginning our first job assignments. Clinicians who may not be in contact with the medical community on a daily basis will find this volume an important reference and source for expanding their philosophical approaches to diagnosis and treatment. We think it is the rare speech/language pathologist who can ignore contact with issues that are medically based, whether in a report from a community hospital concerning a child's recent hospitalization, in a summary from a school nurse about medications whose side effects may impact on communication, or in a referral from a psychiatric social worker who seeks an evaluation of language to differentiate between linguistic delay or psychiatric disturbance.

It has occurred to us that the title, *Medical Speech Pathology,* may be redundant since the discipline of speech pathology is a science that emanates from medical knowledge, concepts, and approaches. In fact, our patients most often evidence disorders of communication secondary to medical complications, and fluctuations in health do have a direct impact on communication effectiveness. It is necessary, therefore, to become intimately familiar with primary medical processes as they relate to, and in some cases dictate, the approach one might utilize in managing any compromise to communication.

In spite of our intended close association with medical science we are not a visible, equal part of it down in the trenches. Agreement among practicing professionals apropos to this point is inescapable and has far-reaching implications for future staffing and funding patterns, because the importance of your contribution in health care is based, in part, on the perceived importance of your contribution to the maintenance of health. The ability to communicate is one of our most cherished skills as humans. Curiously, the inability to communicate has never received an established importance in reimbursement, because it is not a primary disease but usually a consequence of a disease. It is understandable that the speech and hearing sciences must struggle to compete for resources with acute medical concerns, such as maintenance of the basic biologic supports for life. However, they also compete with less acute medically based problems, such as those seen routinely by the general surgeon, ophthalmologist, gastroenterologist, neurologist, and dermatologist, that have less severe consequences than the failure to communicate.

The discrepancies are ascribed most easily to the fact that the speech/language pathologist and other so-called allied health professionals (even this term suggests a certain separation of importance) do not hold M.D. degrees and, by implication, do not have the background and training to be equal partners in overall contributions to health care. Our contention, from which the established need for this book emanates, is that the role the speech/language pathologist plays on the low rung of the ladder is largely the result of our inability to demonstrate to the medical community our real worth, not only with chronic or secondary medical complications but with those problems involving the acutely ill, such as dysphagic patients, or patients who temporarily cannot communicate due to severe respiratory illness.

Our failure to demonstrate our stature in the medical community is partly due to the lack of program emphasis at training institutions in the preparation of students to compete successfully as speech/language pathologists in a medical environment. Perceived lack of training leads to fear of interacting as equal partners with physicians. Unsure of our knowledge, we avoid the very situations we need to educate our medical colleagues about the role of the medical speech/language pathologist. In most cases it is not that clinicians lack the knowledge, but that they fail to recognize how that knowledge might fit into the moment. This book speaks directly to that need.

Most academic institutions are not offering training specific to employment in medical settings, because certification requirements for practice will not allow a student to concentrate on any one area in depth during a two-year master's program. However, philosophies of training should evolve to prepare students better before they enter medical and nonmedical settings. Retrospectively we have come to realize, as we teach our students, that they are unanimous in mistaken perceptions of communication disorders existing outside of other biologic, sociologic, and psychologic functions and physiologic systems. They tend to see direct interaction only with the traditional communicative partners of respiration, articulation, phonation, and language and do not consider how these will be affected by a leg or urinary tract infection, an increased heart rate, or a situational depression. Examples are plentiful of beginning clinicians' lack of understanding between knowledge of how a system works and the potential effects on communication when that system is damaged. We continue to be amazed and somewhat embarrassed (but still empathetic) by this situation because we remember our own predicament. For instance, it is not unusual for the beginning clinician not to understand that dysarthria could be a consequence of something other than cerebral palsy, or that the resonance characteristics of a patient with a cleft palate may be the same as those of another patient with a defective velum secondary to lower motor neuron disease. These misperceptions come from our penchant to separate disorders from the system, rather than to teach the system and all potential consequences to communication that can result from damage to that system. We hope that some of these issues will become less consequential as a result of this book.

Underlying our approach in managing patients with communication disorders seen most often in a hospital setting is the concept that for most patients physicians are in the forefront of entry into the system. Therefore, they are in a position to control the services any given patient receives for any given condition. Skillfully educating physicians to the understanding of the benefits a speech/language pathologist can provide to their patients will be achieved only if the speech/language pathologist first can thoroughly learn, rather than ignore, the world of medicine. This will include not only familiarity with medical terminology and the function of each medical discipline, but an understanding of how we can interface our training to be consonant with medical procedures and expectations. In this way we will continue to support and build our stature not only as speech/language pathologists, but for the field of communication sciences in general.

It should be noted that all examples of patients and case records have been altered to maintain patient confidentiality.

Acknowledgment

We would like to express our appreciation for the expert guidance in our training that was provided by Dr. George L. Larsen. His creativity and vision for our field provided the inspiration for this book.

Part I

The Medical Model

Chapter 1

The Medical Center

INTRODUCTION

The role of the speech/language pathologist in a medical setting often is dependent on the type of setting in which that person is employed and on the perceptions of the employer regarding the duties and responsibilities expected from graduates with an advanced degree in the field. For instance, speech/language pathologists working in long-term care facilities will have different perspectives on their roles than those working in acute care facilities. Similarly, employers may feel that the role of a speech/language pathologist is one of a "therapist," dealing primarily in the rehabilitative aspects of communication and little with the diagnosis of disorders. Different physical settings and popular perceptions of the role of speech/language pathologists always will impact on how they perform their jobs in the medical environment. The successful medically oriented speech/language pathologist will recognize these differences, tailor his or her expertise to the setting, and develop a role that is consistent with training and background. The institution will play a major role in developing responsibilities according to its patient population and its resources, but the medical speech/language pathologist also should take an aggressive role in educating the institution regarding the potential areas of expertise and programs available from those trained in the communication sciences. How a speech/language pathologist can establish a useful role in the medical community and attain its respect is a common theme in this book. Also, how a speech/language pathologist can be utilized most effectively as part of a health care team is demonstrated. Details relating to the definition of the importance of the speech/language pathologist in a medical setting are presented in Chapters 2 and 3.

TYPES OF MEDICAL SETTINGS

Not every medical setting that has patients with communication dysfunction will find it prudent to hire a speech/language pathologist. The institution might find it beneficial to refer its communication-impaired patients to another facility. If the institution employs a speech/language pathologist, it may have in mind a specific function that is dependent on the inherent structure of the setting. The patient population of the institution often may define some specialized roles for the speech/language pathologist. For instance, the duties of a speech/language pathologist working primarily with problems of geriatric medicine in a long-term care facility might be very diverse compared with those of a speech/language pathologist working in a hospital that manages a large population with traumatic injuries, where the population may be younger and the issues of medical care more acute. Not only will specific individual responsibilities be dependent on the setting, but the speech/language pathologist will interact with medical colleagues in different specialties. In some circumstances the speech/language pathologist may spend a great deal of time with the dietitian if the two specialties concentrate on working with patients who evidence swallowing dysfunction. In other settings the speech/language pathologist may work closely with an otolaryngologist (head and neck surgeon) or a neurologist, or even work more with volunteers and families of the communication-impaired than with nurses.

To be successful in any of these interactions, the speech/language pathologist must not only educate colleagues to the role in general, but must be able to tailor his or her performance to the situation and to the interacting discipline. For example, the type and amount of information given to an otolaryngologist on a consult reply may be necessarily different in scope and design than the reply given to a neurologist. Both are physicians, but they may ask for different information and respond differently to what is provided by the speech/language pathologist. Sensitivity to this issue is vitally important in establishing a viable role for the speech/language pathologist who practices in a medical setting.

Medical and Surgical Hospitals

Hospitals can be organized and categorized in a number of ways: (1) by the monetary support they receive (private, nonprofit, or for profit), (2) by their orientation (community service, teaching, or commercial), or (3) by the patient services they offer (general services or specialty services, such as pediatrics or cardiology). Some of these categories often overlap. Most hospitals, regardless of classification, provide general medical and surgical services. In this context, *medical* refers to services that require an internist or family practice physician who is qualified to treat such illnesses as hypertension and diabetes. *Surgical* refers to services provided by a surgeon, such as an appendectomy or a hernia repair. Both types of services typically are provided at small community-based facilities that have under 100 hospital beds with few support staff. These hospitals may not employ full-time speech/language pathologists but utilize their services as consultants.

Specialty Services

Adding specialized surgical services, such as those provided by an otolaryngologist or a neurosurgeon, expands the scope of a hospital and potentially increases its need for other services that may include neurology, speech/language pathology, and audiology. If a hospital is committed to expanding its medical services, it might add other specialists, such as a cardiologist and a gastroenterologist. In general, the closer a hospital gets to acquiring a full complement of specialty services, the more likely it will employ staff speech/language pathologists.

Acute Care Services

Acute care can be defined as a stage in an individual's medical care where symptoms are severe and the duration of the immediate illness is short. Hospitals equipped with emergency room facilities offer acute medical care. Their primary mission may be to diagnose and treat patients only in the acute stages of illness, but leave any future rehabilitation, convalescence, or needed outpatient visits to another facility. The role of the acute care setting is to return the patient as quickly as possible to a medically stable condition. Basically, this includes stabilization of the patient's life support systems, including, but not limited to, the heart, lungs, liver, and kidneys. In selected cases, the acute setting may perform only diagnostic tests and transfer the patient to another facility for treatment not available at the original admitting facility. For instance, it may be determined in a facility's emergency room that the patient is in need of neurosurgery. Transfer of the patient is then warranted if the institution does not support that specialty, or if it is predicted that the patient eventually will need more services than the admitting facility is capable of providing. The length of time a patient is hospitalized in an acute care setting averages less than one week.

Acute care patients usually are managed in specially equipped intensive care units (ICUs). These units may be further divided into medical intensive care units (MICUs), cardiac care units (CCUs), and surgical intensive care units (SICUs). The main goal of acute care is to provide medical stability followed by discharge, rather than the treatment of any residual disability secondary to the illness. The use of full-time services of a speech/language pathologist in this setting may be limited. However, patients who need to remain in an acute care setting for longer than a week because of the uncertainty of their illness may require the diagnostic and rehabilitative services of a speech/language pathologist. Those who cannot swallow or communicate their basic needs are especially appropriate candidates.

Intermediate Care Services

Intermediate care services are those the patient receives while hospitalized that are still required after medical stability has been achieved. Most often these services are needed to assist the patient in adjusting to his or her former life-style. They can range from rehabilitation following stroke or a surgical procedure to specific types of medical treatments, such as certain antibiotic therapies, radiation therapy, and chemotherapy, that require supervision by hospital specialists. Speech/language pathology is an integral part of the rehabilitation effort, and hospitals with intermediate care services utilize the services of a speech/language pathologist.

Chronic Care Services

Chronic care can be defined as services that a hospital offers beyond those provided to ensure medical stability from an acute illness and beyond those needed for the immediate rehabilitation of an illness. The nature of the illness often determines the provision of chronic care. It treats those illnesses that are stable medically or that have achieved maximum effects from intermediate rehabilitative care. Chronic care is often characterized by treatment of an illness with a slowly progressive downhill course, but one not severe enough to require hospitalization of the patient or acute enough to benefit the patient by further direct rehabilitative support. Many chronic care services are provided during regular visits to outpatient clinics or by visits of health care personnel to patients' homes. At any time during chronic illness, patients may require the support of acute or intermediate care services. Many hospitals attempt to combine acute, intermediate, and chronic care support to their patients in order to provide better continuity of care. Such institutions frequently are interested in employing the services of a medical speech/language pathologist.

Major Teaching Hospitals

Teaching hospitals have affiliations with medical schools and other university programs that educate people in the medical professions. Faculties of university programs and hospital staffs cooperate in offering curriculums of medical training that are beneficial to the respective parties. These affiliations usually are established with hospitals that offer a full range of basic and special medical services at the acute, intermediate, and chronic levels of care.

Specialized Centers

Some medical facilities are designated and equipped to manage selective populations of patients, for instance, hospitals or clinics that provide only rehabilitative medicine services offered to those who need intensive physical, communication, and occupational remediation. Other centers may offer both inpatient and outpatient services to special groups, such as patients with cerebral palsy and childhood developmental disabilities or patients recovering from traumatic brain injury. Most general medical and surgical coverage in these specialized centers is done on a consultative or part-time staff basis. Other centers with larger bed capacity employ a limited number of full-time physicians in addition to a full complement of rehabilitation specialists, including speech/language pathologists.

Extended Care Facilities

Commonly referred to as nursing homes, extended care facilities are designed to manage the medical problems of older persons who suffer from chronic illnesses and who usually require 24-hour medical supervision for an extended period of time. The levels of care in these facilities can range from minimal supervision, such as monitoring of medication intake, to more sophisticated care that includes total management of toileting, feeding, dressing, and other activities of daily living. Because patients in these facilities have a high incidence of communication and swallowing impairment,[1] there is a recognized need for the services of speech/ language pathologists. If the institution is large enough, these services may be provided on a full-time, rather than consultative, basis. General medical and surgical coverage usually is provided by consultants, but most patient needs are met by the nursing staff. When acute medical problems arise, patients often must be transferred to local acute care centers, both for diagnosis and treatment. Some extended care facilities have special bed sections to handle acute medical needs.

Many of the specialty medical services that traditionally work closely with speech/language pathologists, such as neurology and otolaryngology, are not readily accessible in the extended care setting. Speech/language pathologists often must make some modifications in their approach to communication management. For instance, they may have to take a more active role in the identification of communication disorders, because they may not be able to rely on the traditional steady source of referrals from these medical specialists. In practice, speech/language pathologists may need to be more aggressive in their screening of patients with suspected communication dysfunction who may require examination by an otolaryngologist or neurologist. This is particularly true when a speech/language pathologist is employed full time in an extended care facility and must rely on medical consultants for supportive diagnostic and treatment services.

Consultative Services

Speech/language pathologists who are self-employed may be hired as consultants by hospitals, clinics, specialized rehabilitation centers, and extended care facilities. They also may service these areas through association with a major medical center that extends its services to smaller institutions. In these circumstances speech/language pathologists often provide services based on demand. The services may be provided at the medical centers or in the private offices of speech/language pathologists. Consultant speech/language pathologists who are not employed full time in any one particular setting must rely on the full-time staffs of client institutions for referrals. Education of the staffs relative to the identification of appropriate candidates for evaluation is a major responsibility of the speech/language pathologist who travels from center to center as a private practitioner.

MEDICAL CENTER ORGANIZATION

Most major teaching hospitals have a full complement of professional and nonprofessional services. This type of organization serves as a model for discussion in this section. Not every service of the hospital is discussed in detail; however, the services with which the speech/language pathologist may have the most interactions are highlighted. In general, the hospital staff can be divided broadly into services that provide direct medical care and those that provide indirect support to the medical care.

Indirect Medical Care

A schematic diagram of departments that provide support to direct medical care services is presented in Figure 1–1. The hospital director has ultimate responsibility of the direct and indirect medical care of patients, but is usually not involved in direct patient care. The director need not be a physician, but frequently is trained in hospital and business administration. Usually the director is responsible to a governing body of selected trustees or to a central, government-regulated authority. It is the director's job to ensure quality medical care at the best possible price. Duties include constant monitoring of the medical and nonmedical services and coordinating the efforts and resources of both.

The director's office is usually supported by related services that assist in daily activities. These may include an automated data processing unit (ADP) with the responsibility of organizing hospital data in permanent records for purposes of observing trends in patient care practices. The data will include information on the quality of care received by patients and on the cost of services. The data are used to structure the hospital's short- and long-range goals and needs. Attention to fair hiring practices and a program of affirmative action and upward mobility in employment opportunity are the responsibilities of the hospital's equal opportunity section (EEO), whose main support and credibility come from the director's office. This section may be organized as part of the personnel department.

The director's office often organizes, participates in, and oversees special hospital committees. In general, the committees' tasks include studies of medical and nonmedical problems in the medical center, recommendation of changes in policy, and approval of changes in policy developed by other committees. Committees usually are composed of department heads who have particular expertise in the matters covered by the committees. Examples of typical committees include

- a clinical executive board, usually composed of department heads who deal with medical issues
- a committee on position management, usually composed of representatives from nonmedical disciplines and one representative from the medical disciplines

INDIRECT PATIENT CARE SERVICES

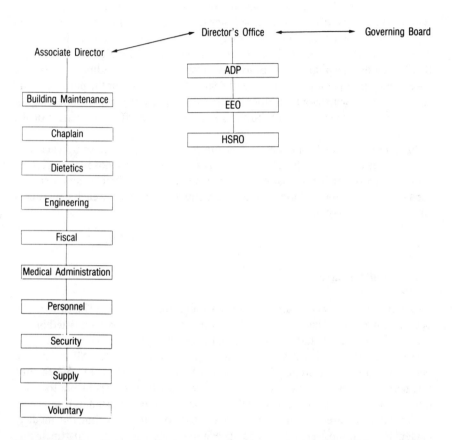

Figure 1–1 Indirect Patient Care Services—example of the organization of hospital departments providing indirect or supportive services.

- an education committee, usually composed of a broad spectrum of hospital occupations
- a budget committee, usually composed of representatives from the nonmedical staff with one or two representatives from the major medical departments

Other committees may have more specific clinical charges and may include a tumor board, geriatric committee, infection control committee, and nutrition committee.

The associate hospital director is responsible for the daily operation of departments that furnish indirect medical services. Building maintenance, dietetics (although this may be a medical responsibility), engineering, medical administration, and personnel departments, among others, may report directly to the associate director. Of these services, the speech/language pathologist is most likely to come into contact with dietetics on issues involving swallowing-impaired patients and with medical administration because it has responsibility for organizing and storing patients' medical records. Frequently, medical administration must send records to other medical institutions and request needed information related to a patient's previous hospitalization. Individuals responsible for the administration of a speech/language pathology service will deal with personnel for the purpose of hiring employees, with supply to order supplies and equipment, with engineering for equipment maintenance, and with the fiscal or finance office in matters of the budget.

In times of financial containment in health care spending, the hospital's accounting department has more direct contact with each section in the hospital. In particular this department is responsible, with guidance from the director and associate director, for devising methods to measure the revenue earned by each department in contrast to its cost of operation.

Direct Medical Care

Direct medical services are organized through the chief of staff's office. The department and sections that generally report to the chief of staff are listed in Figure 1–2. The chief of staff holds an M.D. degree and frequently rises to this position through distinguished service as a major department head. All issues that pertain to patient care are the responsibility of the chief of staff. In a VA facility, this person is supported by two assistants. One assistant is responsible for coordinating the continuing education of the staff, and the other assistant is responsible for monitoring research and development (R&D) activity within the medical center. Because most audiology and speech/language pathology departments report either directly or indirectly to the chief of staff and provide direct patient care services, certain details about the organization of the departments involved in direct patient care activities follows. An understanding of this organization is important, because different disciplines may not relate to the speech/language pathologist in the same way.

First, perceptions of the role of the speech/language pathologist may differ because various disciplines may or may not have had much exposure to speech/language pathology. For instance, the neurologist is most likely to be very familiar with the background and training of the speech/language pathologist, whereas the specialist in endocrinology may have had infrequent contacts. Familiarity with professional roles can influence the number of requests received for services, because individuals unfamiliar with the services offered by a speech/language pathologist may fail to refer a patient who needs the services.

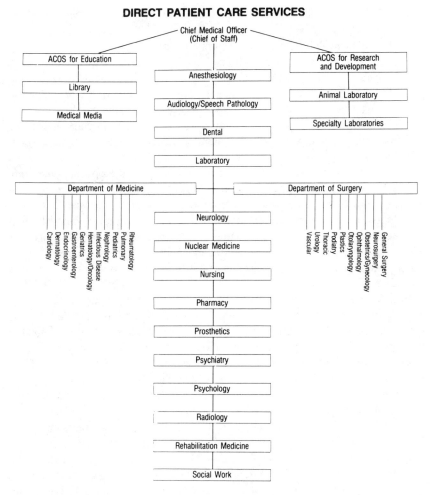

DIRECT PATIENT CARE SERVICES

Chief Medical Officer
(Chief of Staff)

ACOS for Education

Library

Medical Media

Anesthesiology

Audiology/Speech Pathology

Dental

Laboratory

ACOS for Research
and Development

Animal Laboratory

Specialty Laboratories

Department of Medicine

Cardiology
Dermatology
Endocrinology
Gastroenterology
Geriatrics
Hematology/Oncology
Infectious Disease
Nephrology
Pediatrics
Pulmonary
Rheumatology

Neurology

Nuclear Medicine

Nursing

Pharmacy

Prosthetics

Psychiatry

Psychology

Radiology

Rehabilitation Medicine

Social Work

Department of Surgery

Vascular
Urology
Thoracic
Podiatry
Plastics
Otolaryngology
Ophthalmology
Obstetrics/Gynecology
Neurosurgery
General Surgery

Figure 1–2 Direct Patient Care Services—example of organization.

Second, basic knowledge of the roles of the various medical specialties is help-ful because it can aid the speech/language pathologist in the development of diag-nostic evaluations and subsequent reports of findings. For instance, a request for a diagnostic evaluation received from the infectious disease service on a patient who has been diagnosed as having AIDS (acquired immunodeficiency syndrome)-related complex (ARC) would present a different diagnostic dilemma than receiv-ing a consult on a cardiology patient. All possible systemic and neurologic compli-cations of ARC would have to be reviewed in order to plan a thorough evaluation. A consult request from cardiology probably is concerned with voice, because post-surgery patients may evidence peripheral damage to cranial nerve 10 or have compromised respiration due to poor cardiac status. Similarly, a consult received from a gastroenterologist most likely would be concerned with an evaluation of the patient's ability to swallow, not ability to communicate.

Third, if a speech/language pathologist is interested in increasing the number of referred patients, knowledge of the types of patients seen by each specialty is important. A practical example is an understanding of the role of the oncologist, a specialist who treats tumors. An oncologist may see many patients with communication dysfunction secondary to their diseases but not think to consult with the speech/language pathologist, because interaction between the two services is not that common.

Fourth, the medical speech/language pathologist may see patients who complain of specific medical problems during the course of treatment for their communication disorders. They often make these complaints to the speech/language pathologist, because they consider that individual the only professional who will take the time needed to decode complaints. Therefore, a basic understanding of the appropriate discipline to consult for assistance with a patient's complaint is possible if the clinician is knowledgeable about the role and function of the other specialties.

Finally, knowledge of the responsibilities of other direct patient care services is important in understanding the political atmosphere of hospital life. Various specialties have different perspectives on the approaches they take in managing their patients. These perspectives can influence how long a patient stays in the hospital and what types of consultative services the patient will receive. If the philosophy of the psychiatry department includes the belief that a patient who stutters does so because of a psychiatric illness, the chances are minimal that the speech/language pathologist will evaluate that patient. If the resident on the medicine service focuses only on treating the patient's high blood pressure following a stroke, then perhaps that patient will not be referred immediately for needed physical and communication rehabilitation. How the speech/language pathologist identifies and reacts to these differences to improve his or her own practice is discussed more fully in Chapters 2 and 3. Following is a brief summary of the major hospital departments that provide direct medical care. The two largest, and therefore the strongest politically, are the departments of medicine and surgery.

Medicine

The department of medicine may be composed of as many as 11 subspecialties (refer to Figure 1–2). Most of these are concerned with the maintenance of the internal organs of the body. If pathology existing in these organs can be managed by means other than surgical procedures, a patient will remain on a service that is part of the department of medicine. Treatment regimens usually include the administration of medications and other medical procedures that do not require the use of an operating suite. Physicians in the department of medicine identify those patients who require surgery and refer them to the appropriate surgical service. Following surgery, patients may be returned to the medicine service for continued monitoring of their medical condition. An example of this interaction may be seen between a cardiologist and a vascular surgeon. The cardiologist identifies the patient who may need heart surgery, the vascular surgeon performs the necessary operation, and the cardiologist continues to follow the patient for any further signs of cardiac distress. A similar relationship exists between the gastroenterologist (a member of the department of medicine) and the thoracic surgeon. The gastroenterologist may identify a cancer in the esophagus; the thoracic surgeon then removes it and refers the patient back to the gastroenterologist for follow-up or additional medical therapy. This one-to-one relationship does not always exist between a specialty service in medicine and one in surgery; however, it demonstrates the basic differences between these two departments.

Cardiology. The cardiologist diagnoses and treats diseases that relate to the cardiovascular system of the body. The heart is a common source of problems that affect the vascular system to the brain (stroke), and the speech/language pathologist can expect some interaction with the cardiologist. Additionally the cardiologist may see patients following cardiac surgery who evidence voice disorders secondary to distal involvement of cranial nerve 10.

Dermatology. The dermatologist diagnoses and treats diseases of the skin. Interaction with speech/language pathology is usually minimal except in conditions such as dermatomyositis or scleroderma that also may compromise speech production or the ability to swallow.

Endocrinology. The endocrinologist diagnoses and treats those diseases leading to an imbalance of hormonal activity that regulates certain bodily functions. For instance, it is well-known that disorders of the thyroid gland affect not only voice, but can play a role in cognition through their hormonal influence on the cerebral cortex.

Gastroenterology (GI). The gastroenterologist diagnoses and treats diseases that involve the gastrointestinal tract, including the esophagus, stomach, intestines, and rectum. The most common interface with the speech/language pathologist is in consultation on swallowing disorders.

Geriatrics. Not all departments of medicine include the specialty of geriatrics, but it is fast becoming a recognized field in medicine. Many older patients have accompanying communication disorders.[2] The specialist in geriatrics medicine consults the speech/language pathologist for assistance in dealing with these patients who cannot communicate effectively. Because of the multiple medical problems of older persons, the geriatrics specialist utilizes many consultative services of colleagues in medicine, psychiatry, and surgery.

Hematology/oncology. The oncologist, a specialist in the science of the study of tumors, often has a background in hematology, the science of diseases of the blood. The oncologist is responsible for providing chemotherapy regimens that help to control the spread and growth of tumors. Because the side effects of this therapy often emerge as changes in the composition of the body's blood cells, it is desirable for the oncologist to have specialized training in diseases of the blood. Tumors of the brain and the head and neck region, as well as side effects from radiation and chemotherapy treatments, often impact negatively on a patient's communication skills, especially as the disease progresses. The speech/language pathologist may follow the same patients as the hematologist/oncologist.

Infectious disease (ID). The physician with a specialty in infectious disease identifies and attempts to control the spread of disease processes that are easily communicable and may threaten any major body system if left untreated. These specialists have prominent roles in the identification and treatment of patients with acquired immunodeficiency syndrome (AIDS) and diseases that may be related to AIDS. This disease may manifest itself not only in the internal organs, but also in the central nervous system with a potential impact on communication and swallow. The speech/language pathologist may evaluate and treat AIDS patients.

Nephrology. The nephrologist is the medical expert who manages diseases affecting the kidneys. Patients who require long-term dialysis to maintain kidney function may be at risk for cognitive, and therefore communicative, dysfunction.[3] Patients undergoing dialysis are also at risk for other complications involving the vascular system, including compromise to the blood supply to the brain that may result in both communication and swallowing disorders. Therefore, the speech/language pathologist will receive requests for services from the nephrologist.

Pediatrics. The pediatrician will have extensive contact with the speech/language pathologist in referring children with speech and language disorders that are common to the practice of pediatrics. Because this specialty represents the entry point into the medical system for children, it is important that the speech/language pathologist work with the pediatrician in providing early identification and treatment of communication disorders. In one sense, the pediatrician must be familiar with all disorders common to children in order to make a referral to other pediatric specialists, similar to the geriatrics specialist being familiar with all disorders common to older persons.

Pulmonary. The specialist in the pulmonary department manages patients with acute and chronic lung disorders. Because disorders that compromise respiration affect both speech (voice) and swallow, the speech/language pathologist in some settings can expect to interact with this service on a regular basis.

Rheumatology. This is the study of diseases that affect the body's joints and muscles. Patients with diseases of the connective tissue that attaches muscle to joint may be referred to the speech/language pathologist by the rheumatologist if the muscles or joints of articulation or phonation are involved as part of the disease process, for example, in dermatomyositis or arthritis.

Surgery

Physicians in the department of surgery evaluate surgical candidates and, if appropriate, perform the necessary surgery. A patient might remain on the surgery service only long enough to recover from the effects of the surgical procedure or, in some cases, until acute surgical complications have subsided and medical stability re-established. Patients who develop complications that are not correctable with additional surgical management are transferred back to referring services for treatment. Surgical services most commonly in contact with the speech/language pathologist are otolaryngology/head and neck surgery, neurosurgery, plastic surgery, and vascular surgery. The speech/language pathologist interacts less frequently with the thoracic and general surgery services.

Otolaryngology/head and neck surgery. The otolaryngologist who specializes in head and neck surgery is the most common interface for the speech/language pathologist in the department of surgery. Once called ear, nose, and throat specialists (ENT), most physicians in this field now prefer the title otolaryngology/head and neck surgery. Diseases involving the head and neck often compromise the peripheral speech and swallow mechanisms. The speech/language pathologist can expect a great number of referrals from the otolaryngologist, both pre- and postoperatively.

Neurosurgery. The neurosurgeon specializes in surgical procedures involving the brain, spinal cord, and peripheral nerves. Surgical intervention to the central nervous system may leave patients with communication and swallowing disorders requiring the services of the speech/language pathologist. Patients with neurologic disease who later become surgical candidates often are identified and evaluated by the neurologist prior to referral to the neurosurgeon. Some neurosurgeons request pre- and postoperative communication evaluations to assess the effects of surgery on the patient's communicative skills.

Plastic surgery. In some medical settings the plastic surgeon, in addition to providing reconstructive and cosmetic surgery, is responsible for the removal of tumors in the oral cavity, including those of the tongue, mandible, and maxilla. Therefore, their postoperative patients may require the services of the speech/language pathologist.

Vascular surgery. The vascular surgeon is trained to operate on the body's vascular (blood supply) system in every region except the central nervous system. Some patients come to the vascular surgeon with preoperative communication deficits, especially those patients who require surgery to maintain the blood supply to the brain. One typical operation, endarterectomy (increasing the blood supply to the brain via the carotid artery in the neck), may improve the integrity of the vascular system but leave the patient with some residual communication deficits in the immediate posthospitalization period. Risk of stroke and unilateral vocal fold paralysis is possible secondary to this procedure.

Thoracic and general surgery. The thoracic surgeon operates on most of the internal organs of the body including the esophagus, lungs, and stomach. Direct relationships with the speech/language pathologist are infrequent, but there may be interactions regarding patients with swallowing disorders secondary to resections of the esophagus. The speech/language pathologist may come into contact with the general surgeon when a patient with a swallowing disorder requires the surgical placement of a gastrostomy tube. The roles of these two surgical titles vary from hospital to hospital.

Other Hospital Departments

Following are brief descriptions of the majority of the remaining departments that report to the chief of staff. The speech/language pathologist will have contacts with most of these departments while performing routine duties in a medical setting.

Audiology and speech/language pathology. The size of this department can range from two or three staff members to as many as 25 to 30. The larger departments usually exist as freestanding, separate services with their own operating budgets, policies, and procedures. The staff is directly responsible to the department head who usually is responsible to the chief of staff. Smaller departments may be organized under another related service with the staff subject to the decisions of that department head. In this circumstance, audiology and speech/language pathology services might be part of either otolaryngology/head and neck surgery (department of surgery), neurology, or rehabilitation medicine, because the majority of referrals a speech/language pathologist receives comes from these services. Ideally, audiology and speech/language pathology services are organized within one department. In some settings they are separated. Audiology services may be part of otolaryngology/head and neck surgery because of the large volume of hearing assessments required by the otology section, while speech pathology may be part of rehabilitation medicine to support stroke, traumatic injury, and other rehabilitation programs.

Dental. In the process of providing routine dental care, a skilled dentist will identify and refer patients with communication disorders, usually defects of articulation and resonance. Some dental departments offer specialized services such as oral surgery and prosthodontics; both of these services may have steady contact with the speech/language pathologist. In some settings the oral surgeon is part of the operative team to manage patients with tumors in the oral cavity, while the prosthodontist prepares prosthetic devices (usually molded pieces of synthetic materials) used to improve swallowing function by closing a surgical defect or to improve speech intelligibility.

Neurology. The neurologist is a specialist in diseases and conditions that affect the nervous system. This specialist performs essential services involved in diagnosing neurologic diseases and manages patients suffering from these disorders. A significant number of patients with disease of neurologic origin evidence both communication and swallowing disorders. The speech/language pathologist will have significant contact with the neurology department. Patients with communication disorders secondary to stroke often spend the acute stages on the neurology service for diagnostic evaluation, including examination of their communicative skills, before transfer to rehabilitation medicine for treatment focused on restoration of physical and mental abilities.

Nursing. There are very few departments in a hospital that never have direct contact with nursing, and speech/language pathology is not one of these. If the speech/language pathologist is to play a significant role in the medical setting, it is imperative that a portion of diagnostic and treatment time be spent at the patient's bedside. In this setting, there is usually much contact with the nurses who provide 24-hour care to the patient. Because their care involves this time span, they can become partners in communication treatment by assisting the patient's communicative attempts under guidance of the speech/language pathologist. Properly trained nurses also can assist in identifying patients with communication and swallowing disorders and initiate consults with physician concurrence. In this role, they provide an important link to all members of the health care team.

In nursing there are hierarchies of expected proficiency according to education, each with prescribed duties and responsibilities. The *nursing aide* or *nursing assistant* usually has a high school education and learns basic nursing skills while on the job. The *licensed practical nurse* (L.P.N.) holds a two-year degree in nursing science and is capable of providing more direct medical care than the nursing assistant. The *registered nurse* (R.N.) usually has a four-year college degree in nursing science and is responsible for the total coordination of the patient's nursing care in consultation with the patient's physician. The R.N. is solely responsible for the administration of medications and is capable of providing emergency medical care. The *head nurse* or *nursing care coordinator* is an experienced R.N. who is responsible for the nursing care services on any given bed service. Local bed service policy decisions, work schedules, and patient assignments are the responsibility of the head nurse.

Some nurses also hold a master's degree or receive postbaccalaureate training to become *nurse practitioners.* They are trained to perform histories and physical examinations on patients. With physician approval, a nurse practitioner may take a direct role in managing a patient's hospital stay and ensure that all diagnostic tests are ordered and completed. In the VA, long-term and intermediate care services for patients who are medically stable, but who require additional hospitalization, are often administered by nurse practitioners with minimal physician guidance. Because of extensive experience in dealing with patients with similar problems, some nurses choose to specialize in the care that they provide. For instance, some *nurse specialists* work only on surgical services, while others enjoy the demands of an intensive care unit.

Prosthetics. The prosthetics section distributes, by prescription, devices that aid in the physical rehabilitation of patients, such as artificial limbs, suction machines, and special adaptive equipment for the patient's bath, toilet, or shower. Because of its association with efforts at rehabilitation, this section may be organized as part of the department of rehabilitation medicine. The speech/language pathologist will come into contact with the prosthetics section if a patient's needs call for augmentative communication devices or the purchase of an electrolarynx.

Psychiatry. The psychiatrist holds an M.D. degree and diagnoses and treats disorders of the mind that may or may not be secondary to known organic pathology. Treatment generally is by psychotherapy and the use of psychotropic medications. These medications often have side effects that can affect both speech and swallow and require intervention of the speech/language pathologist. In diagnosis, some patients with fluent language disorders may need differentiation by the speech/language pathologist between language deficits related to structural change in the central nervous system, such as Wernicke's aphasia, and the similar language characteristics associated with schizophrenia.

Psychology. The psychologist may work closely with the speech/language pathologist in the diagnosis and treatment of neurobehavioral disorders through the use of projective techniques and the administration of psychometric test batteries. The speech/language pathologist may also work closely with the vocational psychologist in planning a patient's vocational goals consistent with linguistic and speech production skills. The speech/language pathologist and psychologist often are partners in the treatment of patients suffering communication and related disorders due to brain damage.

Radiology. Until the field of speech/language pathology became more involved with patients suffering from dysphagia, the radiologist rarely interacted with the speech/language pathologist, except in some cases of radiographic documentation of children and adults with craniofacial anomalies. The radiologist now is assisted by the speech/language pathologist in the dynamic evaluation of the swallowing mechanism, particularly as it pertains to the mouth and pharynx. Radiologists also are indirectly involved with patients having communication dysfunction secondary to neurologic disease by providing important data on brain function via computerized axial tomography (CAT), magnetic resonance imaging (MRI), and positron emission tomography (PET).

Rehabilitation medicine. The department of rehabilitation medicine provides diagnostic and treatment services for patients with muscular, neuromuscular, and skeletal disease. In particular, its staff assists patients in the rehabilitation of skills lost to disease, such as ambulation, and in activities of daily living (ADL). Services are directed by the *physiatrist* (a doctor of medicine) who prescribes treatment regimens performed by therapists trained in occupational and physical therapy. Occupational and physical therapists are skilled in the physical manipulation (exercise) and retraining of muscle groups to compensate for lost function and in the use of physical agents, such as light, heat, water, and electricity, to improve physical performance. In practice, physical therapists work primarily on issues associated with ambulation (lower extremities and trunk stabilization), while occupational therapists concentrate on restoring lost function in the upper extremities, including the hands and fingers. Both are expert in assisting patients to utilize various prosthetic devices that aid in compensating for the patient's physical deficits. Other therapists involved in recreation and in education also work under the guidance of the physiatrist. Some physiatrists specialize in the care of patients with spinal cord injury. Rehabilitation medicine specialists and speech/language pathologists interact most often with patients who need rehabilitation following stroke, head injury, and other related diseases, because these patients often evidence both communication and physical deficits.

Social work. The hospital-based social worker attempts to meet the patient's immediate social needs (e.g., marital, financial, and psychological adjustment to disability) while in the hospital and also may assist in planning the patient's future social needs (e.g., housing, applications for benefits, job placement, and family counseling). The social worker, by direct interview and historical analysis of the patient's past and present social status, provides an important link between the hospital and the community. Some social workers specialize in working with the homeless or with patients who have either psychiatric or physical disabilities. Determination of the social needs of patients with communication deficits may be difficult and require the assistance of the speech/language pathologist.

Dietetics (food service). The speech/language pathologist and the registered dietitian (R.D.) will often interact as members of the hospital's dysphagia management team. The dietitian will assist the team in the identification of patients with swallowing dysfunction, the documentation of malnutrition, the preparation of special diets, and the calculation of patients' nutritional requirements. For those patients unable to take food by mouth, the dietitian monitors both enteral and parenteral tube feedings. Speech/language pathologists who evaluate patients with swallowing dysfunction have close contact with dietitians in their efforts to assist patients to feed orally.

Other services. The medical speech/language pathologist will have peripheral contacts with the anesthesiology department for advice and consultation on airway tubes that may compromise speech and swallow; the laboratory for biochemical results of patients' nutritional status before and after interventions for swallowing disorders; and nuclear medicine for studies, such as scintigraphy, that document the course and amount of aspirated contents in patients being diagnosed and treated for dysphagia.

The Medical Staff

Individuals who provide direct patient care in a hospital often are divided into two major categories. The smaller group contains services that are part of *allied health,* a term generally used for departments that are staffed by persons with bachelor's degrees, master's degrees, and doctorates. These usually include the departments of audiology and speech/language pathology, dietetics, psychology, pharmacy, social services, and the therapists employed by the department of rehabilitation medicine. The laboratory service is not usually viewed as part of the allied health care team. Its staff includes persons holding the above degrees, as well as M.D.s.

The larger hospital group is comprised of the departments that are staffed by physicians (M.D. degrees) and by dentists (D.D.S. degrees). Nursing service may be included in this grouping because it works closely with physicians; however, some medical centers include nursing as part of allied health. Personnel comprising the medically based departments in a major teaching hospital include attending physicians, fellows, and residents (often referred to as the *house staff*), interns, and medical students.

Attendings. Attending physicians are fully credentialed (often board-certified) physicians who have completed internship and residency training programs. In consultation with their residents, they ultimately are responsible for every aspect of their patients' care. If the institution is affiliated with a medical school, these physicians usually hold teaching appointments on the faculty and are expected to provide guidance and training not only for the residents in their respective specialties but also for residents and attendings in other specialty areas. Ideally their appointments are full time; however, some attendings must divide their time between the hospital and the affiliate medical school. Smaller departments often cannot support full-time services of an attending.

Fellows. Some hospitals receive special funding for fellowships to provide physicians additional experience (usually for one or two years) in specialty fields after the completion of their residencies. A fellow not only assists in the department's routine activities of patient care and resident training, but often is involved in pursuing a research project as a direct requirement of the fellowship stipend.

Residents. Often referred to as the *house staff* because they are responsible for providing 24-hour physician coverage for patient care, residents have completed medical school and are continuing into their chosen specialties, for example, neurology, otolaryngology, or internal medicine. Most residency training programs last three years, but an additional year is required in some surgical specialties. Training experience is not limited to a chosen specialty area. Residents must rotate to different, but related, services to broaden their scope of practice. These rotations can interfere with the continuity of patient care, but it is the attending physician's responsibility to ensure that this continuity is not lost. Residents are distinguished, according to experience, with the designations of first-year resident, junior resident, and senior resident. Generally, one senior resident is chosen as the chief resident. This position involves the additional responsibility of ensuring that each resident is participating fully at expected levels of performance. The senior resident often is responsible for the daily review of patient care and may oversee admissions to the service. In the medical model, first-year residents are trained by more senior residents and the senior residents receive guidance from the fellows or the attending physician.

Interns. Interns have finished medical school and are considering entry into a residency training program in a specialized field. Internship lasts for one year and in many cases serves as the first year of residency. The intern rotates to other services that come into contact most often with the chosen specialty. Interns receive guidance from the residents and attendings.

Medical students/clerkships. After completing four years of undergraduate training, students must complete an additional four years of training to become eligible to receive an M.D. degree. Medical students usually begin their actual hospital experience in their third and fourth years. They attend departmental lectures, make ward rounds, take medical histories, and give physical examinations. Fourth-year medical students are eligible for clerkships, sometimes referred to as subinternships, where they are allowed to manage total care of patients under strict supervision.

Support personnel. Recognition should be given to the secretaries, clerks, and technicians who support each medical and allied health service. While not professionally qualified to provide direct patient care services, they are knowledgeable about the procedures and protocols that pertain to their respective services. Often they are the first contact point for patients and other services. When properly trained, they are valuable allies of those individuals seeking to make their services visible and professional.

SUMMARY

It is the rare beginning speech/language pathologist who enters a medical setting with extensive training and background pertinent to the hospital circumstance. Prior training and experience may offer excellent preparation and give the speech/language pathologist confidence in dealing with patients who evidence a wide variety and severity of communicative disabilities. The application of these skills in a medical setting will be difficult, however, unless the speech/language pathologist is intimately familiar with the organization of services and personnel within the hospital environment. Without an appreciation of hospital organization, his or her expertise will remain unknown and separated from hospital routine. Knowledge of the services of each medical specialty will assist the speech/language pathologist in identifying (1) services that can benefit most from the special services the speech/language pathologist provides (some of the specialties will be unaware of these benefits), (2) specific diagnostic information that is dependent on the orientation of the specialty requesting the services, and (3) appropriate referrals that the speech/language pathologist can make for specific patient complaints.

The organization of the hospital can be divided basically into two categories. The first provides direct patient care services, such as those of the speech/language pathologist. The second category provides services in support of patient care, such as personnel and supply services. Most direct patient care services are part of either the department of medicine or the department of surgery. In general, the speech/language pathologist working in a medical care setting with patients who evidence both communicative and swallowing disorders will have close contacts with the departments of otolaryngology/head and neck surgery, neurology, rehabilitation medicine, gastroenterology, radiology, dentistry, dietetics, and nursing.

NOTES

1. Hillary Siebens et al., "Correlates and Consequences of Eating Dependency in Institutionalized Elderly," *Journal of the American Geriatrics Society* 34 (1986):192–98.

2. Barbara B. Shadden, "Communication and Aging: An Overview." In *Communication Behaviors and Aging: A Sourcebook for Clinicians,* ed. Barbara B. Shadden (Baltimore, Md.: Williams & Wilkins Co., 1988), 3–11.

3. Diane P. Madison et al., "Communication and Cognitive Decline in Dialysis Dementia: Two Case Studies," *Journal of Speech and Hearing Disorders* 42, no. 2 (1977):238–46.

Chapter 2

Specialized Roles for the Speech/Language Pathologist

INTRODUCTION

In most circumstances, speech/language pathology training programs do not offer extensive coursework or practica to prepare the speech/language pathologist for the medical setting. Although some coursework may be offered in affiliated medical schools, the classroom training in most cases is not medically oriented and is taught outside of the hospital setting. The majority of practicum experiences are sponsored either in university speech and hearing clinics, private rehabilitation centers, specialty schools, such as those for the cerebral palsied or hearing impaired, and in the public schools. Most of these settings are not directly affiliated with medical training programs and do not support inpatient hospital bed services.

Consequently, the typical speech/language pathologist who enters a medical setting will have had little exposure to a hospital environment and will not have had a sufficient number of role models to follow. Even though the training program may have given the speech/language pathologist didactic information pertinent to disorders frequently encountered in a hospital setting (e.g., aphasia, dysarthria, dementia, and dysphagia), there is little guidance on how to coalesce this knowledge into the medical model. For instance, the beginning clinician may know how to identify language characteristics consistent with dementia, but may not be cognizant of the fact that the neurologist is seeking help in either confirming or denying a diagnosis of dementia, rather than a description of the language characteristics of someone with dementia. In fact, a neurologist who has a good working relationship with the speech/language pathologist will expect the speech/language pathologist to supply additional diagnoses if the patient's communicative status is not consistent with the supplied or current diagnosis. Role expectations such as this need to be developed over time, but should be included in the practice of the medical speech/language pathologist.

Exposure to the role model is blurred further by the fact that training in the processes of diagnosis and treatment of speech and language disorders usually is done in an office or clinic. This model assumes that the patient comes to the speech/language pathologist and receives services within the confines of the office or clinic. Medical speech/language pathologists are most effective when they are able to expand their services to the patient's bedside and into areas that are more unfamiliar, such as oncology clinics, radiology suites, intensive care units, and, in some cases, operating rooms. Moving outside of the speech/language pathology clinic increases clinicians' exposure and therefore increases the demand for services. The need for contact outside of the departmental confines forces them to become familiar with the roles of many other health care professionals. At the same time, they are able to educate the other professionals regarding the contributions of speech/language pathology to health care management. This should be a top priority in establishing recognizable roles within the medical setting, because knowledge of these contributions is not well-known or understood. Informal relationships with other health care professionals as they care for the same patients eventually will lead to the most practical and beneficial training that speech/language pathologists can offer and other professionals receive.

Establishing a comfortable role for the speech/language pathologist in a medical setting is also compromised because a large majority of the hospital's professional health employees received their training in medical environments and entered the setting with awareness of daily hospital routine. They knew how to write consults and patient progress notes, how to examine patients at bedside, how to participate in team treatment meetings, and how to get information about their patients from the medical records. In short, the speech/language pathologist is entering foreign territory, one with a different language and different customs. Other health care professionals may feel uncomfortable if they are not sure why the speech/language pathologist is there or what he or she will do.

To acclimate, the speech/language pathologist must quickly learn health care language and customs. When these obstacles are out of the way, it will be easier to demonstrate how a speech/language pathologist can be a productive member of the hospital community. This chapter presents an overview of some of the more common roles for the speech/language pathologist in a medical setting. It focuses on a discussion of how role definition is shaped by the disciplines with which the speech/language pathologist interacts, and how he or she can become an equal and valued partner in the medical care of the patients.

TRADITIONAL ROLES

The speech/language pathologist is taught to diagnose and treat disorders of communication. However, many communication disorders tend to be secondary to a primary medical diagnosis, such as the dysarthria that is secondary to the medical diagnosis of amyotrophic lateral sclerosis. The role of diagnostician for the speech/language pathologist in the medical setting is diminished. Because most patients sent to the speech/language pathologist have a medical diagnosis, it is assumed by the referring physician that the speech/language pathologist's "diagnosis" will be limited to whether or not the patient can benefit from communication intervention. The physician does not expect any information that may be relevant to the primary medical diagnosis. It is this misguided assumption (one that speech/language pathologists have only begun to dispel) that in the physician's mind relegates the field of communication science more to aspects of rehabilitation than to the processes of differential diagnosis. In fact, the speech/language pathologist must separate some communication disorders from others (e.g., speech from language) and among subtypes (e.g., Broca's from Wernicke's aphasia) by processes of differential diagnosis.

This is of little consequence to the physician, however, who views the challenge of accurate medical diagnosis as the most important part of what the medical setting can offer. And rightly so. While certain medical treatments are needed to confirm the accuracy of the diagnosis, in most cases a careful diagnostic evaluation will dictate the treatment regime. Consequently, the emphasis in medical school training is on thorough clinical and laboratory investigations in an effort to establish an accurate diagnosis. Once this is done, the treatment, in most cases, requires basic applications of medicine that are more routine than the processes involved in differential diagnosis. Treatments and, by association, "treaters" are viewed as less important in the patient's care. This notion is transferred almost subliminally to the speech/language pathologist and other professionals who are viewed as supplying services that are oriented toward treatment (rehabilitation). Longer-term rehabilitative treatment can be provided while the patient is on outpatient status. Therefore, there is no expectation for the speech/language pathologist, who is considered a long-term treatment provider, to be involved acutely at the patient's bedside. Presence on the patient's floor in the hospital and at bedside is a powerful tool of the speech/language pathologist in establishing a more valued role in a medical setting.

To obtain equal status in the medical setting it is imperative that speech/language pathologists demonstrate how their expertise can be used to solve the problems of establishing medical diagnoses and how their skills can assist physicians in managing patients after and, more importantly, during the hospital stay. Subsequent chapters demonstrate how this involvement can be developed. It comes initially from an understanding of medical disciplines to which speech/language pathologists relate on a regular basis and how to establish a mutual environment of respect as diagnosticians and treatment providers.

Speech/language pathologists in a medical setting will interact most often with the specialties of pediatrics, otolaryngology (head and neck surgeons), neurology and neurosurgery, rehabilitation medicine, and nursing. Those who provide diagnostic guidance and treatment management of dysphagic patients will spend additional time with dietitians, gastroenterologists, radiologists, and dentists. Other specialties, such as cardiology, pulmonology, and surgical specialties, will request their services on a more limited basis. However, speech/language pathologists who spend a great deal of time in intensive care units interact with these professions on a daily basis. In other special environments that provide care to adults and children with developmental disorders, such as cleft lip and palate, speech/language pathologists may spend large amounts of time with dentists and plastic surgeons. To maintain successful interactions with all of these specialties, it is important that speech/language pathologists know what types of patients should be referred to each of these services. This knowledge allows speech/language pathologists to be conversant regarding their findings from the perspective of communication specialists.

Otolaryngology/Head and Neck Surgery

The otolaryngologist/head and neck surgeon evaluates and treats patients with diseases that involve the head (temporal bone and base of skull); mouth, nasal and sinus cavities; pharynx; larynx; upper airway; and the supporting neck tissue. Because these anatomical regions are responsible for the majority of sensory and motor peripheral control to the speech production mechanism, their pathological correlates often involve the combined efforts of the otolaryngologist and speech/ language pathologist in treatment. At large medical centers, some otolaryngologists prefer to subspecialize in the surgical care of disorders related exclusively to hearing and balance (otology and neuro-otology), while others prefer to subspecialize in the management of patients with head and neck tumors. The medical speech/language pathologist will receive the majority of consults from specialists in head and neck pathology. They will include patients with voice disorders who may have had, or who may not require, surgical intervention. In an active head and neck surgery service most referrals are for patients who need surgery to control cancer that has invaded the oropharyngeal and laryngeal spaces. Loss of structure or neural innervation to the structures that effect phonation and articulation impairs both speech intelligibility and swallowing. In general, the head and neck surgeon is interested in controlling the cancer and providing the patient with as little loss of structure and function as feasible. If the patient requires further rehabilitation after surgery, the speech/language pathologist will be consulted.

Unfortunately, not all otolaryngologists involve the speech/language pathologist on a regular basis in preoperative decisions. Part of the reason stems from the surgeon's failure to view the speech/language pathologist in the role of diagnostician. More often, the speech/language pathologist is considered to be a specialist in rehabilitation, and rehabilitation always follows medical (surgical) treatment. Another explanation is that the surgeon typically knows little about rehabilitative technique and does not appreciate the need to know beforehand how well the patient will be able to learn after the operation. The preoperative cognitive assessment (see Chapter 7) of all patients who need rehabilitative care is a necessary part of the preoperative evaluation and should involve the speech/language pathologist who is expected to provide the rehabilitation.

For some patients, the type of operation chosen by the surgeon should be reviewed if preoperative input from the speech/language pathologist reveals that the patient's cognitive skills are not predictive of success in postoperative rehabilitation. Exemplar of this point is the patient who presents with a tumor in the pyriform sinus that extends to the tongue base and involves one arytenoid cartilage. The planned surgical procedure may be a supraglottic laryngectomy to include the arytenoid cartilage. The surgeon feels that this is the procedure of choice, because the tumor can be controlled and voice is not sacrificed. The surgeon is aware of the fact that patients in this category will experience postoperative dysphagia because of an inability to protect the airway. If postoperative irradiation is planned, the patient is further liable for complications from dysphagia. The speech/language pathologist knows that this patient must be able to learn a series of sequential steps in order to swallow efficiently. If the patient were to receive a preoperative cognitive evaluation and the findings revealed that the patient could not easily follow commands and had problems with short-term memory and basic communication skills, the speech/language pathologist would be aware of possible difficulties in teaching the patient how to protect the airway during swallow. If a preoperative conference were held on this patient, a discussion might ensue regarding the acceptability of this patient for supraglottic laryngectomy. It might be decided to perform a total laryngectomy to minimize the swallowing difficulty and to offer the patient postoperative vocal rehabilitation in view of the poor prognosis for swallow rehabilitation.

Another example of necessary preoperative cooperation includes a "voice," motor, and cognitive evaluation of a patient who is scheduled for tracheoesophageal puncture.[1] The patient needs to have adequate phonatory, motor, and cognitive skills to be most successful in rehabilitation following the placement of the prosthesis. Because the surgeon does not receive training regarding issues of rehabilitation technique, every effort should be made to provide education in this area. The surgeon should have the opportunity to improve postoperative results by being cognizant of the variables related to the patient's chances of rehabilitation.

The diagnostic evaluation of potential surgical cases involving the head and neck is completed by the surgeon before the patient is scheduled for the operating room. A typical evaluation includes a clinical examination with possible visualization and biopsy of tissue during anesthesia and a consultation with the radiologist to define the extent of the lesion. Cases that present without a diagnosis, such as those with cranial nerve dysfunction that involve both speech and swallow, should be referred to the speech/language pathologist for a diagnostic impression.

The types of surgical resections to control cancer that should include the speech/language pathologist are glossectomies (partial or complete); extensions of glossectomy that might include the tonsil, bony or soft palate, and floor of the mouth and mandible (commando or composite resection); resections of the pharynx; and procedures involving the larynx, including supraglottic laryngectomy, hemilaryngectomy, and total laryngectomy.[2] During interactions with the head and neck surgeon on postsurgical cases, it is necessary for the speech/language pathologist to become familiar with the indications and possible complications of feeding and airway (tracheostomy) tubes as they impact on voice and swallow (see Figure 2–1).

The speech/language pathologist should have knowledge of related surgical procedures, such as tympanic neurectomy with salivary duct ligation to control sialorrhea (excessive saliva) (see Figure 2–2), Teflon/gelfoam injection for voice improvement and airway protection (see Figure 2–3), cricopharyngeal myotomy (see Figure 2–4) to improve swallow, and, in some cases phonation following laryngectomy.[3] Another procedure to improve swallow in the presence of a noncompliant pharyngoesophageal segment is the nonsurgical approach of esophageal dilatation (see Figure 2–5). This procedure may be supervised by the otolaryngologist or by the gastroenterologist.

The speech/language pathologist's interaction with the otolaryngologist also will involve interactions with patients who are recovering from removal of benign vocal fold lesions, such as polyps or nodules (see Figure 2–6), for the implementation of postsurgical management of the voice. Referrals also are made to the speech/language pathologist for patients who demonstrate vocal pathology not requiring surgical excision, but who need training in vocal hygiene. These patients may present with chronic laryngitis, plica ventricularis (hyperadduction of the false vocal folds), or with no visible changes in the anatomy or physiology of phonation but with obvious perceptual changes in voice.[4] Speech/language

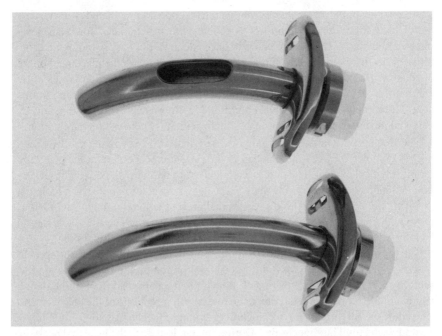

Figure 2–1 (A) Example of two types of metal tracheostomy tubes. The top example is fenestrated to facilitate air flow to the vocal folds above it for speech. *Source:* Reproduced with permission from Michael Groher (Ed.), *Dysphagia: Diagnosis and Management,* Butterworth Publishers, Stoneham, MA, © 1984.

pathologists involved in aural rehabilitation will instruct patients who have had surgically or nonsurgically related hearing loss to maximize their hearing residuals.

Neurology

The role of the medical speech/language pathologist with the neurologist should include diagnostic as well as rehabilitative aspects in the management of communication disorders secondary to neurologic disease. The neurology service often is involved in the differential diagnosis of patients who may present with suspected disease of neurogenic origin, rather than in their nonmedical rehabilitation (rehabilitation that does not require the use of medications). Part of the differential diagnostic process may include the services of the speech/language pathologist, because speech and language processes are sensitive barometers of change in the nervous system. However, the speech/language pathologist should be prepared to offer an opinion regarding the rehabilitation potential of the patient (see Chapters

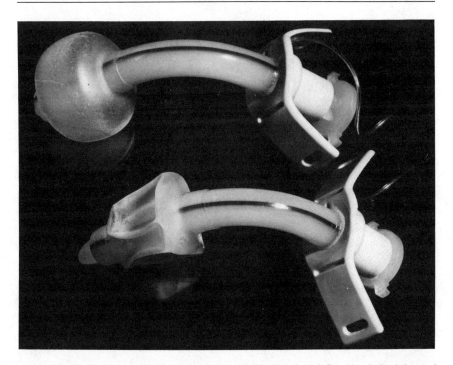

Figure 2–1 (B) Example of a cuffed tracheostomy tube. The top tube is inflated by air that is inserted with a syringe through the narrow tubing toward the right of the tube; the bottom tube is partially inflated. When the cuff is inflated, theoretically food cannot fall past the cuff into the lungs, and air cannot pass superiorly for speech. *Source:* Reproduced with permission from Michael Groher (Ed.), *Dysphagia: Diagnosis and Management,* Butterworth Publishers, Stoneham, MA, © 1984.

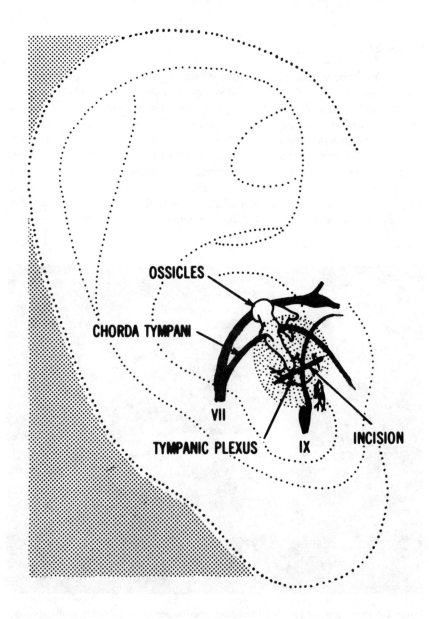

Figure 2–2 Diagram of the parasympathetic nerve supply to the major salivary glands and their accessibility within the middle ear. Tympanic neurectomy can be used to control excessive saliva production. *Source:* Reprinted from *American Family Physician,* Vol. 19, by J.A. DeLisa et al., with permission of the American Academy of Family Physicians, © 1979.

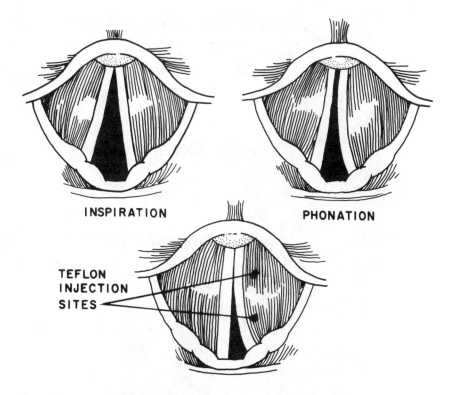

INSPIRATION

PHONATION

TEFLON
INJECTION
SITES

Figure 2–3 During inspiration the paralyzed vocal fold fails to move laterally; during phonation it fails to meet the midline. Teflon is injected at two sites on the paralyzed vocal fold to improve phonation during speech and airway protection during swallow.

7 and 8) to assist the neurologist in the decision of whether to refer the patient for rehabilitative services.

The neurologist who requests the diagnostic services of the speech/language pathologist should be able to receive information about the patient from three perspectives. First, if there is no definitive neurologic diagnosis, it should be the role of the speech/language pathologist to suggest a number of possibilities based on the results of the speech and language assessment. Second, if the patient comes with one or two firm diagnoses, the speech/language pathologist should try to add information that supports one over the other. Finally, it is a valid role to suggest that the speech and language symptomatology is not consistent with any of the stated diagnoses and to offer an alternative impression if the examination warrants.

The speech/language pathologist, while assisting in the assessment of neurologic disease, should understand that the neurologist seeks to differentiate among disorders of neurologic origin based on the neurologist's view of the organization of the nervous system. It is from this view that the discovery and eventual treat-

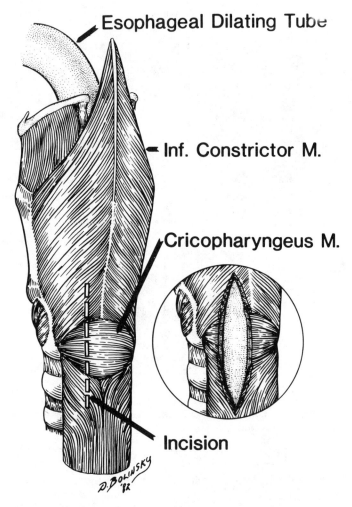

Figure 2–4 A cricopharyngeal myotomy is a surgical relaxation of the pharyngoesophageal segment. The incision is placed in the hypopharyngeal musculature and extends into the upper esophageal musculature.

ment of neurologic disease emanates. For instance, the nervous system is potentially liable to pathology from disease in the motor and sensory systems (peripheral and central), the vascular supply, the ventricular network (cerebral spinal fluid), and the visceral system (autonomic nervous system). After establishing which system may be impaired, the neurologist seeks to establish the level of involvement (muscle, peripheral nerve, spinal cord, brainstem, subcortex, or cortex). The expected symptomological correlates will then emerge (see Figure 2–7). For instance, the neurologist might expect more disorders of speech production and eye

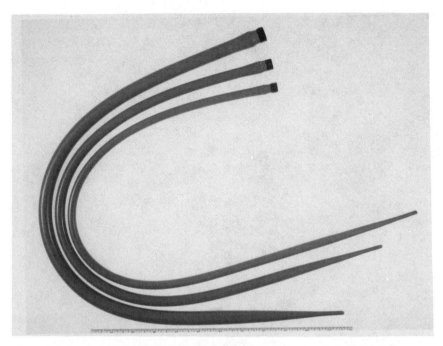

Figure 2–5 Bougie (Maloney-type) dilators used in progressive sizes are swallowed by the patient to widen the esophageal lumen. Shown are sizes 30, 36, and 48 French.

movement with pathology confined to the brainstem and more difficulty with memory and language in the cerebral hemispheres. Similarly, pathology confined to the spinal cord would not affect eye movements, but might affect the respiratory supports for speech production. Having knowledge of which system is impaired and at what level helps to dictate the needed treatment.

An understanding of this approach to differential diagnosis (by system and by level) should help the speech/language pathologist to assist the neurologist in establishing a firm diagnosis. It is necessary for the speech/language pathologist to become familiar with the neurologic diseases that affect speech and language by system and by level. For instance, the medical speech/language pathologist may need to know speech and language characteristics that separate cortical from subcortical disease, those that can be expected in pathology involving the ventricular system, or those associated with endocrine disorders, such as hypothyroidism, and their secondary effects on communication.

Before the evaluation commences, the speech/language pathologist should be cognizant of whether the neurologist is seeking confirmation of a diagnosis, asking for help in providing additional diagnoses, requesting baseline information to chart the progression of a disease, or any combination of these. Baseline evaluations of patients with acute neurologic disease who are expected to change can provide valuable data for the neurologist and the speech/language pathologist as they pre-

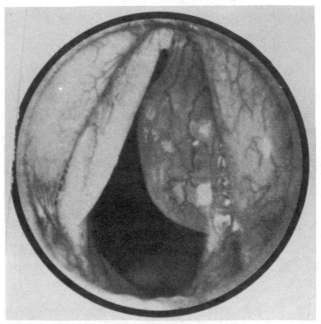

A

B

Figure 2–6 (A) Example of a sessile polyp extending from the anterior commissure down the length of the vocal fold. (B) Example of bilateral polypoid vocal nodules; they commonly are found in this position on the vocal folds. *Source:* From A.E. Aronson in *Clinical Voice Disorders,* 2nd ed., New York, 1985, Thieme Medical Publishers, Inc. Reprinted by permission.

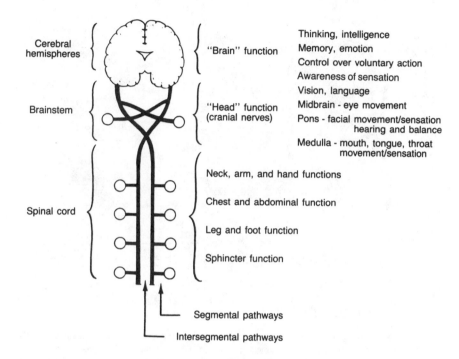

Figure 2–7 Pathologies at different sites within the central nervous system produce deficits characteristic of their functional correlates. Disturbances in language usually are confined to the cortical and subcortical region, whereas disturbances of speech production can occur at any level. *Source:* Reprinted from *Medical Neurosciences,* 2nd ed., by J.R. Daube et al., p. 40, with permission of Little, Brown and Company, © 1986.

sent pertinent prognostic information to the patient and family. In most cases, a review of the medical record will provide the answer (see Chapter 4). The process of differential diagnosis often requires the neurologist to request assistance of various medical specialties in confirming a diagnosis, denying a diagnosis, or suggesting a new line of exploration. The neurologist will use this information in formulating a final diagnosis. This process of confirmation and denial is accepted medical practice. It should be viewed as a viable role for the communication specialist when asked to reply to a consultation.

Because of the large number of neurologic disease processes that potentially impact negatively on communication, it is necessary for the medical speech/language pathologist to be familiar with not only the anatomy and physiology of the central and autonomic nervous systems, but with pathologic processes that may affect communication during their course. To be most effective, the speech/language pathologist should conceptualize the processes, both sensory and motor, that may be affected by disease and the levels of the nervous system manifested by the disease. This information is then tied to structural pathologic correlates, for example, muscle, peripheral nerve, brainstem, subcortex, or cortex (see Figure 2–8).

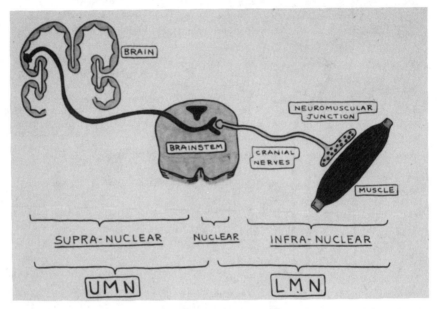

Figure 2–8 The voluntary component (upper motor neuron) for the movements of the muscles in the head and neck begins in the cortex with tracts crossing to the opposite side as they synapse on the lower motor neuron representation in the brainstem. The lower motor neuron is composed of the cranial nerve, the neuromuscular junction, and the muscle. *Source:* Reprinted with permission of George Zito, M.D.

Further, basic knowledge of the expected course and duration of the disease and some notions about its medical management are needed. For instance, Parkinson's disease is a relatively common pathologic process of largely undetermined origin that affects motor output at the level of the subcortex.[5] It is characterized initially by involuntary motor movements and progresses to bradykinesia (slow motor movements) and rigidity, both of which will interfere with speech function. The course of the disease to termination may range from 5 to 20 years. Cognition may be affected in the later stages with a resulting impact on learning and orientation. Treatment largely is through the use of medication that facilitates neural transmission, such as Sinemet (carbidopa/levodopa). The side effects from the medications may either improve or adversely affect both speech production and swallow.

Certain diseases of neurologic origin may affect multiple levels in the nervous system. More than one physiologic process may be involved, but it is the responsibility of the speech/language pathologist to know which diseases present themselves in this manner. For instance, progressive supranuclear palsy (PSP) can initially affect the midbrain and subcortical structures with resulting dysarthria and then progress to concurrent involvement of the cortex with subsequent impairments of language and cognition.[6]

Some patients with neurologic disease evidence disorders of deglutition secondary to impairment of the oropharyngeal muscle complex and, in some cases, to involvement of both the striated and smooth muscle of the esophagus. Evaluation and treatment of these disorders are important to the patients' medical evaluations, and referrals to the speech/language pathologist are appropriate. The evaluation and remediation of disorders of deglutition involve a new, but recognized, role in the field of speech/language pathology.[7] Most physicians are not aware of the fact that a consult to the speech/language pathologist for evaluation of a dysphagic patient could be useful. In the past, most consults were sent to the otolaryngology and gastroenterology services. Cooperation among all four services (speech/language pathology, otolaryngology, gastroenterology, and neurology) often is needed for optimal management of the dysphagic patient.[8,9]

In some cases, the neurologist's process of differential diagnosis will end in consultation with the neurosurgeon who may consider the patient a candidate for neurosurgical intervention. If communication is impaired, the speech/language pathologist should evaluate these patients prior to surgery for postsurgical comparisons and, if indicated, necessary treatment.

Rehabilitation Medicine

Patients who are referred to the rehabilitation medicine service usually have some disability that interferes with the activities of daily living (ADLs). The source can come from disease processes that involve the skeletal, muscular, or neuromuscular systems. The rehabilitation physician (physiatrist) heads a team of other rehabilitation specialists trained to manage these disorders. As indicated in Chapter 1, the speech/language pathologist may be assigned to the department of rehabilitation medicine. The rehabilitation medicine physician evaluates the rehabilitative potential of a patient and prescribes specific rehabilitative techniques as appropriate. The primary role for the speech/language pathologist in conjunction with the physiatrist should provide not only the necessary treatment to improve the patient's communicative deficits, but also basic information on the most efficient methods of communicating with the patient so that learning can be achieved most efficiently. This information should be used by the entire rehabilitation team as a way of reinforcing what the speech/language pathologist provides in individual or group remediation sessions. As the patient improves, all members of the rehabilitation team should comment on the patient's progress in achieving previously discussed rehabilitation goals. If the patient has achieved these goals or has reached a point of maximum benefit from rehabilitation, it should be the role of the speech/language pathologist to instruct the family and others concerned with the patient's care about how best to communicate with the patient (see Chapter 10). The patient may receive additional outpatient care after discharge that requires further documentation of progress. When the patient achieves maximum benefit from the speech/language pathologist, this should be noted in a final summary and the patient discharged.

Nursing

Because the medical speech/language pathologist evaluates and treats patients both in the clinic and on the ward, it is necessary that a portion of this effort be spent in interactions with nursing personnel in mutual attempts to manage communication-disordered patients. Nursing care requires 24-hour patient coverage. Nurses spend the most time in communication interactions with patients as they provide this care. In these interactions they may observe communication or swallowing disorders not evident on routine screening when the patients entered the medical setting. Therefore, nurses should know how to identify swallowing and communication disorders and how to consult with the speech/language pathologist in managing them. In this role, they become an important referral source. Following the evaluation, it is the role of the speech/language pathologist to provide the nurse with the information needed to communicate most successfully with a patient. In most cases this will facilitate nursing care. A patient with a swallowing disorder can be fed more successfully when a nursing care plan is developed mutually between the speech/language pathologist and the nurse.

Most nurses will not have the time to provide direct treatment for communication disorders while the patient is at bedside; however, indirect treatment through facilitation of the patient's communicative strengths is an important role for the speech/language pathologist to direct. For instance, if the speech/language pathologist has determined that the patient is unable to communicate basic needs through any linguistic modality but is able to follow one-step auditory commands, the nurse will not expect the patient to request needs and will meet those needs automatically by following established nursing protocol. The nurse can expect the patient to cooperate more fully by following one-step auditory commands. Also, the nurse can assist the speech/language pathologist in the documentation of the patient's reliability in compliance and note any improvement in communicative status.

The nursing staff spends the most time with patients suffering acute disorders affecting speech and language, and each shift will report observed changes in function. It is imperative that the speech/language pathologist attend to these reports of communication changes in an objective fashion. Frequently the nursing staff reports that a patient with an acute neurologic language impairment is following all verbal commands without difficulty, whereas the objective evaluation of this modality by the speech/language pathologist shows the patient to have very little comprehension for spoken commands. The medically oriented speech/language pathologist must explain these contradictory findings in a satisfactory manner. This does not imply that it is necessary to confront the nurse with these differences in observations. It is important, however, to explain the differences in positive terms that will reinforce good management techniques. For example, the patient who is unable to perform well on an objective test of auditory comprehension may indeed follow verbal instructions when they are accompanied by demonstration or when they are a part of a regimented nursing care schedule. In this circumstance it is likely that the nurse not only stimulated the patient through the auditory modality, but provided accompanying demonstration in the context of a situation that was by now familiar to the patient. The nurse may have repeated the command four or five times before the patient responded. Taken in total, all of these redundancies motivated the nurse to document the fact that the "patient understands everything."

When the nursing staff recognizes that the approach of using a short verbal command together with a visual demonstration enhances the communicative skills of most language-impaired patients, the nurses become allies in educating the family and other care providers regarding management techniques of the communicatively impaired. It is important for the speech/language pathologist to follow the nurses' observations and documentation of patients' communication status. These documentations can be especially useful in collecting empirical data on patients who are unable to cooperate in the traditional testing situation. Working with the speech/language pathologist, for example, the nurse can describe the situation of the communicative exchange, the time, nursing care activity, stimulus, and response. This information can be analyzed to achieve the most appropriate communication care plan.

Medicine

Patients in medical intensive care units often require the exclusive services of the department of medicine for management of cardiopulmonary distress. Communication and swallowing disorders in this setting are prevalent[10] and require the services of the speech/language pathologist. Patients with acute stroke secondary to cardiac complications must be evaluated to determine the best channels for communication interaction. Intensive care patients may have complications of the airway that compromise voice production. These problems can include tracheostomy with or without the support of a respirator, intubation (placement of an airway tube through the mouth and vocal folds) to maintain the airway, and intubation trauma that may cause voice disorders secondary to tissue damage or peripheral neural damage to the vocal folds.[11]

It is the role of the speech/language pathologist to establish the best alternative means of communication for a patient so that medical care can be facilitated. This may include providing paper and pencil for writing, teaching the patient how to occlude the tracheostomy tube for speaking, use of communication devices that attach to the patient's tracheostomy tube, and use of an electrolarynx if the patient's physical and cognitive skills are appropriate. Because of the shared interactions of respiration and deglutition,[12] a patient in respiratory and cardiac distress frequently evidences dysphagia and requires the intervention of the speech/language pathologist. A swallowing disorder in an intensive care unit is frequently ignored due to the acute medical condition of the patient.

Gerontology

The specialist in gerontological medicine usually relies heavily on a multidisciplinary approach to the management of patients. This reliance stems from the fact that older persons typically have more medical problems than their younger cohorts and require the expertise of many specialists. The coordination of these efforts is done under the guidance of the physician trained in the medical and psychiatric problems of older persons. The prevalence of communication disorders among older persons is high,[13] and the speech/language pathologist can play a pivotal role in their delineation and management. These disorders can be the result of an increase in combined system degeneration, with deficits in vision, hearing, cognition, and motor performance all acting to decompensate communication. Other disorders are more obvious, such as communication impairments that result from stroke. Therefore, the clinician must be prepared to evaluate each of these systems as they relate to communication by providing input to the team of specialists managing the geriatric patient. Special testing procedures may be necessary if these patients are to receive the benefit of services from the speech/language pathologist.[14]

Gastroenterology, Radiology, Dentistry, and Dietetics

A common interaction of these services with those of the speech/language pathologist can be found in the management of patients with swallowing disorders. The gastroenterologist evaluates the esophagus and lower gastrointestinal tract and refers patients who need further evaluation to the swallowing disorders team. The speech/language pathologist should work closely with the radiologist in the radiographic assessment of patients with dysphagia to provide dynamic documentation of deglutitory muscle function. Patients with head and neck cancer and problems with speech and swallow frequently receive concurrent services from the speech/language pathologist and the dentist/prosthodontist. Specially designed prosthetic aids for both speech and swallow (Figure 2–9) require the close cooperation of these two disciplines. The dietitian assists in the identification of swallowing disorders and works with the speech/language pathologist by recommending specialized diets that the dysphagic patient can manage more efficiently. Modifications of textures and fluids may achieve a more efficient swallow.

Specialized Roles

The speech/language pathologist in a medical setting normally interacts with many medical specialties, because communication and swallowing disorders can be secondary to a large variety of diseases and disease processes. During these interactions, the speech/language pathologist develops specialized roles that de-

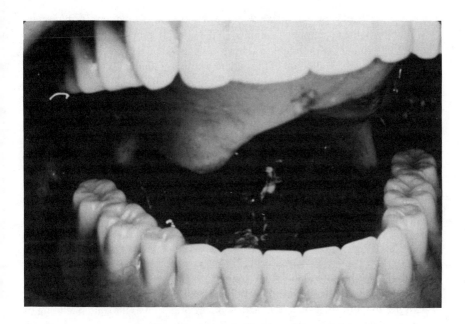

Figure 2–9 An anterior view of a prosthetic device used to fill a large surgical deficit that enabled the patient to channel food down a synthetic tongue surface.

pend on the nature of the request for services and on the type of service that is rendered. These specialized roles include diagnostician, remediation specialist, counselor, educator, and a contributor on a number of interdisciplinary medical management teams.

Diagnostics

The medical speech/language pathologist needs to be well-trained in the process of differential diagnosis. This process should begin routinely with the following five steps:

1. a thorough review of the patient's previous medical history (see Chapter 4)
2. a review of the patient's current medical problems and complaints
3. a review of the results of previously completed consultations during the current hospitalization
4. a review of the current progress notes
5. information by telephone or personal contact with the patient's doctor and nurse that may not be documented in writing.

The use of this process before the speech and language assessment helps the speech/language pathologist to establish the direction in which the assessment will proceed (see Chapter 5). For instance, it may be obvious from the information review that the patient cannot be examined in the clinic but must be seen at bedside. Undoubtedly screening measures will have to be used and a great emphasis placed on observations and evaluation of the patient's physical status as it impacts on communication (see Chapter 6). Or, it may be obvious that the physician is not seeking any new diagnostic information (although this may surface in the examination) but is requesting support of a diagnosis, a management or care plan, or initiation of treatment to facilitate the patient's recovery. After the communication evaluation is completed, the results are summarized and returned to the consulting source (see Chapter 8).

The response to the consultation is based on the speech/language pathologist's perceived need for the reason the physician has requested the service and on the responsibility of the speech/language pathologist to provide objective data to document the patient's communication status. The speech/language pathologist's role in response to consultation should be

- to supply information that relates only to the patient's communication status, including a statement of prognosis and a plan for treatment
- to use this information to add additional information to the understanding of the patient's medical diagnosis by way of confirmation
- to use the communication evaluation to refute the current diagnosis, when necessary, and to offer suggestions for alternate diagnoses
- to refute or correct any error in the previous medical history
- to suggest additional sources of consultation if a problem exists that has not been adequately explored (see Chapter 8 for examples)

On some consultations, all of these factors may be addressed, while on others only one or two will be needed. It is important that the response to the consultation be completed within 48 hours to ensure continuity of care. Failure to respond within this time may unnecessarily lengthen the patient's hospital stay at a time when hospitals are competing to shorten inpatient visits. By way of association, a slow response casts an unfavorable shadow on the value of the speech/language pathologist's role when delays are excessive or frequent. Suggestions for improving or maximizing the patient's communication should be detailed and aimed at decreasing the patient's communication dysfunction or feeding dependency. This type of response will free staff to spend additional time with other patients, enable the hospital to be more productive, and strengthen the status of the speech/language pathology department.

Remediation

Further definition of the specialized role of the medical speech/language pathologist comes from the understanding that remediation for the patient is equally valuable by providing direct behavioral treatment or management suggestions, or both. In this context, *treatment* refers to the more traditional aspects of communication remediation wherein the patient is seen in the clinic or at bedside, and the speech/language pathologist, through techniques of facilitation, stimulation, and reinforcement, attempts to strengthen or improve the patient's communication strategies. There is an interaction between the speech/language pathologist and the patient, and objective measures of change are made. *Management,* however, represents a more indirect mode of remediation wherein the patient is not seen regularly by the speech/language pathologist. Rather, the speech/language pathologist provides the patient's caregivers or family with the best methods of communicating with the patient and is available for additional explanations, demonstrations, and re-evaluations as needed. Providing management suggestions is a useful role for the speech/language pathologist and should not be minimized. It greatly facilitates the patient's care and can free the speech/language pathologist to see more patients in direct treatment modes. Discussions relative to management and treatment decisions are explored further in Chapter 9.

Counseling

A specialized role for the speech/language pathologist in a medical setting relates to his or her skills as a counselor by interpreting medical information to the patient and family. It is important for the speech/language pathologist to be very familiar with both medical terminology and the basics of medical procedure and evaluation. A patient with a communication impairment is often unable either to understand a medical procedure or to ask questions about the purpose or outcome. It should be the role of the speech/language pathologist to assist the patient's interactions with the medical staff in this context. It is the speech/language pathologist who is most familiar with the patient's best channels of communication input and output and, therefore, is in the best position to know the most efficient manner in which to explain information to the patient. The role of counselor can be especially helpful to communication-impaired patients who are scheduled for surgical or diagnostic procedures that they are refusing because of confusion about their purpose and outcome.

Experience suggests that many patients who suffer communication impairment secondary to a stroke or their families rarely receive information about what a stroke is and its etiology, pathology, course, medical treatment, and chance for recurrence. After a patient has stabilized medically, these questions are paramount and require direct, yet simple, answers. When the patient does receive this information from a health professional other than a speech/language pathologist, it usually is given at a rate or complexity level that exceeds both the patient's and family's ability of comprehension. Speech/language pathologists can help fill this void by educating other health care professionals on how best to communicate medical information to communicatively impaired patients and their families. Explanations to families regarding patients' communication status often overlap with necessary basic medical information. For instance, they may entail discussions of what brain damage is and what part of the brain could be involved in communication impairment. Explanations offered to a patient's family also should focus on how family members can facilitate the patient's communicative strengths. This may require actual demonstration of some concepts with observations by the family and follow-up critiques by the speech/language pathologist.

The speech/language pathologist also should play a counseling role in providing information relative to patients' avocational or vocational futures based upon the patients' communication potentials. Many times patients are referred to vocational training programs that involve relearning or learning new skills through the basic processes of reading and writing. These modalities may not be appropriate for the language-impaired patient, unless they are geared toward the level that the speech/language pathologist recommends. Further, it may be the opinion of the speech/language pathologist that the patient be encouraged to pursue a future that does not place a high emphasis on communication skills. Proper counseling of the patient and family regarding job selection as it relates to communication impairment and interactions with vocational placement specialists will ensure that the patient is not placed in a setting where he or she will fail because of the inability to communicate.

Another specialized role for the speech/language pathologist as counselor is to facilitate interactions between the patient and other medical specialists. For instance, the patient may have a medical complaint that cannot be verbalized during medical rounds due to lack of time or because the patient cannot respond to questions as the doctor seeks to explore the complaint. Often a patient identifies with the skill of the speech/language pathologist in being able to communicate successfully with patients, and soon recognizes that the complaint can be communicated best to the speech/language pathologist. Therefore, the speech/language pathologist should be prepared to explore a patient's concerns and complaints about medical care with the patient's physician. This communication should take the basic form of determining the nature of the complaint, the duration, the general impact on the patient's health as the patient perceives it, and whether or not the complaint is acute or chronic. It is helpful in this circumstance for the speech/language pathologist to be familiar with the basic procedure involved in exploring a patient's subjective complaint. For instance, if a patient complains of leg pain, he or she should be asked to localize it, determine if it is sharp or dull and intermittent or constant, note if it changes with position, and indicate if it is relieved or exacerbated with any medications.

Additional details relating to the speech/language pathologist's role as counselor in a medical setting are discussed in Chapter 9.

Contributions to Interdisciplinary Teams

The speech/language pathologist often participates in meetings where health care professionals come together to discuss the patient's care from the viewpoints of the represented disciplines. In particular, the patient's current medical status and prognosis are presented from each discipline's standpoint, together with recommendations for treatment and any reports on the effects of treatment already completed. An example of an interdisciplinary team meeting often can be found associated with the department of rehabilitation medicine. This meeting usually is attended regularly by the physiatrist, speech/language pathologist, physical therapist, occupational therapist, nurse, social worker, and psychologist. The speech/language pathologist should be prepared to present the patient's communication strengths and weaknesses and be able to give the other team members specific suggestions on how to communicate with the patient to facilitate their interactions and to assist the patient in learning new skills.

In order to participate successfully in a multidisciplinary team, the speech/language pathologist must remain cognizant of the roles and perspectives of each team member. For example, in some settings a psychologist working on the rehabilitation team may be concerned only with the emotional and affective aspects of the patient's condition. All neuropsychological testing and assessment of cognition may be left to the speech/language pathologist. However, in another setting the psychologist may prefer to evaluate the patient's neuropsychological status in addition to providing other psychosocial information. In this instance there is the potential for conflict between the two disciplines. This can be avoided when they both view their information as complementary, confirmative, and supportive. In some cases, disagreement benefits the team and the patient. It can open new avenues for achieving the patient's rehabilitative goals. It also is imperative that the speech/language pathologist understand the perspective from which the physical and occupational therapists are viewing the patient's function. For example, what represents independence in ambulation or self-care activities will differ from therapist to therapist. For one, independence may refer to the patient's ability to carry out a task when the environment is safely structured and the patient verbally initiated or directed. A second therapist may view independence in stricter terms, whereby the patient must be able to perceive dangers in the environment and be self-initiating. The dynamics and the interaction of the various team members are variable, and it is incumbent upon the speech/language pathologist to recognize the roles played, the individual biases, and the potential conflicts that can exist on any team.

The medical speech/language pathologist should be prepared to assume the unique position as team leader in the management of patients with swallowing disorders. This role may entail directing the evaluation of the patient with dysphagia and providing treatment at the bedside by facilitating the feeding process. Since the diagnosis and evaluation of the patient with dysphagia require the services of many medical disciplines, their inputs often must be coordinated by the speech/language pathologist in the role of team leader, either by consultation or through regular interdisciplinary meetings. After receiving the consult, the speech/language pathologist screens the patient at bedside and in consultation with the referring physician and schedules additional consultations as needed. These consultations usually are made to other key members on the dysphagia team, including otolaryngology, radiology, gastroenterology, dietetics, nursing, and neurology. By consultation or in regular meetings, members decide on appropriate diagnoses and arrange for treatments. Recommendations for additional evaluation by specialists in other related fields, such as pulmonology, dentistry, and rheumatology, can be made at this time. The advantages of the multidisciplinary process in the management of these patients are well documented.[15-17]

Depending on the medical institution, the speech/language pathologist may be involved with other interdisciplinary teams including those in neurology, gerontology, and otolaryngology/head and neck surgery. In all team meetings, the focus should be maintained on providing patients with the best possible care through the contributions of many experts who are sharing their expertise for one common goal. That goal is not only to provide patients with quality medical care, but to provide care that involves aspects of their psychosocial well-being. It is anticipated that this approach eventually saves health care dollars by providing care that is more organized and therefore more efficient, while at the same time ensuring patient and family satisfaction.

STAFF EDUCATION

A major role for the speech/language pathologist in a medical setting is to provide staff education. For the purposes of this book, staff education that takes place in a medical environment can be divided broadly into two sections: (1) in-service training and (2) continuing education. *In-service training* is distinguished further by two primary areas of emphasis: (1) training on a regular, scheduled basis that provides an orientation to the department's services to new hospital employees or to nurses and physicians still in training and (2) training that department personnel receive from sources outside and within the department. The latter may consist of orientations given by other, related hospital services or of more in-depth information of general interest to the department, such as a lecture presented by a neurologist on the examination of the nervous system. In-service training presentations usually are limited to one hour.

Continuing education, while often overlapping in principle with in-service education, usually is provided by sources not located within the medical setting. Outside lecturers on contract may offer continuing education, or staff members may travel to another medical setting for a sponsored conference on an issue of interest. These conferences may last from one to three days. Topics usually are geared toward specific departmental needs, such as a presentation of new technology or a complete review of well-known information from a different perspective. Participants often receive credits from an accrediting body that assist the individuals in demonstrating that they have maintained current interest in their fields. Some professions require continuing education credits in order for the professional to remain licensed to practice.

In-service education is discussed in the next section. Other aspects of continuing education as it relates to the medical speech/language pathologist are discussed in Chapters 10 and 11.

In-Service Training

It is well-known that the public, or indeed the medical community, is not fully aware of the potential contributions to the maintenance of health care that can be provided by speech/language pathologists. Many of their contributions in a medical setting are grossly misunderstood, and the consequences can result in an under-utilization of their services that eventually will have impact on the economic and political well-being of the department. Part of the problem is due to the fact that speech/language pathologists have not had training in a medical setting to assist them in defining their role to others in that setting. A great deal of impetus for this book occurred as a result of this aspect of the problem. An ongoing, active, hospital-wide, in-service training program that focuses on orienting other professionals to the role of the speech/language pathologist is perhaps the most feasible way to increase departmental visibility and credibility. A successful orientation program, in turn, will increase the need for services, because each department that receives the training will be able to recognize clinical problems that require the expertise of the medical speech/language pathologist. If a high standard of service is maintained, the value of the service will continue to grow.

The concept of in-service training in most medical settings that provide educational opportunities for their health care professionals is tied to a commitment of providing quality health care. Orientation to other hospital services, both by lecture and by demonstration, is a common occurrence for medical students, nurses, and residents as they rotate through each designated department. They discover what each department has to offer and in what circumstances they should utilize that department's services. Another aspect of in-service training involves presentations given within a department by its staff or students, such as gastroenterologists speaking to their colleagues. Topics for this training usually fall into three categories: (1) a review of information basic to the profession (tutorial in nature), (2) a report by a staff member on new technological information that may have been acquired by attendance at a recent meeting outside of the medical setting, and (3) a journal club where a staff member is responsible for the critical review of a recently published piece of research or presents his or her own research.

The model for this type of training is established firmly in the medical setting. Most departments must develop their own programs one year in advance. It is necessary only to contact the training coordinator for each targeted department and request that the speech/language pathology service become involved in that department's in-service training program. Depending on its needs, the sponsoring department may schedule lectures for the orientation of its personnel to speech/language pathology on a regular basis. This is particularly common when a service has a large turnover rate, as in nursing, and in a teaching hospital that sponsors residency training programs.

Targeted departments in need of in-service training/orientation by the speech/language pathologist will include those disciplines with which the department is likely to have the most contact: nursing, dietetics, otolaryngology/head and neck surgery, neurology, gerontology, and rehabilitation medicine. There should be an active in-service education program pertinent to the role of the speech/language pathologist in a medical setting for all medical students and first-year residents, most of whom will have had little contact with speech/language pathology or may have developed gross misperceptions regarding its services. If the in-service presentation is designed to elucidate a specific topic, such as the speech and language characteristics of patients presenting with dementia, it is appropriate that the entire department, including attendings and fellows, be present.

The Orientation

This section will assist the medical speech/language pathologist in designing an in-service program that defines the potential roles of a speech/language pathologist in a medical environment. Inherent in the presentation is a philosophy of the role of the speech/language pathologist in a medical setting. It can be adapted to fit any philosophical approach. Not all of the slides demonstrated here will be used for every audience in every setting. The presentation is designed to last for 50 minutes and allows 10 minutes for discussion and questions. It can be adapted to any size or type of audience. The level of sophistication of information and the vocabulary are chosen to appeal to all types of audiences. Experience shows that in most cases serious concern about vocabulary is not necessary; the same information and terminology are appropriate for the orientation regardless of the educational level of the audience. The program is designed to be presented in 2×2 slide format. This format is the most common teaching format in the medical model. By association, the choice presupposes that the presenter is part of that model. This first impression helps to orient the audience to the fact that the speech/language pathologist has not come as an "outsider."

If designed properly, the slides serve as the speaker's notes. They free the audience from the boredom of listening to written presentations and ensure the spontaneity necessary for the speaker to "sell the product." Videotaped demonstrations can be utilized if they are well-edited; however, securing the videotape hardware in a busy setting often is more difficult than reserving a carousel slide projector. Various props and demonstrations can be used in its place and are discussed later. Because the "orientation to services" lecture may be given routinely, some may choose to put the entire presentation on videotape. However, a videotaped presentation only serves to further alienate the speech/language pathologist from other health care professionals. The live presentation not only provides interest and spontaneity, but allows the speaker to pause and answer questions, and to interject appropriate amounts of interest when the five o'clock audience is demonstrating signs of extreme ptosis (drooping eyelids).

The following slide presentation is similar to those used at the Seattle and New York VA medical centers to orient health care professionals to the duties and goals of the medical speech/language pathologist. It is designed to be comprehensive in nature. Avoiding specific detail on any one issue aids in comprehension, interest, and retention.

Slide 1, processes involved in the production of speech (Figure 2–10). Consider the complexity involved in producing a phrase like "Wow, I'm surprised." First, the language is formulated in response to something seen, heard, or felt. The input is interpreted and then responded to with this phrase of exclamation. The language of the remark is formulated in the left brain, with the right brain contributing an emotional intonation to give the comment the intended meaning. The motor execution is begun by eliciting a sequential motor pattern (a learned sequence of muscular events initiated in the left frontal lobe) that utilizes the systems of respiration, phonation, and articulation. The power source for speech production is the lungs. When disease decompensates the lungs, the strength of the speech signal, or how loud one is, can be affected. After air is taken in during the inspiratory cycle, the expiratory cycle pushes air up the trachea to the vocal cords. The controlled rushing of air and the neural connections to the vocal cords bring the vocal cords together. The vibrations that result from the cords' cyclic opening and closing are the sound source for speech. The sound is altered and shaped as the size and shape of the pharynx and mouth are modified by the position of the soft palate and tongue. Changes in the cavity size help to shape the vowels and stop, constrict, or redirect the air stream to form the consonants. The size of these resonating cavities and the way sounds are articulated by moving the tongue and lips are what give each individual a characteristic vocal quality.

The phrase "Wow, I'm surprised" is composed of both voiced and unvoiced sounds, or phonemes. The voiced sounds include all of the vowels and about one-

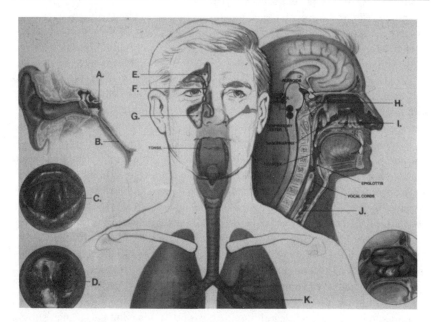

Figure 2–10 Processes Involved in the Production of Speech (Slide 1).

half of the consonants. However, a number of the sounds are produced without voice, like the initial "s" in surprised. If the "s" were voiced, one would say "zurprised." Yet the brain's control of our speech is so remarkable that it is possible to turn on and off the voice instantaneously in order to execute properly this type of phrase. If the speech and brain mechanisms were unable to perform this complex motor patterning, one would not be able to differentiate between words like "Sue" and "zoo," "pop" and "Bob," or "cot" and "God," all of which differ only in the fact that the consonants are unvoiced in the first word of each pair, and voiced in the second.

Speech and language for the most part are functions laid upon the central nervous system. The peripheral controls for the production of speech come from the spinal column and from the cranial nerves that are housed in the pons and the medulla of the brainstem. Volitional controls for speech and language reside in the subcortex and cortex at the top of the central nervous system. It has been calculated that there are about 100 muscles contributing to speech at any given time, and that there are about 100 motor units firing throughout an utterance. Additionally, one produces approximately 14 speech sounds per second in conversation. Therefore, there are about 140,000 neuromuscular events occurring during every second of running speech. This behavior is so complex and precise that a disturbance in the neuromuscular system is likely to produce a change in the speech of the individual. Speech, therefore, is a sensitive barometer to measure change in the neuromuscular system.

Slide 2, glossopharyngeal breathing (Figure 2–11). With an understanding of the complexity of the speech mechanism, one can begin to consider how this system can deteriorate. The first mechanical component necessary to produce speech is respiration. When respiration fails completely, patients require mechanical systems, or respirators, in order to survive. If respiration is not completely lost, but impaired by damage to the nervous system or lungs, the following functions will be affected. (At this point, the speaker repeats the phrase "Wow, I'm surprised" with maximum and minimum breath support and points out the change in voice. The speaker might ask members of the audience to exhale, and repeat the phrase on residual air.)

Patients who sustain high cervical damage to the spinal cord often are rendered quadriplegic. In quadriplegia, the muscles of respiration are compromised, and so is the power needed to speak and produce an efficient cough. An efficient cough is essential for these patients since their inactivity often leads to respiratory complications. Teaching the patient a technique called glossopharyngeal breathing, originally developed in the days of the poliomyelitis (polio) epidemic to free victims temporarily from an iron lung, may help to improve both the strength of the voice and the strength of the cough.

Glossopharyngeal breathing (GPB), or frog breathing, is accomplished by taking a maximum inspiratory effort and then gulping and pumping air into the lungs beyond that inspiration while holding the breath. (At this point the speaker should

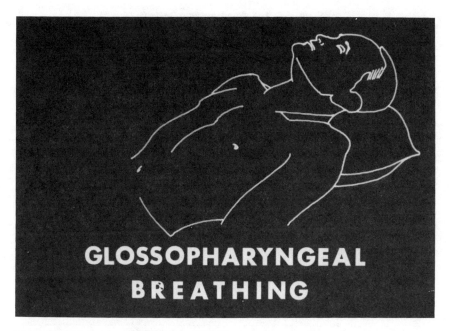

Figure 2–11 Glossopharyngeal Breathing (Slide 2).

demonstrate the technique by exhaling all air from the lungs, beginning the glossopharyngeal technique, and then speaking. This demonstrates that air can be pumped into the lungs for use in speech and cough beyond what the patient normally can inspire.)

Slide 3, effects of GPB (Figure 2–12). After a patient was taught to use GPB, a series of measurements was made that compared the patient's vital capacities before and after GPB. In all but one measure, the patient demonstrated he could improve his vital capacity. If the situation demanded increased vocal volume or an improved cough, the patient utilized his GPB technique to accomplish it.

Slide 4, another patient on GPB (Figure 2–13). This patient learned the glossopharyngeal breathing technique so well that he continued to improve his vital capacity after ten weeks. Before treatment his vital capacity was so low that speech was barely audible, and he required constant suctioning. By improving his vital capacity to over two liters, his speech was now audible, and he could clear his own secretions with an adequate cough.

Slide 5, fiberoptic view of the vocal cords (Figure 2–14). This is what examiners see when they look down a patient's airway. At the top of the picture is the epiglottis in its resting position that allows a view of the false and true vocal cords. As mentioned earlier, the true vocal cords come together under neural impulses

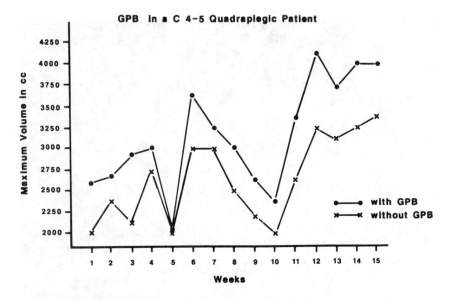

Figure 2–12 Effects of Glossopharyngeal Breathing (Slide 3).

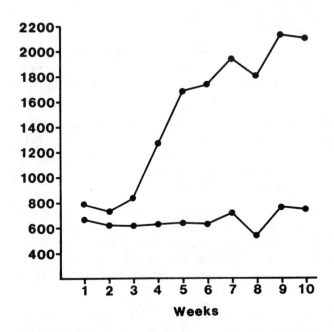

Figure 2–13 Vital Capacity of a Patient Using the Glossopharyngeal Breathing Technique (Slide 4).

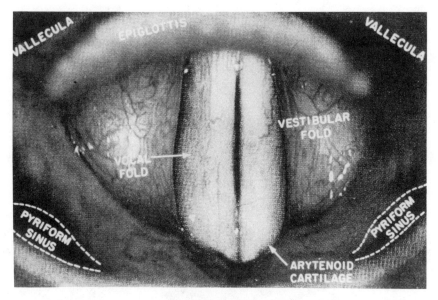

Figure 2–14 Fiberoptic View of the Vocal Cords (Slide 5). *Source:* Reproduced with permission from Michael Groher (Ed.), *Dysphagia: Diagnosis and Management,* Butterworth Publishers, Stoneham, MA, © 1984.

and by air pressure sucking them together and setting them into vibration. On either side of the larynx are the pyriform sinuses and the vallecular spaces (between the tongue base and epiglottis) through which food and fluid pass on their way to the esophagus. During swallow, the vocal cords remain closed, and the epiglottis is turned down in maneuvers to momentarily block and protect the airway.

Slide 6, bilateral vocal fold nodules (Figure 2–15). Some people misuse their voices and put undue stress on the vocal cords that results in small blisters called vocal nodules. Such stress can come from excessive yelling, poor breath support for speech as when a person runs out of air and continues to talk, or from speaking at an inappropriate pitch level. Other patients develop larger lesions called polyps as the result of the chemical abuses of smoking or alcohol or sometimes from acid reflux associated with heartburn. These growths on the vocal cords create irregular vibrations and may prevent the cords from coming together. The result is a harsh or hoarse voice that is breathy due to the air escape. Many of these patients can be taught to use their voices more effectively and reduce the size of these growths. Patients that do not respond to remediation may need to have the polyps surgically removed. Following surgery, the patients should be evaluated by the speech/language pathologist for follow-up voice treatment. Another vocal cord problem is paralysis of one or both vocal cords, usually due to neurologic disease. Following heart or carotid artery surgery, patients may have a paralyzed vocal cord that makes them hoarse, because the tenth cranial nerve that innervates the vocal cords is stretched in some procedures involving the heart. In unilateral paralysis, some pa-

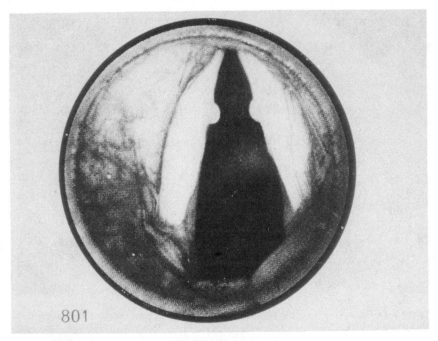

Figure 2–15 Bilateral Vocal Fold Nodules (Slide 6).

---

tients can be taught special techniques to help the normal vocal cord meet the damaged one to make a more acceptable voice.

Slide 7, cancer of the vocal fold (Figure 2–16). The growth on the vocal cord shown in the slide is cancerous. Cancerous lesions in the larynx require immediate attention. Any patient who complains of hoarseness or swallowing difficulty should have the larynx examined. Cancer of the larynx is often caused by irritation of the tissues from inhalation of tobacco smoke, frequently in combination with alcohol abuse. Cancer of the larynx usually is not painful, and patients may wait a long period of time before having an examination. Some are treated for laryngitis before the larynx is ever visualized and the tumor discovered. Changes in voice and difficulty in swallowing are important warning signs.

Slide 8, laryngectomy (Figure 2–17). When cancer has invaded the larynx, the patient may be a candidate for total removal of the larynx. In some cases, only one vocal cord is removed. This is called a hemilaryngectomy. When the surgeon removes the larynx, the procedure is called a total laryngectomy; the airway and the foodway are functionally separated. The patient must breathe through a permanent tracheostomy, called a stoma, but has lost voice and the ability to speak. The speech/language pathologist counsels the patient before the operation and discusses the communication alternatives following removal of the vocal cords. In the immediate postoperative phase, patients may find it difficult to move their bow-

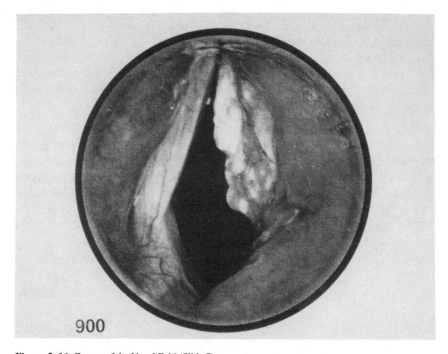

Figure 2–16 Cancer of the Vocal Fold (Slide 7).

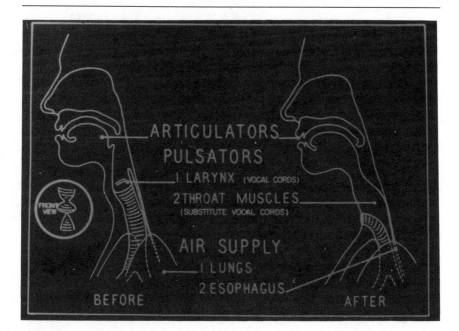

Figure 2–17 Laryngectomy (Slide 8).

els because they cannot hold a column of air to push against (valsalva) for normal defecation. By teaching the patient to valsalva by occluding the stoma, the use of harmful laxatives can be avoided. Patient education in this regard is important. The speech/language pathologist provides the patient with pencil and paper or with an electronic communication device for use in communicating basic needs in the immediate postoperative phase of recovery.

Slide 9, electrolarynx, an option for vocal rehabilitation (Figure 2–18). Prior to total laryngectomy, the speech/language pathologist counsels the patient regarding the options for communication. Following surgery, the speech/language pathologist provides the necessary training in vocal restoration. One method is the use of an electrolarynx. The electrolarynx is an artificial sound source that can be placed on the side of the neck or cheek or introduced into the oral cavity if the patient has excessive neck edema, radiation fibrosis, or surgical scarring on the

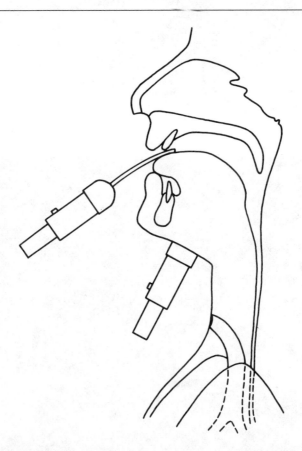

Figure 2–18 Electrolarynx, an Option for Vocal Rehabilitation (Slide 9). *Source:* Reprinted from *Cancer: Principles and Practice of Oncology,* Vol. 2, 2nd ed., by V.T. DeVita, S. Hellman, and S.A. Rosenberg, p. 2172, with permission of J.B. Lippincott Company, © 1985.

neck. For neck use, the sound source must be flush against the skin. The patient must be taught to move the articulators in a distinct pattern, as well as certain aspects of phrasing and maintenance of eye contact. (Now the speaker would demonstrate the use of the electrolarynx using the phrase "Wow, I'm surprised" and pointing out how the electrolarynx produces only voiced phonemes and how the meaning is filled in by the context. If the audience is small enough, participants may attempt to use it.) A patient can be issued an electrolarynx for use approximately seven days following the operation. The patient may choose to use this mode of communication after this time or in special speaking situations, such as on the telephone or in situations where there is excessive background noise. The electrolarynx also may be used for tracheotomized patients with cuffed tracheotomy tubes who have the motor strength in their hands and articulators to manipulate it. It is appropriate for patients in intensive care units who have been temporarily tracheotomized secondary to cardiopulmonary complications, but who retain their cognitive and motor skills.

Slide 10, esophageal voice (Figure 2–19). Another option for communication following total laryngectomy is esophageal voice. The patient is taught to trap and inject air and take it down to the level of the top of the esophagus. By gently tightening the stomach muscles, while at the same time relaxing the upper esophagus, the patient is taught to produce a controlled belch-like voice. This voice serves as the new sound source for speech. By controlling the voice, the patient eventually can articulate four or five words at a time before it is necessary to take in additional air. In an accomplished esophageal speaker the intake of air is not noticed by an observer, but the speaker's voice sounds somewhat hoarse and low-pitched. (The speaker now demonstrates some esophageal voice or uses a recorded sample).

Slide 11, tracheoesophageal puncture (Figure 2–20). A third option for vocal rehabilitation following total laryngectomy is tracheoesophageal puncture (TEP). The procedure can be done either at the time of laryngectomy or as a secondary procedure at any time following laryngectomy. The otolaryngologist makes a small puncture at the top of the patient's stoma, and the patient then is fitted with a prosthesis by the speech/language pathologist. The prosthesis extends through the airway and into the esophagus where the voice for speech is made. The front of the prosthesis is taped to the patient's neck. The patient must be taught to clean and insert the prosthesis. Patients who do not have the preoperative cognitive or motor skills necessary to manage the prosthesis independently are not candidates for this procedure.

Slide 12, TEP prosthesis (Figure 2–21). A closer view of the TEP prosthesis helps to explain how voicing is achieved. Before beginning to speak, the patient must seal off the stoma with the thumb. (The speaker demonstrates.) This directs the air through the small hole in the open end of the prosthesis. The air travels down the tube to the tip that is located in the esophagus. The tip has small slits, or a valve, that allow air to flow into the esophagus. As the air moves up the esophagus toward the mouth, it passes an area of resistance at the pharyngoesophageal seg-

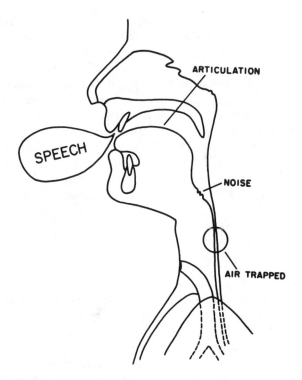

Figure 2–19 Esophageal Voice (Slide 10).

ment that is vibrated just as in esophageal speech and produces a voice. This vocal sound is articulated in the same way as in a person who speaks normally. The tip of the tube is designed to stay tightly closed when the patient swallows to avoid any leakage into the airway. It is recommended that the patient receive a new tube every few months as the strength and turgor in the valve decrease. Proper cleaning and disinfecting of the prosthesis are necessary to avoid any bacterial or fungal contamination of the airway.

Slide 13, dysarthria (Figure 2–22). Disorders of speech articulation and resonance usually result in dysarthria. Dysarthria is a reduction of speech intelligibility that compromises the processes of articulation, resonation, phonation, and respiration. The muscles involved in these processes are either weak or uncoordinated, conditions usually secondary to damage in the central nervous system. It is very important to distinguish between a patient who cannot be understood because of dysarthria and one who is unintelligible because of aphasia. The slide illustrates that the dysarthric patient comprehends well and can formulate all language responses, whereas the aphasic patient's expressive disorder may be one of language and not speech production. The treatment for each is very different.

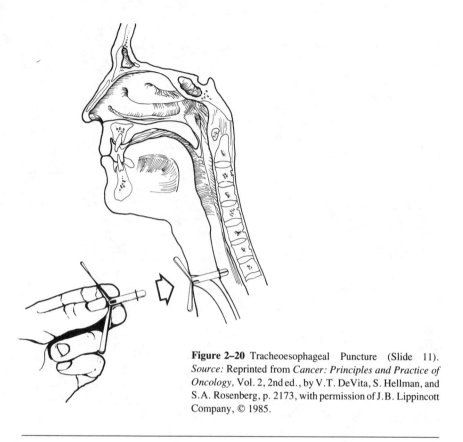

Figure 2–20 Tracheoesophageal Puncture (Slide 11). *Source:* Reprinted from *Cancer: Principles and Practice of Oncology,* Vol. 2, 2nd ed., by V.T. DeVita, S. Hellman, and S.A. Rosenberg, p. 2173, with permission of J.B. Lippincott Company, © 1985.

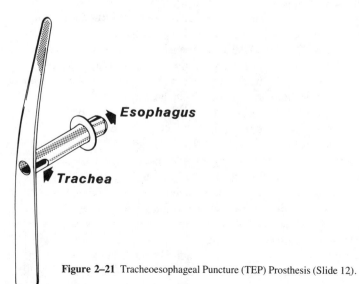

Figure 2–21 Tracheoesophageal Puncture (TEP) Prosthesis (Slide 12).

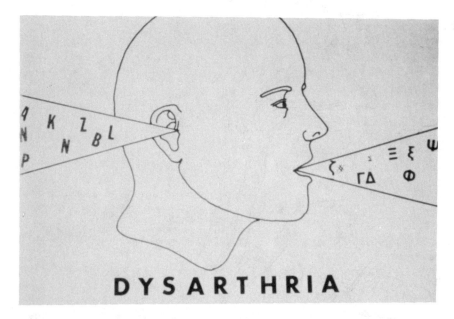

Figure 2–22 Dysarthria (Slide 13).

Patients with central nervous system damage may have both dysarthria and aphasia. It is the job of the speech/language pathologist to differentiate and distinguish between the two. The dysarthric impairment usually coincides with the site and level of damage to the nervous system. For instance, a patient with an ataxic dysarthria will have coincident damage to the cerebellum or its connecting tracts. The cerebellum helps to coordinate the processes of articulation and respiration. In pathology, the lack of the coordination causes irregular bursts of loudness and abnormal stress patterns. It is akin to the speech pattern that can result from imbibing too much alcohol. Patients who have spastic limbs that are slow and uncoordinated also may have spastic speech with the same signs of slowness and incoordination. Flaccid dysarthrics show little or no movement in the articulators with severe compromise in intelligibility. (The speaker then can imitate some of these dysarthric types while using the same short phrase as in the other examples.)

Treatment for the dysarthrias largely involves principles of perceptual training in which the patient must listen to his or her speech pattern and make the appropriate adjustments. It is the responsibility of the speech/language pathologist to determine which process (articulation, resonation, phonation, or respiration) most interferes with speech intelligibility and focus on changing it as an immediate goal in treatment. For some patients, such as those with flaccid dysarthria and reversible disease, muscle strengthening exercises may be appropriate. For patients with progressive neurologic disease, such as amyotrophic lateral sclerosis or myasthenia gravis, these exercises are contraindicated.

Slide 14, nonvocal communication (Figure 2–23). Some patients with dysarthria do not improve in their speech but do retain their ability to think and use language. For these patients, a nonvocal or augmentative communication device may be appropriate. There are many electronic communication devices available today. Not all of them are dependent on good motor control. For instance, the patient in this slide could not move his arms, but could move his head. Therefore, a pointer was attached to a headband, and the patient could select the proper letter or word. Other special selection mechanisms, such as switches that need minimal strength or movement to operate, are also available. Establishing viable communication systems for these patients greatly facilitates their care and provides them with an essential human behavior.

Slide 15, dysphagia (Figure 2–24). A recently recognized role for the speech/language pathologist is the management of patients with dysphagia. In many centers, the speech/language pathologist facilitates the multidisciplinary evaluation that these patients require by involving the services of the neurologist, otolaryngologist/head and neck surgeon, dietitian, radiologist, occupational therapist, and gastroenterologist as they are needed. For discussion purposes, dysphagia can be divided into three major categories. Mechanical dysphagia is largely the result of an inability to move food and fluid into the esophagus due to resections of the mouth or pharynx secondary to carcinoma or to surgical alterations in these structures. The patient has lost portions of the upper aerodigestive tract and also has

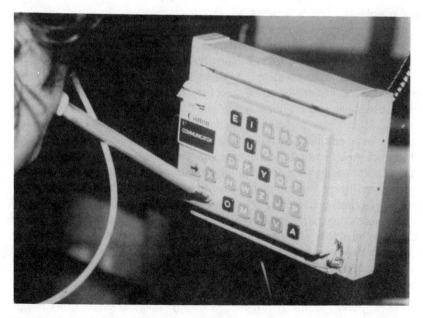

Figure 2–23 An Electronic Device for Nonvocal Communication (Slide 14).

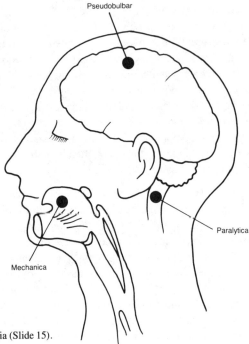

Figure 2–24 Dysphagia (Slide 15).

some peripheral nervous innervation to those structures. Treatment involves prosthetic management and instruction in bolus control and propulsion, as well as airway protection drills. The second category, dysphagia paralytica or paralysis, is the result of damage to the lower motor neurons of the brainstem. The patient's musculature is so weak that there is no strength to move the bolus. In many cases the patient is tracheotomized and has accompanying respiratory problems. Treatment involves management of the airway and strengthening exercises in reversible conditions. Some patients may be taught to swallow their own feeding tube as a way to maintain nutrition without having the tube inserted on a 24-hour basis.

The third group consists of patients with pseudobulbar or supranuclear dysphagia. These patients have lost the ability to coordinate a swallow reflex and often have accompanying behavioral disturbances that disrupt the feeding process. These deficits in cognitive integrity, such as distractibility, forgetting to chew and swallow, and taking inappropriate bite sizes, as well as the patient's diet, must be managed in treatment. It is important to remember that patients with swallowing dysfunction can have problems in the entire aerodigestive tract, including the mouth, pharynx, esophagus, and stomach, and that a complete evaluation will include an investigation of each.

Slide 16, pureed food tray (Figure 2–25). An important aspect of dysphagia treatment is the patient's diet. Patients with swallowing dysfunction typically are

Figure 2–25 A Sample Tray of Pureed Food (Slide 16). *Source:* Reproduced with permission from Michael Groher (Ed.), *Dysphagia: Diagnosis and Management*, Butterworth Publishers, Stoneham, MA, © 1984.

given a tray similar to the one pictured. Food has no taste, temperature and texture are unappealing, and the food lacks sufficient pressure to stimulate a swallow reflex. Additionally, thin textures and fluids tend to be the most difficult items for some patients with oropharyngeal dysphagia to swallow. It is necessary to provide a diet that stimulates a swallow reflex and often the fluids should be thickened for easier control. Each patient deserves an individual assessment and diet recommendations customized to his or her particular needs.

Slide 17, brain damage (Figure 2–26). As mentioned earlier, speech and language are processes that have their roots within the central nervous system. Because these functions are highly organized, they often are the first affected when the nervous system is compromised. Changes in speech and language functions may signal impending changes in the integrity of the nervous system. Similarly, monitoring the improvement in these functions can help document positive changes in nervous system activity. The slide illustrates some common etiologies that potentially can interfere with ability to communicate. A *thrombosis* is a buildup of clotted material in the wall of the artery that, if severe enough, can cause a stroke with subsequent loss of communicative skills. Likewise, other vascular etiologies that temporarily reduce the oxygen supply to parts of the brain include *embolism* (a floating clot from a large vessel, such as the heart, that becomes lodged in a smaller one) and a *hemorrhage* (where a blood vessel breaks and the

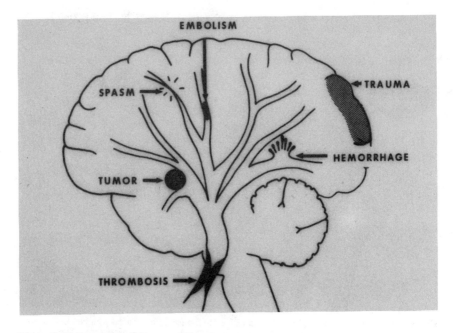

Figure 2–26 Types of Brain Damage (Slide 17).

bleeding must be controlled). Some patients experience a vessel *spasm* (a temporary change in the hemodynamics of the artery) and suffer mild brain damage. A blow to the skull (*trauma*) can cause brain damage at the site of the blow or in areas away from the impact and create diffuse or bilateral brain damage. Brain damage results not only in pathology to speech and language, but also to the patient's behavior. The central nervous system's role in controlling aspects of behavior and cognition is to facilitate emotional expression, thought, or movement by inhibiting unwanted behaviors and allowing others to manifest themselves. Loss of inhibition that is a frequent accompaniment of brain damage will make it difficult for a patient to control previously well-inhibited functions. Therefore, it is not unusual for brain-damaged patients to make errors of judgment, tear or laugh easily, have a difficult time in accessing words, or be unable to remember and learn new information.

Slide 18, aphasia (Figure 2–27). One consequence of brain damage that is familiar to speech/language pathologists is aphasia. For most individuals, the language centers are located in the left brain. Even the majority of left-handers, whose leading hemisphere is on the right, have their language centers located in the left hemisphere. Since most individuals have their language centers in the left brain, damage to the left cerebral hemisphere is most likely to cause disturbances in the ability to communicate. For the majority, the right hemisphere is more responsible for the integrative aspects of vision and music. It is known that this hemisphere

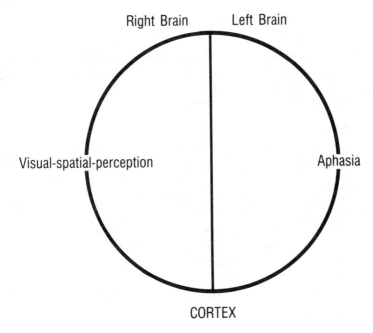

Figure 2–27 Aphasia (Slide 18).

takes a leading role in orienting individuals to their environment. Therefore, it is not unusual for those patients with right hemisphere dysfunction to have some disturbance in spatial orientation.

Slide 19, definition of aphasia (Figure 2–28). As the slide indicates, aphasia is the result of localized brain damage, usually to the left hemisphere, that compromises the propositional aspects of both expressive and receptive language. There are three major points that must be remembered in classifying a patient as aphasic. First, the true aphasic patient will demonstrate only *localized,* not *bilateral,* brain damage. The implications of this distinction are clearer when observing the demented patient who also may have language impairment but no evidence of focal brain dysfunction (see discussion under Slide 23). Second, aphasia is a disturbance of *propositional* language, a term that refers to using language creatively. Most people use many of the same words all day long, but in different circumstances, in different sentences, and on demand. This is opposed to *nonpropositional* language that is characterized by automatic expressions, such as "I'm fine" and "O.K.," counting, and swearing. For example, when hitting his thumb with a hammer, a man would not stop and think of what to say. The utterance would be an expletive like "darn" or "phooey" or perhaps something more demonstrative.

It is these nonpropositional language utterances that typically are retained by the aphasic patient, whereas the propositional ones are impaired. When the family member tells you that the patient is talking, it is wise to judge the quality of the

APHASIA: Definition

An acquired impairment of propositional language functioning in persons who have suffered localized (usually left) cerebral damage that results in a reduced capacity to understand and produce recognized communicative symbols.

Figure 2–28 Definition of Aphasia (Slide 19).

utterance before concurring that this represents a change in communicative status. For example, patients may say only "be-be-be" with good inflection or "plca-blab eufast glibport" that sounds as if they are talking in a foreign tongue. Some caregivers and family members do feel that this is another language, particularly when the patient is a polyglot. The final point regarding the definition of aphasia is that both expressive and receptive language disturbances will be found in all patients. It may be that the patient has a more obvious receptive or expressive problem; however, with the use of a sensitive testing instrument deficits in both modalities are observed. Caregivers must recognize this fact in order to interact in the most therapeutic manner.

Slide 20, integrated functions in aphasia (Figure 2–29). Within the expressive and receptive communication modalities are the functions of speaking, comprehension, reading, and writing. These centers are located in known sites in the left hemisphere and are connected by associational fiber tracts. Therefore, any pathology within a center or within a connecting fiber tract often affects other centers. This explains why aphasics often have brain damage in the comprehension centers and concurrent deficits in writing and thought formulation.

Slide 21, complications of aphasia (Figure 2–30). The slide lists some of the more common complications of aphasia. First, the aphasic patient may have difficulty remembering what is said for a sufficient period of time in which to identify the information or to respond if the situation requires it. For instance, a speaker may say to an aphasic, "John, did you talk on the phone today with Bill or Fred?" John might not be able to remember that the response would have to be either Bill or Fred, because that information was at the end of a long sentence. Second, the aphasic patient may not have access to as large a vocabulary as before the brain insult. The patient also may have difficulty retrieving the desired word (*anomia*). In most cases this difficulty is most obvious with nouns. (Here the speaker can provide examples of anomia: the anomic who gives up, the one who circumlocutes, and the one who uses paraphasia to finally hit the intended target.) Faulty syntax may be evident by the inability to combine words into a correct order within the sentence or by the omission of parts of speech. (Again, the speaker can interject some examples.)

Poor channel selection is characterized by the inability to comprehend internally information that may be coming into the brain from a number of various mo-

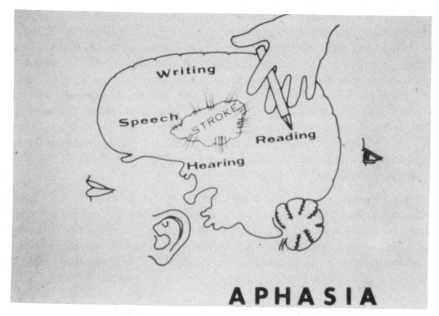

Figure 2–29 Integrated Functions in Aphasia (Slide 20).

Complications of Aphasia

1. Reduced auditory memory

2. Reduction in vocabulary

3. Faulty syntax

4. Poor channel selection

5. Processing delays

Figure 2–30 Complications of Aphasia (Slide 21).

dalities, such as by listening, watching, feeling, or reading. The confusion this brings to the brain-damaged mind makes it difficult to sort out the relevant inputs. When the patient tries to respond to an input, the inability to select the correct output mode also is evident. Finally, the aphasic patient will experience marked delays both in processing and responding to information. In treatment it is necessary to tolerate these delays at first and work toward improving the time between stimulus and response.

Slide 22, the aphasia profile (Figure 2–31). In evaluating the patient with communication dysfunction it is important to assess all of the modalities utilized in the performance of the communicative act. The modalities are those cognitive constructs that allow an individual to communicate with the environment. Included are the processes of language comprehension, language expression, auditory memory, visual motor perception, visual motor memory, and ideation (creative problem solving). The slide shows a typical profile of the aphasic patient and demonstrates that weakness in communication is restricted to the modalities of language expression, reception, and retention, while the processes involving the visual and thinking (nonlinguistic) modalities remain intact. (See Chapter 7 for details of the mental status examination.)

Slide 23, aphasia versus dementia (Figure 2–32). It is necessary to distinguish between a person with a communication disorder related to aphasia and a person with a communication disorder secondary to dementia. The distinction is important, because the aphasic patient will benefit more from direct therapeutic interventions and therefore is a better rehabilitation candidate. The demented patient shows the following characteristics:

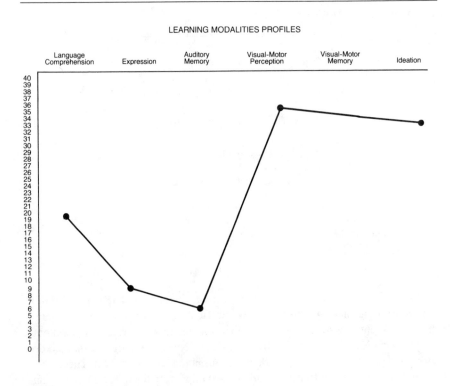

Figure 2–31 The Aphasia Profile (Slide 22).

APHASIA VS. DEMENTIA

APHASIA	DEMENTIA
1. Oriented	1. Disoriented
2. Learns by demonstration	2. Learning impaired in all modalities
3. Relevance intact	3. Often irrelevant, rambling
4. Appropriate behavior	4. Inappropriate behavior

Figure 2–32 Aphasia versus Dementia (Slide 23).

- is not oriented
- does not learn well through any modality
- is usually fluent in the early stages
- lacks relevance in conversation
- demonstrates anomia
- demonstrates inappropriate behaviors, such as indifference to self-care skills, inattention to the current task, and failure to interact in a socially appropriate manner

A person with aphasia, for example, can decide what to eat for dinner, go to the store, buy the groceries, return home, cook the meal, and clean up. A person with dementia, on the other hand, may know what he or she wants to eat, but does not have the skills to find or remember the items when at the store, gets lost when coming home, and cannot sequence the necessary steps to cook. As the disease progresses, the demented patient shows signs of faulty syntax and inappropriate use of words. The pragmatics of language, such as turn-taking, also are impaired.

Slide 24, aphasia versus language of confusion (Figure 2–33). The language deficits of aphasia also should be differentiated from those associated with confusion. The language of confusion usually is associated with patients who have communication deficits secondary to traumatic brain injuries, such as those sustained in motor vehicle accidents. Traumatic injury may cause deficits not only in language, as in aphasia, but in other cognitive functions, including attention, vigilance, perception, orientation, and memory. This is attributed to the diffuse involvement of the brain often seen following traumatic injury. Residual deficits of behavior control and memory are barriers to communication and learning after the acute stages of recovery. Because trauma often compresses the brainstem, a patient who suffers traumatic injury usually evidences an accompanying dysarthria.

Slide 25, recovery profiles (Figure 2–34). This slide shows a sample communicative recovery profile measured immediately following a stroke and after

APHASIA	LANGUAGE OF CONFUSION
1. Usually vascular	1. Usually traumatic
2. Older in age	2. Younger in age
3. Focal deficits	3. Diffuse deficits
4. Specific language impairment	4. Cognitive impairment
5. Memory may be good, oriented	5. Residual memory disorders, disoriented
6. Behavior appropriate	6. Behavioral problems

Figure 2–33 Aphasia versus Language of Confusion (Slide 24).

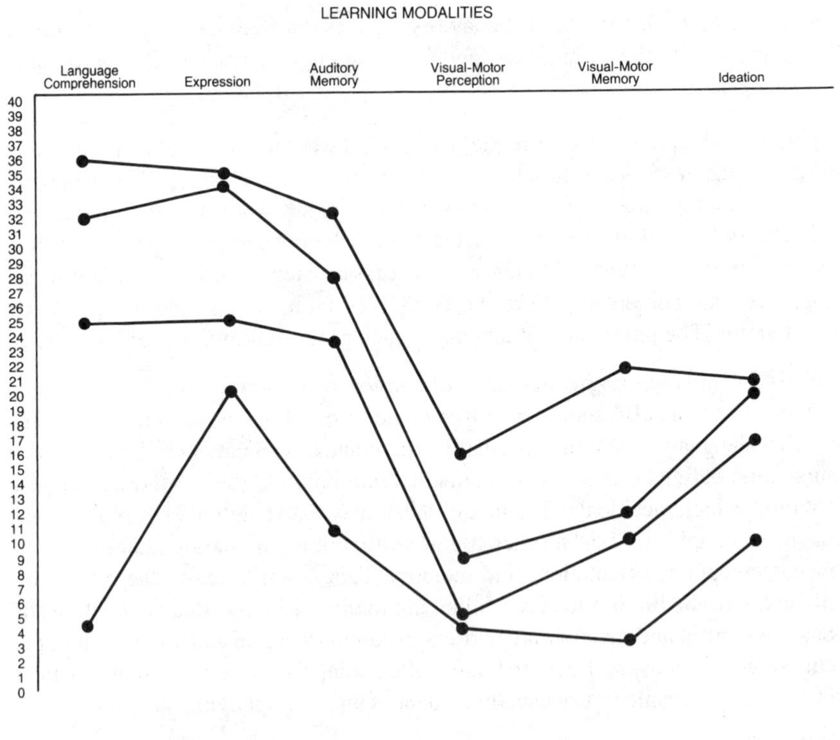

Figure 2–34 Recovery Profile of a Stroke Patient (Slide 25).

one and two months of speech and language remediation. Following stroke, the patient had severe language deficits, moderately severe visual integration disabilities, and severe ideation, or problem-solving, deficits. Because the patient could not communicate basic needs, it was recommended that all of the patient's needs be anticipated, and that the patient's rehabilitation schedule be routinized so the patient would be able to anticipate more communicative needs. The visual modality was the strongest, and the health care team was instructed to combine all communication to this patient with the liberal use of gesture and demonstration. Using this structure, the patient's ideational skills made marked improvement after the first month. By the second month, as language comprehension improved, the health care team was instructed to use less demonstration, because the patient was now able to understand most auditory information. This approach served to move the patient into a role of more independence, while reinforcing the speech/language pathologist's suggestion that the patient be allowed to rely more on the auditory system. With a major residual deficit in auditory memory, the patient still had to rely on the frequent repetition of information and on written lists.

Slide 26, individual language remediation (Figure 2–35). Individual speech and language remediation should focus initially on strengthening the patient's strongest learning modality. Part of this remediation is ensuring that the rest of the health care team is taking the same approach with the patient and working through the patient's strongest learning modality to reach a desired goal. It is important that the patient is helped to understand communication limitations and immediate goals at the outset of remediation. Early remediation is geared toward improving a patient's receptive and expressive vocabulary with words and concepts that are part of the immediate hospital surroundings. Other potentially useful sources for vocabulary include known hobbies, occupations, or special interests of the patient. Having the patient repeat sentences or relearn the alphabet usually does not have any therapeutic benefit. As the patient progresses, the focus of remediation should continue in the direction of strengthening the best learning modalities and allowing the patient to use these modalities more in interactive, structured conversation. Most patients never fully regain their former communicative levels and must work within the confines of their disabilities.

Slide 27, group remediation (Figure 2–36). In addition to individualized speech and language remediation, many patients benefit from the therapeutic advantages of a group process. It can assist patients to make adjustments to their communication disabilities. First, they see other patients with similar disabilities who are struggling to communicate. Second, they see others who are able to communicate at levels above themselves. A skillful group leader can use this latter point as a strong motivator to achieve higher goals. The group situation provides a forum for communicatively impaired patients to talk to their peers and not feel embarrassed by their hesitancies or mistakes. In this regard the group experience can serve as a bridge between hospital life and returning home. Many medical centers sponsor aphasia groups on an outpatient basis with the same goals in mind. Pa-

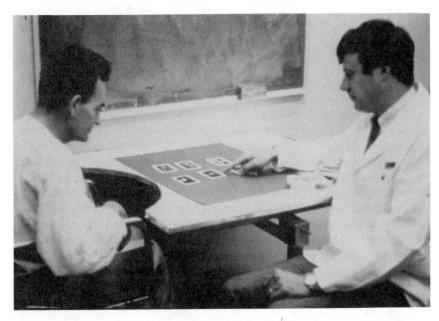

Figure 2–35 Individual Language Remediation (Slide 26).

Figure 2–36 Group Remediation (Slide 27).

tients can continue to improve their communicative interactions in a familiar environment.

Slide 28, family counseling (Figure 2–37). Patient treatment should include the family as part of the process. The family should be educated on how best to communicate with its loved one. If the patient can understand but is unable to express himself or herself, the family should know that it is important to talk to the patient in simple, straightforward terms at an adult level and not expect anything in return. If the patient is capable of making yes/no judgments, the family can communicate with the patient in this fashion. It is important to emphasize that the aphasic patient will need additional time to understand information and formulate responses. Family members must be indulgent and allow the patient extra time. They should not fill in missing words or provide information at a complex level or rapid speaking rate. Due to the patient's physical and mental limitations caused by the stroke, family members may find themselves in different roles. For instance, if the husband, who did all of the household business before, is the stroke patient, the wife probably will assume this role. (See Chapter 10 about issues in counseling.)

Slide 29, right hemisphere damage (Figure 2–38). Because of the right hemisphere's role in visual integration and because the visual modality is important both in normal communication and in compensating for the deficits of aphasia, it is important for the speech/language pathologist to evaluate the patient with right hemisphere brain damage. This is a typical learning modality profile of a patient with right hemisphere pathology. It is almost the exact opposite, or a mirror image, of the patient with left hemisphere damage. This patient has good expressive and receptive language skills, but has decreased visual motor memory and perception abilities.

Patients with right hemisphere damage frequently have disturbances of visual integrative skills, such as the inability to put together the necessary steps in getting dressed, yet they can explain exactly how to do it. It is this discrepancy between good communication skills and poor visual-motor performance that interferes with this group's ability to learn. However, the knowledge that the patients' strength in learning is through the linguistic modality can be used to their advantage in treatment. Rather than trying to demonstrate new learning tasks, the correct procedure is to place the emphasis during instruction on the auditory and graphic (writing) modalities. Besides visual integration problems, patients with right hemisphere damage frequently evidence difficulty in comprehending the emotional content of an utterance, understanding idioms, and expressing their emotions. (The speaker can say, "Wow, I'm surprised," with little emotion or intonation.) These characteristics manifest themselves behaviorally in a certain concretism of social interaction, and often the patients are viewed as uncaring or unsympathetic, even to their own disabilities.

Slide 30, drawings by patients with right hemisphere damage (Figure 2–39). The inability of these patients to integrate information through the visual modality

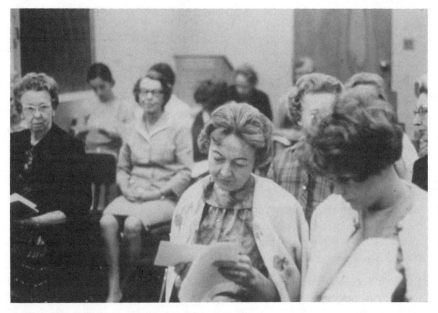

Figure 2–37 Family Counseling (Slide 28).

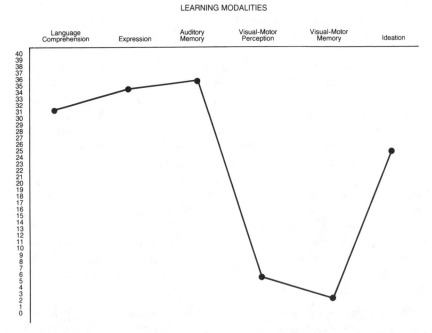

Figure 2–38 Learning Modality Profile of a Patient with Right Hemisphere Damage (Slide 29).

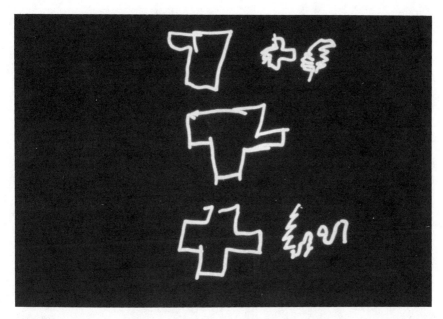

Figure 2–39 Drawings by Patients with Right Hemisphere Damage (Slide 30).

can be tested in part by having them copy geometric figures. This slide shows attempts by three patients to copy a cross. All three drawings show various distortions of the intended target. The patients were using their dominant, unimpaired hands for copying.

Slide 31, summary of right hemisphere damage (Figure 2–40). This summary of patients with right hemisphere damage indicates three general characteristics. First, the patients are apparently unable to look at something through the visual modality and to integrate it into a learning format. For instance, the occupational therapist may demonstrate a sequence of motor acts for upper extremity strengthening, but the patients will not be able to put them into the proper order to obtain the desired effect. The second characteristic is their propensity to be able to convince someone verbally that they can perform on visual-motor tasks, but they fail to demonstrate that they can. When asked by their physicians if they have learned to dress themselves, they will indicate that they can and describe the steps, often in greater detail than necessary. The accuracy of their verbalizations serves to convince the listener until the actual performance is requested. Even after failure, they often do not recognize their apparent limitations. Finally, they will compensate best for these deficits if they are talked through a sequence of motor steps, rather than if they are shown how to perform.

Slide 32, optokinetics (Figure 2–41). Some patients with brain damage, particularly those with damage to the right parietal lobe brain, will neglect one-half of

SUMMARY OF RIGHT HEMISPHERE LESION

1. Impaired ability to make visual-spatial judgments.
2. Patients talk a good story, but perform poorly.
3. Capitalize on language skills by talking them through activities.

Figure 2–40 Summary of Right Hemisphere Damage (Slide 31).

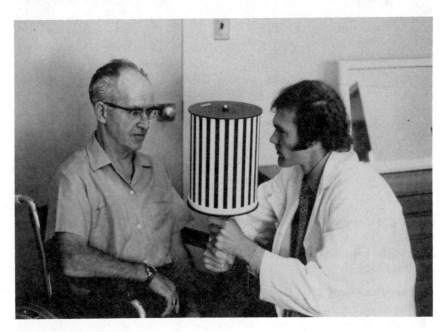

Figure 2–41 Optokinetics (Slide 32).

their immediate space. This makes communication attempts from that side impossible. In the early stages, communication can be enhanced by approaching the patient from the side of non-neglect. Confirmation of neglect can be done by eliciting optokinetic nystagmus. Optokinetic nystagmus is a rhythmic movement of the eyes that is seen when a moving target is passed in front of them, such as the eye movement of a person who is watching a train pass. The movements can be elicited by a tape with equally spaced black lines. When testing for the presence of optokinetics, the examiner is testing the ability of the cerebral cortex to integrate sensory information. When the tape is brought in from the patient's right visual field, the integrity of the sensory integrative cortex in the left hemisphere is being evaluated. Conversely, the right hemisphere is tested from the left visual field. (At this point the speaker may want to demonstrate optokinetics with a member of the audience or show an optokinetic tape.) Patients who have no response from one side or the other tend to have neglect, and their rehabilitation prognosis will be affected by this devastating loss. They should be approached from the strong side and placed on a very repetitive schedule to enhance any chances of learning. As the response returns, patients may begin to improve their attention. This may allow them to learn new information. The physiologic response can be used to predict who may gain the most benefit from intensive rehabilitation. Unfortunately, the predictive value of this reflex only applies when the response is absent. When it is present, there is no assurance that the patient is a good rehabilitation candidate.

Slide 33, clock face (Figure 2–42). The clock face is an example of a drawing by a patient with right hemisphere damage and left spatial neglect. This can be assessed by asking the patient to complete the conceptually based task of putting the numbers on a clock face. In this example the patient attended only to the right half of the clock (intact left hemisphere) while totally ignoring the left (damaged right hemisphere). This patient also would forget to shave half of his face, to put both arms into a shirt, or to put on two shoes.

Slide 34, neglect demonstrated by writing (Figure 2–43). This is the writing of a patient who initially had a total neglect, but had recovered to the point of being able to compensate if cued verbally to do so. When asked to write single words he did so but placed them on the right-hand side of the paper. While the words are

Figure 2–42 Drawing by a Patient with Right Hemisphere Damage and Left Spatial Neglect (Slide 33).

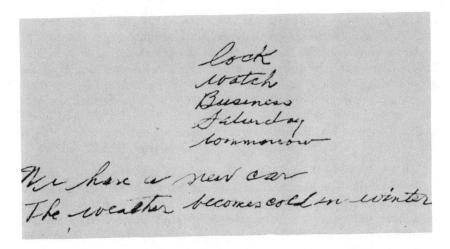

Figure 2–43 Neglect Demonstrated by Writing (Slide 34).

spelled correctly, the patient demonstrates residual attentional errors in his failure to dot the i's and cross the t's. When his neglect of the left visual space was pointed out to him, he was able to write the sentences with the proper orientation. Treatment, then, focuses on forcing the patient to attend to the visual space being neglected, first using cues on every stimulus and gradually working toward fewer reminders if learning is demonstrated.

Slide 35: (For the summary, show Slide 1 again. See Figure 2–10.) Communication is a complex process. Disorders can affect any component of speech production, including respiration, phonation, resonance, or articulation. The subcortical and cortical connections to these peripheral systems house the language centers that understand and formulate the message to be spoken. As seen in the presentation, there is a wide variety of communication disorders in need of interventions by the speech/language pathologist. Each patient should receive a full evaluation of his or her disability. The results should be communicated to the patient and the family if they are to receive maximum benefits from the services of the speech/language pathologist.

The presentation should end with the speaker indicating to whom and where consults for the services of the speech/language pathologist can be sent. The location of the service in the medical setting should be indicated, as well as telephone and beeper numbers. The speech/language pathologist will wish to emphasize that this is a general orientation intended to give the audience an interest in the subject so they will want to explore specific topics such as language disorders, dysphagia, dysarthria, and laryngectomy, in future presentations.

SUMMARY

Most training institutions currently are not providing the background necessary for speech/language pathologists to enter the medical environment. Therefore, speech/language pathologists may have difficulty adjusting to a hospital setting. Part of the difficulty will stem from the hospital staff's uncertainty regarding the role of speech/language pathologists, and part will come from the speech/language pathologists' own lack of preparation for entering a medical environment. Most medical specialists assume that the main function of speech/language pathologists is to provide rehabilitation for communication disorders. In order to assume a more prominent place in the medical environment, speech/language pathologists must expand their roles as diagnosticians. Additionally, they need to be more aggressive in their roles as translators of medical information to and from communication-impaired patients, and as counselors to patients' families. This chapter explores roles for medical speech/language pathologists and suggests methods of educating others to these roles.

The most common interfaces for medical speech/language pathologists on issues involving both communication and swallow will be with otolaryngology/head and neck surgery for patients with disease involving the head and neck, with neurology for patients with the many neurologic diseases that impact negatively on communication, and with rehabilitation medicine for the rehabilitation of patients with stroke (both right and left brain) and trauma. Direct contact with the nursing service at patients' bedsides is important because nurses can assist in the identification of both communication and swallowing disorders and in the reinforcement of management suggestions. Speech/language pathologists must be familiar with other services concerning issues of communication and swallowing disorders. These services include medicine, gerontology, dietetics, dentistry, gastroenterology, and radiology. Another important role of speech/language pathologists is coordinating the medical center's dysphagia team that consists of gastroenterology, radiology, and dietetics. These are services with which speech/language pathologists previously may have had little contact.

The role of medical speech/language pathologists must be communicated to the majority of hospital sections if their services are to be utilized fully. A suggested format to provide this communication through in-service training focuses on the processes of speech production and of language, how they may be impaired, and how they can be managed.

NOTES

1. S.J. Wetmore, M.E. Johns, and S.R. Baker, "The Singer-Blom Voice Restoration Procedure," *Archives of Otolaryngology* 107 (1981):674–76.

2. Michael E. Groher, "Mechanical Disorders of Swallowing." In *Dysphagia: Diagnosis and Management*, ed. Michael E. Groher (Stoneham, Mass.: Butterworth Publishers, 1984), 61–84.

3. Mark I. Singer and Eric D. Blom, "Selective Myotomy for Voice Restoration after Total Laryngectomy," *Archives of Otolaryngology* 107 (1981):670–73.

80   MEDICAL SPEECH PATHOLOGY

4. Arnold E. Aronson, *Clinical Voice Disorders: An Interdisciplinary Approach* (New York: Thieme Inc., 1985),·57–76.

5. Raymond D. Adams and Maurice Victor, *Principles of Neurology* (New York: McGraw-Hill Book Co., 1977), 832–33.

6. Ibid.

7. "Ad Hoc Committee on Dysphagia Report," *American Speech and Hearing Association* 29 (April, 1987):57–58.

8. William J. Ravich et al., "The Swallowing Center: Concepts and Procedures," *Gastrointestinal Radiology* 10 (1985):255–61.

9. Martin W. Donner, Editorial, *Dysphagia* 1, no. 1 (1986):1–2.

10. Michael E. Groher and Rochelle Bukatman, *"The Prevalence of Swallowing Disorders in Two Teaching Hospitals,"* *Dysphagia* 1, no. 1 (1986):3–6.

11. John L. Stauffer et al., "Complications and Consequences of Endotracheal Intubation and Tracheotomy: A Prospective Study of 150 Critically Ill Patients," *American Journal of Medicine* 70 (1981):65–76.

12. James F. Bosma, "Functional Anatomy of the Upper Airway During Development." In *Respiratory Function of the Upper Airway*, eds. Matthew P. Oommen and Guiseppe Sant'Ambrogio (New York: Marcel Dekker, Inc., 1988), 47–85.

13. Barbara B. Shadden, "Communication and Aging: An Overview." In *Communication Behaviors and Aging: A Sourcebook for Clinicians*, ed. Barbara B. Shadden (Baltimore, Md.: Williams & Wilkins Co., 1988), 3–11.

14. Michael E. Groher, "Modification in Speech and Language Procedures for the Older Adult." In *Communication Behaviors and Aging: A Sourcebook for Clinicians*, ed. Barbara B. Shadden (Baltimore, Md.: Williams & Wilkins Co., 1988), 248–60.

15. Ravich et al., "The Swallowing Center," 255–61.

16. Donner, Editorial, 1–2.

17. Pamela L. Jones and Sherry L. Altschuler, "Dysphagia Teams: A Specific Approach to a Nonspecific Problem," *Dysphagia* 2, no. 4 (1987):200–05.

Chapter 3

Communication and Disease

INTRODUCTION

The ability to communicate by use of conventional symbols is a trait unique to humans. It is an achievement of ontogenesis, by anatomic and physiologic adaptions of the airway and articulators from newborn to infancy to mature adult, culminating in the development of the cerebral cortex. It is by this specialized development that the manipulations of language and the sensory/motor aspects of speech are combined. And even though the communicative act is overlaid on, and largely subject to, the operative control of the central nervous system, it does not function in a vacuum or outside of influences imposed on it by the environment, the human psyche, and basic biologic processes. In total, human communication is understood best when the communicative act is viewed as a consequence of the integrated performance of external and internal forces that potentially impact on central nervous system activity. Within the complexity of these integrations lies the strength of its operations—to be able to produce an unending chain of thoughts, each with a unique syntax, and to be able to solve problems by reasoning with words. In essence, language allows one to control the environment. Its weakness also emanates from its complexity; to function optimally it requires an exact homeostasis. To evaluate and treat speech and language disorders, the speech/language pathologist must recognize this vast array of associated functions and be prepared in assessment to discover the impact of each process (biological, environmental, or psychological) on communication.

COMMUNICATION: A DYNAMIC PROCESS

A frequent question from the spouse of a language-impaired adult is "How come John did so well with his talking yesterday, but can't say a thing today?" Behind this inquiry is the unspoken fear that something terrible has happened to John: that

81

he had another stroke, that one is coming in the near future, or that he must need some type of medical attention. In fact, she may be right, but most often it is not the explanation for his perceived, sudden nonexpressiveness. The answer lies, in part, in understanding the concept that one's ability to communicate is not a static, but a dynamic process.

Humans have the capacity to produce what Jackson called propositional utterances.[1] The result of human propositions is evidence for a communicative system that is creative and adaptive, and designed to respond to exchanges of information that move in time, always in different patterns and directions but rarely repeated in perfect duplication. Language has an inherent flexibility, subject to performance by interactions among often unobserved internal (physiological) variables and among more observable (but not always well-recognized) external variables. Internal factors include those that affect metabolism, such as the state of fatigue, nutrition, the emotional state (sadness, joy, anger, or reflection), and medications. Other potential physiologic decompensators such as a head cold or urinary tract infection influence metabolism both directly by their effect on body temperature and the immune system and indirectly by altering energy levels, hydration, and nutrition. External factors that impact on the communicative act include the situation (lighting, noise, number of speakers), the topic, the time of day, and the persons involved. Acting together, these internal and external forces play a role in helping to explain why John did so well one day and not so well the next. Rarely do the requirements of the situation remain stable, even though one may talk to the same person about the same topic. A strict analysis of the two situations would undoubtedly reveal the answer. In short, the two circumstances were not the same and therefore are not comparable.

Under close scrutiny, the dynamic properties of human communicative exchange rarely duplicate one another. Examples of the immense possibilities for variation in the effects of these internal and external forces abound in everyday communicative exchanges, yet the generality always comes forth because it is easier to observe; John talked better yesterday than today. In fact, perhaps John's wife talked better yesterday than today, but the difference was less noticeable because her nervous system was able to perform the necessary compensations. In the brain-damaged patient, the decompensated cortex does not respond as easily, and the differences that emerge are more obvious. The speech/language pathologist who attempts to describe objectively the communicative ability of those with brain damage should be cognizant of the fact that a sample of behavior is being collected at one particular time and in one particular situation. This may or may not accurately reflect the patient's communicative capacities. The skillful examiner will assess communication effectiveness at a point in time by simultaneously recording pertinent clinical observations, physiological responses, and mental status measures for comparison purposes (see Chapters 5, 6, and 7).

Communication: A Barometer

Because the efficiency of the communicative act is subject to alteration by an almost infinite number of forces with unknown strength, speech and language become an important barometer for detecting change in a patient's mental or physical health. Therefore, when a patient complains of communication incompetence it becomes necessary not only to examine the central nervous system where speech and language have most of their operative genesis, but to be prepared to understand and look for other biologic, psychologic, and environmental factors that might influence the diagnosis or that might impact on treatment decisions. In his writing on the human nervous system, Jackson often returns to the concept that more complex behaviors, such as speech and language and the cognitive constructs they support, are frequently the first to be affected in pathology.[2] Inherent to this highly organized structure is a sensitive barometer that may signal impending disease. Sometimes subtle changes in communication will precede the demonstrable appearance of structural damage[3] such as in the patient with lower motor neuron disease who first complains of a change in vocal quality, assuming it is secondary to an upper respiratory tract infection. Therefore, careful attention to changes in communicative patterns may be a more sensitive indicator of decompensation in health than more sophisticated objective clinical or laboratory measures. Knowing how to focus one's attention on those aspects of the communicative process that may signal change in health is part of the responsibility of the medical speech/language pathologist.

Communication and Decompensation

The same neural networks that subserve speech and language are indicators of change in health because of the complexity of their circuitry. They are programmed to be sensitive to a great number of incoming signals, similar to the factors that impact on communication. This complexity also serves to protect the integrity of its function by providing some redundancy in the network system. It allows the organism to remain flexible enough to respond consistently in both favorable and unfavorable circumstances. It maintains a homeostasis.

Fatigue, anger, nutritional deficiency, and the conversational topic and speakers involved may interact to reduce communication effectiveness. In most cases, the normal brain automatically acts to compensate for any potential negative factors. For instance, an extemporaneous speaker knows that the presentation on the following day will be more effective if a good night's rest is followed by a hearty breakfast. Because compensations are available, however, the speaker is capable of giving the same quality talk to the same audience without that audience perceiving any adverse effects from the speaker's having been up all night and not eating before the presentation. The speaker was able to do well in spite of the apparent obstacles of little sleep and food. The audience was provided with an excellent performance because of the plasticity of the central nervous system, brought about as a consequence of its complex, redundant circuitry for communication. In this case involving a normal brain, the central nervous system was able to adapt to adverse physiologic influences that potentially could decompensate its overall effectiveness. However, when the nervous system is damaged, these compensations are more difficult to achieve. How well the damaged brain is able to make these compensations is what the speech/language pathologist must first measure and then treat.

The relative ability of the nervous system (and communication function) to protect itself from destruction means that it is prepared to combat assaults on its integrity from a variety of sources (biologic, psychological, and environmental) and can remain functional as it makes the necessary compensations. However, there comes a point where the additive effects of multiple insults will decompensate the whole organism as if the organism had suffered one major event, such as a cerebrovascular accident. Therefore, in pathology, the patient's speech and language disorder need not be the result of one obvious catastrophic event, but it may be the result of a number of minor insults that, in total, tip the scale enough to decompensate function. Too often the burden to explain a patient's communication deficits must be on the existence of one demonstrable brain lesion, when in fact multiple "lesions," both obvious and occult, serve as the etiologic explanation. The medical speech/language pathologist will do well to review and understand all of the physiologic mechanisms that impact on communication in an attempt to document those systems that are normal, those in compensation, and those that have been decompensated.

Communication and Emotion

Changes in one's emotional state can affect both speech and language. These changes may not be pathologic, such as the effect on one's voice during brief fits of anger, or in the selection of words (more nonpropositional utterances) under the same stresses. How a person intones an utterance or uses facial and body gestures can convey meaning beyond the words themselves. Loss of the use of this faculty is a frequent accompaniment to right brain damage.[4] In psychiatric disease or in response to terminal systemic disease, such as cancer, patients can become so depressed that they make no attempt to communicate, or they may present with inaudible voices. Even relatively minor situational depressions can be enough to decompensate patients with aphasia and to exacerbate their impaired performance on all language functions. Patients who take medication to control psychoses may show parkinsonism-like disturbances in speech production as a side effect of the drug. Patients troubled by chronic anxiety may present with problems in articulation with noticeable repetitions and difficulties in regulating their rates. The language of patients with schizophrenia needs to be differentiated from that of patients with aphasia (usually fluent) and dementia.[5]

Communication and Environment

Social situations can influence the quality of communicative exchanges that take place during the course of human interactions. Alluded to earlier, these situations provide an array of external forces on individuals that may facilitate or detract from the interactions. For instance, most people feel they communicate best when they are in familiar surroundings with familiar faces or when they are in leisure activities as opposed to being at work. Conversations with authority figures often are identified as situations that impede normal communicative exchanges in both amount and quality. Some people find that an environment free of noise is conducive to their most successful communicative exchanges.

The normal brain tries to compensate for these variations in social situations. A person may feel uncomfortable speaking to a boss, but that person nonetheless does communicate a message. Perhaps it is even communicated seemingly with no undue stress. However, for the brain-damaged patient or even for the normal brain that may be temporarily decompensated, making the necessary adjustments during stress that is related to environmental factors may not be within the capacity of the nervous system. When the brain is unable to compensate, communication falters. Correct pronunciation, word selection, thought sequencing, and sentence word order may emerge as insurmountable obstacles or as difficulties that once may not have been so obvious.

Communication and Aging

As stated previously, a major role of the speech/language pathologist is to identify those aspects of a person's communication that are normal, in compensation, or are decompensated. In evaluation, normality is relative and needs to be defined as a comparison of the diseased state to a known level of prior competencies, usually determined by education and age. Speech and language changes associated with the aging process are well-known.[6] They include physiologic changes in the end organs of hearing and vision as they impact on auditory discrimination, reading, writing, voice, and articulation and changes in the cognitive processes as they affect language (naming skills, linguistic problem solving, auditory processing speed, and expressive response times). It is inappropriate to identify a recommended treatment for a patient whose skills are considered to be in the normal range relative to age and educational level. Determinations of when communicative decrements fall below expected normative levels and the documentation of the suspected reasons for the decline are concerns of the speech/language pathologist.

The combination of the impact of emotions, environment, and the aging process often interact to decompensate the elderly patient beyond what any one factor alone could explain. For instance, Mr. Z was an 80-year-old patient in good health except for a cataract in his right eye and a bilateral sensorineural hearing loss for which he refused hearing aids. Although he lived alone, he had many friends at a senior center that he attended daily. He suddenly developed right-sided weakness and aphasia. While he was hospitalized his friends came to visit, but they found him angry and frustrated by his communication loss, and soon they stopped coming. In spite of excellent motor recovery, his communication functions lagged far behind and kept him home for most of each day. An evaluation of his communication skills determined that several factors were combining to exacerbate his difficulties. He was fitted with bilateral hearing aids and the appropriate corrective glasses. He was given an antidepressant, and his friends at the senior center were instructed in the most efficient ways to compensate for his aphasia in the context of his favorite activities. Without formal traditional language treatment, the patient's communication skills improved dramatically. He returned to the senior center and took part in most of his usual activities.

DISEASE AND DISEASE PROCESSES

The speech/language pathologist working in a medical setting must be aware of diseases and disease processes that most often interfere with a patient's ability to communicate. Particular knowledge of the course and prognosis of the disease is helpful in treatment decisions. The speech/language pathologist should know if and when intervention is appropriate. It must be determined whether the patient can benefit from intervention or whether treatment is contraindicated, such as exercising the muscles of a patient with myasthenia gravis. In some cases, a characteristic speech or language pattern may help the physician to differentiate one disease from another or to recognize when the services of the speech/language pathologist should be considered.

The majority of disorders that may impact negatively on communication are either those that are the direct result of damage to the central nervous system (neurologic disease), such as a tumor in the cerebral cortex, or those that arise outside of the central nervous system (systemic). Systemic disorders affect structures under the control of the central nervous system, such as extreme muscle weakness (myopathy) from endocrine disorders that may alter the production of speech. A frequent role of the neurologist is to differentiate between the two types of disorders. For instance, the neurologist must decide if a patient's acute facial weakness represents damage from within the nervous system, as from a stroke, or from cranial nerve involvement from a malignant lung lesion (outside the central nervous system) that has metastasized to the head and neck and compromised vocal fold integrity secondary to involvement of cranial nerve 10.

The challenge for medical speech/language pathologists is to broaden their knowledge base of disorders that affect communication and arise from central nervous system pathology. They also must strive to become more familiar with those physiologic systems outside of the central nervous system that act to decompensate it. A brief review of disorders of central nervous system origin that affect communication is presented below. The most common systemic diseases that may involve the central nervous system during the course of their manifestations are discussed in the next section.

It is not the intent of these sections to provide exhaustive detail about each disorder, but to call to the attention of the practicing speech/language pathologist a method of viewing a disease and its potential relationship to the communicative process. It should be remembered that the signs and symptoms mentioned are not always present in the same degree in every patient. Some progressive diseases in the early stages may not compromise communication but may affect it during later stages. Similarly, mild forms of a disease such as meningitis may not affect communication; however, severe forms may result in communication disorders. Overgeneralizations should be avoided. Communication disorders should be supported or denied only after considering the available data from the medical record, interview, and examination.

No one classification of disease can account for each disorder that may impact on the central nervous system and, by implication, on the speech/language pathologist. Some diseases, like scleroderma, often interfere with the physiology of the nervous system. Scleroderma is often classified and discussed as a disorder of neurogenic origin, but it is also described as a disorder of the body's connective tissue that interferes with neurologic control over the muscles it affects. Therefore, classifications often overlap without total agreement into which category a disease is best placed.

Neurologic Disease

Broadly speaking, all symptoms of a disease can be classified as neurologic if one takes the position that to perceive illness requires, first, intact sensory receptors and, second, an intact cortex to recognize that the illness represents a departure from a previous state of health. Neurologic disease results when there is structural (loss of functioning cells) or physiologic (inadequate functioning of cells) damage in the central (brain and spinal cord) or peripheral (spinal and cranial nerves) nervous system. Headache that arises from extracranial, nonneural sources and pain secondary to muscle and joint disease are exceptions and typically are considered to be neurogenically based.[7]

Disorders of Consciousness

An individual must maintain a reasonably alert level of consciousness to communicate. Disease that can impact on that individual's level of consciousness, such as a severe infection, may interfere with communication. In general, disorders of consciousness deny the patient access to, or proper use of, the cerebral cortex. Most frequently both hemispheres are involved. The patient does not appreciate any incoming stimuli, and output for communication is nonfunctional. The patient often may be difficult to arouse or become agitated and combative in an attempt to respond to stimuli. Disorders of consciousness include coma, stupor, obtundation, delirium, confusion, the vegetative state, and the locked-in syndrome. In locked-in syndrome (bilateral interruption of the cortical-spinal tracts at the midbrain-pontine level) patients may be able to achieve communication with vertical eye movements as they usually have access to the cortex.[8] Patients with certain psychiatric diseases, such as catatonic schizophrenia, severe depression, hysteria, and malingering, also may evidence marked changes in their levels of consciousness and arousability. More common central nervous system pathologies that cause changes in consciousness with concomitant reduction in communicative ability include encephalitis, neoplasm, infarct, hemorrhage, and hematoma (see Table 3–1).

Cortical Disorders

Many diseases of central nervous system origin and others from outside the central nervous system can impact on the cortex. Not all of these diseases are mentioned in this section; some are noted in other portions of this chapter.

Behavioral disorders. Abnormal changes in mood and behavior most likely are due to changes in the brain's chemistry and electrical activity and, therefore, can be considered representative of cortical disorders. In most circumstances, however, the physician tries to distinguish between disorders that affect the psyche as the result of structural brain lesions and those where there is no demonstrable pathology. The distinction often is difficult because psychogenic reactions (schizophrenia, anxiety disorders, or affective and dissociative disorders) can follow or be a part of organicity. In general, psychiatric disturbance causes loss of responsiveness to the environment and, with it, a failure to communicate. Schizophrenic language disorders need to be distinguished from those secondary to dementia or aphasia. Speech characteristics of patients with acute anxiety attacks may mimic those of patients with disease of the basal ganglia. Medications (phenothiazines) given to control these disturbances may have side effects that involve the orolingual-facial structures (tardive dyskinesia). Usually seen as uncontrollable movements of the articulators at rest and volitionally, they can impair both speech intelligibility and swallow. Patients in severe depressive states may have disturbances in the volume and clarity of speech and in their memory and concentration. Those in manic states evidence excessive rates of speech that interfere with intelligibility. In both of these states, patients may complain of inability to eat and swallow, either from disinterest (depression) or from choking sensations as in panic and hysterical states. Patients who demonstrate neurologic symptoms in the absence of physical findings may convert psychologic feelings into organic "realities" (conversion reaction). These often include problems with voice (usually aphonia and breathing difficulty) and swallowing (globus hystericus and rumination) disorders. It is important to realize that a patient without a history of psychiatric disease who complains of a lump-in-the-throat feeling (globus hystericus) most often has an organic etiology for the complaint. A complete swallowing evaluation is indicated.[9] The patient with true globus hystericus complains of the lump as a sticking sensation during periods not involved with swallowing, and the complaint often is relieved by a swallow.

Table 3–1 Central Nervous System Pathologies That Affect Consciousness/Communication

Level of Lesion	Mechanism
Supratentorial	
Directly invading or destroying the posterior ventromedial diencephalon	Neoplasm
	Infarct
	Encephalitis
Compressing or herniating diencephalon against the upper brainstem	Cerebral hemorrhage
	Large cerebral infarction
	Subdural hematoma
	Epidural hematoma
	Brain tumor
	Brain abscess
Subtentorial	
Compressing or destroying the midbrain-upper pontine reticular formation	Pontine or cerebellar
	hemorrhage
	Infarction
	Tumor
	Cerebellar abscess

Source: Reprinted from *Cecil Essentials of Medicine* by C.J. Carpenter, F. Plum, and L.H. Smith with permission of W.B. Saunders Company, © 1986.

Focal disease. Focal disease, usually from vascular etiologies of thrombosis and emboli that involve the cortex, often results in aphasia when it presents in the left hemisphere and in disorders of affective language and perception when it involves the right hemisphere. The speech/language pathologist should evaluate both groups of patients to determine their strongest learning modalities in preparation for the most efficacious rehabilitative interventions (see Chapter 7). Focal disease with vascular etiologies also may involve the subcortex and produce "atypical aphasias" and disturbances of speech production ranging from hesitations and stuttering-like behaviors to complete mutism. Infarcts in the brainstem can affect the cranial nerves that innervate the muscles needed for speech production.

Diffuse disease. Diffuse involvement of the cerebral cortex affects the cognitive process of language and memory. It is thought that destruction of the hippocampal centers is responsible for reduced memory skills.[10] Often compromised by alcohol abuse (chronically as in *Korsakoff's psychosis*, acutely as in *Wernicke's encephalopathy*), hippocampal involvement produces disorientation combined with memory and general intellectual impairments. If left untreated it will destroy the patient's ability to use thoughts and ideas to communicate.

Patients who are considered to be demented from neurologic sources may show the characteristic decrements in speech, language,[11] and swallow as the disease progresses to termination. Most primary neurogenic causes of dementia are summarized in Table 3–2. They can be divided into those that are not treatable and primarily involve the cortex (Alzheimer's disease, Pick's disease, Creutzfeldt-

Table 3–2 Major Causes of Progressive Dementia

Cause	Percentage of Cases
Senile dementia, Alzheimer type	50
Multi-infarct (arteriosclerotic)	20
Combination of Alzheimer type and multi-infarct	
Communicating hydrocephalus	5
Alcoholic or post-traumatic	5
Huntington's chorea	5
Intracranial mass lesions	5
Uncommon or mixed with above: chronic drug use, Creutzfeldt-Jakob disease, metabolic (thyroid, liver, nutritional), degenerative (spinocerebellar, amyotrophic lateral sclerosis, parkinsonism, multiple sclerosis, Pick's disease, Wilson's epilepsy), static dementia	10

Source: Reprinted from *Cecil Essentials of Medicine* by C.J. Carpenter, F. Plum, and L.H. Smith with permission of W.B. Saunders Company, © 1986.

Jakob disease, and multi-infarct) and those that involve the subcortex (Parkinson's disease, Huntington's chorea, Wilson's disease, and progressive supranuclear palsy). Other treatable dementias that also can interfere with central nervous system cortical activity, mostly from etiological sources outside of the nervous system, include acute depression, alcoholism, electrolyte disturbances (salt and water imbalances), renal and hepatic (liver) disease, cardiopulmonary disease, toxins (including misuse of medications), and endocrine disorders.[12]

Sensory Disorders

Impairments in the sensory (input) function of the central nervous system can be both acute and chronic. Some, such as those associated with visual and hearing impairment, may go unnoticed until they reach a stage where the individual no longer can compensate for the loss. Others, such as acute pain, are more obvious and require immediate attention. In addition to the primary loss of the effectiveness of the sensory apparatus, often there are secondary psychological effects.

Pain. Some patients will complain of pain that primarily can involve those structures involved in speech and hearing. If intense and chronic (not always relieved by analgesics), the pain may be diagnostic of neurologic disease and may interfere with speech intelligibility and swallowing efficiency. Pain in the vicinity of the ear may come from neurologic involvement of the glossopharyngeal nerve (glossopharyngeal neuralgia), from herpes zoster involving cranial nerves 5 and 7, or from disease involving the teeth, tonsils, larynx, or nasopharynx. Encountered most often is trigeminal neuralgia in which the patient experiences sudden, sharp pain and spasms over the facial distribution of cranial nerve 5 that are precipitated by talking or eating.[13] Similarly, patients with glossopharyngeal neuralgia complain of pain in the distribution of cranial nerves 9 and 10 with the focal point of pain in the tonsil or oropharynx. When neoplastic lesions have been ruled out as a primary source, patients receive some relief from their pain with Tegretol (carbamazepine).

Smell and taste. Disorders of smell (anosmia) and taste (ageusia) can serve to decompensate a patient's swallow, particularly if they are overlaid on other neurologic etiologies that are known to produce swallowing dysfunction. Neurologic diseases that have been known to alter smell and taste include Parkinson's disease,[14] multiple sclerosis, viral infections, herpes zoster, seizure disorders, and trauma. The anticholinergic side effects from some medications also may interfere with taste by reducing the amount of saliva (xerostomia) that plays a role in exciting the taste buds.

Vision. Since vision is the primary sensory input system for the majority of treatment approaches for speech and language disorders, it is helpful to be aware of the type of visual disturbance the patient has in an effort to try to compensate for the deficits. Damage in the visual system is a frequent accompaniment of neurologic disease. It may result from tumor, vascular insufficiency in the brainstem and cortex, infectious processes (neurosyphilis), or demyelination disease (multiple sclerosis) or as a secondary effect of diabetes. Disorders can include unilateral or bilateral blindness, scotomas (blind spots), diplopia (double vision), and ophthalmoplegia (from botulism, Guillain-Barré syndrome, or myasthenia gravis). Involvement of cranial nerves 3, 4, and 6 from neurologic disease is common.

Motor Disorders

Motor disturbances resulting from central nervous system pathology usually affect the muscles needed for speech production in the same manner that they involve muscles needed for ambulation and upper extremity functions. For instance, spasticity seen in the arms and legs may be found in the articulators, although it may not be as apparent in the head and neck due to the brain's bilateral representation of the midline (speech) musculature. Ataxic involvement of the extremities also can be noted in the patient's ataxic speech. The motor disturbances that affect the intelligibility of the speech signal (dysarthria) may or may not occur coincidentally with linguistic disorders, depending on the level of involvement in the central nervous system. For instance, disease that affects the upper motor neurons in the cortex also may involve language centers, whereas involvement of the upper motor neurons at the midbrain level would most likely produce only disruption of speech. Dysarthria can result from either upper or lower motor neuron disease. Other disorders of the motor system, such as those resulting from damage to the cerebellum and basal ganglia, usually exist in isolation, reflecting the fact that the disease process is located predominantly in that one structure.

A common feature of pathology that produces motor disorders is a disruption of normal muscle physiology. The pattern of behavior often will be consistent with a particular disease entity or site of lesion. *Spastic muscles,* consistent with disease in the upper motor neuron, result in discoordination and slowness of voluntary movements in the absence of significant muscle weakness. Deep tendon reflexes are exaggerated. *Flaccid muscles,* consistent with lower motor neuron disease, are severely weakened muscles with loss of tone. Deep tendon reflexes are diminished, and atrophy and fasciculations (fine muscle bundle twitchings) usually are present. *Myotonia* is a prolonged contraction of a group of muscles during any voluntary effort. *Tremor* can be abnormal movements of muscle groups seen at rest, as in Parkinson's disease, or as an *intention tremor* seen only during voluntary movement, as in cerebellar disease. *Asterixis,* a flapping tremor that can involve the tongue, is seen most often as a consequence of metabolic encephalopathy (see metabolic disease in the next main section on systemic disease). *Dystonia* refers to involuntary contractions (usually of basal ganglia origin) lasting for a second or more, briefer than the same contortion-like movements seen in *athetosis.* In *chorea* these movements are rapid and nonrhythmic. *Tics,* such as those associated with Gilles de la Tourette's syndrome, are rapid contractions of muscle groups that are quick, sudden, and more irregular than those of chorea. *Myoclonus* is an abrupt muscle contraction, usually involving the limbs and trunk. It may be seen in the palate and is associated with certain lesions at the pontine level.

Diseases of muscles. Disease of the muscle body when it involves the muscles of respiration and the head and neck has an impact on speech production. Such disorders are classified as *myopathies.* An inherited myopathy that can affect speech intelligibility is muscular dystrophy, although in most cases the weakness is confined to the support musculature (strap musculature) important in phonatory adjustments and in swallow. The facial musculature also may be involved. There are a number of varieties of muscular dystrophy including Duchenne-Landouzy dystrophy, limb-girdle dystrophy, oculopharyngeal dystrophy, and myotonic dystrophy. The latter two commonly affect speech production.

Myotonic dystrophy interferes with the intelligibility of the speech signal, since it has a predilection for involvement of the cranial nerves and facial muscles. Weakness of the sternocleidomastoid muscles further compromises both speech and swallow. Blindness in later stages may interfere with attempts at rehabilitation. Patients' known sensitivity to cold suggests special diet management to facilitate their efforts to produce normal swallows. Oculopharyngeal dystrophy is a rare disease most frequently found in French Canadians that affects the muscles of the eyes and pharynx.[15]

The inflammatory myopathies of dermatomyositis and polymyositis are discussed under musculoskeletal and connective tissue diseases in the next main section on systemic disease. The endocrine-based myopathies that impact on the central nervous system are discussed under metabolic disorders in that section.

Diseases of the neuromuscular junction. Myasthenia gravis is the primary disease involving the neuromuscular junction that can affect both speech and swallow by compromising the head/neck and respiratory muscles. Due to an abnormally rapid fatigability of the muscle strength, the patient will not be able to move the articulators or produce enough continuous movement for swallow. Treatment usually is accomplished by the administration of an anticholinesterase agent, such as Prostigmin (neostigmine) or Mestinon (pyridostigmine bromide). An intravenous injection of either medication can improve lost muscle function in a matter of minutes. Use of these anticholinesterase agents in excess, however, can precipitate a cholinergic crisis characterized by sudden muscle weakness and potential respiratory failure. Some patients receive relief of symptoms through intermittent use of steroids. Current thinking suggests that myasthenia gravis is an autoimmune disease, and it often is associated with disorders of the thymus gland. In addition to medication, other treatment approaches include plasmapheresis and thymusectomy.

Botulism, usually resulting from eating contaminated foods, also can compromise the integrity of the neuromuscular junction with symptoms of bulbar paralysis. This can produce respiratory failure, with an accompanying loss of both speech and swallow.

Diseases of the peripheral nerves. Diseases involving the peripheral nerves are broadly classified as *neuropathies.* Their etiologic sources vary, from idiopathic, such as demyelinating neuropathy; to focal neuropathy from trauma (effects of compression); to infectious neuropathy, as in herpes zoster; to vascular neuropathies, as in periarteritis nodosa; and to inflammatory/immune polyneuropathies, as in Guillain-Barré syndrome. Not all neuropathies will involve the services of the speech/language pathologist. In some there is extensive cranial nerve involvement, which may be a possibility in the neuropathies discussed in this section. In particular, Guillain-Barré syndrome can rapidly involve the muscles of respiration, speech, and swallow, in addition to those of the arms and legs. As the patient recovers, assistance with both speech and swallow is a necessary part of rehabilitation. Idiopathic unilateral paralysis of the peripheral aspects of cranial nerve 7 is called Bell's palsy. Depending on the level of involvement, patients may experience hearing loss, interruption of lacrimal function, loss of taste, and upper and lower facial weakness. Both speech (bilabial productions) and swallow (loss of taste, lip seal, and inner cheek sensation) can be affected. For most patients the effects of the paralysis are transitory; however, the paralysis may recur on the same or opposite side.

Disorders of the lower motor neuron. The most common progressive disease involving both the upper and eventually the lower motor neurons is amyotrophic lateral sclerosis (Lou Gehrig disease). Typically, it is marked by progressive, unrelenting weakness in the extremities and in respiratory or bulbar musculature (or in both), although plateaus do occur. There is anecdotal evidence that the disease may go into remission. Symptoms usually progress from involvement of the upper motor neurons to involvement of the lower motor neurons. Symptoms occur at different rates and in different patterns. Some patients who are ambulatory have unintelligible speech and difficulty in swallowing, while others maintain these skills but are unable to walk until they expire.[16] However, in most cases, the compromise to both speech and swallow requires the expertise of the speech/language pathologist. Almost all patients remain cognitively intact. When the lower motor neurons are affected without involvement of the upper motor neurons, the disease is referred to as either *progressive spinal atrophy* or *progressive bulbar palsy.* Both upper and lower motor neurons must be involved for the disease to be diagnosed as amyotrophic lateral sclerosis.

Diseases of the basal ganglia. Most diseases of the basal ganglia impact on the patient's speech intelligibility. In the progressive basal ganglia diseases, the ability to swallow also is affected. Since the basal ganglia has close cortical ties, patients may also evidence a concurrent dementia that interferes with their ability to compensate for their speech production and swallowing disorders. The most frequent referrals to a speech/language pathologist in this category are patients with Parkinson's disease, Huntington's chorea, Wilson's disease (a disorder of copper metabolism that is also called hepatolenticular degeneration), and cerebral palsy. Progressive supranuclear palsy is an idiopathic, uncommon disorder of middle age that also affects speech production due to degenerative changes in the basal ganglia and cerebral nuclei. As the disease progresses, dementia is a frequent accompaniment.

Because the side effects of many psychotropic medications (both by institution and by withdrawal) may produce dyskinetic release phenomena similar to those movements seen in basal ganglia disease, patients with tardive (refers to late-occurring) dyskinesia may need the assistance of a speech/language pathologist.

Diseases of the cerebellum. Involvement of the cerebellum, and in particular any of its connections to the cortex/subcortex, brainstem, or spinal cord, can affect the volume and timing of speech. Most affected will be the processes that coordinate respiration, phonation, and articulation. A summary of the primary diseases that affect the cerebellum and its connecting tracts is presented in Table 3–3.

Diseases of the upper motor neuron. Disease that primarily involves the upper motor neurons, usually affecting both speech production and swallow, include multiple sclerosis and primary lateral sclerosis. The course of both is progressive and often involves other motor systems. In primary lateral sclerosis, there is a progressive degeneration of the descending pyramidal tracts with accompanying spasticity, without involvement of the lower motor neurons. This usually progresses to amyotrophic lateral sclerosis, as do progressive spinal atrophy and progressive bulbar palsy. Multiple sclerosis is a progressive demyelinating disease that is discussed later in this section.

Stroke Syndromes

Ischemic stroke caused by either embolic or thrombotic occlusion of the major blood vessels can compromise any structure at any level in the central nervous system and produce combinations of both speech and language deficits. In total, it is perhaps the most common etiologic agent producing speech, language, and swallowing deficits in the medical setting. A summary of the vascular factors that contribute to stroke is provided in Table 3–4.

Table 3–3 Principal Diseases of the Cerebellum and Its Connections

---

I. Primarily spinocerebellar

  A. Inherited spinocerebellar ataxias (childhood or adolescent onset, chronic course, few positive sensory symptoms)

    1. Molecular genetic defect uncertain: Friedreich's ataxia and its variants; Roussy-Levy

    2. Genetic defect known: phytanic acid α-oxidase deficiency (Refsum); abetalipoproteinemia (Bassen-Kornzweig): arylsulfate and other deficiencies

  B. Acquired spinal sensory ataxia (acute, subacute, or insidious onset): polyneuropathy; sensory polyradiculopathy (tabes dorsalis); vitamin B_{12} deficiency; spinal cord damage (multiple sclerosis, neoplasm, etc.)

II. Primarily cerebellar

  A. Inherited degenerative (course progressive): restricted olivopontocerebellar atrophy (young to mid-adulthood); ataxia-telangiectasia (childhood onset)

  B. Developmental abnormalities (onset of signs varies, progressive): basilar impression; Arnold-Chiari malformation

  C. Nutritional-immunological (mostly adult onset, acute or subacute course)

    1. Acute, parainfectious cerebellar ataxia of children

    2. Alcoholic-nutritional cerebellar degeneration

    3. Paraneoplastic cerebellar-brainstem degeneration

  D. Structural cerebellar lesions (acute or subacute course): trauma, neoplasms, hemorrhage, anoxia-ischemia, etc.

  E. Intoxication (acute or subacute or chronic): alcohol; sedatives, anxiolytics; phenytoin, anticancer agents

III. Cerebellar-plus disorders

  A. Inherited-degenerative system degeneration (middle adult onset, gradual progression)

    1. Olivopontocerebellar atrophy plus, variable spasticity, parkinsonism, sensory changes, optic atrophy, retinitis pigmentosa, ophthalmoplegia, dementia

    2. Shy-Drager syndrome

    3. Generalized mitochondrial dysfunction with ataxia, ophthalmoplegia, myopathy

  B. Acquired disseminated disorders affecting cerebellar and other systems (disseminated cancer, abscess, etc.)

Source: Reprinted from *Cecil Essentials of Medicine* by C.J. Carpenter, F. Plum, and L.H. Smith with permission of W.B. Saunders Company, © 1986.

Transient ischemic attacks. Transient ischemic attacks (TIAs) produce temporary deficits in nervous system function including aphasia and dysarthria. Characteristic of a TIA are a temporary loss and then complete recovery of function within a period of a few hours. Most TIAs, thought to be embolic in nature, are quickly dissolving clots that do not leave any demonstrable evidence of infarction. Some transient effects that begin as focal deficits can spread to larger areas, usually in the middle cerebral and basilar artery distribution. These attacks that result from

Table 3–4 Vascular Factors That Contribute to Stroke

I. Mural abnormalities
  A. Extracranial-intracranial atherosclerosis
    1. Thrombotic narrowing or occlusion of cervical vessels
    2. Ulcerated aortocervical plaques generating platelet-fibrin or cholesterol emboli
    3. Thrombotic occlusion of intracranial vessels
  B. Inflammatory-immunological vascular occlusions
    1. Extracranial only—cranial arteritis
    2. Extracranial and intracranial
    3. Intracranial only
      a. Accompanying bacterial or granulomatous arteritis
      b. Amphetamine–cocaine-like drugs
      c. Idiopathic
  C. Invasion or compression of arterial or venous vascular walls by trauma, neoplasms, etc.

II. Embolic disorders
  A. Artery to artery: platelet or cholesterol emboli from aortocervical atherosclerotic plaques
  B. Cardiogenic
    1. Mural (postmyocardial infarction)
    2. Atrial
    3. Valvular
      a. Septic (endocarditis)
      b. Nonseptic (rheumatic, atherosclerotic, mitral prolapse, marantic)
    4. Neoplastic-arterial myxoma, etc.

Source: Reprinted from *Cecil Essentials of Medicine* by C.J. Carpenter, F. Plum, and L.H. Smith with permission of W.B. Saunders Company, © 1986.

---

the internal carotid artery distribution (most common) and are caused by emboli from the heart that block the major sensorimotor zones of the cerebral cortex. Since the internal carotid artery feeds the middle cerebral artery that, in turn, supplies the major speech and language zones, transient aphasic symptomatology is frequent. TIAs precede symptoms of major stroke due to occlusion of the internal carotid artery in about 20 percent of the reported cases.[17]

Other transient effects on communication can come from vasospasm of an artery that usually is associated with thrombosis or narrowing of major vessels in the neck. While not definitively proven, migraine may be a form of vasoconstrictive disease. Usually associated with severe headache, nausea, and photophobia, some forms of migraine produce transient aphasia, dysarthria, dysphagia, and paresthesias in the articulators.

Cerebral artery occlusion. Occlusions of the middle cerebral artery in the left hemisphere that involve one lobe produce fluent and nonfluent aphasias. When two lobes are involved, global aphasia often results. Involvement of the right hemisphere in the middle cerebral artery distribution produces confusional states, spatial neglect, and accompanying disorientation. Occlusion of the anterior cerebral artery also produces nonfluent aphasia in its anterior distribution and fluent aphasia in its posterior distribution into the parietal lobe. While posterior cerebral artery occlusions may cause reading and writing disturbances, they also can produce primary visual field and sensory deficits. Temporary confusional states following infarction of this artery also have been described.[18]

Lacunar (small cavitations) disease results in small infarcts by occlusions of smaller arteriolar branches, usually in the deeper circulatory beds of the middle cerebral and basilar arteries. Often occurring bilaterally in the internal capsular region, they will impair speech production. The occlusions are caused by sustained hypertension that accelerates the effects of atherosclerosis. In lacunar stroke there are some characteristic syndromes, including "dysarthria-clumsy-hand syndrome."[19]

Dementia following occlusive cortical disease that produces multiple small and large infarcts in any distribution and in any part of the brain often is referred to as multi-infarct dementia (MID). The usual course is of cumulative episodes of focal neurologic worsening. It often is associated with hypertension and diabetes mellitus. While frequently decompensating the processes of both speech and language, it is distinguished from those dementias of the Alzheimer's type by its preponderance of focal signs and radiographic demonstration of infarcted tissue.

Vertebral-basilar artery occlusion. Loss of blood supply to the posterior brain can involve structures as high as the cortex and produce dementia and memory loss, and to structures in the brainstem involving the cranial nerves that affect vision, speech, and swallow. Disorders of respiration and regulation of consciousness are not infrequent in vertebral-basilar insufficiency. Since the vertebral-basilar branches supply the cerebellum, speech and gait ataxia can be evident. Lesions of the posterior inferior cerebellar artery (PICA) typically produce Wallenberg's syndrome that involves both the motor and sensory aspects of cranial nerves 9, 10, and 12. Such involvement often decompensates swallow.

Hypertensive encephalopathy. Long-standing hypertensive disease can cause a series of microhemorrhages and ischemia in the cerebral cortex. Hypertensive encephalopathy can be marked by sudden attacks of headache, visual loss, confusional states (affecting communication), and, if focal in nature, specific language disorders. The sudden nature of these events is thought to be due to a high systemic intravascular pressure that is exerting abnormal pressure on the brain's arterioles.[20]

Progressive subcortical encephalopathy. Progressive subcortical encephalopathy (Binswanger's disease) is a rare disease marked by arteriosclerotic involvement of the white matter of the cerebral cortex and an accompanying demyelination of the subcortex that produce a slowly progressive dementia. As the disease progresses, patients frequently have memory loss with seizures and some focal signs including hemiplegia and aphasia. Pseudobulbar dysarthria is a frequent finding in the end stages.

Hemorrhage. Bleeding into the spaces that cover the brain can occur at any level of the central nervous system, including the cerebellum. Common sites are

the thalamus and internal capsule/basal ganglia regions. Bilateral capsular (lacunar) lesions frequently compromise speech production and produce dysarthric vari-
ants with pseudobulbar and hypokinetic features. Atypical aphasias and motor
speech disturbance following thalamic lesions have been described.[21]

Aneurysms. Most aneurysms are thought to be congenital weakness in the proximal walls of the cerebrovascular vessels that fill with blood, usually creating
symptoms of severe headache. Other aneurysms may develop in the distal cerebral
arteries from infected emboli secondary to bacterial endocarditis (inflammation of
the heart lining and valves). Some are asymptomatic and are only detected after
they rupture and hemorrhage into the subarachnoid space. Aneurysms create potential problems with communication and other functions. Neurosurgery may be
required to control the bleeding or to bypass an aneurysm. Patients may be left
with communication deficits, including aphasia, and remain at risk for an extension (rebleeding) of their lesion in the immediate postoperative phases.

Arteriovenous malformation. An arteriovenous malformation (AVM) is a
tumorlike mass that is an abnormal entanglement of the veins and arteries in the
cerebral cortex (Figure 3–1). As they grow larger neurologic abnormalities, including communication deficits, may be apparent. Patients who are candidates (some
are inoperable because of their location) for removal of these lesions may be left
with postoperative communication complications, especially if the malformation
has invaded the primary speech and language areas in the left hemisphere.

Traumatic Injury

Traumatic brain injury (TBI) often produces generalized central nervous system
damage causing speech, swallowing, and cognitive deficits of which communication is a part. The patient's early course and prognosis can be complicated by posttraumatic coma and neurosurgical interventions to control bleeding and infection.
Early communication sequelae include attentional problems, linguistic deficits,
disorientation, memory loss, perceptual deficits, behavioral deficits, and dysarthria. As patients improve, they are left with residual communication deficits,
including word-finding deficits, linguistically based problem-solving deficits,
memory loss, perceptual disturbances, and dysarthria. Swallowing disorders are
prevalent and need to be managed, although prognosis for oral feeding is good.[22]

Communication and swallowing disorders also must be considered in local
trauma to the head and neck. This may involve the face, mouth, pharynx, or larynx
with complications of neurologic dysfunction. In particular, fractures of the mandible and larynx impact negatively on communication and swallow. Local traumatic
injury to the airway may be the result of emergent or prolonged intubation. In addition to local irritation, bleeding, edema, and vocal fold paralysis are all potential
causes of dysphagia.[23] Granulomas may form on the vocal folds and interfere with
normal voice production, airway protection during swallow, and breathing (see
Figure 3–2).

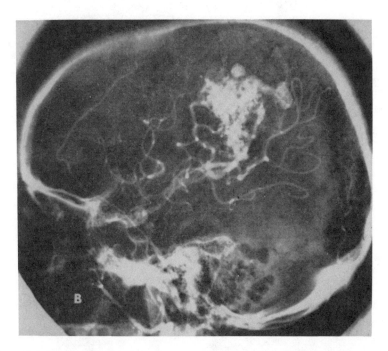

Figure 3–1 An angiogram showing enlargement of branches of the middle cerebral artery abruptly terminating in a plexus of abnormal arterioles and venules (arteriovenous malformation). *Source:* Reprinted from *A Textbook of Neurology* by H.H. Merritt with permission of Lea & Febiger, © 1967.

Neoplasms

Tumors, whether benign or malignant, involving the peripheral and central nervous system at any level can affect the processes of speech, language, and swallow. They do so through (1) direct invasion of the structures necessary for communication and swallow, (2) exertion of pressure on those structures (remote effects), or (3) the absence of those structures following surgery. Patients with neoplasms in the cortex, both within and outside of the classic speech and language zones, show progressive mild forms of aphasia with anomia as the major presenting symptom.[24] Involvement of two brain lobes, however, is more predictive of marked aphasia than involvement of one.[25] After surgery the patient's communication is temporarily decompensated secondary to postsurgical edema but returns to preoperative levels in a short period of time. Language skills worsen with recurrence of the tumor or if the tumor is inoperable. Malignancy alone is not a predictor of recurrence or the amount of potential tissue destruction. For instance, meningiomas (usually benign) can become large before producing symptoms or reappear after removal and cause new symptoms.

Patients with slow-growing neoplasms rarely develop the focal signs of aphasia or dysarthria but show other signs of cognitive decline, such as confusion and dis-

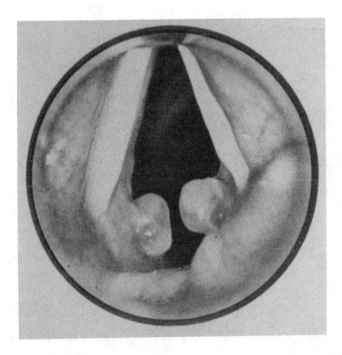

Figure 3–2 Postendotracheal anesthesia granulomas from trauma. *Source:* From A.E. Aronson in *Clinical Voice Disorders,* 2nd ed., New York, 1985, Thieme Medical Publishers, Inc. Reprinted by permission.

orientation, forgetfulness, apathy, and depression. Patients with accompanying hydrocephalus (increased pressure within the ventricles) secondary to the compressive effects of the neoplasm show the classic symptoms of mental confusion, apractic gait, and urinary incontinence. After shunting (draining the cerebral spinal fluid) the mental status and communication should improve. The cerebral spinal fluid usually is shunted through tubing from the lateral ventricle down the neck to a valve behind the ear and into the atrium of the heart (V-A shunt), or into the peritoneal cavity of the stomach (V-P shunt) where it is reabsorbed. Postoperative shunting also may be needed to control hydrocephalus.

Postoperative changes in a patient's communication skills can be excellent indicators of neurologic change and impending hydrocephalus. In the immediate postoperative period, the patient may be placed on corticosteroids to reduce excessive brain edema. The patient's communication skills may recover quickly during this period. However, the withdrawal of steroids, particularly if done too quickly, may produce a temporary depression in communicative ability. This is noteworthy as a point of explanation to the medical staff and family.

The speech/language pathologist must be aware of the fact that patients can have primary tumors outside of the central nervous system, such as in the lung, liver, or prostate gland, that metastasize to the nervous system and cause further destruction. In general, the effects are diffuse, but they can be focal, such as an isolated cranial nerve involvement. Speech and language are decompensated as part of the reduction in responsiveness and intellect. Since patients often receive radiation and chemotherapy in efforts to control the neoplasm, side effects can be expected. These are discussed in the next section of this chapter, as are the remote effects of cancer (those that impact on the central nervous system without actually invading it).

Seizures

Seizures are abnormalities in the brain's electrical activity that can express themselves as abnormal sensory, motor, or psychological behavior. They can occur as a complication of many diseases that affect the central nervous system, such as encephalitis, dementia, head trauma, neoplasms, and cerebrovascular accidents. They can be precursors of undetected disease, such as in hepatic encephalopathy, neoplasms, central nervous system infections, and drug withdrawal. Particularly in children, they may occur in the absence of any detectable central nervous system pathology. In general, the seizure itself causes few consequences to speech and language unless the condition has been present since childhood, although postictal (immediate period following the seizure) mutism and aphasia have been described in some patients.[26] In focal seizures (Jacksonian type) communication may be temporarily lost if focal discharge begins in the dominant temporal lobe. In prolonged petit mal seizure activity, a patient can become confused, forgetful, and incoherent. Abnormal twisting and writhing movements of the articulators that compromise speech production can be seen in patients who have psychomotor attacks (unclassifiable seizures).

Control of seizures usually is by use of pharmacological agents and may be difficult in some patients. These antiepileptic medications, with their accompanying depressive effects on the central nervous system, may cause mental slowing and in some cases dysarthria. Superimposed on any aphasic or dementing syndromes, these side effects act to reduce previous levels of communicative capacity. Therefore, some patients are able to compensate, while others are not able to communicate at previous levels. Family members who witness seizures following stroke may need counseling regarding the differences between the two conditions. In most cases, seizures that are reasonably well-controlled do not extend structural brain damage, whereas a cerebrovascular accident does. Recurrent seizures in the absence of any initial structural or metabolic pathology (epilepsy) must be differentiated from those whose source is known.

Demyelinating

The most common demyelinating disease requiring the services of the speech language/pathologist is multiple sclerosis. The disease is now thought to be due to autoimmune mechanisms that cause a demyelinization of axons with accompanying sensory and motor disturbances. Typically diagnosed in the third and fourth decades of life, multiple sclerosis is characterized by exacerbations and remissions with a downward progression of function. The typical presentation of the speech disturbance is a mixed ataxic (scanning) and spastic dysarthria. Although involvement of the cortex is not uncommon, this rarely produces focal language deficits, but it interferes with memory, orientation, abstract thinking, conversational pragmatics, and the ability to maintain a topic with relevancy. It is important for the speech/language pathologist to obtain baseline measures of speech function (including respiration, phonation, and articulation) and cognition. Diagnosis of the disease often is difficult and by exclusion. However, diagnosis has been facilitated through the use of magnetic resonance imaging,[27] and analysis of visual- and auditory-evoked potentials.

Systemic Disease

It is necessary for the medical speech/language pathologist not only to be aware of pathology arising within the central nervous system that affects communication and swallow, but to be familiar with the negative effects on nervous system integrity that may be secondary to diseases and disease processes arising outside of the central nervous system. These processes may or may not actually invade the nervous system. For instance, local involvement of the lungs from chronic obstructive pulmonary disease may impair the respiratory supports for speech without invading the central nervous system. Some cancers that begin in the lung may eventually invade the central nervous system and cause communication and swallowing impairments. Most of the systemic disease processes discussed in this section impact on nervous system activity and communication. They are divided into six major areas:

1. metabolic disease
2. infectious disease
3. toxins
4. musculoskeletal and connective tissue disease
5. cardiopulmonary disease
6. gastrointestinal disease

Metabolic Disease

Metabolic disease results when the metabolism is altered in reaction to specific chemical changes within the living organism. These reactions are either anabolic (energy-requiring) or catabolic (energy-yielding). Changes in metabolism can be due to a large number of systemic disease processes, some of which are specifically alluded to under other headings in this section. Diseases of metabolism that attack the central nervous system may include anoxia and insufficiencies of the hepatic, renal, pancreatic, and pulmonary organs. They are summarized in Table 3–5.

Systemic abnormalities that affect the central nervous system are referred to collectively as *metabolic encephalopathies*. They are characterized by acute changes in central nervous system activity that may affect any anatomic level, although they have a predilection for the cortex. Abnormal changes in speech and language can be precursors to their detection and require close cooperation between the speech/language pathologist and the attending physician. If the cortex is involved, patients often become confused and disoriented. Language output is irrelevant and tangential. Tremor may be present, and focal neurologic signs can be found. Due to the acute progression and the presence of focal signs, ischemic episodes must be ruled out. Most symptoms will abate after medical intervention.

Endocrine disorders. The principal neuroregulator of autonomic nervous system activity is the hypothalamus. Local damage to the hypothalamus can interfere with mechanisms of arousal, heat and water regulation, appetite, and endocrine function. With hypothalamic connections to the pituitary gland, these organs serve as the endocrine control centers to the thyroid, parathyroid, and adrenal glands. In general, abnormalities in any of these glands can result in myopathy and affect the muscles needed for speech production. These include both hyper- and hypothyroidism, hyperparathyroidism, hyperadrenalism, and hyperpituitarism. Most endocrine disorders, whether acquired or congenital, have effects on the patient's vocal quality as in the low voice of those with hyperadrenocorticism; the stridulous voice of those with hypoparathyroidism (secondary to hypercalcemia); the breathy, soft voice of those with hyperthyroidism; and the low, husky voice of those with

---

Table 3–5 Metabolic and Diffuse Lesions and Communication

A. Anoxia or ischemia
B. Hypoglycemia
C. Nutritional deficiency
D. Hepatic, renal, pulmonary, and pancreatic insufficiency
E. Exogenous poison
F. Infections:
   Meningitis
   Encephalitis
G. Ionic and electrolyte disorders
H. Mixed encephalopathies:
   Aging
   Postoperative state systemic infection
   Drugs in combination
I. Multifocal small structural lesions (e.g., metastases, emboli, and thrombi)
J. Concussion and postictal states

Source: Reprinted from *Cecil Essentials of Medicine* by C.J. Carpenter, F. Plum, and L.H. Smith with permission of W.B. Saunders Company, © 1986.

hypothyroidism. In the severe form of hypothyroidism (myxedema), articulation also is affected due to a thick, edematous tongue. Cognitive changes in long-standing disease, such as mental slowness, reduced memory, and confusion, also are described in hypothyroid conditions and have an effect on the patient's overall communicative effectiveness. Most endocrine disorders can be treated by replacement hormones that delay the negative effects on central nervous system integrity if the diseases are detected early.

Diabetes. *Diabetes insipidus* is distinguished from *diabetes mellitus.* Diabetes insipidus, resulting from absence of the antidiuretic hormone, causes excessive urination but rarely has negative impact on the nervous system. Diabetes mellitus is an endocrine disorder in which insulin is not secreted by the pancreas or is not in proper balance. The disorder may produce secondary effects on the nervous system, often through occlusive disease of the peripheral and cerebral arteries. This atherosclerotic process reduces circulation and impedes wound healing. In patients recovering from surgical procedures affecting communication, as in laryngectomy, who have a prior history of diabetes mellitus, slow healing may delay the onset and eventual success of speech and language remediation. The systemic complications of diabetes mellitus are presented in Figure 3–3. Complications most frequently involve the distal peripheral nerves in the arms and legs, but complications important to the speech/language pathologist include diabetic neuropathies involving the cranial nerves. Their involvement probably is on a vascular basis. Cranial nerves 3, 4, and 6 are frequently affected, although the symptoms may be transitory. Peripheral effects on vision are well-known and may need to be compensated for in treatment. Though less likely, peripheral involvement of cranial nerve 10 has been described.[28] It is important for the speech/language pathologist treating patients with dysphagia to be knowledgeable about sugar-restricted diets for these patients and the possibility of autonomic neuropathies that affect the gastrointestinal tract with symptoms of diarrhea and dysphagia.

Aphasic patients with a history of hypertensive disease and stroke may have accompanying diabetes mellitus. The speech/language pathologist should be aware that changes in blood sugar levels affect a patient's ability to communicate. Acute changes in sugar metabolism may cause marked communication dysfunction and must be separated from the occurrence of another cerebrovascular accident. A consequence of acute stroke or other central nervous system insults may be increased blood sugar levels. If treated too rapidly with insulin the patient may become hypoglycemic and develop complications. Therefore, patients with known diabetes mellitus prior to stroke are difficult to treat in the acute stages. They often will have a fluctuating communication performance until their sugar levels stabilize.

Cancer. Cancers can be divided broadly into three major categories: (1) carcinomas that affect the epithelial tissues, skin, and mucous-lined membranes; (2) sarcomas that attack the connective tissue of bone, muscle, and cartilage; and (3) hematologic cancers of the lymph system (lymphoma) and of the blood (leukemia).

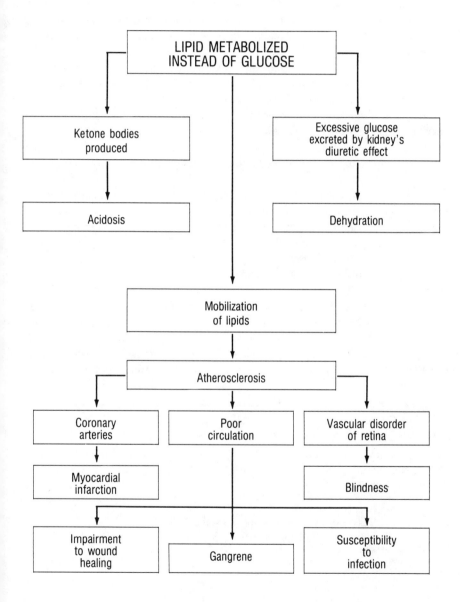

Figure 3–3 Complications of diabetes mellitus. *Source:* Reprinted from *Human Diseases: A Systemic Approach,* 2nd ed., by M.L. Mulvihill with permission of Appleton & Lange, © 1987.

Squamous cell carcinoma commonly invades the structures of the head and neck and interferes with both speech production and swallow by decompensating structures and peripheral nervous innervations in the mouth, pharynx, and larynx. Primary tumors of the head and neck infrequently metastasize to the central nervous system.

Invasive cancers to the central nervous system can involve the cranial nerves and the higher cortical centers in irregular patterns. Primary tumors of the lungs, liver, pancreas, and kidneys have been known to metastasize to the central nervous system. Focal language effects are rare. Noninvasive (paraneoplastic) effects of cancer on the central nervous system are widespread and the mechanisms poorly understood. The central nervous system effects can precede the discovery of the primary source. To the experienced clinician, communication dysfunction in the absence of structural neurologic pathology can dictate examination of other systems to explain the decline of function. Paraneoplastic effects can include involvement of muscle, the neuromuscular junction, and the peripheral nerves innervating the speech musculature. Cortical effects usually are diffuse, but can be focal if vascular disease is suspected. The potential remote effects that precipitate nervous system involvement are summarized in Table 3–6.

A negative effect on the patient's appetite in both invasive and noninvasive cancers is common; however the exact mechanism is unknown. Since patients may have accompanying destruction of the support structures for swallow, they are at nutritional risk. Compromise to nutrition can result in poor immunological defenses leading to infection whose secondary effects, as in encephalitis, can attack the central nervous system. Nutritional deficiencies also precipitate poor wound healing following surgery that delays rehabilitation efforts and recovery of function.

Table 3–6 Nonmetastatic Effects of Cancer on the Nervous System

---

I. Remote effects
   A. Brain and cranial nerves
      1. Dementia
      2. Bulbar encephalitis
      3. Subacute cerebellar degeneration-opsoclonus
      4. Optic neuritis-retinal degeneration
   B. Spinal cord
      1. Grey matter myelopathy
         a. Subacute motor neuropathy
         b. Autonomic insufficiency
      2. Subacute necrotic myelopathy
   C. Peripheral nerves and roots
      1. Subacute sensory neuropathy (dorsal root ganglionitis)
      2. Sensorimotor peripheral neuropathy
      3. Acute polyneuropathy, Guillain-Barré type
      4. Autonomic neuropathy

    D. Neuromuscular junction and muscle
      1. Polymyositis and dermatomyositis (dermatomyositis in older men)
      2. Myasthenic syndrome
      3. Myasthenia gravis (thymoma)
      4. Neuromyotonia

II. Metabolic encephalopathy
    A. Destruction of vital organs
      1. Liver (hepatic coma)
      2. Lung (pulmonary encephalopathy)
      3. Kidney (uremia)
      4. Bone (hypercalcemia)
    B. Elaboration of hormonal substances by tumor
      1. Parathormone (hypercalcemia)
      2. Corticotropin (Cushing's syndrome)
      3. Antidiuretic hormone (water intoxication)
    C. Competition between tumor and brain for essential substrates
      1. Hypoglycemia (large retroperitoneal tumors)
      2. Tryptophan (carcinoid)
    D. Malnutrition

III. Infections (usually associated with lymphomas)
    A. Parasites
      1. Toxoplasma cerebral abscess
    B. Fungi
      1. Meningitis (cryptococcosis)
      2. Encephalitis (aspergillosis, mucormycosis)
    C. Bacteria
      1. Meningitis (Listeria monocytogenes)
    D. Viruses
      1. Herpes zoster (radiculitis, myelitis, encephalitis, granulomatous vasculitis)
      2. Progressive multifocal leukoencephalopathy

IV. Vascular disease
    A. Intracranial hemorrhage
      1. Subdural hematoma
      2. Subarachnoid hemorrhage
      3. Intracerebral hemorrhage
    B. Cerebral infarction
      1. Thrombotic (due to hypercoagulability)
      2. Embolic nonbacterial thrombotic endocarditis

V. Side effects of therapy
    A. Chemotherapy
      1. Central nervous system
      2. Peripheral nervous system
    B. Radiation therapy

Source: Reprinted from *Cecil Essentials of Medicine* by C.J. Carpenter, F. Plum, and L.H. Smith with permission of W.B. Saunders Company, © 1986.

The potential effects of sarcomas of the connective tissues as they relate to communication disorders are discussed in another section of this chapter. Hematologic cancers, such as leukemia and lymphoma, frequently invade the meninges with resultant communication decompensation if the disease remains uncontrolled. Communication disorders secondary to the side effects of irradiation and chemotherapy to control cancers are prevalent.

The combination of irradiation and chemotherapy to control malignancies in the central nervous system will decompensate both communication and swallow. Radiation therapy to the head and neck can cause pain, edema, and xerostomia in the mouth and pharynx and make it difficult for the patient to swallow. Combined with loss of appetite, nutritional depletion eventually leads to poor immunosuppressive function and subsequent infection. Loss of body mass decompensates respiration and affects vocal volume and airway protection during swallow. The effects of irradiation to the central nervous system can act on both the peripheral and central control mechanisms. Effects may be immediate, as in acute encephalopathy, or more delayed, as in dementia, cranial nerve tumors (sarcoma), cerebral infarction, and metabolic encephalopathy, all of which can create specific speech and language deficits. Irradiation also can produce side effects on the endocrine system, such as hypothyroidism or hyperparathyroidism.

Infectious Disease

Infections can compromise communication and swallow by acting to decompensate the central nervous system from such sites as the lungs, kidneys, and urinary tract. Infection also can arise from within the central nervous system as in the formation of brain abscesses (a pus-filled cavity formed by the disintegration of tissue). Local infections that attack the aerodigestive tract also must be recognized as etiological sources that are capable of decompensating speech production and swallow. Both focal and diffuse involvement at any level in the central nervous system are possible, although acute involvement of the peripheral nervous system is rare. The impact of infection on communication and swallow usually is acute and reversible if detected early. Sources for infection are bacterial, viral, and fungal. In many cases, infection decompensates all metabolic activity through the secondary effects of fever or sepsis (bacterial organism in the blood). If untreated, either can lead to changes in the individual's consciousness level that result in unresponsiveness, obtundation, and a failure to communicate.

Bacterial and viral disease processes that decompensate communication by attacking the central nervous system include meningitis, encephalitis (often via the herpes simplex virus), rabies, and intracranial abscesses. When left untreated, patients rapidly become unresponsive and confused. Early treatment helps to avoid permanent structural deficits. The bacterial infections associated with neurosyphilis and meningeal invasion by the tuberculin pathogen (tuberculosis) can cause focal and diffuse brainstem and cortical pathology. Neurosyphilis can cause focal and multifocal infarction resulting in linguistic abnormalities and cranial nerve involvement in the tongue and face. Tuberculosis can attack the cranial nerves (particularly cranial nerve 8), and produce focal cortical disturbances that appear similar to tumors or abscesses on computerized tomography. If the lesions involve the speech and language zones, resultant complication of language will follow. Other infective processes thought to be viral in origin include Creutzfeldt-Jakob disease (discussed under cortical dementia), acute polymyositis, herpes zoster with its characteristic predilection for cranial nerves 5 and 7 (see Figure 3–4), and progressive multifocal encephalopathy. Poliomyelitis, another viral infection, characteristically attacks the lower motor neurons controlling the muscles of ambulation, respiration, speech, and swallow. Although once controlled well by inoculation, some patients inflicted with poliomyelitis in the 1940s and 1950s who have had remissions are now having recurring symptoms.

Infections originating outside of the central nervous system eventually may invade it and cause changes in communicative capacities. Patients with bacterial endocarditis are at risk for embolic stroke that creates states of lethargy with the chance for transient focal (aphasia and dysarthria) symptoms. Emboli usually lodge in the distal, rather than proximal, vascular distributions, thus sparing the speech and language zones.

Viruses originating outside of the central nervous system also produce neurologic complications such as those secondary to acquired immune deficiency syndrome (AIDS). Toxoplasmosis presenting as single or multiple brain abscesses

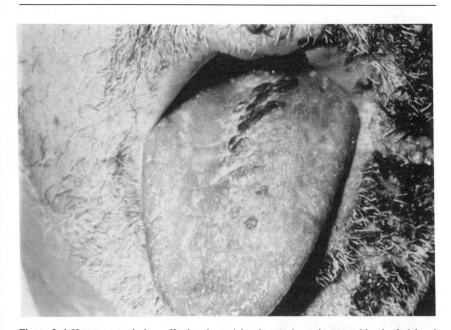

Figure 3–4 Herpes zoster lesions affecting the peripheral musculature innervated by the facial and hypoglossal cranial nerves.

produces deficits in both speech and language if properly located. Both disorders can be reversible with treatment of the abscess. Progressive multifocal leukoencephalopathy (PML) causes cortical demyelination resulting in dementia with its characteristic effects on language.

The immune/inflammatory disease of Guillain-Barré (acute postinfectious polyneuropathy) produces a generalized weakness of voluntary motor muscles. Symptoms usually follow a mild respiratory infection and progress rapidly to total weakness in a few hours or days. Recovery is complete in a few weeks to several months in 85 percent of cases. Respiratory involvement often becomes emergent and requires tracheostomy with concomitant negative effects on both speech and swallow.

Infections localized to the aerodigestive tract, such as moniliasis (thrush), may compromise both speech and swallow, particularly if they are superimposed on pre-existing pathology, such as loss of innervation due to neurologic disease or loss of structure secondary to surgery. When the underlying cause of infection is determined, the effects on communication usually can be reversed with treatment. Secondary to nutritional and other primary infections, stomatitis causes pain and swelling of the tongue, making both speech and swallowing difficult. Commonly seen as milky white lesions in the oral cavity that bleed when scraped, moniliasis is an infection caused by the *Candida* species of fungi. If left untreated, the lesions can spread into the pharynx and esophagus and cause difficulty with swallow secondary to pain. These lesions frequently appear in patients with immunodeficiencies, such as AIDS, and in patients on chronic antibiotic therapy. AIDS patients also may develop Kaposi's sarcoma (neoplastic skin lesions) with accompanying tumorlike growths that can invade the tongue, pharynx, and esophagus and compromise both speech and swallow.

Patients complaining of pain on swallow with accompanying swelling of the floor of the mouth may have Ludwig's angina, an inflammatory process usually secondary to dental injury and caused by streptococcal infection. Other infections that must be considered in impairment of function in the oropharynx include the inflammatory lesions of herpes simplex, syphilis, pharyngitis (bacterial and viral), and histoplasmosis (fungal). Infections in the oropharynx, as in peritonsillar abscess, present with a sore throat, pain radiating to the ear, and difficulty in swallowing. Inflammatory processes affecting adenoid tissue can cause denasality. In patients complaining of sore throat without pharyngeal erythema, swallowing difficulty, or labored breathing (possible laryngeal stridor), acute epiglottitis (bacterial) must be ruled out.

Normal senescent changes in the oral cavity and laryngopharynx need to be differentiated from those secondary to infection.[29] Loss of taste perception, chronic ulcerations from ill-fitting dentures, and a decrease in saliva production have been described as disorders, normally seen in elderly persons, that may affect both speech and swallow.

Infections associated with the airway and compromise of laryngeal function include viral pharyngitis and acute and chronic laryngitis. Both can be associated with hoarseness and cough. Tuberculosis and other diseases can impact on laryngeal function by invasion of the vocal folds. If not detected early, lesions can cause airway obstruction. The presence of laryngeal stridor and possible accompanying changes in vocal quality can be consistent with infectious and noninfectious disease processes that compromise the airway.

Toxins

In general, toxic effects on the central nervous system present as sensorimotor polyneuropathies involving both the peripheral and cranial nerves.

Bacterial toxins. Some infectious disease processes, such as diphtheria, tetanus, and botulism, are associated with bacterial toxins that attack nervous tissue and decompensate central nervous system activity. The toxins from these diseases have a predilection for the lower motor neurons, resulting in disorders of both speech production and swallow. Diphtheritic and tetanus toxins have a potential effect on the peripheral nerves, particularly in the pharynx, larynx, and esophagus; in the jaw (tetanus); and in the motor nerve endings. Severe respiratory complications requiring tracheostomy create secondary effects on communication and swallow. If detected early, patients can recover, but they may have residual weakness requiring the interventions of the speech/language pathologist.

Metallic toxins and other poisons. Toxic effects from ingestion of or exposure to metallic poisons can act on the central nervous system to decompensate communication. Most metals that affect the central nervous system produce variations of a polyneuritis (widespread inflammation of the peripheral nerves); some of these may affect the innervations to the speech musculature. For instance, arsenic and lead poisoning can involve the cranial nerves. Lead can cause an acute encephalopathy and ataxic dysarthria with accompanying poor communication skills.[30] Complications from manganese and mercury may create choreiform movements of basal ganglia origin affecting articulatory intelligibility.[31] Patients who are exposed to lead and bismuth (formerly used to treat neurosyphilis) may evidence stomatitis with resultant speech and swallowing difficulty.[32]

The inhalation of carbon monoxide fumes can cause acute perivascular hemorrhage and a dyskinesia of basal ganglia origin that may appear months or years after the original insult.[33] The inhalation of any noxious fumes or the heat from fire can cause local damage to the structures used in swallow and voice. Ingestion of toxic chemicals, such as lye, also creates secondary effects on the mucosa of the aerodigestive tract. The secondary scarring can cause fixation of the jaw and lips (trismus) and affect articulator movement, as well as occlude the cervical esophagus to prevent completion of a swallow. Certain tick bites can result in ataxic speech and, if the ticks are not removed within two days, may progress to a bulbar paralysis and anarthria.[34]

Medications. Patients who take too much of a medication or who mistakenly mix medications, either with one another or with alcohol, can become toxic. Toxic side effects from improper use of medications can range from mild changes in physical performance, such as in speech production, to marked changes in mentation characterized by disorientation, memory loss, and confused language. Some medications have side effects whose impact on speech production is well-known. These side effects include the hypokinetic effects on speech from phenothiazines and the potential for generalized myopathy from chronic use of corticosteroids.

Medications rarely are given specifically to improve communication skills. Since communication disability usually is secondary to disease, medications that treat or control the disease often have positive effects on communication. For instance, antibiotics used in treatment of a bacterial infection that has compromised articulation or voice should improve the speech condition as they combat the infection. Some medications act to decompensate communication; that is, the intended effect of the medication is achieved but at a cost to communicative effectiveness. For instance, valium (diazepam) might be used effectively to reduce muscle spasticity but impact on dysarthric speech by making it more unintelligible, because the muscles have lost some of the strength needed to achieve the articulatory contacts.

Medications also impact negatively on communication and swallow through their side effects. For instance, patients taking antipsychotic medications, such as thorazine (chlorpromazine), may develop severe xerostomia and tardive dyskinesia, both of which affect speech and swallow. It is particularly important for the speech/language pathologist to know the actions and dosages of medications that their communication-impaired patients are taking, because the patients may not be able to read the labels or tell their physicians they are experiencing side effects or that they forgot to take the medication. Counsel from the speech/language pathologist in this regard can be very important to ensure that a patient is receiving the proper medication and dosage. Acute changes in a patient's communication ability can be related to an increase, decrease, withdrawal, or change and should be one of the first considerations when the speech/language pathologist observes reduction in the patient's skills.

Some commonly used medications are listed in Table 3–7, together with their effects on communication and swallow. Not all patients show reactions to these medications. Their effects on communication may relate to the dosage and the patient's general health. High dosages for long periods of time are usually required to affect communication, whereas normal or even subtherapeutic dosages can affect swallow.

Alcohol. The toxic effects of alcohol abuse impact directly on central nervous system function (loss of neurons with atrophy) and indirectly as the alcohol decompensates the liver (hepatic encephalopathy). Smaller dosages impact on the cortex and limbic system, while larger dosages act on the brainstem and affect sensation and arousal.[35] Cerebellar disease with resultant ataxic dysarthria is common in heavy abusers. Memory is the first cognitive function to become impaired, with increasing signs of generalized dementia if the toxin is not withdrawn. Diseases

Table 3–7 Effect of Medications on Communication and Swallowing

Drug (Brand)	Drug (Generic)	Possible effect on communication and swallowing
Antianxiety		
Equanil	Meprobamate	′ Drowsiness
Librium	Chlordiazepoxide hydrochloride	Organizes thoughts, ataxia, nausea/vomiting
Valium	Diazepam	Increased dysarthria, ataxia
Antiarthritic		
Clinoril	Sulindac	Gastrointestinal bleeding
Decadron	Dexamethasone	Myopathy, personality swings
Dolobid	Diflunisal	Gastrointestinal symptoms, vertigo
Antibiotics		
Achromycin	Tetracycline	Glossitis, dysphagia, nausea/vomiting
Flagyl	Metronidazole	Seizures, peripheral neuropathy, thrush, stomatitis
Principen	Ampicillin	Stomatitis, laryngeal stridor
Anticonvulsants		
Dilantin	Phenytoin	May help to organize language, painful gingivitis, ataxia, dysarthria
Luminal	Phenobarbital	May organize language, lethargy
Mysoline	Primidone	Ataxia, drowsiness
Tegretol	Carbamazepine	Dyskinesias, irregular breathing, mental confusion
Antidepressants		
Adapin	Doxepin hydrochloride	Xerostomia, drowsiness, extrapyramidal symptoms
Elavil	Amitriptyline hydrochloride	Confusion, disorientation, xerostomia
Ritalin	Methylphenidate hydrochloride	Dyskinesias, may help in communication initiation
Sinequan	Doxepin hydrochloride	Extrapyramidal symptoms, xerostomia
Anesthetics		
Cetacaine Lozenges (general)	none (topical)	Epithelium dehydration Can temporarily decrease oral sensation
Xylocaine	Lidocaine	Can relieve oral pain at risk of reducing sensation, drowsiness, confusion

Table 3–7 continued

Antihistamines

Actifed	none	Xerostomia, distractibility, nausea
Benadryl	Diphenhydramine hydrochloride	Drowsiness, thickens bronchial secretions
Phenergan	Promethazine hydrochloride	Xerostomia

Antihypertensives

Dyazide	Triamterene (with hydrochlorothiazide)	Xerostomia, gastrointestinal disturbances
HydroDIURIL	Hydrochlorothiazide	Xerostomia, muscle spasm, anorexia
Lasix	Furosemide	Xerostomia, electrolyte imbalance

Antiparkinsonians

L-Dopa	Levodopa	Increased extrapyramidal signs, xerostomia
Parlodel	Bromocriptine mesylate	Xerostomia
Sinemet	Levodopa	Increased extrapyramidal signs, if dose not adjusted or withdrawn

Antipsychotics (Neuroleptics)

Compazine	Prochlorperazine maleate	Tardive dyskinesia, xerostomia
Haldol	Haloperidol	Dyskinesias, xerostomia
Prolixin	Fluphenazine hydrochloride	Tardive dyskinesia, xerostomia
Thorazine	Chlorpromazine hydrochloride	Organizes language, tardive dyskinesia, xerostomia

affecting the peripheral and cranial nerves and the muscles they innervate (myopathies) can interfere with both speech and swallow. Secondary effects of alcohol abuse, including nutritional (loss of thiamine) and vitamin (B_{12}) deficiencies, also are causative factors precipitating myopathy and dementia. In general, alcohol abuse will exacerbate any pre-existing nervous system pathology. The acute form of alcoholism (Wernicke's encephalopathy) and the chronic phase (Korsakoff's psychosis) are discussed under cortical disorders at the beginning of this chapter. The generalized physiologic effects of alcoholism are summarized in Figure 3–5.

Drug abuse. The recreational use of street drugs not only creates a psychological dependence but may have secondary effects on communication and other biologic functions. Susceptibility to drugs varies depending on environmental and inherited factors. Combining drug abuse with alcohol usually magnifies the symptoms. In general, the effects on communication are through alterations of consciousness affecting both language and speech production (dysarthria).

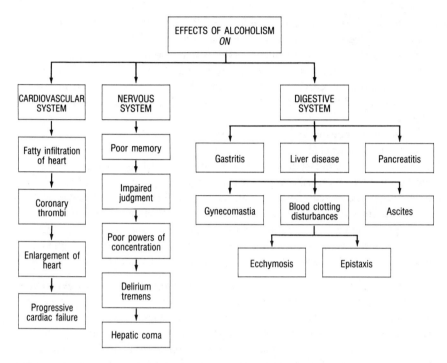

Figure 3–5 Complications of chronic alcoholism. *Source:* Reprinted from *Human Diseases: A Systemic Approach,* 2nd ed., by M.L. Mulvihill with permission of Appleton & Lange, © 1987.

Symptoms range from confusion and stupor to coma secondary to the use of cocaine, opiates, central nervous system depressants, and phencyclidine (PCP). Ingestion of PCP may cause severe confusion and ataxia, in addition to prolonged psychotic states, convulsions, and coma. Damage localized to the peripheral mechanism from inflammation secondary to marijuana and "free-base" (inhalation) cocaine use may impact on articulation and voice.

Musculoskeletal and Connective Tissue Disease

Diseases that involve the body's cartilage and bone and the supportive and connective tissue that joins them can impact negatively on speech and swallow. A majority of these disorders produce inflammatory/immune responses in tissue or joints that may be localized or systemic. Those that involve the connective tissue often are referred to as collagen-vascular disorders. Many of the signs and symptoms of each disease may overlap, making differentiation difficult and treatments imprecise. In some patients, symptoms often disappear (as in rheumatoid arthritis), and only after their reappearance can the diagnosis be made. In general, the incidence of all collagen-vascular disorders is higher in women than men.

Aging and skeletal changes. Observed most often in elderly persons, hyperostosis of the spine can impact on swallow. Impingement of cervico-vertebral spurs on the pharynx[36] and thoracic spurs[37] on the esophagus can impede or misdirect the bolus. Patients complain of a sticking sensation at the level of impingement. Impingement from the cervical spine into the pharynx also may result in inflammatory disease of the prevertebral space that limits pharyngeal movement during swallow.[38]

Senescent changes in the laryngeal support musculature cause the larynx to descend from the normal level, C-3 to C-6, to levels between C-7 through T-1 (laryngoptosis). This can impact on the patient's ability to protect the airway during swallow, because the laryngeal complex has to be pulled a greater distance to meet the tongue base. The increased need for elevation is further decompensated by failure of the suspensory muscles to provide sufficient contraction to achieve the necessary superior movement as a function of aging or changes in posture secondary to aging. Changes in esophageal motility secondary to aging (presbyesophagus) may impede the normal movement of the bolus from the pharynx to the stomach.

Rheumatoid arthritis. This disease attacks primarily the body's synovial joints bilaterally. Secondarily, rheumatoid arthritis involves other systems, such as the heart, skin, lungs, and nervous system. In the initial stages of the disease the joints become inflamed with resultant hypertrophy (swelling) causing pain and decreasing movement. In some cases granulomatous lesions form in the heart, brain, and lungs. Involvement of the arytenoid masses is not common but may occur. Failure of the arytenoids to perform their function affects airway competence and voice.

Systemic lupus erythematosus. This is an inflammatory disease that attacks the central nervous system and predominantly occurs in women. Systemic lupus erythematosus (SLE) is characterized by skin lesions, painless oral lesions, and central nervous system involvement, including seizures, stroke, cranial nerve damage, chorea, and peripheral neuropathy, all of which can compromise communication and swallow. Like many of the inflammatory disorders involving the connective tissue, symptoms may be present to create acute changes, and then remit or disappear.

Sjögren's syndrome. The primary form of Sjögren's syndrome is characterized by inflammation of the salivary and lacrimal glands impacting negatively on the patient's ability to swallow. Drying of the mucosal-lined structures of the gastrointestinal tract impedes esophageal motility; in the lung it results in chronic bronchitis and pneumonia with their accompanying effects on voice. Xerostomia in the mouth impedes bolus transport, creates dental caries, and causes pain and difficulty in swallow.[39] The secondary form of Sjögren's syndrome is associated most often with rheumatoid arthritis and systemic lupus erythematosus.

Polymyositis and dermatomyositis. These are inflammatory myopathies that affect proximal striated muscle and therefore can involve the muscles of the head and neck. In dermatomyositis there is a coincidence of a skin rash and myopathy.

Polymyositis and dermatomyositis can suddenly involve the pharyngeal and respiratory musculature with resulting compromise of speech and swallow. Both disorders are marked by exacerbations and remissions. When not of primary idiopathic origin, they are seen together with progressive systemic sclerosis (scleroderma).[40]

Progressive systemic sclerosis (scleroderma). Progressive systemic sclerosis causes inflammatory and fibrotic changes in smooth muscles. The fibrotic changes important for the speech/language pathologist are those involving the lungs and heart for respiratory support and the gastrointestinal tract for swallow. Involvement of the distal esophagus reduces peristaltic wave activity and slows the movement of the bolus. Esophagitis with stricture and gastroesophageal reflux disease can be common manifestations. The characteristic loss of muscle bulk combined with dysphagia adds to weight loss. The fibrotic changes are characterized by swelling, followed by a tightening with malfunction of the connective tissue. Bitemporal muscle atrophy and a pursed-lip posture may be observed secondary to loss of subcutaneous tissue in the head and neck. In most cases this does not interfere significantly with speech intelligibility. The disease is most frequently associated with rheumatoid arthritis.

Polyarteritis nodosa. An inflammatory disease of the medium-sized arteries, polyarteritis nodosa can invade the central nervous system. When central nervous invasion is seen, it is most often in the form of encephalopathy secondary to hypertension. However, focal and multifocal deficits of cognition, including aphasia, can be a finding.

Wegener's granulomatosis. Wegener's granulomatosis is a vasculitis that presents primarily in the upper and lower respiratory tract and results in necrotizing granulomata formation. The granulomata frequently invade the lungs and can be seen as nodular, reddened lesions in the nose, sinuses, and pharynx. When they are present in the lungs, respiratory support for speech is poor. If invasion from the lungs extends into the pharynx, swallow will be painful and require great effort.

Sarcoidosis. Sarcoidosis is an inflammatory disease of unknown origin that can invade the connective tissue by the formation of granulomas in the heart, lungs, skin, eyes, liver, spleen, muscle, and central nervous system. When it is in the nervous system, cranial nerve palsies and subacute meningitis are findings. Poor respiratory support for speech is a consequence when involvement is confined to the lungs and heart. The disease can be associated secondarily with carcinoma and lymphoma.

Osteoarthritis. This is the most common connective tissue disorder causing joint and cartilage erosion. The symptoms of osteoarthritis usually appear in the sixth through the ninth decades. Changes in posture secondary to involvement of the spine can affect respiratory capacities for speech and the ability to protect the airway during swallow. In vertebral spine degeneration, the thoracic cage is allowed to shrink with the coincident loss of vital capacity. Hyperostotic (bony protuberance) changes in the spine secondary to the loss of cartilage can affect swallow by their impingement into the aerodigestive tract. Amyloidosis (fibrotic tissue deposits) has been associated with osteoarthritis. These deposits can affect the normal mobility of the tongue and lungs and interfere with speech and voice production. Idiopathic amyloidosis should also be considered in a thickened, enlarged tongue when other infections have been eliminated from the diagnosis.

Cardiopulmonary Disease

Patients with disease localized to the lungs or with cardiac disease as it might impact on respiratory drive are at risk for changes in their speech production efforts. Lack of respiratory efficiency from these two organs (lungs and heart) can affect speech output by changing the rate (short breath groups), the intensity (loss of sufficient expiratory capacity), and the pitch (loss of air flow and vocal fold tension). In general, pitch is lower than expected for sex and age.

Compromise to respiratory capacities (vital and forced expiratory capacities) is the result of a number of pulmonary diseases, including chronic obstructive pulmonary disease (COPD), emphysema, asthma, mediastinitis, sarcoidosis, and pneumonia. For the speech/language pathologist treating cardiopulmonary patients with dysphagia, the importance of differentiating between pneumonia resulting from pathogens that were not aspirated and those that were can be an important distinction. In aspiration pneumonia, the patient may have an undetected swallowing disorder in need of further diagnostic evaluation. If the patient was previously being fed and was known to have dysphagia, it will interfere with treatment because the patient will not be allowed to eat while antibiotics are being administered to combat the infection. If the source for the pneumonia is determined not to be from aspiration, the patient may be allowed to continue eating. Unfortunately, the distinction between the two sources of infection is not easily made. Patterns seen on x-ray are not always predictive and sputum cultures not always reliable.[41] Invasive procedures into the lung to document the aspirant are potentially hazardous and difficult to perform.[42] The distinction often must be made on judgment of the patient's overall health and disease manifestations. If the patient is in a category of high risk for aspiration, it will be assumed and treated accordingly.

Patients with decreased respiratory efficiency will have poor vocal volume and may not be able to form a cough strong enough to clear the airway. Those with respiratory rates above 30 per minute will have difficulty maintaining airway closure for a sufficient length of time to protect the airway as a bolus passes through the pharynx, because the inspiratory/expiratory ratio will not allow the vocal folds to remain closed for the required minimum of one second. When there is not enough respiratory reserve to form a sufficient cough to clear secretions, patients will need respiratory supports.

Respiratory failure may require immediate intervention by way of tracheal intubation. The secondary effects of tracheal intubation on the vocal folds, including local trauma and paralysis, are discussed under traumatic injury earlier in this chapter. Following extubation other local irritation, including edema and lacerations in the pharynx, can interfere with both speech and swallow. Surgical management of patients in respiratory distress is by tracheostomy. Redirection of the airway by the placement of a tracheostomy tube interferes with speech production, although patients with good expiratory reserve can speak "around" the tubes if they are instructed to occlude them. Long-term placement of tracheostomy tubes may interfere with the laryngeal closure reflex needed to protect the airway during swallow.[43] Some patients will require cuffed tracheostomy tubes. When inflated, they will interfere with speech production since pulmonary air cannot travel past the inflated cuff to vibrate the vocal folds. They also anchor the larynx and inhibit normal elevation for airway protection during swallow. Tracheostomy cuffs that are overinflated or that remain in the airway for an extended period of time may cause tracheal stenosis or erosion of the tracheoesophageal wall with subsequent aspiration through a tracheoesophageal fistula.

In general, cardiac disorders that compromise respiration are of most concern to the speech/language pathologist because of their effects on voice. Patients who become anoxic during cardiac arrest may suffer diffuse cortical disease characterized by severe memory and disorientation deficits. Patients who undergo cardiac bypass surgery or procedures that may compress the recurrent laryngeal branch of the vagus nerve as it wraps around the aorta in its distal extension are at risk for postoperative vocal hoarseness (see Figure 3–6). Unilateral left laryngeal paralysis with accompanying breathiness can be a finding secondary to cardiac surgery.

Patients with swallowing disorders who complain of chest pain that is thought to be atypical should have both esophageal and cardiac etiologies investigated.[44] Some esophageal pain is indistinguishable from cardiac angina.

Gastrointestinal Disease

The speech/language pathologist who assists in the evaluation and treatment of swallowing disorders must be aware of disease processes that can impact on the patient's ability to eat by mouth. This knowledge is important because:

- A patient with unexplained dysphagia requires a complete evaluation of mouth, pharynx, and esophagus.
- Disorders of the esophagus can affect structures above it that are necessary for swallow.[45]
- Disorders of the mouth and pharynx can affect the efficiency of the esophagus.[46]
- Separate disorders of the mouth, pharynx, and esophagus can exist to explain a patient's swallowing complaint.[47]

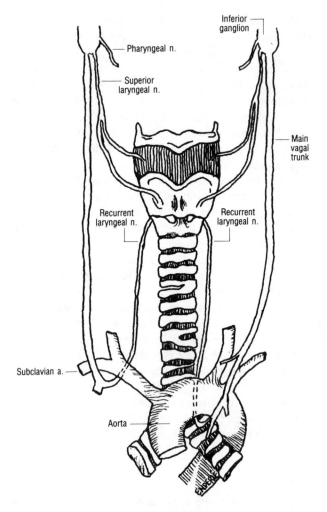

Figure 3–6 The left recurrent laryngeal nerve (branch of the vagus) is liable to damage from cardiac disease and procedures because of its distal approximation to the aorta.

The differential diagnosis of esophageal lesions begins by taking a history from the patient. The differential diagnostic process based on the patient's report is best accomplished by the use of a decision tree[48] (see Figure 3–7). In the majority of cases, patients with esophageal lesions complain of difficulty either with solids only or with solids and liquids, without frank choking or nasal regurgitation. When esophageal dysphagia is suspected, the direction of the diagnosis can be established by using the decision tree.

Esophageal rings and webs. Lower esophageal rings are found when the patient complains of intermittent difficulty with solid foods only. The complaints

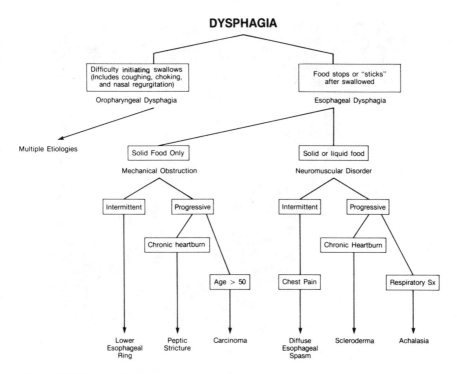

DYSPHAGIA

Figure 3–7 The use of a decision tree to differentiate among swallowing disorders of suspected esophageal origin. *Source:* Reprinted from "Evaluation of Dysphagia: A Careful History Is Crucial" by D.O. Castell and M.W. Donner, *Dysphagia*, Vol. 2, No. 2, p. 67, with permission of Springer-Verlag, New York, © 1987.

may have persisted for years without a clear diagnosis, because there can be periods of time when the patient is asymptomatic. Rings usually are found in the region of the squamocolumnar junction and are sometimes referred to as Schatzki's rings. Treatment involves instruction to the patient to masticate food completely and the dilatation of the esophagus. Dilatation usually involves having patients swallow rubber dilators of progressively greater diameter to gradually stretch the narrow lumen. Webs in the esophagus may cause more bolus impedance than rings, and usually are in the proximal one-third. Plummer-Vinson syndrome is characterized by an upper esophageal web (see Figure 3–8) with dysphagia and is associated with iron-deficiency anemia.

Peptic stricture. Patients complaining of a mechanical obstruction to solid food that is progressive with heartburn may develop a peptic stricture causing esophageal narrowing and dysphagia. Chronic heartburn and long-term antacid use may be part of the history. Some patients develop Barrett's esophagus from the chronic irritation that appears as a stricture with ulcerations surrounded by colum-

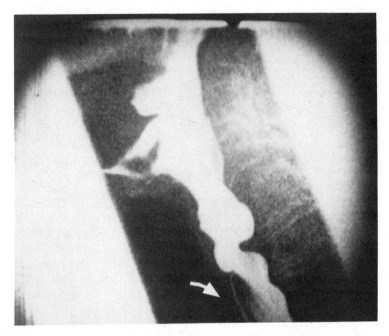

Figure 3–8 An upper esophageal web (curved arrow) secondary to Plummer-Vinson syndrome.

nar mucosa instead of squamous cells. These metaplastic changes may be a precursor to carcinoma.[49]

Carcinoma. Progressive solid food sticking retrosternally, without chronic heartburn and in patients over 50 years of age, is suggestive of esophageal carcinoma. Heavy ethanol and tobacco abuse, with or without significant weight loss, is usually a part of the history. Pain on swallow is infrequent, except in the later stages when the carcinoma has invaded the mediastinum. If the patient is a surgical candidate (involvement of the distal one-third), parts or all of the esophagus are removed, and the gastric tract is reconnected superiorly to the pharynx and inferiorly to the stomach. The patient is liable for postoperative strictures or fistula at the site of reanastomosis. With the loss of the normal protective functions of the upper and lower esophageal sphincters, the patient also is at risk for gastroesophageal reflux.

Diffuse esophageal spasm. In this neuromuscular (motility) disorder the patient complains intermittently of difficulty with solids and liquids and accompanying chest pain. In the circumstance of true dysphagia without a cardiac source for pain, the diagnosis of diffuse esophageal spasm is most probable.

Scleroderma. Patients with progressive dysphagia for liquids and solids and chronic heartburn may evidence scleroderma. The presence of skin tightness over the face (see progressive systemic sclerosis under musculoskeletal and connective tissue disease in this section) may or may not be present in conjunction with the dysphagia. Primary peristaltic waves often are absent, more distally than proximally. The presence of reflux and heartburn may help to distinguish scleroderma from achalasia.

Achalasia. This disease of unknown etiology is characterized by a lack of peristalsis in the body of the esophagus. Patients complain of both solids and liquids failing to pass into the stomach. In most cases, the lower esophageal sphincter fails to relax properly. Symptoms of achalasia are progressive and usually found in patients over 40 years of age. Nocturnal cough and choking, sometimes with resultant pneumonia, are frequent findings due to failure of the fluid-filled esophagus to empty in the supine position.

Gastroesophageal reflux. A mixture of food, fluid, and acid from the stomach that retropulses into the esophagus, pharynx, or mouth, gastroesophageal reflux is a common consequence of esophageal disease. It creates symptoms within the esophagus, such as dysphagia, chest pain, and hiccups; in the oropharynx, such as glossalgia (tongue pain), halitosis, and odynophagia (painful swallow); and in the airway, such as hoarseness, vocal fold granulomas, subglottic stenosis, and aspiration.

One or more of the following five symptoms is characteristic of the patient with gastroesophageal reflux:

1. a decrease in the production of saliva (which normally acts to maintain proper esophageal pH)
2. an absence or decrease in the tone of the lower esophageal sphincter
3. an inappropriate relaxation of the lower esophageal sphincter during swallow
4. a decrease in acid clearance due to impaired secondary peristalsis
5. a history of smoking, alcohol abuse, caffeine use, obesity, voice disorders, and pneumonia

SUMMARY

The two major components of communication are speech production and language. The processes of speech production and swallow share the same peripheral mechanisms, but are accomplished through different processes and through different, but sometimes shared, central and peripheral control centers. Speech and language largely are processes overlaid on the central nervous system. Communication is a dynamic process that is subject to external and internal forces from the environment, as well as the individual's psychological health and biologic system. These forces act in varying degrees to affect communication. Swallowing also is a dynamic process, more patterned in performance than communication, but adapting to change in the eating circumstance (bolus size, texture, and fluid versus solids). The potential for negative effects from change in either communication or swallowing is well-compensated in the normal brain by redundancy of systems. However, because of their complexity, even in subtle pathology these processes may become decompensated in time. Failure in their performance can be indicative of underlying disease. Therefore, alterations in an individual's usual communication or swallowing abilities are important signals of either positive or negative changes in health.

In general speech/language pathologists who work in a medical setting learn about disorders of nervous system origin that may impact on communication. However, the disorders are taught as disease entities separate from underlying neurologic mechanisms that they represent and usually not as a part of other biologic systems that, when diseased, can impact on or invade the nervous system.

This chapter focuses on a method to organize and expand the speech/language pathologist's view of neurologic disorders that can impact on communication and swallowing disorders. It also reviews those systemic diseases that impact on the central nervous system and, in turn, affect communication and swallow.

Neurologic diseases of central nervous system origin are discussed as they might impact on a general level of consciousness. Disturbances in consciousness and affect secondary to psychogenic etiologies also can impact negatively on communication.

Communication disorders secondary to cortical disease are both focal (aphasia) and diffuse (dementia). Dementia can be divided broadly into disorders that are treatable (depression, electrolyte imbalance, and alcohol intoxication), and those that are not. Nontreatable dementia includes disorders that involve the cortex (Alzheimer's) and those that are subcortical (parkinsonism-related).

Damage to the central nervous system can affect both sensory and motor processes. Sensory disorders impacting directly on communication and swallow include diseases that affect the end organs and the processes of vision, smell and taste; generalized pain response; and balance and hearing. Sources for motor disorders resulting in distortion of the speech signal and in swallow inefficiency can be found at every level of the nervous system: upper motor neuron, basal ganglia, brainstem, cerebellum, peripheral nerve, neuromuscular junction, and in the muscle. Some disease entities that affect these levels of function include stroke, hypertensive encephalopathy, progressive subcortical encephalopathy, aneurysms, arteriovenous malformation, trauma, neoplasms, and demyelinating disease.

Pathology can affect communication and swallowing skills by remote effects on the central nervous system, by local effects on the peripheral mechansim, and from direct invasion from outside sources. The systemic disease categories discussed in this chapter include communication and swallowing disorders secondary to metabolic disorders, infection, toxins, musculoskeletal and connective tissue disease, cardiopulmonary disease, and gastrointestinal disorders.

Impacting communication through metabolic disease are endocrine disorders, such as hypothyroidism, diabetes mellitus, and cancer (with its invasive and noninvasive effects), and the side effects of irradiation and chemotherapy. Both bacterial and viral in origin, infectious diseases attack the central nervous system and locally involve the structures for speech production. Toxic effects on communication result from medications, metals, bacteria, alcohol, and street drugs.

Connective tissue diseases that affect communication and swallow include skeletal changes in the spine, rheumatoid arthritis, systemic lupus erythematosus, Sjögren's syndrome, polymyositis, dermatomyositis, progressive systemic sclerosis, polyarteritis nodosa, Wegener's granulomatosis, sarcoidosis, and osteoarthritis. Diseases that act to decompensate lung tissue, such as asthma and pneumonia, and cardiac disorders that decompensate respiration with their secondary effects on voice are discussed in this chapter, as well as local damage to the vocal folds from intubation and tracheostomy.

Gastrointestinal diseases that affect swallow include esophageal rings and webs, peptic stricture, carcinoma, diffuse esophageal spasm, scleroderma, and achalasia. Gastroesophageal reflux, a common manifestation of patients with esophageal disease, and dysphagia are also included in the discussion.

NOTES

1. J. Hughlings Jackson, *On Affections of Speech from Disease of the Brain: Selected Writings,* vol. 2 (New York: Basic Books, 1984), 184–204.

2. Ibid.

3. Nina A. Simmons, "Experimental Analysis of a Treatment Program for Alexia Without Agraphia." In *Clinical Aphasiology Conferences Proceedings,* ed. R.H. Brookshire (Minneapolis: BRK Publishers, 1984), 166–72 .

4. Daniel M. Tucker, Robert T. Watson, and Kenneth M. Heilman, "Discrimination and Evocation of Affectively Intoned Speech in Patients with Right Parietal Disease," *Neurology* 27 (1977):947–50.

5. Robert T. Wertz, "Language Disorders in Adults: State of the Clinical Art." In *Language Disorders in Adults: Recent Advances,* ed. Audrey L. Holland (San Diego: College-Hill Press, 1984), 29–33.

6. Barbaranne J. Benjamin, "Changes in Speech Production and Linguistic Behaviors with Aging." In *Communication Behavior and Aging: A Sourcebook for Clinicians,* ed. Barbara B. Shadden (Baltimore, Md.: Williams & Wilkins Co., 1988), 58–78.

7. Fred Plum and Jerome F. Posner, "Neurologic Disease." In *Cecil Essentials of Medicine,* eds. Thomas E. Andreoli et al., 644–793 (Philadelphia: W.B. Saunders Co., 1986).

8. Ibid.

9. Wataru Nishijima, Shoji Takoda, and Makoto Hasegawa, "Occult Gastrointestinal Tract Lesions Associated with the Globus Symptom," *Archives of Otolaryngology* 45 (1984):246–47.

10. Plum and Posner, "Neurologic Disease," 644–793.

11. Kathyrn A. Bayles, "Language and Dementia." In *Language Disorders in Adults: Recent Advances,* ed. Audrey L. Holland (San Diego: College-Hill Press, 1984), 209–44.

12. John D. Tonkovich, "Communication Disorders in the Elderly." In *Communication Behavior and Aging: A Sourcebook for Clinicians,* ed. Barbara B. Shadden (Baltimore, Md.: Williams & Wilkins Co., 1988), 204–06.

13. Plum and Posner, "Neurologic Disease," 644–793.

14. Richard L. Doty, Daniel A. Deems, and Stanley Stellar, "Olfactory Dysfunction in Parkinsonism: A General Deficit Unrelated to Neurologic Signs, Disease Stage, or Disease Duration," *Neurology* 38, no. 8 (1988):1237–44.

15. Plum and Posner, "Neurologic Disease," 644–793.

16. Joel A. DeLisa et al., "Amyotrophic Lateral Sclerosis: Comprehensive Management," *American Family Physician* 19, no. 3 (1979):137–42.

17. H.J.M. Barnett, " Cerebrovascular Diseases." In *Cecil Textbook of Medicine*, 17th ed., eds. J.B. Wyngaarden and L.H. Smith (Philadelphia: W.B. Saunders Co., 1985), 2086–3111.

18. Orrin Devinsky, David Bear, and Bruce T. Volpe, "Confusional States Following Posterior Cerebral Artery Infarction," *Annals of Neurology* 45 (1988):160–63.

19. H. Houston Merritt, *A Textbook of Neurology* (Philadelphia: Lea & Febiger, 1973):200–01, 570–763.

20. Benjamin, "Changes in Speech Production," 58–78.

21. N.R. Graff-Radford and A.R. Damasio, "Disturbance of Speech and Language Associated with Thalamic Dysfunction," *Seminars in Neurology* 4 (1984):162–68.

22. Carolee J. Winstein, "Neurogenic Dysphagia: Frequency, Progression, and Outcome Following Head Injury," *Physical Therapy* 63, no. 12 (1983):1990–97.

23. John L. Stauffer et al., "Complications and Consequences of Endotracheal Intubation and Tracheotomy: A Prospective Study of 150 Critically Ill Patients," *American Journal of Medicine* 70 (1981):65–76.

24. Michael E. Groher, "Prevalence and Type of Communication Disorders Following Removal of Malignant Brain Tumor," *Journal of Neurological Communication Disorders* 2, no. 1 (1985):14–19.

25. Ibid.

26. Merritt, *A Textbook of Neurology*, 200–01, 570–763.

27. Martin R. Farlow et al., "Multiple Sclerosis: Magnetic Resonance Imaging, Evoked Responses, and Spinal Fluid Electrophoresis," *Neurology* 36 (1986):828–31.

28. Plum and Posner, "Neurologic Disease," 2086–3111.

29. H. Heeneman and D.H. Brown, "Senescent Changes in and about the Oral Cavity," *The Journal of Otolaryngology* 15, no. 4 (1986):214–16.

30. Merritt, *A Textbook of Neurology*, 200–01, 570–763.

31. Ibid.

32. Plum and Posner, "Neurologic Disease," 2086–3111.

33. Ibid.

34. Merritt, *A Textbook of Neurology*, 200–01, 570–763.

35. Plum and Posner, "Neurologic Disease," 2086–3111.

36. Elias A. Zerhouni, James F. Bosma, and Martin W. Donner, "Relationship of Cervical Spine Disorders to Dysphagia," *Dysphagia* 1, no. 3 (1987):129–44.

37. Steven Willing and Taher El Gammal, "Thoracic Osteophyte Producing Dysphagia in a Case of Diffuse Idiopathic Skeletal Hypertrophy," *American Journal of Gastroenterology* 78, no. 6 (1983):381–83.

38. Ibid.

39. G. Kjellen et al., "Esophageal Function, Radiography, and Dysphagia in Sjögren's Syndrome," *Digestive Diseases and Sciences* 31, no. 3 (1986):225–29.

40. Plum and Posner, "Neurologic Disease," 2086–3111.

41. Linga Raju and Faroque Khan, "Pneumonia in the Elderly: A Review," *Geriatrics* 43, no. 10 (1988):51–62.

42. Ibid.

43. Clarence T. Sasaki et al., "The Effect of Tracheotomy on the Laryngeal Closure Reflex," *Laryngoscope* 87, no. 9 (1977):1428–33.

44. Michael G. Lee et al., "Chest Pain: Esophageal, Cardiac, or Both?" *American Journal of Gastroenterology* 80, no. 5 (1985):320–24.

45. Carlos J. Sivit et al., "Pharyngeal Swallow in Gastroesophageal Esophageal Reflux Disease," *Dysphagia* 2, no. 3 (1988):151–55.

46. David L. Curtis et al., "Abnormal Solid Bolus Swallowing in the Erect Position," *Dysphagia* 2, no. 1 (1987):46–49.

47. David W. Buchholz and Bernard R. Marsh, "Multifactorial Dysphagia—Looking for a Second Treatable Cause," *Dysphagia* 1, no. 2 (1986):88–90.

48. Donald O. Castell and Martin W. Donner, "Evaluation of Dysphagia: A Careful History Is Crucial," *Dysphagia* 2, no. 2 (1987):65–71.

49. John Dent, "What's New in the Esophagus?" *Digestive Diseases and Sciences* 26, no. 2 (1981):161–73.

Part II

The Evaluation Process

Chapter 4

The Medical Record

INTRODUCTION

In order to utilize and appreciate the information in a medical record it is necessary to recognize the processes that led to the compilation of facts, interpretation and analysis of data, and conclusions. The organization of a medical record may differ from setting to setting, but the processes involved in obtaining the data are consistent. In some institutions a nurse practitioner or physician's assistant obtains and records preliminary data; however, the complete evaluation is the responsibility of a physician. The same basic system is used to obtain historical information, a statement of the current complaint, and a record of the examination. Whether the data were compiled by a medical student or a staff attending, the medical record differs only in the degree of knowledge and experience that the practitioner brings to the interview and examination.

The medical speech/language pathologist, in most cases, uses the medical record as the starting point for collecting diagnostic data. The interpretation of the information presented in the medical record will be dependent upon at least two factors. The first factor is the speech/language pathologist's experience in reading medical records and his or her familiarity with medical terminology. The second factor is the speech/language pathologist's knowledge of the interrelationships among various physiologic systems, patient complaints, symptoms, diseases, and findings. Assuming the speech/language pathologist is working on a consultative basis and is evaluating a patient in order to make either a diagnostic statement or to determine the appropriate treatment modalities, the medical record gives the clinician a starting point for the formulation of assessment hypotheses.

The active clinical chart of a hospitalized patient is usually divided into sections containing orders, admitting history and examination, progress notes, laboratory and x-ray reports, and consults. For the outpatient or inactive patient, the clinical record will contain each of the above elements for each admission, plus discharge summaries from each hospitalization and a report or progress note from each outpatient, or ambulatory care, visit.

It must be recognized that the central figure in compiling the medical record is the physician, and to the physician go certain responsibilities and privileges that are not granted to other members of the health care team. For example, society has granted to the physician the privilege to ask very personal questions and to delve into the most intimate aspects of the patient's life. The physician is allowed to touch, manipulate, and explore the patient's body in a manner that is not granted to any other health professional. It is from this privileged examination that the clinical record takes shape.

The speech/language pathologist is a nonphysician specialist and is generally granted privileges relating to the acquisition of historical, social, psychological, physical, and behavioral data related to the patient's communication or associated functions. Clear boundaries cannot be drawn to define the limits of privileges applying to all speech/language pathologists. Individual clinicians and institutions must work out their own guidelines (see the discussion of credentialing/privileging in Chapter 10). In a given circumstance, however, the speech/language pathologist's clinical judgment will determine the appropriateness of actions.

CLINICAL PROCESSES

The medical record is a reflection of specific clinical processes that the physician has been trained to execute. Major's classical text on physical diagnosis describes three primary steps in the clinical process that are necessary for the study of a patient.[1]

The first step is the process of taking the patient's history, executing the physical examination, and documenting the information in a systematic manner. The specifics of these processes are elaborated later in this chapter.

The second component in the clinical process is the analysis of all data regarding the patient. This analytical step is necessary to develop a diagnosis and a prognosis. The process, combining intellect with intuition, begins with the formulation of diagnostic hypotheses followed by the correlation of facts, the discrimination and interpretation of signs, and the elimination or eventual confirmation of a diagnosis.

The third necessary step is the development of a treatment or management plan. Most patients go to the physician not to obtain a diagnosis but to gain relief from symptoms or suffering. The physician is trained to apply certain basic tenets, such as "primum non nocere" (first do no harm), and "what can be done is not necessarily what should be done." There are many times when it must be tempting to use a recipe for the treatment of a disease each time it is met, but skilled clinicians recognize that each disease process creates an infinite variety of illnesses, and they respond accordingly.

The speech/language pathologist also is faced with the temptation to use a recipe for the treatment of a particular disorder. In fact, many programmed approaches have been developed and touted as breakthroughs in treatment. While there is nothing wrong with programmed therapies, and in fact many are appropriate and effective, their application must be judicious. Too often the treatments of speech and language pathologies are viewed as benign, with little consideration given to the fact that a patient's perception of the experience may have a profound impact on his or her sense of worth and well-being.

In theory, the medical record should reflect the three steps of the clinical process, as well as other aspects of the physician's thinking. For example, the physician should understand that disease is a necessary abstraction that is used time and again to label a set of pathologic signs.[2] Illness, on the other hand, is a process that takes into consideration the individual patient's responses to disease, not just tissue reaction but social, psychological, and reciprocal physiologic responses to pathology.

In order to understand disease, it is necessary only to study pathology, learn to recognize signs, and associate these signs with the physiologic changes that occur within the bodily tissues. Over 2500 years ago the Greeks, while maintaining a philosophy that all disease stemmed from an imbalance in the "Four Humours" (yellow and black bile, blood, and phlegm), described physical signs so precisely that even today accurate diagnostic labels can be provided for most of their cases.

Yet it is apparent that even the best diagnosticians must combine their knowledge and skill at recognizing diseases with an understanding of illness if they wish to become skilled clinicians. The training of the physician endeavors to combine the study of pathology and disease with the clinical training necessary to respond to patients' illnesses. An imbalance in the training can lead to obvious shortcomings. A good physician recognizes the interplay of science and art. Systematic recordings of clinical facts, hard laboratory data, and correlations with clinical literature help the diagnostician to label accurately and to develop prognoses. Sensitivity, patience, and the intuitive processes help the physician to go beyond the science of disease to an awareness of the humanistic elements of illness. It is the melding of the scientist and the artist that leads to sound clinical judgment.

These same tenets apply to the speech/language pathologist and most other professionals dealing with health care. With an understanding of physicians' privileges and responsibilities and with a knowledge of the basic tenets of their training, the speech/language pathologist can begin to look at the medical record in a more meaningful way.

ESSENTIALS OF THE MEDICAL RECORD

For each patient admitted to a medical center there should be documentation of a medical history. At some point, a thorough history usually is taken, but for some minor complaints the history may be abbreviated. The description that follows includes all of the elements that are explored in a thorough medical history. As the medical record is described, areas are indicated that may have particular relevance to the medical speech/language pathologist. It is counterproductive to discuss each point in the record that is potentially relevant, as indeed each notation has the potential to be relevant in a given case. The notations, therefore, refer to recorded data that have been found useful but omit other more obvious or obscure associations.

Identification and Vital Statistics

This information usually is obtained by a receptionist or through hospital registration forms. Some reference usually is given about the source of the information, whether it is from the patient or from a significant other. Descriptions of the complaint vary tremendously depending upon the source of information. The essential information includes the patient's name, residence, telephone number, date of birth, stated age, place of birth, nationality and race, marital status, and occupation. The same identifying information should be maintained in speech/language pathology records if they are kept separately from the medical records.

Chief Complaint

The chief complaint (CC) consists of a concise statement that describes the symptoms causing a problem. Complaints should be tabulated on separate lines and each described in terms of the duration in time; locus of discomfort or pain; progression of the symptoms; the character of the symptoms, such as a dull or sharp pain; and the relationship of the symptoms to other physiologic functions, such as walking, talking, and breathing. Complaints are usually stated in the patient's own words, and most physicians will not accept a diagnosis from the patient as a chief complaint.

The complaints that relate to the speech, language, swallow, and associated functions should be noted by the speech/language pathologist. As a clinician gains experience, complaints and symptoms that may have had little meaning at one time will take on new significance. There can be no substitute for an expanding experience base in the development of diagnostic sophistication, and unfortunately there is little that the beginning clinician can do to speed up the process required to build a base.

Patients with speech or language impairments often are unable to describe their complaints to the physician. The speech/language pathologist can assist the physician in describing or clarifying these patients' observations.

Present Illness

Under the heading of present illness (PI) the physician records a description delineating the chronology of the illness. It often begins at a point in the past and continues up to the time when the patient seeks medical attention. The purpose of the PI is to furnish clues for diagnosis. The information is obtained by asking the patient a general question such as, "Tell me about your problem," rather than a specific question such as, "What is the matter with you?"

The PI includes data regarding the onset of the problem, the situation in which it developed, the manifestations of the symptoms, all treatments attempted, and the impact that the problem has had on the patient's behavior and life-style. Each symptom is described in terms of the location, subjective quality, severity, duration, frequency, setting, exacerbating factors, and associated perceptions. Relevant laboratory reports also are included in the PI as well as significant x-ray negatives that may aid in the differential diagnosis. A description of current medications often is included following a description of the present illness. Some physician examination handbooks recommend that the medication list include all drugs currently taken, their generic names, doses, and known effects. A notation of past medications that may be pertinent to the present illness also is advised. Clearly the completeness of the PI section of each chart is dependent upon the experience and training of the physician preparing the record.

Most speech/language pathologists have little or no training in the interpretation of laboratory data and only rudimentary knowledge of drug actions, interactions, and side effects, but experience with specific speech and language pathologies will allow clinicians to associate bits of data with clinical observations. Examples include the association of certain laboratory data, for example, pre-albumin with a dysphagia patient's state of dehydration or malnutrition, or relating a history of a patient having taken a prescribed phenothiazine (antipsychotic) medication to the presence of choreatic oral-facial movements (tardive dyskinesia).

Past Medical History

Several outlines are utilized to record a patient's past medical history (PMH). Following is an outline of a comprehensive history from an adult patient:

- description of the patient's general health, including body weight and any significant changes
- past illnesses, with particular attention to communicable diseases and their sequelae
- immunizations
- allergic reactions, including hypersensitivity to specific drugs
- operations, injuries, accidents, and prior hospital admissions, including dates and circumstances
- drugs, medications, and habits
- diet and sleep patterns
- family history, including age and general health or cause of death of all immediate family members
- psychosocial history, including life-style, home situation, and significant others

Whenever possible, the physician records data regarding grandparents and grand-children, if applicable, in the record. Most physicians pay particular attention to family conditions, such as diabetes, tuberculosis, heart disease, hypertension, stroke, renal disease, cancer, arthritis, anemia, headaches, and mental illness. Specific questions are asked about symptoms of other family members that are similar to those of the patient. In some instances a physician also records in fair detail how the patient spends a typical day. Clues are noted regarding the patient's exercise, schooling, education, marriage, financial status, retirement, job history, and military service.

The speech/language pathologist should particularly note weight, weight changes, and diet in patients with swallowing disorders. Notations regarding allergic reactions and hypersensitivities should be noted in the clinic records for patients with communication deficits, because the speech/language pathologist may assist the patient in communicating these facts to unfamiliar health care providers in the future. Previous injuries, accidents, and surgeries that may have a bearing on present complaints or problems should be recorded. Neurologic family history is particularly significant in patients with neurogenic speech, language, or swallowing disorders.

Review of Systems

Physician examination handbooks include detailed descriptions of the review of systems.[3,4] The outlines differ in the order of review; however, an attempt is made to be as thorough and as systematic as possible. Most experienced physicians perform examinations of the pertinent body parts or systems as they complete the inventory. The review itself is completed by asking relevant questions, recording general observations, and by physical inspection.

Although the speech/language pathologist should pay attention to the observations made by the physician at the time of the initial or admitting examination, some of the findings may have changed by the time the speech/language pathologist examines the patient. Except for the limitations imposed by clinical privileges and sound clinical judgment, it is not inappropriate for the speech/language pathologist to record observations and inspect specific areas related to the specialty to confirm the previously recorded data. For example, a patient admitted with a suspected stroke or stroke in evolution may have evolved to a completely different sensory and motor state within hours after the initial examination. A repeat motor and sensory examination can give the clinician significant clues regarding the patient's prognosis. The new data may help to dictate procedures that can be used for early communication and swallowing management.

General

Under the heading of general, the following elements are considered: appearance, hygiene, grooming, odors, usual weight, recent weight change, stature, posture, gait, manner, motor activity and habits, state of awareness or level of consciousness, fever, chills, sweats, fatigue, and weakness.

Skin

The review for skin includes the following: lesions, rashes, itching, moles, sores, hives, dryness, color or pigment changes, and changes in hair or nails. *Dryness of the skin may be related to chronic states of dehydration when found in patients with chronic or progressive dysphagia.*

Lymph Nodes

A review of lymph nodes considers enlargement, pain, suppuration (formation of pus), and draining. Palpation of the neck may be a part of the speech/language pathologist's routine oral-peripheral examination. Enlarged neck lymph nodes often are associated with head and neck cancer and abnormal findings should be referred for medical diagnosis.

Head and Neck

The review of head and neck structures and functions includes a consideration of general symptoms and a specific inventory of the eyes, ears, nose, mouth, throat, and neck. The amount of detail in any one section varies depending on the specialty of the examining physician.

General. The general head and neck review describes symptoms of headache, trauma, pain, stiffness, and swelling.

Eyes. The elements reviewed in this section include the following: vision, glasses or contact lenses, date of last examination, pain, itch, swelling, redness, excessive tearing, nystagmus (abnormal, involuntary rapid eye movements), diplopia (double vision), scotoma (blind spot), glaucoma, and cataracts. *Identification of a visual impairment has significance both in speech and language diagnosis and in treatment planning; the speech/language pathologist should carefully note the physician's observations. Examination of the eyes and extraocular muscles can yield important information related to the cerebrovascular system and cranial nerves (see Chapter 6).*

Ears. The examination of the ears considers hearing, tinnitus, vertigo, pain, infection, discharge, mastoiditis, and operations. *Again, the speech/language pathologist must have specific knowledge about the functioning of these primary sensory organs in order to make an appropriate diagnosis and to develop management and treatment plans for communication problems. Particular attention should be paid to any prior history of ear disease.*

Nose. The review of the nose includes the following symptoms and functions: dryness, stuffiness, epistaxis (nosebleeds), pain, discharge, obstruction, smell, sneezing, hay fever, sinus trouble, and frequency of colds. *A complaint of frequent epistaxis can have significance for patients with hypertension. Bleeding from any source can be serious when patients are medicated with anticoagulants (blood thinners). These medications are commonly given to patients who are at risk for cerebrovascular accident or myocardial infarction caused by the formation of an embolis or a thrombosis.*

Mouth. In the review of the mouth, the symptoms of pain, ulcers, dryness, sialorrhea, and bleeding gums are considered, along with facts regarding the date of last dental examination, condition of teeth, and presence of dentures. *An oral examination is a significant part of the speech/language pathologist's workup and often is more thorough than that of the admitting physician (see Chapter 6).*

Throat. The review of symptoms and functions related to the throat includes soreness, infection, hoarseness or other voice change, and swallowing. *Inspection of the pharynx should be an essential component of the speech/language pathologist's oral-peripheral examination (see Chapter 6). Descriptions of vocal characteristics also should be included in the examination report and swallowing complaints described in appropriate detail.*

Neck. Swollen glands, goiter, pain, and limitation of motion or stiffness are reported in the section on the neck.

Breasts

The review of breasts considers information on lumps, pain, nipple discharge, nipple change, bleeding, infection, and lactation.

Respiratory

Date of last chest x-ray, cough, pain, sputum, occupational exposures, asthma, wheezing, dyspnea (labored breathing), bronchitis, pneumonia, hemoptysis (expectoration of blood), tuberculosis, emphysema, and pleurisy are all reviewed under the respiratory heading. *The condition of the respiratory system should be of essential importance to the speech/language pathologist. Almost any symptom related to breathing has a relationship to speech, particularly voice, and to swallowing. Obstructive pulmonary diseases (such as emphysema) and restrictive pulmonary diseases (such as pleurisy) have direct impact on the resultant phonatory pattern of the patient. The presence of pre-existing pulmonary conditions will influence eventual management decisions when dealing with dysphagic patients.*

Cardiac

In the cardiac review the physician comments on the following: known heart disease, date of past electrocardiogram or other heart tests, exercise limitations, infarction, heart failure, murmur, rheumatic fever, palpitations, edema, angina, orthopnea, and paroxysmal nocturnal dyspnea. *Conditions such as heart failure can result in pulmonary edema that, in turn, leads to increased respiratory rate, restricted phonatory production, and difficulty in protecting the airway during swallow.*

Gastrointestinal

The gastrointestinal system review considers the following: appetite, swallowing, anorexia, nausea, vomiting, belching, vomiting of blood, indigestion, food intolerances, gas, frequency of bowel movements, change in bowel habits, rectal bleeding or black tarry stools, constipation, diarrhea, abdominal pain, hemorrhoids, hernia, use of laxatives or antacids, jaundice, liver trouble, hepatitis, and gall bladder. *When the speech/language pathologist engages in a specific examination for swallowing disorders, the information contained in this section of the systems inventory can be invaluable. Specific questioning about symptoms associated with the swallow complaint may further elucidate this area. For example, a patient's response may allow the clinician to separate oropharyngeal disorders from those involving the gastrointestinal tract.*

Renal and Urinary

A renal and urinary review notes the following: frequency of urination, polyuria (passage of a large volume of urine), nocturia (excessive urination at night), dysuria (painful or difficult urination), hematuria (blood in the urine), urgency, hesitancy, incontinence (poor voluntary control), urinary infections, stones, nephritis (kidney inflammation), and color of urine.

Genito-reproductive

The genito-reproductive system review is specific for the sex of the patient. In a male, the physician considers discharge from the penis, sores on the penis, history of venereal disease and treatments, hernia, testicular pain or masses, potency, frequency of intercourse, libido, sexual difficulties, sexual preference, and tumor.

For a female, the physician reviews the following: age at menarche; regularity, frequency, and duration of periods; Pap smear with date and results; menopause age; menorrhagia (excessive uterine bleeding); metrorrhagia (irregular uterine bleeding); spotting; discharge; itch; contraceptive use; frequency of intercourse; libido; sexual difficulties; sexual preference; venereal disease; tumor; number of pregnancies; live births; and abortions.

Musculoskeletal

A musculoskeletal review investigates joint pain or stiffness, arthritis, gout, backache, muscle pain, cramps, weakness, trauma, sprains, fractures, and tenderness. *A number of diseases, such as dermatomyositis and arthritis, affect connective tissues and can have symptoms that include compromise to articulation, resonance, voice, and disorders of swallowing (see Chapter 3).*

Hematological

In the hematological review the physician considers anemia, easy bleeding, bruising, malignancies, and past transfusions and reactions.

Endocrine and Metabolic

The endocrine and metabolic systems are reviewed together and specifically include the following elements: thyroid dysfunction, heat or cold intolerance, excessive sweating, diabetes, excessive thirst, hunger, urination, weight change, temperature intolerance, and hair change. *Hormonal imbalance and hypothyroidism are among conditions that can cause excessive mucosal swelling, particularly laryngeal, and result in voice changes (see Chapter 3).*

Peripheral Vascular

Intermittent claudication, cramps, varicose veins, and thrombophlebitis are symptoms documented in the review of the peripheral vascular system. *Patients with known peripheral vascular disease who complain of pain in a leg, for example, should receive attention due to the risk of thrombophlebitis and possible emboli dislodging and traveling to the brain. Speech/language pathologists might encounter situations that require them to interpret the vague complaints of patients with severe communication disorders. Therefore, they must be cognizant of the potential for serious complications in any given patient and be able to communicate relevant patient complaints to appropriate health care providers.*

Nervous System

The review of all neurologic conditions and the report of all neurologic symptoms are included in this section. It is further subdivided into sections on general state, cranial nerves, motor system, sensory system, autonomic nervous system, and mental status. *All aspects of the neurologic history and inspection deserve the special attention of the speech/language pathologist, particularly for patients with neurogenic speech and language disorders. Much of the specialized speech/language examination involves a modified neurologic examination and supplements the medical record by adding detail and a nonphysician perspective (see Chapter 6).*

General. In the general review of the nervous system the physician may report on syncope, seizures, memory change, and confusion.

Cranial nerves. The cranial nerve inventory includes the following: disturbances of smell (cranial nerve 1), visual disturbances (cranial nerves 2, 3, 4, and 6), orofacial paresthesias and difficulty in chewing (cranial nerve 5), facial weakness and taste disturbance (cranial nerve 7), disturbances in hearing and balance (cranial nerve 8), speech impairment, swallowing difficulty, taste change, hoarseness (cranial nerves 9, 10, and 12), and limitation in neck motion (cranial nerve 11).

Motor system. The motor system review reports paresis, paralysis, atrophy, involuntary movements, convulsions, gait disturbance, and incoordination.

Sensory system. The sensory system review considers pain, paresthesia, hyperesthesia, and anesthesia.

Autonomic nervous system. The autonomic nervous system review relates to control of urination and bowel, sweating, heat and cold tolerance, erythema, cyanosis, and pallor.

Mental status. The mental status review reports on mood, lability, hallucinations, orientation, confusion, language disturbance, and memory change.

Emotional and Neuropsychiatric

The elements that relate to an emotional and neuropsychiatric review are psychoses, neuroses, anxieties, sleep, depression, thoughts of suicide, self-image, and life satisfaction. *Emotional states may influence many speech and language parameters, particularly phonatory characteristics, rate of speech, and content.*

The Physical Examination

The art of physical examination has been refined through the years with the addition of laboratory tests, radiological studies, and new technologies to evaluate the various biologic systems. At one time the physician used all of the sense modalities, sight, hearing, touch, smell, and taste, to assess the physical state of a patient. Taste, once used to detect sugar in urine, has been replaced by objective laboratory tests. Smell, although it remains an important tool, often is neglected.

Physical examination is dependent on the examiner's knowledge. Examiners attend only to what is known or has meaning for them. A finding that has significance for one clinician may be overlooked by another until it becomes associated through experience with some abnormality, pathology, or disease. The four basic maneuvers most frequently described for physical diagnosis are inspection, palpation, percussion, and auscultation.

Inspection is literally the art of observation. Usually an inspection will move from the general to the specific; from noting facts such as body build, motor behavior, and speech to surveying local anatomic regions such as the skin, eyes, or ears. In some instances the physician uses special tools to aid in the inspection of local areas. For example, the ophthalmoscope allows the eyes to be inspected in detail, the otoscope permits visual inspection of the ears, and the flashlight illuminates the mucous membranes of the mouth and throat.

Palpation is the act of feeling. It may confirm or extend the observations made by inspection. Palpation allows the physician to perceive such qualities as temperature, moisture, vibration or pulsation, and resistance. The physician attempts to evaluate muscle tone; areas of tenderness; crepitus (the sensation of grating) in bones, joints, and subcutaneous tissues; and the characteristics of masses. The clinician's hands are the primary tools of palpation.

Percussion is the technique of striking the body surface in order to elicit sounds and assess the resistance encountered. The sounds elicited by percussion are described relative to the density of the region tapped. Tympanic sounds are encountered in the least dense region, for example an air-filled stomach. Resonance is elicited by tapping air-filled lungs. Dullness will be elicited over the liver or from a hepatized (liver-like) lung. Flatness, a woody quality, will be elicited when tapping the effused or fluid-filled lung. A reflex hammer or the fingers are used in percussion.

Auscultation is the technique of detecting sounds emitted from various organs by listening at the body's surface. Auscultation is usually aided by the use of a stethoscope. The lungs are evaluated by auscultation. Breath sounds, when abnormal, may be described with terms such as rales, rhonchi, and wheezes. Rales may be further defined in terms such as fine, medium, or coarse and may be distinguished as dry or moist depending on the absence or presence of fluid in the air passages. The heart also receives considerable attention through auscultation. Heart sounds are generally described as S1 through S4, with S1 representing the first heart sound and S4 the fourth and last sound. For example, S1 represents the sound associated with closure of the mitral (M) and tricuspid (T) valves, with M1 usually preceding T1. Additional sounds associated with the heart are gallops, snaps, and clicks. Auscultation also is used to assess vessels of the neck and skull for bruits (abnormal sounds) and the abdomen for bowel sounds, aneurysms, and stenotic arteries.

The physical examination described in a medical chart may vary greatly depending on the specialty of the physician conducting the procedure. For instance, the cardiologist spends additional time in detailed evaluation of the heart, while the neurologist expands the section pertaining to the neurological assessment. Table 4–1 outlines a routine examination and the usual order in which it is approached. There is great overlap between the physical examination and the review of systems described above; therefore, most examiners combine the two surveys into one thorough history and examination.

THE PROBLEM-ORIENTED RECORD

In 1969, Weed published *Medical Records, Medical Education, and Patient Care: The Problem-Oriented Record As a Basic Tool.*[5] The system he described calls for the recording of the conventional history and examination, followed by an analysis of the available data. The analysis results in a numbered problem list. Problems may be symptoms, signs, laboratory findings, or combinations of factors that are associated with a particular disease. Each problem is then addressed in three distinct ways: (1) plans are developed to elucidate the diagnosis, (2) therapies are described, and (3) the education of the patient and significant others relative to the problem is defined.

Table 4–1 Outline for Routine Biologic Systems Examination

Order of examination	Elements examined	Basic maneuvers
Vital signs	Pulse rate Respiratory rate Blood pressure Temperature Height and weight	Inspection Palpation Auscultation
Appearance and behavior	Level of consciousness Language Posture Physique Dress and hygiene	Inspection
Integument	Skin Hair Nails	Inspection Palpation
Lymph nodes		Inspection Palpation
Head	Hair Scalp Skull Face	Inspection Palpation
Eyes	Acuity Fields Alignment Pupils Conjunctivae and cornea Fundi Extraocular movements	Inspection
Ears	Auricles Canals Drums Acuity	Inspection Palpation
Nose and sinuses	External Mucosa Septum Turbinates	Inspection Palpation
Mouth and pharynx	Lips Buccal mucosa Gums Teeth Palate Tongue Pharynx	Inspection Palpation

Table 4–1 continued

Order of examination	Elements examined	Basic maneuvers
Neck	Cervical nodes Masses or pulsations Trachea Thyroid gland	Inspection Palpation Auscultation
Breasts	Axillae Axillary nodes Epitrochlear nodes	Inspection Palpation
Back	Spine Back muscles	Inspection Palpation
Chest and lungs	Breath sounds	Inspection Palpation Auscultation Percussion
Heart	Heart sounds Pulses	Palpation Auscultation Percussion
Abdomen	Liver Spleen Kidneys Bladder	Inspection Palpation Auscultation Percussion
Inguinal area	Femoral arteries Inguinal nodes	Palpation
Rectal and genitalia (men)	Anus Rectum Prostate Penis Scrotal contents Hernias	Inspection Palpation
Rectal and genitalia (women)	External genitalia Vagina Cervix Uterus Adnexa Rectum	Inspection Palpation
Extremities	Joints Limitation of motion Length Alignment of legs Gait	Inspection Palpation
Musculoskeletal	Range of motion Posture	Inspection Palpation

Table 4–1 continued

Order of examination	Elements examined	Basic maneuvers
Peripheral vessels	Equality of pulsations Color and temperature of feet Edema Varicose veins	Inspection Palpation Auscultation
Nervous system	Cranial nerves Motor system Reflexes Sensation Coordination Autonomic nervous system	Inspection Palpation Auscultation Percussion
Mental status	Psychomotor activity Affect and mood Thinking Orientation and memory	Inspection

Weed also describes the process of entering progress notes into the record. Each note is titled and numbered corresponding to the problem being addressed. The acronym SOAP is used to title the four subheads included in each note:

1. Subjective data
2. Objective data
3. Assessments
4. Plans

Subjective data are the symptoms, the patient's or significant others' complaints, or the patient's perception of a response to treatment. Objective data are the physical signs, radiological findings, and the laboratory results. Assessments are the analyses, interpretations, and impressions (diagnoses) made by the examiner. Plans include the therapies and education needed by the patient and significant others.

In this problem-oriented approach to recording, all numbered problems are continued throughout the chart. New problems may be added as they arise, and they are listed in sequence. When a problem is resolved by cure, the disappearance of symptoms, or by inclusion in another diagnosis, a progress note is entered to document its elimination from the list.

Since the introduction of the problem-oriented record, there have been many modifications and compromises. The individual characteristics of a medical center (size, teaching versus nonteaching, public versus private, and acute versus chronic) to a great extent dictates the recording methodology employed. Because the Weed method generally adds paperwork and requires consistent adherence, it is rare to find the system used in its pure form.

THE COMPONENT PARTS

The organization and specific component parts included in the inpatient's medical chart vary among institutions. However, these differences are reflected more in the types of forms on which information is coded, rather than in the content. In other words, a clinician can move from institution to institution and feel comfortable in finding and reading comparable information in spite of the differences in appearance or organization of the record. For ease of recognition, most inpatient hospital records are divided into sections that are separated by tabular dividers. These sections include, but are not limited to:

- general identifying information, including next of kin, occupation, social and financial status, hobbies, expectations of hospitalization, and reason for admission
- complete history and record of physical examination
- consultation replies
- doctor's order sheet
- records of temperature, pulse, respiration, and blood pressure
- consents for operative procedures and operative reports
- patient progress notes (in some institutions notes from nursing and rehabilitation have separate sections)
- results of laboratory tests, such as blood, urine, and x-ray, and other special tests, such as pathology reports
- continuing medication record

Reading the Medical Record

There are many challenges for the speech/language pathologist in reading the medical record. These challenges revolve around four major issues:

1. unfamiliarity with medical terminology
2. unfamiliarity with the format of medical terminology
3. unfamiliarity with medical shorthand and its accompanying jargon
4. difficulty encountered in decoding the illegible handwriting that seems to be inherent in medical practice

Decoding handwriting is facilitated greatly if the speech/language pathologist is familiar with medical terminology and medical abbreviations. Knowledge of the format of the history and physical or progress notes also adds additional cues that assist in deciphering illegible script. For instance, if the undecipherable handwriting is in a section that should be discussing the central nervous system and not the cardiopulmonary apparatus, the terminology and medical shorthand for neurology would be used, thus providing a known context that aids in decoding the message. Decoding medical shorthand can be facilitated by reading beyond the term in question in an effort to establish a more extensive context and then rereading the sentence with the larger context in hopes that the meaning will be clearer. In general, an understanding of medical shorthand comes only after reading hundreds of medical folders. The process of decoding abbreviated terms will be facilitated by using the glossary of medical abbreviations in the back of this book. The excessive use of medical shorthand combined with illegible writing styles should be discouraged because it can delay patient care.

An example of a consult reply that is difficult to read, and therefore the information is difficult to understand, is presented in Exhibit 4–1. The request for services is from neurology to rehabilitation medicine. The history is presented on a 21-year-old patient who approximately one month earlier sustained a traumatic head injury. Presently he is conscious and mute. The request for services indicates that the evaluation must be done at bedside. Responses to a consult request such as this usually follows the format of a brief history review, the physical evaluation, the diagnosis, and the treatment plan. Knowledge of the specialty of the responder (in this case a physiatrist) also is useful in decoding information. For example, a reply from a neurologist would focus on an evaluation of a different set of systems than one that is provided by an otolaryngologist. Therefore, different terminologies, different emphases in content, and sometimes differences in format can be expected. It is assumed that the consult presented in Exhibit 4–1 would be answered from the perspective of a rehabilitation specialist. The information would focus on an evaluation of mental status, the sensory and motor evaluation of the musculoskeletal system, and comment on the patient's rehabilitation potential. The aspects of the consult that are decipherable are as follows:

The consult begins with a brief history: 21 y/o (year old) S/P (status post) severe head injury 7/13/87, S/P V-P (status post ventriculoperitoneal) shunt 7/31/87 for hydrocephalus, R (right) hemiplegia. Admitted (to) neuro (neurology) 8/11/87. Pt's (patient's) mother was (remainder undecipherable). In the section beside "O" (for objective) the reply continues: No verbalizations, NG in (nasogastric tube in place), does not follow commands. Eyes open L (left). (The remainder of the consult is mostly undecipherable except for terms such as "spastic" and "UE" (upper extremity) that lead one to believe there was an assessment of motor and sensory ability.)

In effect, the response to this consultation is rendered useless by its illegibility. It does not contain a legible assessment or treatment plan. In all likelihood, the neurologist was interested in finding out if the patient was a suitable rehabilitation candidate. The information now will have to be obtained either by personal contact

Exhibit 4–1 Example of a Consult Reply That Is Difficult to Read

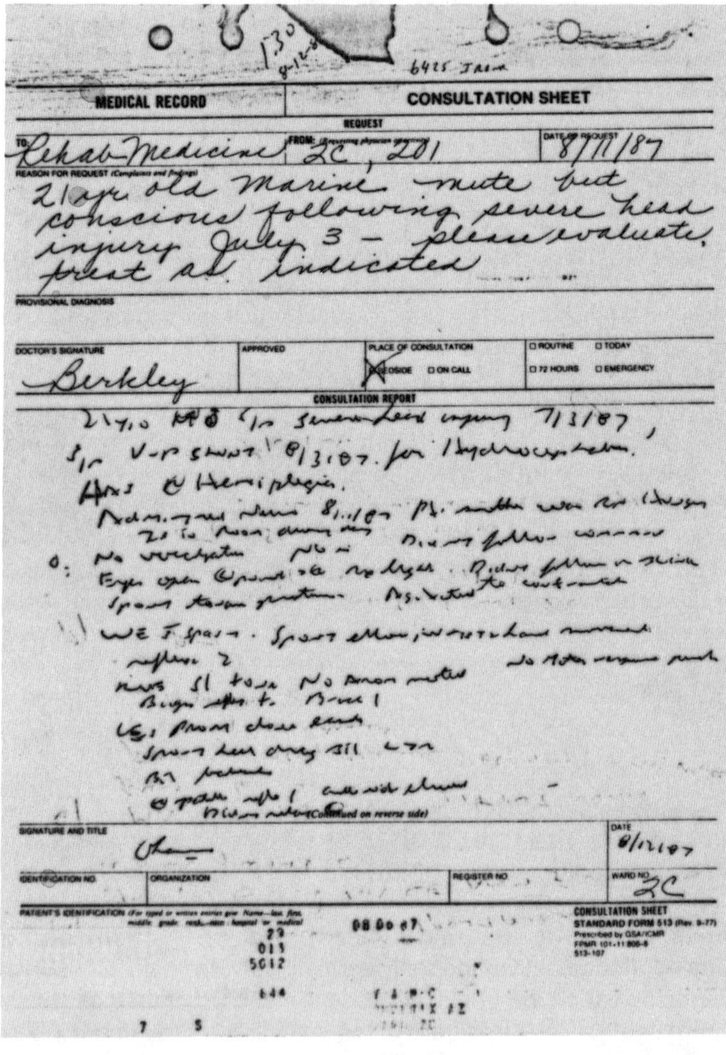

or on the telephone. This will require additional time on the part of all of the caregivers involved and delay the patient's care.

The History and Physical Examination

The history and physical examination include a systematic review of the patient's past medical history and current medical complaints, together with the results of the current physical evaluation (see Chapter 6) and the plan for further assessment and treatment. Often it is the first section that the medical speech/language pathologist reviews in order to become familiar with the patient and to have a guide for development of strategies to be used in his or her evaluation (see Chapter 5). After extensive experience in patient evaluation, the clinician may choose not to review the medical record before evaluating the patient, so as not to bias the evaluation by reviewing the evaluations of others. Reminiscent of the fable about the emperor's new clothes, this bias is frequently seen in medical records where consecutive examiners tend to "see" things as being normal or pathological due more to the fact that another has made the observation than whether or not the findings were present. The best clinical evaluation is the one that seeks to objectify the findings based on the present examination. If the findings do not agree with previous evaluations, the differences need to be resolved as part of the process of differential diagnosis. An unbiased evaluation of the patient is in the examiner's and the patient's best interests.

Examples of a thorough history and a physical examination by a neurologist are presented in Exhibit 4–2. The examples are useful because they represent the classic evaluation format as it reviews the patient's history, documents the physical findings, and reaches some conclusions. The examples contain the usual amount of medical shorthand, combined with a certain amount of illegibility. The consult begins in Exhibit 4–2, (Parts A and B) with a thorough review of the patient's complaint and history. As an exercise in becoming familiar with this important part of the medical record, a translation is provided. The translation of the medical shorthand is in parentheses. Translations of recurring terms are given only once. Colons represent the end of a line. The translation of Exhibit 4–2(A) is as follows:

CC (chief complaint), ↑ ed (increased) confusion: Informant (patient, chart, family): One of multiple MVAH (Manhattan VA)/admissions: 57 y/o (year old) R H (right-handed) BM (Black male) IDDM x 35 yrs. (insulin dependent for diabetes mellitus for 35 years), HTive x 25 yrs. (hypertensive for 25 years) PVD (peripheral vascular disease): mother CVA (his mother died of a stroke), smoker, neurological Hx (history) of SzD (seizure disorder) prob 2° to ↓ glucose (probably secondary to decreased glucose levels) W/U 7/ 87 c̄ ncCT nml. (workup of 7/87 with a noncontrast CAT scan was normal); EEG nml (electroencephalography normal); refused CCT and LP (refused contrast CAT scan and lumbar puncture); started on DPH (dilantin): but was noncompliant. The patient was in usual state of health until about 1 month PTA (prior to admission): when he claims increased confusion, got lost traveling e.g. (for example): 195th (street)→ (was) Manhattan Veterans Administration Hospital (location is at 23rd Street) for clinic appt (appointment). Also c/o (complains of): decreased memory and forgetting appointments: One week prior to admission, the patient's family

Exhibit 4–2 (A through E) Example of a Complete History and Physical Examination on a Patient with Suspected Neurologic Disease

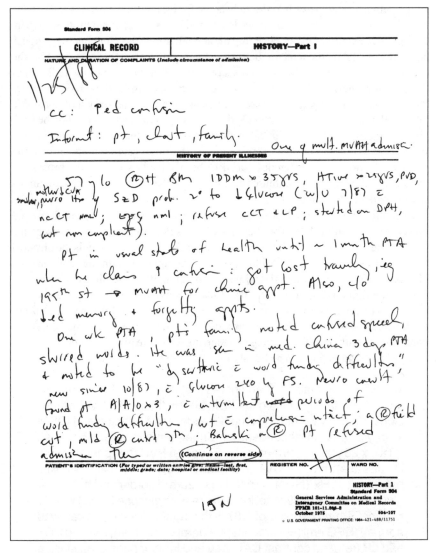

noted confused speech: slurred words. He was seen in med. (medical) clinic 3 days prior to admission: and noted to be "dysarthric with word finding difficulties,": new since 10/87, with glucose of 240 by FS (fasting sugar). Neurology consult: found patient A/A/Ox3 (awake, alert, and oriented to time, person, and place), with intermittent period of: word finding difficulties, but with comprehension intact; a right field: cut, mild right central 7th (upper motor neuron

Exhibit 4–2 B

damage to cranial nerve 7); Babinski on the right (a right plantar/
extensor Babinski reflex). The patient refused: admission then:

The translation of the history, as depicted in Exhibit 4–2 (B), continues:

states now he wanted to see a boxing match on TV: Patient has a
H/O (history of) head trauma secondary to LOC (loss of consciousness), but none: recently. No Si/Sx of Sz (signs/symptoms of seizures) No N,V, D, D, CP (No nausea, vomiting, dyspnea, diplopia,
or cardiopulmonary-related symptoms) △ (change) in: vision, but
chronic infraorbital HA (headaches). He does not: complain of limb
weakness or difficulty walking: His history is also sign. (significant)
for noncompliance: with meds (medications) D/Ced DPH on own
(discontinued dilantin on his own), but: claims to take hypertensive
and DM (diabetes mellitus) medications regularly: but not compliant with diet: Medications NPH (intermediate-acting) insulin 25
units SQ qAM (subcutaneously every morning) Minipress 5 mg
(milligrams) PO BID (by mouth, twice a day): Ecotrin 325 milligrams PO qD (by mouth, every day).

Exhibit 4-2 C

Standard Form 505

CLINICAL RECORD	HISTORY—Part 2

PAST HISTORY

INSTRUCTIONS.—*Include (1) OCCUPATION (Civilian and military), (2) MILITARY HISTORY (Include geographic locations and dates), (3) HABITS (Alcohol, tobacco, and drugs), (4) FAMILY HISTORY, (5) CHILDHOOD ILLNESSES, (6) ADULT ILLNESSES, (7) OPERATIONS, (8) INJURIES, and (9) DRUG SENSITIVITIES AND ALLERGIC REACTIONS.*

PmH: IDDm x 35 yrs   ⊖ Asthma   ⊖ STD
      HTN x 25 yrs   ⊖ MI
      PVD
      DICA 1965   ⊕ Szp (2° ↓ Glu.?)
                              Prostatitis 1983
PSH: Ⓡ Leg, femoral Art. bypass 1985

Allergies : ?

SH: retired mastr sgt. after 18 yrs in Army
      Divorced x 5 yrs
      ↑ son   } lives alone in elevated bldg
      ↑ daughter   } on 60% Disability
      Smokg ½ - ↑ PPD x 30 yrs
      Social EtOH

FH: F ↓ 37 unk. cause
      m ↓ 75 IDDm , CVA
      Brother ↓ MI

(Continue on reverse side)

PATIENT'S IDENTIFICATION (For typed or written entries give: Name—last, first, middle, grade; date; hospital or medical facility) | REGISTER NO. | WARD NO.

HISTORY (Parts 2 and 3)
Standard Form 505

The history continues in Exhibit 4–2 (C) as follows:

PMH (primary medical history) of insulin-dependent diabetes mellitus for 35 years (without) asthma, without STD (sexually transmitted disease): HTN (hypertension) for 25 years, without MI (myocardial infarction), peripheral vascular disease, DICA (Doppler of internal carotid artery) in 1965, positive history of seizures secondary to reduced glucose levels, and prostatitis in 1985: no known, or questionable allergies: SH (social history) retired master sgt. (sergeant) after 18 years in the Army: Divorced for 5 years: T son (one son), and one daughter, lives alone in elevated building on 60% disability (from the Army): smoking 1/2-TPPD x 30 yrs (smokes 1/2 total packs per day for 30 years): social ETOH (drinks alcohol socially): FH (family history) F 37 unk. cause (father died at 37 of an unknown cause): M (mother) died at 75, had a history of stroke and insulin-dependent diabetes mellitus, his brother died of a myocardial infarction.

Exhibit 4-2 D

Standard Form 506

CLINICAL RECORD			PHYSICAL EXAMINATION			
DATE OF EXAM.	HEIGHT	WEIGHT	TEMPERATURE	PULSE		BLOOD PRESSURE
1 X 88		AVERAGE · MAXIMUM · PRESENT				

INSTRUCTIONS — Describe (1) *General Appearance and Mental Status*; (2) *Head and Neck (General)*; (3) *Eyes*; (4) *Ears*; (5) *Nose*; (6) *Mouth*; (7) *Throat*; (8) *Teeth*; (9) *Chest (General)*; (10) *Lungs*; (11) *Cardiovascular*; (12) *Abdomen*; (13) *Hernia*; (14) *Genitalia*; (15) *Rectum*; (16) *Prostate*; (17) *Back*; (18) *Extremities*; (19) *Neurological*; (20) *Skin*; (21) *Lymphatics.*

[Handwritten clinical notes:]

Thin black male in NAD

200/90   65 reg   14/min   98°

Skin: mult. scars   (R) LE surg scar from bypass

Lymph: ⊖

HEENT: NCAT   no injection or discharge

Neck: supple   ⊖JVD   ⊖bruits   carotids 2+ bilat

Lungs: Clear

Heart   RRR S₁S₂   s̄ MRG↑

Abd   ⊕ BS   SNT   s̄ HSM

Ext   s̄ CCE   pulses 2+ UEs   1+ LEs

Rectal   NML tone   guaiac ⊖

Neuro: A + A/O x 3   speech fluent, naming difficulty, follows simple commands, but not 2 steps. Slow cognition + poor short term memory (1/3 at 5 min.) No suicidal TS. Knows pres & V.P. Constructional apraxia

CN: I smells but cannot ID cinnim

II discs flat   20/40 bilat.   to/from vessels AV nicking   2(R) field cut

III, IV, VI   EOMI ⊖nystagmus   PERRLA

V, VII   ⊕ corneals   ⊖asymmetry

(Continue on reverse side)

PATIENT'S IDENTIFICATION (*For typed or written entries give: Name — last, first, middle; grade; date; hospital or medical facility*)	REGISTER NO.	WARD NO.

PHYSICAL EXAMINATION
Standard Form 506

In Exhibit 4–2 (D), the examiner begins the physical evaluation starting with a review of general biologic systems and focusing in detail on the neurological assessment. The translation begins:

Thin black male in NAD (no acute distress): 200/90 (blood pressure is systolic 200, diastolic 90) 65 reg 14/min 98 (pulse rate of 65 per minute and regular respirations at 14 per minute and a body temperature of 98 degrees): Skin multi (multiple) scars on the R LE surg. (right lower extremity with a surgical) scar from bypass. Lymph (no palpable nodes in the lymph chain): HEENT: (head, ears, eyes, nose, and throat) NCAT (normocephalic and atraumatic), no injection (swelling) or discharge. Neck supple, no JVD (jugular vein distension, cardiac insufficiency), no bruits, carotids 2+ (patency, on a scale of 4) bilaterally: Lungs clear: Heart RRR S1,S2 s̄ MRGT(the heart has a regular rhythm and rate, without murmur, rub, gallop, or thrill) Abdo (abdomen) positive BS (bowel sounds heard) SNT (soft, nontender) without HSM (hepatosplenomegaly): Ext (extremities) without CCE (cyanosis, clubbing, or edema), pulses 2+ UES, 1+ LES (blood flow rate judged as 2+ in the upper extremities and 1+ in the lower extremities): Rectal normal tone and guaiac (blood in the stool) is not present. Neuro (neurologic systems), awake, alert, and oriented to time, person, and place, speech is fluent, naming and repetition are good, follows simple commands: but not two steps. Cognition is slow and poor short-: term memory (remembers 1 of 3 test items after five minutes), No serial 7s (could not count backward from 100 by seven): knows the President and Vice-President. Constructional apraxia (is present): CN (cranial nerves) I, smells, but cannot ID (identify) cinnamon: II discs flat (no papilledema), 20/40 bilat. (vision screening almost is normal bilaterally), tortuous vessels with AV (arteriovenous) nicking (sign of peripheral vascular disease) and a questionable right field cut (deficit in the right field of vision): III, IV, VI, EOMI (extraocular movements are intact for cranial nerves III, IV, and VI), no evidence of nystagmus, PERRLA (the pupils are equal, round, and react to light and accommodation): V, VII positive corneals (the corneal reflexes are present bilaterally) without any asymmetry (in the appearance of the muscles innervated by cranial nerves 5 and 7).

The neurological examination continues in Exhibit 4–2 (E).

VIII hears watch (ticking) at 2 inches, Weber/Rinne are normal (normal tuning fork screening): IX, X gag (reflexes are present and the muscles symmetric to inspection) and uvula (also midline) XI

Exhibit 4–2 E

PHYSICAL EXAMINATION

√III   hears watch at 2"   weber / Rinne NML
IX, X   ⊕ symetric gag ↓ uvula
XI   5/5
XII   midline s̄ fascics

motor: 5/5 NML walk + toe , Heel + toe walks.
          ⊖ drift   Good tandem.

cerebellar : L UE s̄ mild dysmetria , dysdiadochokinesia.

reflexes :   [2 0 2 / 2 2]   Sensory intact to PP, LT
              ↓ o 5 ↓   ↓ vib in plane & stocking dist.

⊖ Frontal release signs   Intact 2 pt discrimination , graphesthesia.

Labs: 132 | 99 | 27   ⟨500   8.4 ⟩13.8⟨ 116
        6.0 | 23 | 2.0   41.1

        PT 11.8   Ketones ⊖   mcv 90   61° 35 ↓ y m
        PTT 26   ABG (RA) 7.38 | 40 | 101 | 97%

Imp: 57 y/o IDDM, HTN , ? S≠D , now c̄ P+d confusion, dysarthria, constructional apraxia
(L) UE dysmetria + dysdiadochokin , c̄ glucose = 500 + s̄ DKA.
Focal deficit ((L) cerebellar / (R) ventricular nuclei) may be 2° to
Ketoacidosis / myelinolysis , but pt has confusion + dysarthria c̄ mildly
depressed but did 10/87 c̄ glucose = 240. Therefore, will w/u
for possible CVA; embolic , subdural , infarct … ; +/- dementia .
will control Glu , HTN now, get c/ncCT m m to f/u neurology
INITIAL IMPRESSION   or mass , infarcts …

SIGNATURE OF PHYSICIAN ———— 1/25/88

5/5: (normal strength on a scale of five) XII midline without fascics
(fasciculations): Motor strength in all extremities is judged to be
normal, as in walking and fine (fine coordination maneuvers usually tested by touching each finger to the thumb in rapid succes-
sion), heel and toe walks (test of coordination on the heels and
toes): without drift (arms did not fall on extension with the eyes
closed, a sign of subtle weakness) good tandem (walks a straight
line placing one foot directly in front of the other): Cerebellar, the
left upper extremity shows mild dysmetria and dysdiadochokine-

sia: Reflexes (interpretation of the stick figure): 0 = no reflexes elicited at the brachioradialis and Achilles tendons, the remaining reflexes were judged at 2 on a 4-point scale. The downward pointing arrows indicate normal Babinski reflexes. Sensory intact to PP, LT (pin prick, light touch) decreased vib (vibratory) sensation in glove and stocking dist. (sensory distribution of the hands and ankle to toes) without frontal lobe (bilateral) release signs. Intact 2 pt (point) discrimination, and graphesthesia. The laboratory data are translated as follows: 132 = sodium, 99 = chloride, 27 = blood urea nitrogen (BUN), 6.0 = potassium, 23 = bicarbonate, 2.0 = creatinine, and 500 = glucose, ketones negative (patient does not have acidosis). The results of the blood count were: 8.4 = white blood cell count (an indicator of infection if abnormal), 13.8 = hemoglobin, 41.1 = hematocrit, and 156 = platelets. PT = 11.8 is the prothrombin time, PTT = 26 is the partial prothrombin time, ABG's, RA (arterial blood gases, room air) are 7.38 = the pH, 40 = CO_2, 101 = O_2, and 97% is the percent of oxygen saturation. The MCV = mean corpuscle volume, 61P = 61 polycytes, 35L = 35 lymphocytes, and 4M = 4 monocytes. Imp: (impression) This is a 57-year-old insulin-dependent diabetic who is hypertensive, with a questionable seizure disorder, now with increased confusion, dementia, dysarthria, and constructional apraxia: he has left upper extremity dysmetria and dysdiadochokinesia with a glucose of 500 without DKA (diabetic ketoacidosis): Focal deficits in the left cerebellum and left lenticular nucleus may be secondary: to hypoglycemia, but the patient has confusion and dysarthria with mild: dementia noted in 10/87 with a glucose of 240. Therefore will have to work up: for a possible stroke, subdural, infarct . . . whether or not dementia is present: will control glucose, hypertension now, get a contrast/noncontrast CAT scan in the morning to R/O (rule out, or eliminate) hemorrhage: or mass, or infarcts.

The aspects of the history and physical examination just presented that are especially noteworthy from the perspective of the speech/language pathologist include the evaluation of a patient, age 57, with possible extensive (probably bilateral) brain damage that may have affected speech production, language, memory, and perception. Of immediate concern is the fact that the patient has a long history of hypertension and diabetes that are uncontrolled as evidenced by the high glucose and blood pressure (see Table 4–2 for normal acceptable ranges of laboratory values) with accompanying peripheral vascular disease (absent peripheral reflexes and pulses, arteriovenous nicking seen in the fundus). The high glucose may be a result of a new cerebrovascular event in which the body dumps amounts of sugar into the blood as a defense mechanism. However, since the patient is without signs

Table 4–2 Sampling of Normal Laboratory Values

Laboratory test	Normal values
Blood	
Bicarbonate:	24–32 mEq/L
Blood urea nitrogen:	6–22 mg/100 ml
Chloride:	95–105 mEq/L
Creatinine:	0.7–1.4 mg/100 ml
Glucose:	65–115 mg/100 ml
Potassium:	3.5–5.0 mEq/L
Sodium:	135–145 mEq/L
Hematology	
Hematocrit:	Male 40–52%
	Female 38–40%
Hemoglobin:	Male 13–18 gm/100 ml
	Female 12–16 gm/100 ml
Mean corpuscle volume:	80–95 cubicmicrons
Platelets:	150,000–450,000/mm^3
White blood cells:	4,500–11,000/mm^3
Differential	
Lymphocytes:	35–70%
Monocytes:	2–14%
Polycytes:	35–70%
Coagulation	
Prothrombin time:	11–13 seconds
Activated partial thromboplastin time:	26–40 seconds
Arterial blood gases	
pH	7.35–7.45
HCO_3	23–29 mEq/L
PO_2	80–90 mm/Hg
PCO_2	35–45 mm/Hg

of ketoacidosis, he probably will not receive additional insulin as a corrective factor at the risk of further decompensation by hypoglycemia. However, the speech/language pathologist should be aware of the possibility for daily changes in communication in this patient based on fluctuations in metabolic activity. The patient's nervous system is further decompensated by the history of trauma, possible alcohol abuse, and a seizure disorder. More recently, the patient became confused during travel (possible right brain focal insult) and now presents with increased word-finding difficulty, increased loss of memory, and dysarthria. There has been new documentation of focal disease that was not present by CAT scan in 10/87 to include a left cerebellar and left lenticular (subcortical) lesion. In this case, the speech/language pathologist must be prepared to differentiate between communication deficits secondary to dementia and those of aphasia. And at what level, and in what structures in the nervous system, does the communication disorder manifest itself? Apropos of this point is the consideration of differentiation between word-finding difficulty secondary to left focal brain involvement, generalized (nonlocalizing involvement), and/or memory loss. A description of the impact on communication secondary to any perceptual involvement of the right brain also is appropriate and must be considered. With such an involved history, marked by multiple medical problems, the speech/language pathologist should begin by describing all of the patient's communication strengths and weaknesses. Placing this patient into one single diagnostic category would be difficult, and might interfere with a complete evaluation. The speech/language pathologist's reply to the consultation on this patient will be presented in another section of this chapter.

Not all history and physicals will be as complete as the one presented in Exhibits 4–2 (A through E). Exhibit 4–3 (A and B) represents a more abbreviated admission physical prepared by an otolaryngologist. In this example, note that the plan and assessment are summarized in the section at the beginning that is reserved for the patient complaint. Also, there is a greater emphasis on the head and neck without a specific review of the nervous system. Exhibit 4–3 begins:

> 55-year-old male, status post RT (radiation therapy) for Ca (cancer) with positive neck: node admitted for radical neck dissection: chart not yet available (assume that the history was taken from the patient and from previous contact with the admitting physician). 55-year-old smoker and alcohol abuser: who had several years' history of hoarseness: with v.c. (vocal cord) plaque and no dx (diagnosis) and several: endoscopies. Finally in 5/85 the patient: was noted to have a left pyriform (sinus) lesion and left neck node: He had Rtx (radiation treatment) for 6 weeks with some resolution of hoarseness: and a decrease in node size.

Exhibit 4–3 (B) presents the following abbreviated information about the physical examination.

> WN (well-nourished) thin male in no acute distress: Skin, warm dry: H (head), normocephalic, without trauma, E (eyes) anicteric, noninjected, with extraocular eye movements intact, E (ears) apparently were unremarkable: oc/op (oral cavity/oropharynx) poor dentition without mucosal lesions: neck supple, submandibular glands: easily palp. (palpable) left upper jug (jugular) L.N. (lymph node): about 1–2 cm (centimeters) mobile: lungs, clear: ca (cardiac) regular first and second heart sounds: abdomen is unremarkable, and the extremities show no signs of cyanosis, clubbing, or edema.

From this physical examination, the speech/language pathologist may assume that the patient has had a recurrence of cancer. Presently, the patient is able to communicate. The speech/language pathologist now must wait for the patient's pathol-

Exhibit 4–3 Examples of an Abbreviated History (**A**) and Physical Examination (**B**) on a Patient with a Head and Neck Tumor

Standard Form 504

CLINICAL RECORD	HISTORY—Part I

NATURE AND DURATION OF COMPLAINTS *(Include circumstance of admission)*

55yo♂ s/p RT for Ca c̄ ⊕ neck node admitted for Radical neck dissection

CHART not available YET

HISTORY OF PRESENT ILLNESSES

55yo♂ smoker Etoh abuser who had several yr. h/o hoarseness c̄ v.c. plaque and no dr x several endoscopies. Finally in 5/85 pt was noted to have ⊕ ° pyriform lesion and ⊕ neck node.
He had RT x 4–6 weeks c̄ some resolution of hoarseness and + node size

(Continue on reverse side)

PATIENT'S IDENTIFICATION *(For typed or written entries give: Name—last, first, middle; grade; date; hospital or medical facility)*	REGISTER NO.	WARD NO.

HISTORY—Part 1
Standard Form 504

ogy report to know what the surgeon will plan to control the cancer. Depending on the extent of the cancer's invasion into adjacent tissue, the patient probably would receive either a partial (supraglottic) laryngectomy or a total laryngectomy. In the former case, the surgeon would not sacrifice communication; however, the patient probably would have postoperative swallowing difficulty requiring the services of the speech/language pathologist. With a total laryngectomy, the patient would need voice restoration. In either case, preoperative involvement by the speech/language pathologist is essential.

Exhibit 4–3 B

Standard Form 506

CLINICAL RECORD				PHYSICAL EXAMINATION		
DATE OF EXAM.	HEIGHT	WEIGHT: AVERAGE	MAXIMUM	PRESENT	TEMPERATURE	PULSE	BLOOD PRESSURE
					984	84	120/80

INSTRUCTIONS.—Describe (1) General Appearance and Mental Status; (2) Head and Neck (General); (3) Eyes; (4) Ears; (5) Nose; (6) Mouth; (7) Throat; (8) Teeth; (9) Chest (General); (10) Lungs; (11) Cardiovascular; (12) Abdomen; (13) Hernia; (14) Genitalia; (15) Rectum; (16) Prostate; (17) Back; (18) Extremities; (19) Neurological; (20) Skin; (21) Lymphatics.

WD thin ♂ in NAD
Skin warm dry
H: NC A/T
E anicteric non-injected EOMI
E:
O/OP: poor dentition ē mucosal lesions
neck: supple. submand glands
easily palp. Ⓛ upper jug L.N.
~ 1-2 cm mobile
lungs: clear
cor Reg S1 S2
abd
Ext: no CCE

(Continue on reverse side)

PATIENT'S IDENTIFICATION (For typed or written entries give: Name—last, first, middle; grade; date; hospital or medical facility)	REGISTER NO.	WARD NO.

PHYSICAL EXAMINATION

The Consultation Reply

When the primary physician requests an opinion from another specialty, a consultation request, as illustrated in Exhibit 4–4, is filled out and sent to the other specialty. The recommendations and opinions of the consultations are weighed by the patient's attending physician from the perspective of the patient's current health problems and acted upon or integrated into the patient's health care plan as warranted. Exhibit 4–4 is the response to a consultation initiated by the physician who was managing the patient presented in Exhibit 4–2. In the request, the physician

Exhibit 4–4 A Consultation Reply from a Speech/Language Pathologist on a Patient with Suspected Neurologic Disease

---

MEDICAL RECORD	CONSULTATION SHEET

REQUEST

TO: Speech Pathology   FROM: *Requesting physician or service* Neuro   DATE OR REQUEST: 1/29/88

REASON FOR REQUEST (*complaint and findings*)

57 y/o IDDM, HTN c̄ L parietal infarct, c̄ visual field deficit and

expressive aphasia. Please eval.

PROVISIONAL DIAGNOSIS

DOCTOR'S SIGNATURE

CONSULTATION REPORT

S– pt's hx reviewed. Apparently c̄ confirmed (L) parietal infarct. pt oriented, reports he had some college education, cooperates during exam

O– oral peripheral: (R) central VII, tongue deviates (R), palate midline, rest of exam WNL. Speech: ↓ rapid alt. movements, prolongs vowels abnormally c̄ consonant imprecision, & poor coordination between respiration & phonation. Language: Follows 3 step complex commands accurately but c̄ delay. Names objects, describes function c̄ hesitancies, some paraphasic errors. Writes names of objects c̄ spelling errors & some perseveration. Matches pictures to objects c̄ delay. Difficulty copying geometric forms. Repeats high & low probability phrases. Functional expression is fluent but c̄ word finding problems not evident during naming. Conversation. Expression lacks content, but c̄ time makes needs known.

A– Anomic aphasia c̄ ataxic dysarthria. Parietal lesion c̄ay explain aphasis but not dysarthria – suspect cerebellar that involvement of infarct superimposed on ETOH hx.

P– 1) Further eval of comprehension skills, reading & writing
2) suggest OT w/u of perception
3) pt good rehab candidate if well comp

SIGNATURE

IDENTIFICATION NO.

PATIENT'S IDENTIFICATION

M. Maher Phy 1-2-88
Speech Path X7515

CONSULTATION SHEET
STANDARD FORM

---

presented a brief description of the patient and noted that the patient now had a confirmed left parietal lobe infarct with expressive dysphasia. The response follows the SOAP (Subjective, Objective, Assessment, Plan) format. In the opinion of the examiner, the patient did have localizing left brain signs as evidenced by the right facial and tongue weakness (that was not present on the physical examination at admission) with evidence of word-finding difficulty and perceptual disturbance. Additionally, the patient had dysarthria that was characterized by poor coordination between phonation and respiration, consistent with cerebellar involvement (and consistent with the previously documented left cerebellar focal pathology).

The impression for this patient was that the pathology, as it related to the patient's communication dysfunction, could not be explained by one lesion but rather by multiple lesions superimposed on an historically decompensated brain. The plan from the speech/language pathologist's perspective was to evaluate the patient's comprehension in detail, to evaluate the patient's reading and writing skills, and to recommend an occupational therapy evaluation to explore documentation of the patient's perceptual deficits as they might impact on his ability to perform the activities of daily living. The consult reply is signed, dated, and returned to the consulting physician to be included in the medical record.

The Doctor's Order Sheet

The doctor's order sheet is a good source of information for following the progress of a hospitalized patient's treatment. For instance, if the speech/language pathologist made some recommendations for additional consultations or for a special diet for a dysphagic patient, a check of the doctor's orders would reveal if the recommendations had been followed. In short, anything that pertains to the patient, whether for a change in medications, scheduling of a special test, or a weekend pass, must be documented and approved on the doctor's order sheet. If the doctor's order requires that nursing follow a prescribed regimen of treatment, the order will be initialed by the nurse after it is completed. Exhibit 4–5 is an example of a doctor's order sheet for the patient who was admitted for a left neck mass. Note that the orders indicate that the patient is to receive anesthesia on August 19 and should be NPO (nothing by mouth) after midnight, with Robinul given at 0.2 mg IM (intramuscularly) after the patient is summoned to the operating room. This order was written by the anesthesiologist. On the same form are the postoperative orders written by the patient's otolaryngologist. They include admission to the RR (recovery room) and to the patient's floor (4 South) and ask that the patient's diet be NPO (nothing by mouth) until fully awake and alert, at which time he could have clear liquids. This is followed by an order to start medications, with their dosages and times of administration.

Consent for an Operation

Before the patient (described in Exhibit 4–3) could enter the operating room for the purpose of confirming or denying the presence of recurring cancer, he had to sign a form indicating that he understood the type of operation to be performed and what it involved (see Exhibit 4–6). Obtaining a patient's consent for an operative procedure is a necessary part of a hospital's quality assurance and risk reduction program (see Chapter 11). The consent for procedures form must indicate in lay

Exhibit 4–5 An Example of a Doctor's Order Sheet

Exception to Standard Form 508
Approved by OMB

MEDICAL RECORD | **DOCTOR'S ORDERS**

NOTE: Physician's signature must accompany each entry including standing orders. Date and time for instituting and discontinuing the orders must be recorded.

DATE AND TIME	PROB. NO.	ORDERS (Another brand, equal in quality, of the same basic drug may be dispensed, UNLESS checked.)	√	NURSE'S SIGNATURE
8/18 6AM		Anesthesia Pre-Op Orders		
		① NPO p̄ midnite		
		② Robinul 0.2 mg. IM		
		on CALL		
		Brody		DMR
8/19		Postop		
		Admit to RR, then 4S		
		Dx: S/P laryngoscopy & bx		Ile
		Cond		
		V.S. routine		
		Allergies NKDA		
		Activities ad lib when fully awake & alert		
		Diet NPO til fully awake & alert		nib
		IVF $D_5\frac{1}{2}NS$ @ 100 cc/h		nib
		Cool mist 35% O_2		
		Clear liquid when fully awake		
		Ampicillin 1 gm IVSS q 6h x 24 hr		
		Trach set @ bedside		

Enter in space below: PATIENT IDENTIFICATION – TREATING FACILITY – WARD NO. – DATE

Solomon

MEDICAL RECORD

DOCTOR'S ORDERS

VA FORM 10-1158
OCT 1975

EXISTING STOCK OF VA FORM 10-1158, MAY 1973 AND VA FORM 10-1158c, NOV 1972, WILL BE USED.

terms that the patient was notified of the type of surgery to be performed and its attendant risks and complications. Exhibit 4–6 indicates that the patient was to be scheduled for a direct laryngoscopy and esophagoscopy with biopsies, taking tissue from the larynx and esophagus. The form is signed by the patient and physician and is witnessed, usually by a nurse. The form then becomes a part of the patient's medical record.

Exhibit 4–6 An Example of a Signed Consent for an Operation

MEDICAL RECORD	REQUEST FOR ADMINISTRATION OF ANESTHESIA AND FOR PERFORMANCE OF OPERATIONS AND OTHER PROCEDURES

A. IDENTIFICATION SURGICAL TEAM *SCULLERAST STROSCHEIN, LIU, BERG KAUFMAN(S)*

1. OPERATION OR PROCEDURE *DIRECT LARYNGOSCOPY AND ESOPHAGOSCOPY WITH BIOPSIES*

B. STATEMENT OF REQUEST

1. The nature and purpose of the operation or procedure, possible alternative methods of treatment, the risks involved, and the possibility of complications have been fully explained to me. I acknowledge that no guarantees have been made to me concerning the results of the operation or procedure. I understand the nature of the operation or procedure to be *(Description of operation or procedure in layman's language)*

looking at larynx and esophagus and taking tissue for biopsies

which is to be performed by or under the direction of Dr. ___SUPERVISING ATTENDING* *KAUFMAN (S)*

2. I request the performance of the above-named operation or procedure and of such additional operations or procedures as are found to be necessary or desirable, in the judgment of the professional staff of the below-named medical facility, during the course of the above-named operation or procedure.

3. I request the administration of such anesthesia as may be considered necessary or advisable in the judgment of the professional staff of the below-named medical facility.

4. Exceptions to surgery or anesthesia, if any, are: ___*NONE*___
(If "none", to state)

5. I request the disposal by authorities of the below-named medical facility of any tissues or parts which it may be necessary to remove.

6. I understand that photographs and movies may be taken of this operation, and that they may be viewed by various personnel undergoing training or indoctrination at this or other facilities. I consent to the taking of such pictures and observation of the operation by authorized personnel, subject to the following conditions:

   a. The name of the patient and his/her family is not used to identify said pictures.

   b. Said pictures be used only for purposes of medical/dental study or research.

(Cross out any parts above which are not appropriate)

C. SIGNATURES *(Appropriate items in Parts A and B must be completed before signing)*

1. COUNSELING PHYSICIAN/DENTIST: I have counseled this patient as to the nature of the proposed procedure(s), attendant risks involved, and expected results, as described above.

_____ M.D.
(Signature of Counseling Physician/Dentist)
M. STROSCHEIN MD PGY3

2. PATIENT: I understand the nature of the proposed procedure(s), attendant risks involved, and expected results, as described above, and hereby request such procedure(s) be performed.

_____ RN
(Signature of Witness, excluding members of operating team)

John Doe
(Signature of Patient)

(Date and Time)

3. SPONSOR OR GUARDIAN: (When patient is a minor or unable to give consent) I, _____ sponsor/guardian of _____ understand the nature of the proposed procedure(s), attendant risks involved, and expected results, as described above, and hereby request such procedure(s) be performed.

_____
(Signature of Sponsor/Legal Guardian)

(Date and Time)

REGISTER NO.	WARD NO.

STANDARD FORM 522 (Rev. 10–76)
General Services Administration &
Interagency Comm. on Medical Records
FPMR 101–11.806–8
522–109

*U.S. GOVERNMENT PRINTING OFFICE 1983 381–488/2995

Laboratory Reports

A section of the medical record is reserved for the results of laboratory investigations. Exhibit 4–7 shows the radiographic report on the patient who was admitted for the left neck mass. The examination requested is a CXR (chest x-ray) and is part of a normal routine in hospital admissions. All laboratory reports, including results of blood and urine analyses, are contained in this section. Also included

Exhibit 4–7 Example of an X-Ray Laboratory Report

519-218-01

PATIENT IDENTIFICATION *(For typed or written entries give: Name — last, first, middle, Medical Facility)*	AGE	SEX	SSN *(Sponsor)*	WARD/CLINIC	REGISTER NO.
John Doe	55	M	—	4-N	
	EXAMINATION REQUESTED *(Use SF 519-B for multiple exams)* CXR				
	REQUESTED BY V8pp				TELEPHONE NO. X682
LOCATION OF MEDICAL RECORDS	FILM NO.			DATE REQUESTED 8-13-86	PREGNANT ☐ YES ☒ NO

SPECIFIC REASON(S) FOR REQUEST *(Complaints and findings)*

New admit: (L) Neck MASS

DATE OF EXAMINATION *(Month, day, year)*	DATE OF REPORT *(Month, day, year)*	DATE OF TRANSCRIPTION *(Month, day, year)*
		DD: 8/21 DT:8/22/86

RADIOLOGIC REPORT

CHEST(PA AND LATERAL) 8/20/86: Loss of the normal curve of the spine is noted with straightening of the back. The lung parenchyma are clear. The mediastinal shadow is within normal limits. No interval changes from previous film of 7/08/86.

SIGNATURE M. Johnson, M.D.

LOCATION OF RADIOLOGIC FACILITY

1 – MEDICAL RECORD **RADIOLOGIC CONSULTATION REQUEST/REPORT** EXCEPTION TO SF 519a APPROVED BY GSA/IRMS 6/86 008583

U.S. GPO: 1986-181-819 (40031)

would be the results of any pathology requests following biopsy, such as the example that is illustrated in Exhibit 4–8 for the patient with the left neck mass. It is noted that the patient was suspected of having laryngeal carcinoma, with a $T_4N_{2A}M_O$ lesion (a lesion involving both the true and false vocal folds, with two neck nodes, and no known metastasis). The results of the pathology report revealed that the patient did have moderately differentiated in-situ and focally invasive squamous cell carcinoma.

The Operative Report

A partial operative report for the patient with the left neck mass is presented in Exhibit 4–9. It shows that the patient underwent direct laryngoscopy and biopsy to discover the type and extent of the lesion. If the speech/language pathologist is interested in discovering what structures were surgically removed, a review of the operation report may be useful. At times, however, a detailed reporting of the structures rearranged or removed will not be included in the operative report, and the information will have to be obtained in conversation with the physician who performed the surgery. For instance, the report may note that the patient underwent a supraglottic laryngectomy, but not indicate whether or not, or how much of, the tongue base was resected. This information is important to the speech/language

Exhibit 4–8 Example of a Report from the Pathology Laboratory

---

515–109

MEDICAL RECORD	TISSUE EXAMINATION

SPECIMEN SUBMITTED BY	DATE OBTAINED
Dr. Sculerati	(8-19-85)

SPECIMEN
Left vocal cord.

BRIEF CLINICAL HISTORY (Include duration of lesion and rapidity of growth, if a neoplasm)
65 year old Black male underwent radiation therapy for transglottic, laryngeal carcinoma. Rule out resistant disease.

PREOPERATIVE DIAGNOSIS
$T_4N_{2A}M_0$ squamous cell carcinoma. (See previous path, Spring 1985).

OPERATIVE FINDINGS

POSTOPERATIVE DIAGNOSIS	SIGNATURE AND TITLE
Same	

PATHOLOGICAL REPORT

NAME OF LABORATORY	ACCESSION NO(S).
VAMC, NEW YORK, NEW YORK 10010	S-2912-85

(Gross description, histologic examination and diagnoses)
GROSS DESCRIPTION (DR. VAZQUEZ): Received in formalin, in a container labelled "Left Vocal Cord", are multiple fragments of tan tissue with focal areas of hemorrhage, measuring 0.9 x 0.6 x 0.2 cm in aggregate. The entire specimen is submitted.

DIAGNOSIS: Left Vocal Cord, Biopsy: Moderately Differentiated In-Situ And Focally Invasive, Squamous Cell Carcinoma.

(Continue on reverse side)

SIGNATURE OF PATHOLOGIST	DATE
GURDIP S. SIDHU, M.D., PATHOLOGIST	8-21-85 msw

	AGE	SEX	RACE	IDENTIFICATION NO.

or written entries give: Name—last, first,
.... ade; date; hospital or medical facility)

WARD NO.
4 South

TISSUE EXAMINATION

STANDARD FORM 515 (REV. 9–77)
Prescribed by GSA and ICMR, FPMR 101-11.806–8

---

pathologist in predicting how well the patient may be able to protect the airway during swallowing rehabilitation.

The Continuing Medication Record

An example of the continuing medication record is presented in Exhibit 4–10. This is a consecutive record of the types and amounts of medications that are given

Exhibit 4–9 Example of a Report Following a Surgical Procedure

---

516–107

MEDICAL RECORD	DD.9/5/85 DT.9/12/**OPERATION REPORT** #1424

PREOPERATIVE DIAGNOSIS

Laryngeal carcinoma.

SURGEON	FIRST ASSISTANT	SECOND ASSISTANT	
Dr. Sculerati	Drs.Stroschein/Berg	Dr. Kaufman(5)	

ANESTHETIST	ANESTHETIC	TIME BEGAN	
Dr's. Statile/Grady	General	TIME ENDED 8:45am	

SURGICAL NURSE	INSTRUMENT NURSE	TIME OPERATION BEGAN	TIME OPERATION COMPLETED
A. Alvarado RN	O. Hodge RN	9:10am	9:20am

OPERATIVE DIAGNOSES	DRAINS (*Kind and number*)	SPONGE COUNT VERIFIED
Direct Laryngeal carcinoma.		

MATERIAL FORWARDED TO LABORATORY FOR EXAMINATION

Vocal cord.

OPERATION PERFORMED

Direct laryngoscopy and biopsy.

DESCRIPTION OF OPERATION (*Type(s) of suture used, gross findings, etc.*)	MAJOR	MINOR	DATE OF OPERATION
POSTOPERATIVE CONDITION: GOOD COMPLICATIONS: NONE		X	8/19/85

FINDINGS: The patient had a left vocal cord which was completely replaced with what appeared to be carcinoma. This was biopsied multiple times.

PROCEDURE: The patient was brought to the Oprating Room, placed on the operating table in the supine position and general anesthesia was smoothly induced and the patient was intubated with a small, #7 endotracheal tube. THE neck was palpated and a left neck mass was noted which was mobile. THIS was a left mid to upper jugular mass approximately 2 x 3 cm. in size. THE floor of the mouth, tongue and tonsils felt normal to palpation. THE anterior commissure scope and then the Dedo scope were properly used to examine the base of tongue, vallecula, epiglottis, left and right piriforms down to the apex, using the anterior commissure scope only, and the left and right arytenoids. THESE all appeared normal. THE left AE fold appeared somewhat thickened but there was no gross evidence of tumor. THE lft vocal cord, however, appeared entirely replaced with tumor. It should be noted that on the preoperative indirect exam, the left vocal cord did not move. THE right vocal cord appeared normal. THE sbglottic area appeared normal. Multiple

SIGNATURE OF SURGEON	DATE
NANCY SCULERATI, M. D.	9/12/85

PA ——— *pcd or written entries give: Name—last, fir. grade; date; hospital or medical facility)*	WARD NO. 4S

OPERATION REPORT

STANDARD FORM 516 (REV. 9–77)
Prescribed by GSA and ICMR, FPMR 101–11.806–8

---

to a patient. The record indicates the medications ordered, when they are administered, for how long, and when they are discontinued. If a patient with a communication disorder suddenly changes in the ability to communicate, the medication record should be inspected to note if there has been a change in medication rate or dosage that might explain the sudden change in the patient's communication ability. Also noted in the medication record would be the type and dosages of recommended feedings. Exhibit 4–10 illustrates the recommendations for the dosages

Exhibit 4–10 Example of a Continuing Medication Record

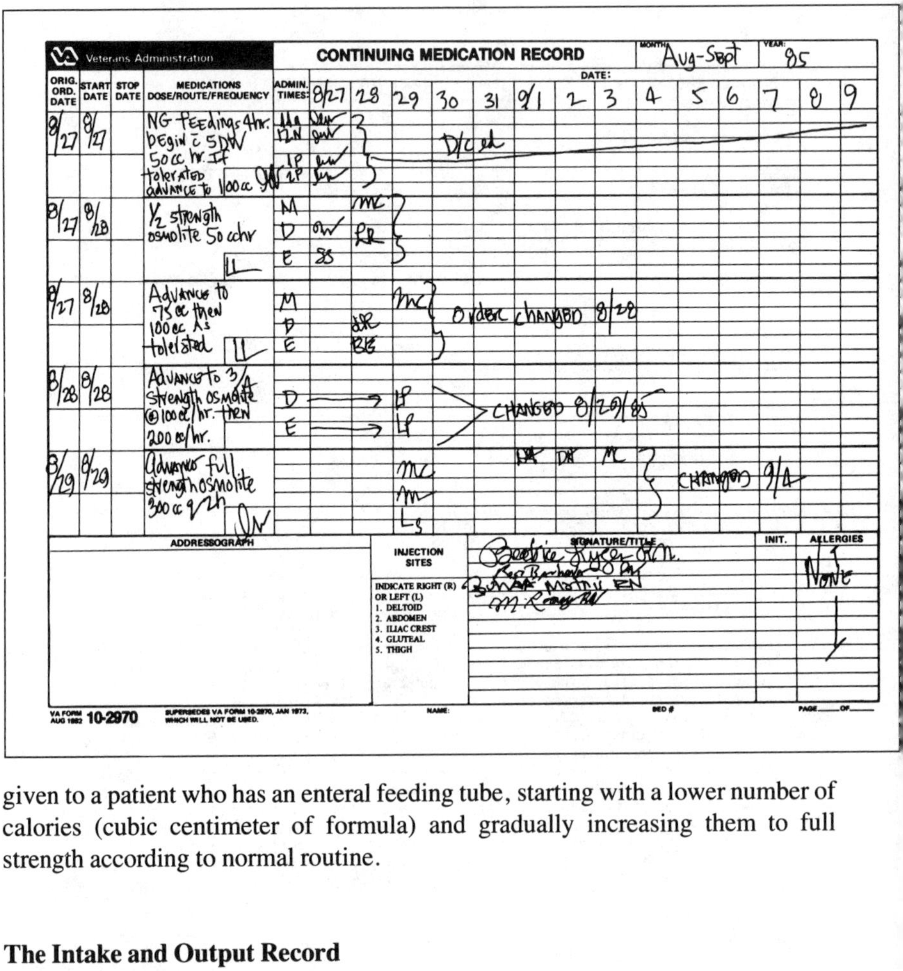

Veterans Administration

CONTINUING MEDICATION RECORD

MONTH: Aug-Sept YEAR: 85

ORIG. ORD. DATE	START DATE	STOP DATE	MEDICATIONS DOSE/ROUTE/FREQUENCY	ADMIN. TIMES	DATE: 8/27	28	29	30	31	9/1	2	3	4	5	6	7	8	9
8/27	8/27		NG feedings 4hr. Begin c̄ 5DW 50cc hr. If tolerated advance to 100cc					D/C'ed										
8/27	8/28		½ strength osmolite 50 cc hr	M D E														
8/27	8/28		Advance to 75cc then 100cc as tolerated	M D E			order changed 8/28											
8/28	8/28		Advance to ¾ strength osmolite @ 100cc/hr. then 200cc/hr.	D E			CHANGED 8/29/85											
8/29	8/29		Advance full strength osmolite 300cc q 2h												CHANGED 9/4			

ADDRESSOGRAPH

INJECTION SITES

INDICATE RIGHT (R) OR LEFT (L)
1. DELTOID
2. ABDOMEN
3. ILIAC CREST
4. GLUTEAL
5. THIGH

SIGNATURE/TITLE | INIT. | ALLERGIES: None

VA FORM AUG 1982 10-2970 SUPERSEDES VA FORM 10-2970, JAN 1973, WHICH WILL NOT BE USED.

NAME: BED # PAGE __ OF __

given to a patient who has an enteral feeding tube, starting with a lower number of calories (cubic centimeter of formula) and gradually increasing them to full strength according to normal routine.

The Intake and Output Record

The intake and output record (I and O sheet) may not always be kept in the patient's medical record. More often, it is kept on a clipboard at the patient's bedside. It contains the documentation of how much fluid and food a patient takes in during a 24-hour period (intake) and how much is excreted (output). An example of a form on which this information is documented is presented in Exhibit 4–11. This form usually is completed by the nursing staff. It is divided into three 8-hour shifts. The nurse records the amount of food and fluids taken either by mouth or by tube during each shift. In the lower right-hand corner of the sheet are the guidelines for estimating how much a patient has ingested based upon the size of the containers in which the food was served. Food and fluid given by intravenous infusion or by feeding tubes also are recorded as intake. Output is recorded as urine excreted, emesis, and

Exhibit 4–11 Example of an Intake and Output Record

INTAKE				OUTPUT				
Veterans Administration								
SOLUTIONS Time-Type-Amt.	AMT-ABS	OTHER	TUBE P.O.	TIME	URINE	EMESIS	DRAINAGE	OTHER
				7 A.M.				
				8 A.M.				
				9 A.M.				
				10 A.M.				
				11.A.M.				
				12 P.M.				
				1.P.M.				
				2 P.M.				
				3 P.M.				
8 HOUR-TOTAL 7-3 PM				TOTAL				
				4 P.M.				
				5 P.M.				
				6 P.M.				
				7 P.M.				
				8 P.M.				
				9 P.M.				
				10 P.M.				

STANDARD LIQUID MEASUREMENTS AS OF JUNE, 1981

8 HOUR-TOTAL 3-11 PM

Water Pitcher   100 mls.
Plastic Drinking Cup   200 mls.
Styrofoam Coffee Cup   200 mls.
Styrofoam Soup Bowl   130 mls.
Juice Container   120 mls.
Milk Container   240 mls.
Jello   120 mls.
Ice Cream   120 mls.
Pleated Paper Cup   80 mls.

8 HOUR-TOTAL 11-7 AM

Travenol Administration Sets

24 HOUR TOTALS

Regular 10 gtts/ml

NAME

Minimeter 60 gtts/ml

VA FORM JAN 1981   7051b **DATA SHEET**

Fluid Balance (Measurements on other side)

estimates of drainage from wound sites (usually postsurgical sites or decubitis ulcers). The I and O sheet becomes an important document if the speech/language pathologist is following a patient with dysphagia and there is a question of the patient taking adequate nutrition by mouth. Often the amounts of by-mouth intake are not documented regularly, and it is necessary to reinforce the importance of this measure as a method of monitoring the patient's health care status.

The Vital Signs Sheet

The patient's vital signs are taken at least once during every nursing shift. Temperature, pulse, and respiration (TPR) and blood pressure (see Exhibit 4–12) are documented. It is important for the speech/language pathologist to check these recordings to note if the patient is in metabolic decompensation during the evaluation, while being followed after the evaluation, or during treatment. Changes in metabolic competency, as indicated by the vital signs, can affect communication

Exhibit 4–12 Example of a Vital Signs Record

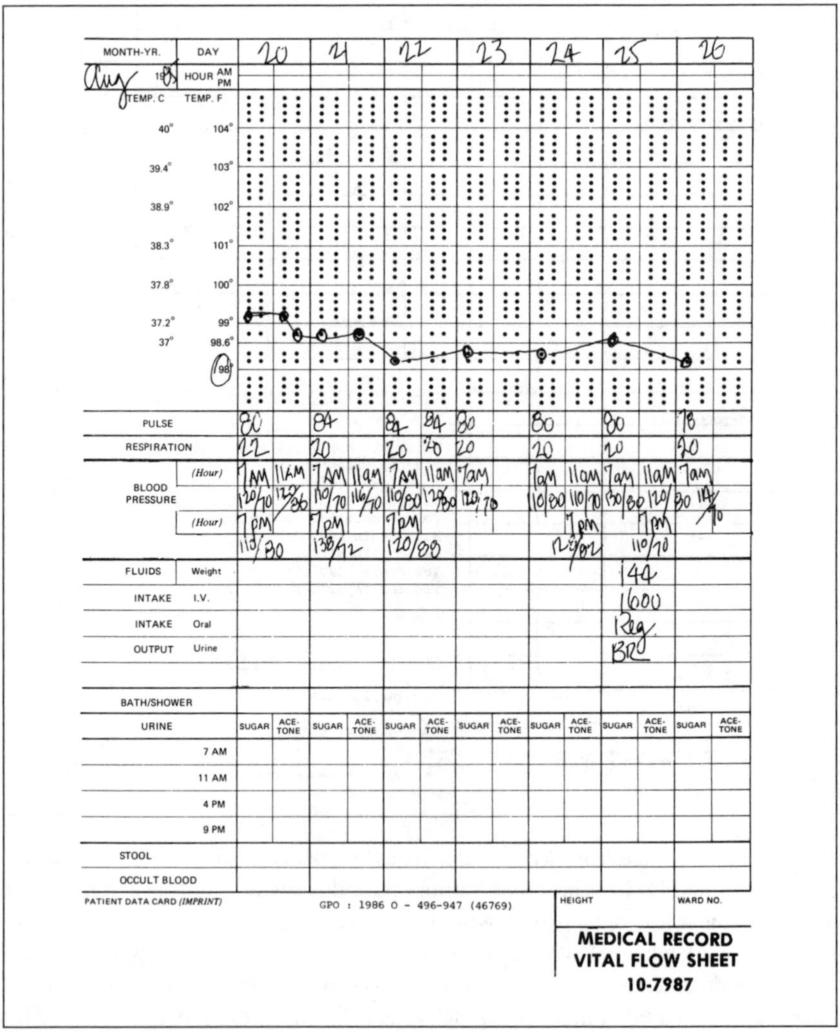

MONTH-YR. | DAY | 20 | 21 | 22 | 23 | 24 | 25 | 26
HOUR AM PM
TEMP. C | TEMP. F
40° | 104°
39.4° | 103°
38.9° | 102°
38.3° | 101°
37.8° | 100°
37.2° | 99°
37° | 98.6°
PULSE | 80 | 84 | 84 84 | 80 | 80 | 80 | 78
RESPIRATION | 22 | 20 | 20 20 | 20 | 20 | 20 | 20
BLOOD PRESSURE (Hour) | 7AM 11AM 120/70 | 7AM 11am 110/70 116/70 | 7AM 11am 110/80 | 7am 120/70 | 7am 11am 110/80 110/70 | 7am 11am 130/80 120/80 | 7am
(Hour) | 7pm 110/80 | 7pm 138/72 | 7pm 120/88 | 7pm | 7pm 110/70
FLUIDS | Weight | 144
INTAKE | I.V. | 1600
INTAKE | Oral | Reg.
OUTPUT | Urine | BRO
BATH/SHOWER
URINE | SUGAR | ACE-TONE | SUGAR | ACE-TONE | SUGAR | ACE-TONE | SUGAR | ACE-TONE | SUGAR | ACE-TONE | SUGAR | ACE-TONE | SUGAR | ACE-TONE
7 AM
11 AM
4 PM
9 PM
STOOL
OCCULT BLOOD
PATIENT DATA CARD *(IMPRINT)*
GPO : 1986 O - 496-947 (46769)
HEIGHT | WARD NO.
MEDICAL RECORD
VITAL FLOW SHEET
10-7987

competence and may explain why a patient is not performing as expected. In Exhibit 4–12, the temperature, pulse, respiration, and blood pressure are recorded on a daily basis as noted at the top of the record. Temperature is recorded by circling the appropriate dot on the matrix. Numbers indicating respirations and pulses per minute are recorded in the appropriate boxes below the temperatures. The time that the blood pressure was recorded, together with the actual reading, is noted below the pulse and respiration measurements.

The Progress Notes

One of the most important sections of the medical record contains the patient's progress notes. This section represents a continuing record of the patient's medical care. It is the vehicle used most often for correspondence between persons who are contributing to the patient's care. The progress notes are used for the documentation of the effects of patient treatment, the results of an evaluation, and the need for the primary physician to request additional services or to begin a treatment modality. Ideally, an entry in the progress notes should be completed each time the patient receives an intervention from an outside service.

The progress notes inform the primary physician about the status of the patient from the perspective of the services that have been consulted, and they serve as a reminder that the patient is continuing to be followed by the services that make entries. Each progress note should reflect the patient's complaint or history of the illness from the specialist's perspective, the type of intervention, the results of the intervention, and the plan for the future. An example of a progress note from a dietitian is presented in Exhibit 4–13. In this note, the dietitian presents the patient's past dietary history and current status, summarizes the current nutritional status by reporting pertinent laboratory values, and indicates that the patient requires an 1,800-calorie diet, with 2 g sodium and cholesterol restrictions. A progress note should be labeled at the top with the topic of the note or name of the service (in this example it is nutrition), dated, and signed with the writer's name and title. If the writer of the note feels that the primary physician may wish further contact, it is a courtesy to leave a telephone or beeper number after the signature.

A Medical-Legal Document

Each component part of the medical record is considered to be a medical-legal document. After all notations and reports are entered, they become a permanent part of the record. Care should be taken by all professionals entering notes to ensure that data are objective and impressions are so labeled.

In teaching hospitals, philosophical discussions regarding a line of diagnostic reasoning or the rationale for a specific treatment plan frequently are entered into the patient's chart. These are acceptable in this setting, but may be inappropriate in

Exhibit 4–13 Example of a Progress Note Regarding the Status of a Patient's Nutritional Status

PROGRESS NOTES

DATE	
	Nutrition
1/26/88 S	Reports poor appetite and weight loss over p̄ year (~25#). Has been instructed on diabetic, low salt diet but unable to follow due to "always burning the food". Does omit [ ] sweets from diet. Usual wt 165#.
O	Dx Dementia, HTN, IDDM, ? seizure disorder. Ht 5'10½" Wt 140# IBW 169 ± 19#. Meds include NPH insulin 15u q AM, Minipress, Halcion. Labs: Glu 171 (↓ from 492) BUN 23 Cr 1.6 K 5.6 (down from 6.0) Cholesterol 303 ALB 4.4 Diet: 2gm Na ADA.
A	57 yo B ♂ 85% of usual body weight c̄ a 15% wt Δ over p̄ year. Labs c̄ nutritional significance reflect hyperglycemia, hypercholesterolemia and elevated K⁺. Calorie needs 1820 Kcal/day, 2070 Kcal/day if slow weight gain is desired. Would recommend diet level be set at 1800 cal/day until BS decreases, ↑ to 2100 pending result of f/u and labs. Observed at lunch yesterday - fair po intake noted.
P	1) Recommend 1800 calorie ADA 2gm Na Decreased Cholesterol diet. If K⁺ remains ↑ a Decreased Potassium diet can be ordered in conjunction c̄ other reductions. 2) Weekly wts recommended. 3) Close F/u of labs, po intake, nutritional status. Pt Ed: Additional diet instruction pending d/c plans and result of f/u. J Curran, R.D.

★U.S.GPO:1987-0-706-172 STANDARD FORM 509 BACK (Rev. 11-77)

others. It also is understood that errors in diagnosis or the misinterpretation of data will be recorded in charts of teaching centers, as these are accepted as part of the learning process. The speech/language pathologist should recognize that the physician, like all professionals, is fallible. When observations or data differ, efforts are needed to resolve the conflict. It is important that speech/language pathologists view their contributions to medical records as no less important or less significant than those of physicians; they are contributions from nonphysician specialists who assist in the maintenance of a patient's health.

SUMMARY

The medical record is the single most important legal document in a medical setting. Within its structure can be found all of the past and current medical information that describes the patient's health status. The progress notes provide a chronological documentation of each aspect of the patient's care and contain information pertaining to the patient's progress or lack of progress, the patient's complaints and desires, the treatment plans, the treatment administered and the patient's response, the discharge plans, and the final disposition (hospital summary). Within these broad categories, the medical record should reflect the thinking that went into each decision and the methods that were utilized to establish the conclusions reported.

For convenience in finding a particular set of data, a medical record is divided into sections. Of primary importance are the patient's past medical history (that includes a review of all biologic and psychosocial systems), a statement of the reason for the current hospitalization, and the results of the present physical evaluation. A standard format for the physical evaluation of the patient by a physician entails a complete review of all biologic systems by the mechanisms of visual inspection, palpation, percussion, and auscultation.

Some medical centers utilize a problem-oriented medical record format, in which the patient's problems are listed as they occur and are referred to by number in subsequent progress notes so that the flow of care can be easily reviewed. Other institutions' progress notes and reports often use a subjective, objective, assessment, and plan (SOAP) format. The format is a sequential presentation of the patient's complaint (S), the examiner's objective findings (O), the interpretation of the findings (A), and the plans for treatment or management (P).

The speech/language pathologist working in a medical setting will contribute to the permanent medical record through consultation replies, progress notes, and discharge summaries. After receiving a consultation, a review of the patient's medical record often becomes the point of departure in evaluation. The speech/language pathologist often will not be able to understand the medical record due to lack of familiarity with medical terminology and shorthand. Familiarity with formats used in the history and physical examination, with terminology generally expected from the specialists making the entries, and with the patient's past medical history will help clinicians to decode important information. A number of examples are provided in this chapter to assist in the development of skills needed to understand the entire medical record, in addition to suggestions and examples of information that may be appropriately used by speech/language pathologists.

NOTES

1. M.H. Delp and R.T. Manning, *Major's Physical Diagnosis: An Introduction to the Clinical Process* (Philadelphia: W.B. Saunders Co., 1981), 12.

2. Ibid.

3. Barbara Bates, *A Guide to Physical Examination,* 3rd ed. (Philadelphia: J.B. Lippincott Co., 1983), 31–33.

4. Richard L. DeGowin, "The Medical History." In *Bedside Diagnostic Examination,* eds. Elmer L. DeGowin and Richard L. DeGowin (New York: Macmillan Publishing Co., 1987), 18–30.

5. Lawrence L. Weed, *Medical Records, Medical Education, and Patient Care* (Cleveland: Press of Case Western Reserve University, 1969).

Chapter 5

The Consultation
and Interview

INTRODUCTION

The plan for the clinical evaluation of the patient should begin as soon as the clinician receives a request for services. This request usually is accomplished on a standard form that states the referring physician's name and service, a brief description of the reason for the request (usually accompanied by some medical history), and a stated diagnosis or, in some cases, a preliminary or working diagnosis stated as R/O (rule out). Exhibit 5–1 illustrates an example of a typical consultation.

It is possible to form hypotheses relative to the patient's speech and language diagnosis without having examined the patient and without any review of the patient's medical record. Attempts to form these hypotheses will assist the examiner during the subsequent review of the medical record, the patient interview, and the actual physical and mental status evaluation. Examples of the process of forming initial diagnostic impressions and how they may assist the examiner in the evaluative process are presented in the next section of this chapter.

Developing the skill of early hypothesis testing is at the crux of the differential diagnostic process. This skill is usually achieved only after the clinician has had exposure to a wide variety of communication disorders and referrals from various medical disciplines. In essence, after receiving a consult, the clinician should make a list of known facts about the patient as indicated by the brief history. The clinician should review what he or she knows about the stated diagnosis as a disease, syndrome, or disorder. For example, if the diagnosis is parkinsonism, what are the concomitant speech and language characteristics, and what are the avenues of investigation that should be pursued? In this stage the clinician "plays the odds." If the consult says the patient is dysarthric, the clinician can assume the patient is not aphasic; or if it says the patient is demented, the patient probably is not aphasic but may have other deficits in communication not related to focal disease. There is less probability of a vascular problem in a young patient. If the patient is completely anarthric, there is a higher probability of bilateral lesions that may suggest the possibility of decrements in cognition and require investigation as part of the assessment plan.

Exhibit 5–1 Sample of a Consultation Sheet (Case Example 1)

MEDICAL RECORD		CONSULTATION SHEET
	REQUEST	

TO:
Speech Therapy (135)

FROM: *Requesting physician or activity*
Psychiatry (16N)

DATE OF REQUEST
12-30-88

REASON FOR REQUEST *(Complaints and findings)*
64 y/o man with Parkinson's, R facial and trouble swallowing past 2 months. Coughs when eating solids and sometimes even liquids. Please evaluate and advise.

PROVISIONAL DIAGNOSIS
Parkinson's disease, acute depression

DOCTOR'S SIGNATURE
CC icS

APPROVED

PLACE OF CONSULTATION

☒ BEDSIDE   ☐ ON CALL

☒ ROUTINE   ☐ TODAY

☐ 72 HOURS   ☐ EMERGENCY

CONSULTATION REPORT

This preliminary mental exercise usually is followed by a thorough review of the medical record that may answer some of the clinician's questions or bring up new ones that need to be resolved. If the examiner has begun to form preliminary diagnostic impressions before evaluating the patient, the circumstance of the patient interview and clinical evaluation will be a planned exercise designed to confirm or deny the initial impressions. The entire differential diagnostic process will be focused on probing those areas that have been preconceived, thus adding authority and clarity to the final diagnosis.

INITIAL CONSULTATION

The request for services of the speech/language pathologist usually comes with a brief, and at times unreliable or incomplete, history of the patient's current hospitalization. This history may or may not be accompanied by a preliminary or final medical diagnosis. For instance, a typical request might be worded: "60-year-old female, S/P [status post] L CVA [left brain cerebral vascular accident] June 1988 now with dysarthric speech." The accompanying preliminary diagnosis might be "Embolic L CVA, resolved, residual dysarthria." Other requests may be more ambiguous, and may dictate a different set of assessment strategies. For example, a consult stating, "80 y/o [80-year-old] ♂ [male] reported sudden confusion on 8/9/88 with word-finding difficulty only; please R/O [rule out] dementia," presupposes that a definitive diagnosis of dementia is being entertained but has not been established. Further, it presupposes that the services requested of the speech/language pathologist should be designed to provide the medical care team with information that either confirms or denies this working diagnosis.

Both of these consult requests potentially set the stage for two different types of evaluations and probably for two different types of consult replies. In the first example, the diagnosis has been confirmed (although one should not always trust its accuracy), and the consult request requires that the speech/language pathologist be prepared to assess in detail those aspects of speech production that affect intelligibility. In the second example, an assessment of both speech and language components is appropriate in an effort to confirm or deny the diagnosis of dementia based on the patient's speech and language characteristics. Additional tests of cognition (orientation, memory, and perception) as they are manifest in daily communicative circumstances also may be appropriate. After this evaluation, the speech/language pathologist may decide that the working diagnosis of dementia is not consistent with the communication evaluation and should state this on the consult reply. Ideally, alternate diagnoses should be suggested with a statement such as "the speech, language and cognitive performances of the patient are most consistent with normal aging."

FORMING HYPOTHESES

Teaching a methodology for the formulation of an initial diagnostic impression that will help guide and define the assessment process is best accomplished through examples. When the clinician receives the consult with the basic information, he or she should begin to make mental lists that fall into three broad categories: (1) what is known about the patient and the presenting symptomatology of the stated diagnosis, (2) what additional information the clinician would like to gather based on these preliminary facts and assumptions, and (3) early speculations about the patient's speech and language diagnosis that need to be confirmed or denied. These speculations often guide the medical record review and clinical assessment.

Case Example 1

A summary of the three main processes used in establishing early clinical hypotheses that will assist in planning the assessment and in formulating a diagnosis is presented in Table 5–1. The information in the summary refers to the patient described in Exhibit 5–1.

After reviewing the brief history provided on the consult, it is possible for the clinician to review what is known and to begin asking questions about additional information needed to provide a complete evaluation of the patient's disorder from the perspective of the speech/language pathologist. Case example 1 in Table 5–1 lists the known (but not necessarily confirmed) medical history as reported on the consultation requesting assistance from the speech/language pathologist. The consult primarily is a request for information and advice on how best to manage the patient's swallowing disorder. The clinician then should review those items from the patient's history or subsequent evaluation that would be useful in establishing

Table 5–1 Summary of Hypotheses Formulation Process for Case Example 1

What Is Known (Process I)	Need To Know (Process II)
1. Age: 64.	1. Progression of Parkinson's disease:
2. Has Parkinson's disease.	a. Length of time since diagnosis.
3. Hospitalized for depression.	b. Recent exacerbation?
4. Has right facial weakness.	c. Effects on communication.
5. Can't swallow solids and liquids for two months; coughs when he tries to do so.	d. Effects on mentation.
	e. Effects on motor skills (e.g., ambulation, self-care).
	2. Seriousness of depression.
	3. Etiology of right facial weakness.
	4. Effect of swallowing complaint on health, weight, and depression.
	5. Previous history of dysphagia? Progress of current complaint.
	6. Social situation (e.g., lives alone, family, other supports).
	7. What is current diet?
	8. What are current medications?

Preliminary Speculations (Process III)

1. The patient's dysphagia for both solids and liquids can be a finding in patients with increasing symptoms from Parkinson's disease.

2. Acute changes in swallowing may be related to alterations in the patient's medications to control symptoms of Parkinson's disease.

3. The patient's dysphagia may be exacerbated by acute depression and/or change in social situation.

4. The patient may have had a new neurological event superimposed on Parkinson's disease (e.g., stroke or head injury from a fall).

5. The patient may have a communication disorder that also needs to be evaluated even though it was not specifically requested.

6. If the patient has a swallowing and/or speech disorder, does mentation contribute and does it allow for rehabilitation if needed?

---

a diagnosis. Some of the items in the "Need to Know" section will be answered after the clinician reviews the medical history. For instance, how long the patient has had Parkinson's disease and its course as it affects ambulation and speech production might be part of the history that was documented at the time of the patient's admission. Additional information, such as the seriousness of the depression for which he was hospitalized, his diet, current medications, and the social history, most likely will be found in the patient's admission data. Since the patient was not admitted to the psychiatry service for a swallowing disorder, it is unlikely that the historical background of his swallowing complaint will be documented in the historical data, although it might appear in the progress notes. Information relating directly to the patient's swallowing complaint probably should be gathered in the patient interview and examination.

In the third process of assessment planning the clinician begins to formulate preliminary diagnoses that assist in planning potential directions for the physical and mental status evaluation. These speculations are based in part on information available from three sources: (1) information obtained from the consultation request; (2) what the clinician knows about the existing diagnoses, for example, depression and Parkinson's disease; and (3) the clinician's experience with the conditions of depression and Parkinson's disease and knowledge about how they can interact and affect swallowing.

In case example 1 the clinician notes that the patient complains of dysphagia for both liquids and solids. Complaints of solids alone should make the clinician more suspicious of esophageal disease, whereas complaints about liquids alone suggest oropharyngeal dysfunction. The complaint of frank choking on both substances makes the clinician suspicious of oropharyngeal pathology.[1] However, Parkinson's disease can result in both oropharyngeal and esophageal pathology.[2,3] Knowledge of these facts should lead the examiner in the direction of planning or recommending a thorough evaluation of the entire aerodigestive tract. The clinician also must be cognizant of the fact that an acute depression could exacerbate an organic swallowing problem and that the patient's social situation (in particular if he was living alone without family support) could add further to a diminished appetite followed by complaints in eating. How much of the patient's swallowing complaint is secondary to organic pathology and how much is secondary to psychological decompensation should be the thrust of this evaluation. Also needing resolution is the initial finding of an isolated facial weakness. This is cause for a thorough evaluation of either cortical or brainstem disease possibly related to vascular insufficiency. Screening of motor speech competence and cognition would be appropriate. Finally, the known effects of Parkinson's disease on speech production require evaluation even though the consult did not focus on these aspects. It is most likely that the patient's motor speech production skills are either unimpaired or unrecognized, or they may not be considered immediately problematic by the physician.

Case Example 2

The consult request describing case example 2 is presented in Exhibit 5–2. The three processes in assessment planning for the second example are summarized in Table 5–2.

In this case, as in case example 1, some of the information on the referral probably can be found in the medical record, such as the integrity of other arterial vessels, previous history of communication deficits, and the postoperative course. Poor blood flow to the brain from previous or current occlusive disease could reduce oxygen proliferation in the brain and compromise the patient's communica-

Exhibit 5–2 Sample of a Consultation Sheet (Case Example 2)

MEDICAL RECORD	CONSULTATION SHEET

	REQUEST	
TO: Speech Pathology	**FROM:** *(Requesting physician or activity)* Medicine/Cardiology	DATE OF REQUEST 11-12-87

REASON FOR REQUEST *(Complaints and findings)*

55 y/o WM c hx of atherosclerotic HD. Had CABG x 3 6 mo. ago.
Now c/o problems communicating at work. Your eval. please.

PROVISIONAL DIAGNOSIS

S/P CABG, stable now

DOCTOR'S SIGNATURE	APPROVED	PLACE OF CONSULTATION	ROUTINE TODAY
(signature)		BEDSIDE ON CALL	72 HOURS EMERGENCY

CONSULTATION REPORT

tive ability. Since anoxia usually decompensates the brain bilaterally, the clinician might expect diffuse rather than focal deficits of language. This would be more consistent with anomic and memory deficits than specific aphasic symptomatology. Preparations for the assessment to investigate these areas would be appropriate. Information specific to the patient's complaint of communication would be elicited in the interview. One can assume that the deficits are not severe enough to keep the patient from work, but probably have disrupted the patient's work performance. The length of time the patient has noticed these communication deficits is important. They may not be coincident with the surgery, but rather a new finding that needs further investigation. If a review of the patient's operative course and postoperative course reveals either a possible involvement of cranial nerve 10 (left recurrent laryngeal nerve encircles the aorta) by surgical intervention or a prolonged airway intubation (with traumatic effects to the vocal folds), the patient may require an otolaryngological consult and thorough evaluation of voice, rather than specific attention to language. If cranial nerve 10 is involved, the patient interview also should include questions about swallowing difficulty. Poor vocal fold closure may predispose the patient to poor airway protection and subsequent intrusion of food or liquid into the airway.

When hypotheses relative to an assessment strategy and initial diagnostic impressions are formed, the clinician must find supporting and confirming data in order to define the speech/language problem. The eventual diagnosis will be based on a review of the medical record, clinical observations, patient interview, the physical examination, and mental status evaluation. Chapters 6 and 7 discuss the physical examination and mental status evaluation that will be added to the clinical picture to complete the data base. This combination of data provides a solid foundation upon which to form an impression and develop a subsequent management plan. In essence, the accuracy and completeness of the diagnostic impression is a

Table 5–2 Summary of Hypotheses Formulation Process for Case Example 2

What Is Known (Process I)	Need To Know (Process II)
1. Age: 55.	1. Any history of stroke or event involving brain, head, or neck.
2. Has a history of lipid collection in his arteries requiring bypass surgery.	2. The patient's operative and postoperative course.
3. Has returned to work.	3. The patient's interpretation of what constitutes difficulty in communication.
4. Complained to his cardiologist about inability to communicate.	4. The time of onset of the complaint and its relationship to the surgery.
	5. Any prior history of deficits related to communication.

Preliminary Speculations (Process III)

1. "Problems communicating" could mean anything from a voice disorder caused by damage to the recurrent laryngeal nerve during surgery to a cognitive impairment with word-finding difficulty as a result of a cerebral vascular event.
2. The patient is young to have had triple bypass surgery and, therefore, may have disease in other arteries affecting the cerebrum.
3. Since the complaints are initiated by the patient and he has returned to work, his communication deficits may be subtle and not apparent to others, even his cardiologist.

---

prerequisite to a successful approach in the patient's communication treatment. The more tools and information available to the speech/language pathologist, the better the quality of the contribution to the medical team.

CLINICAL OBSERVATIONS

The patient interview and examination are performed for the purpose of obtaining diagnostic and assessment data that can be used to specify the nature of a particular disorder, the patient's prognosis, and potential treatment techniques. A maxim in medicine states that an examination must not await the removal of the shirt. In other words, an experienced examiner recognizes that observations made at the time of the initial contact with each patient are registered and processed in such a way that certain immediate diagnostic hypotheses are formed. This sense may appear to be intuitive; however, it is apparent that certain characteristics correlate closely with specific disorders. An unexperienced examiner may even recognize many of these characteristics, but not relate them to specific disordered entities because they are not registered and processed as meaningful observations. When a beginning clinician encounters a patient with Parkinson's disease, the tremors, masked face, and stooped posture will not be recognized as interrelated symptoms, but simply as characteristics of this patient. In fact, the novice may not even attend to many of these features, because they are not yet meaningful clinical signs. When these features are pointed out and the pathology explained, the clinician will be able to recognize these symptoms instantly and eventually will relate them to probable speech characteristics.

A good exercise for a supervisor to use with speech/language pathology interns in a medical setting is to have them enter a room where a referred patient is residing, introduce themselves to the patient, and indicate that they will return momentarily to perform an examination. Upon exiting the room the interns are asked to tell the supervisor everything they can about the patient. When initially faced with this exercise, most unsuspecting interns will indicate they are unable to say anything about the patient's state. However, the supervisor will ask specific questions, such as:

- Can you describe the patient's mental status?
- Can you describe the patient's general behavior in terms of appropriateness?
- In what kind of general medical state did you find the patient?
- What assumptions can you make about the patient's orientation?
- What kinds of prostheses, medical devices, and assistive devices did you observe in the proximity of the patient?
- Can you describe the patient's grooming and hygiene?
- Did you observe any abnormal movements, facial expressions, or postures?

The interns will then begin to recognize that a number of observations indeed had been made, and only the significance of the observations had been overlooked. This exercise also can be used by experienced examiners to force themselves to remain attentive to clinical clues. The list of significant observable factors should continue to expand with quality experience.

Table 5–3 lists the clinical observations that should be made about each patient. Clinicians should not feel bound by the examples given below each observational heading in the table. These are only guidelines that can be used to describe the patient's condition.

The patient's level of consciousness may be described as alert, awake, drowsy, obtunded, inattentive, comatose, or in any number of other descriptive terms. Observations of posture may be generally noted as lying in gurney (rolling stretcher) or in a wheelchair. More specific observations could include descriptions like slumped in the wheelchair, arm dangling, or completely neglecting one side. A patient's orientation to the environment may be presumed to be normal or impaired based upon observations. Patients who have obvious indications of confusion are presumed to be disoriented, while others are presumed to be completely oriented based upon their interaction, communication, and general behavior. A patient's abnormal posture, disheveled dress, neglect of personal hygiene, agitated behavior, or the presence of body restraints may lead to a judgment of impaired orientation. Whenever there is doubt about a patient's orientation and the individual is capable of responding to questions, each element of orientation should be questioned spe-

Table 5–3 Suggested Outline for Clinical Observations

Level of consciousness		General behavior		Orientation
_____	alert	_____	cooperative	_____ place
_____	drowsy	_____	uncooperative	_____ city
_____	lethargic	_____	agitated	_____ day
_____	stuporous	_____	depressed	_____ month
_____	semicomatose	_____	anxious	_____ year
_____	coma	_____	labile	_____ circumstance

Posture		Prosthetics		Medical devices
_____	bed	_____	glasses	_____ catheters
_____	gurney	_____	hearing aid	_____ restraints
_____	wheelchair	_____	limb	_____ tracheostomy tube
_____	ambulatory assist	_____	denture	_____ feeding tube
_____	ambulatory	_____	other	_____ intravenous apparatus

cifically. These include the traditional person, place, and time questions, plus circumstance. The latter sphere of orientation may be assessed by asking the patient to explain why he or she is in the hospital.

There are clinical observations beyond those listed in Table 5–3. For example, the patient's general medical condition usually is noted. This may range from "no apparent distress" (NAD) to evidence of pain, discomfort, agitation, or other signs of distress. The more experienced the examiner, the more significance these clinical observations have. Some clinicians assess various aspects of the patient's condition by touching the skin, looking for signs of dehydration, diaphoresis (excessive sweating), chills, or fever. A clinician may check the pulse for rate and regularity and count the respirations in order to screen the acute medical state of the patient. This can be particularly important for those working in acute medical settings, where they may be asked to evaluate and treat patients at high risk for medical complications or patients who are medically unstable at the time of referral. Because patients' conditions can change so rapidly in the acute circumstance, speech/language pathologists and other health professionals cannot rely on the medical chart or a verbal report for current data.

When the clinician is comfortable with the clinical observations made during each patient contact, a determination about how to proceed with an interview and examination can be made. In some cases a clinician may decide that an interview will not be possible or that it will not yield reliable information. Therefore, the clinician proceeds with an examination without attempting to obtain a first-person history or other verbal information. In another instance the clinician may determine, based upon clinical observations, that the patient is too ill to undergo further interviewing and examination. It should be noted, however, that gathering information relative to communication usually is possible and helpful even with very ill patients. Whatever the observations, the clinician who attends to all significant and applicable pieces of data will attain a higher degree of accuracy in clinical judgment.

INTERVIEWING PRINCIPLES

The interview is an essential step in obtaining diagnostic information. Often it is this first contact with the patient that establishes a lasting clinical relationship. A medical speech/language pathologist should recognize the factors that influence the development of patient rapport. In order to establish an effective style for conducting interviews, the clinician should conduct a self-assessment. This will help to recognize and avoid many of the behaviors that interfere with rapport and hinder the acquisition of important facts. Even in difficult situations, a skillful clinician can proceed with an assured manner.

Rapport

Just as the clinician makes initial clinical observations and develops certain hypotheses about the patient, so does each patient who is alert and cognizant develop certain impressions about the clinician. This is based upon both conscious perceptions and unconscious attitudes. Just as the clinician brings his or her own biases and preconceptions to each patient contact, so does the patient view the clinician. The patient's perception of a clinician will be influenced by certain factors that are beyond the clinician's control. For example, a patient may be angry because a nurse failed to respond to a request just prior to the clinician's visit. The patient may be agitated by innumerable examinations by medical students, residents, and staff attendings prior to the speech/language pathologist's visit. The patient may be upset or depressed by a diagnosis just received or be apprehensive or frightened by an impending examination. Some older patients may have preconceived notions that young clinicians have little to offer their generation. Conversely, other patients may view older clinicians as jaded and uncaring. A male patient may be embarrassed or otherwise reluctant to submit to an examination by a female clinician, whereas a female patient may prefer examination by a female clinician. Whatever the biases and the preconceived attitudes may be, the task is to present oneself as a professional who has a job to perform and who is concerned about that individual patient and the particular condition.

As a general rule, patients should be addressed by surname, such as Mr., Mrs., or Ms. Clinicians should introduce themselves using titles such as Dr., Mr., Miss, Ms., or Mrs. It should be noted, however, that there are exceptions to this policy. At times patients may insist on being greeted by their first names or nicknames. Under certain circumstances a clinician may feel that the use of a title is too formal for the surroundings, the local policy, the patient's condition, or the circumstances of the interview. It is best to begin the interview process with an explanation of the professional discipline represented and the reason for the clinical visit.

The interviewer should avoid being too cold or too remote. The patient should be approached in an unhurried, sympathetic, and interested manner. Eye contact should be maintained. The clinician should write few notes but listen actively to the patient's message and behavior. The tone of the interviewer's voice is important. Condescending attitudes, facetiousness, exaggeration, allusion, and ambiguities of language should be avoided. The goal during the interview is to obtain information by asking questions that are clearly worded and that accurately communicate the intent of the interview. The vocabulary should be appropriate to the patient's level of education and experience. The interviewer should be alert to any behaviors or questions that suggest the patient has misunderstood a question or misinterpreted a message.

Throughout the interview care must be taken to avoid reactions that betray distrust, disapproval, embarrassment, impatience, boredom, or even disgust. There are times when patients communicate information, attitudes, or prejudices that may elicit these emotions. It is not the emotion that should be repressed, but rather the overt reaction that communicates the clinician's emotion to the patient. To some extent the speech/language pathologist is insulated because the purpose of the interview is to obtain data that is pertinent to the patient's communication or swallow disorder. It is important to keep in mind that speech/language pathologists do not have the same license and privilege as physicians to delve into aspects of personal history that are not related to speech, language, intellectual, or swallowing problems. However, in the course of an interview patients may offer personal information, especially if they have communication difficulties and recognize that it is easier to communicate with a communication specialist.

In establishing rapport, as in almost every aspect of professional practice, a clinician's acumen is often measured by his or her clinical judgment. To some extent this cannot be taught, but it can be enhanced. Perhaps the statement "patient care requires caring for the patient" best summarizes an effective approach to establishing rapport.

Interview Style

There is an art to eliciting information from patients. For example, a clinician should ask one question at a time and give patients adequate time to respond in their own words without interjecting biases. The questions should be directed to the patient to increase the specificity of the focus. This allows the clinician to pinpoint the subjective impressions of the patient. At times it is helpful to offer multiple choices. For example, in interviewing a patient who has complaints of swallowing difficulty it is advisable to ask "Do you have the most trouble with solids, liquids, or soft foods?" Questions also should be asked in such a way that the patient can give a quantitative estimation to a particular problem. For example, asking the patient "How many times do you choke while drinking a glass of water?" will provide more information than "Do you choke while drinking water?"

By listening actively the interviewer will gain experience in helping and guiding patients without diverting them from delivering accurate accounts. The clinician must learn to avoid answering for patients or leading them into answering in unintended ways. In the following example a clinician elicits responses from a patient that obscure the patient's true symptoms:

Clinician:	Do you have more trouble swallowing liquids or solids?
Patient:	About the same.
Clinician:	Do you mean you choke as much on solids as you do on liquids?
Patient:	Well, I guess liquids tend to go down the wrong way more often.
Clinician:	So you choke mostly when drinking liquids?
Patient:	Yes, I guess so.

In another example, a clinician can inadvertently put words into the patient's mind that will lead the patient to an unintended description:

Clinician:	How does your throat feel when you're talking?
Patient:	Tight.
Clinician:	Like you have a lump in your throat?
Patient:	Well, yes, I guess you might say that.
Clinician:	So, how long have you had this lump in your throat?

The data received from patients will be defined not only by their words but also by their emotional reactions. During the course of an interview the clinician should observe the patient closely for feelings imparted by facial expression, changes in posture, tone of voice, and general emotional behavior. Perhaps one of the most dramatic examples of this was seen while interviewing a voice patient who had just been informed about his normal otolaryngological examination:

Clinician:	What did the doctor tell you about the examination?
Patient:	He said I did not have a tumor. But he didn't say anything about cancer and that's what I think I have down there.
Clinician:	What the doctor was telling you is that you have no evidence of a tumor or cancer. In this case they are the same thing.
Patient:	You mean there is no sign of cancer?
Clinician:	That's right.
Patient:	I see.

The patient's final words were quite neutral. However, the emotional reactions included a dramatic reduction in behaviors associated with anxiety, a complete change in facial expression, and, perhaps not unsurprisingly, a dramatic improvement in vocal quality. These reactions told more than any words he could have chosen.

It should be expected during the course of interviews that patients will ask questions regarding their medical condition. Speech/language pathologists should become accustomed to the fact that patients will seek to use them as interpreters of information given by other health professionals. This role is not one that should be denied or even de-emphasized. However, limitations of knowledge should be recognized when responding to patients' questions. Care must be taken to avoid responses that may conflict with the information given to patients by their primary physicians.

It is tempting with certain patients to become more personal, perhaps less formal, in the interviews. Clinicians should guard against imparting too much information about themselves. For example, it is easy to empathize verbally with patients' complaints by mentioning similar sensations that have been personally experienced. These temptations should be avoided. Patients may see this behavior as making light of their symptoms and complaints. This is vividly illustrated in the following example of a patient who eventually was diagnosed as having a serious neurologic disease:

Patient:	When I'm trying to speak, I can't seem to make my tongue move fast enough and the words catch in my throat.
Clinician:	You know, that happens to me when I get tired or I'm nervous!
Patient:	Well, I'm not concerned with your fatigue and nervousness. My difficulty is frightening, and it's interfering with my ability to earn a living.

As a general rule clinicians also should avoid discussing their own health, even when patients invite such discussions. As an example, on resident teaching rounds, a bedridden patient was greeted by the attending neurologist and asked how he was feeling. The patient responded, "I'm just fine, but I've been worried all night about poor Dr. Jones over there. Were you aware, Doctor, that he's been working the last three days with what he described to me as an unexplained, periodic pain in his chest and a persistent headache? He tells me he had to work late last night and hasn't been home before 8 p.m. in a week. I think you need to give him some time off!" Meanwhile, the attending glared at "poor Dr. Jones" standing across the bed looking completely abashed.

Difficult Patients

Difficult patients may be encountered in all manner and form. Some may be overly loquacious, some reticent. Some patients are willfully uncooperative, while others do not have the ability to cooperate. The approach that is taken for each is based upon that individual's manner and behavior. It requires the clinician to make a rapid assessment of the situation and the reasons for the patient's behavior.

When an overly talkative patient is asked questions, the patient may elaborate to such a degree that the answers to specific questions are obscured. If the clinician senses that the patient simply is unable to organize thoughts in a concise manner, the questions can be worded in such a way that multiple choice answers or yes/no responses will suffice. The clinician must remain focused on the speech, language, or other specific problem that is being explored. The speech/language pathologist must determine the most important information to extract from the patient and then focus on the essentials. Many times the clinician must lower his or her goals and accept a less comprehensive history from the patient. When the patient persists in a long discourse, the clinician must courteously interrupt and redirect the questioning. Sometimes verbally summarizing what the patient has just said will allow the clinician to change the topic and move ahead in the interview. In these cases it is imperative that the clinician hide any impatience.

Angry patients present significant problems for speech/language pathologists. Once again, clinicians must assess patients' behavior in order to determine whether or not their anger is specifically directed at them, all hospital personnel, a certain individual, or any available human target. Clinicians also must simultaneously assess these situations for potential danger. Hospital security should be alerted immediately to irrational patients, such as an obstreperous, inebriated individual. Small rooms should be avoided when facing angry patients. Discussions should take place in open spaces, if possible. The clinician should avoid challenging a patient and try to maintain a posture that is relaxed and nonthreatening. Listening carefully and avoiding arguments may help the patient to calm down. In these situations there is no substitute for composure and rational judgment on the part of the clinician.

Another problem frequently encountered is the patient who cries easily or frequently. Again, an assessment must be made as to the reason for the crying, whether it is sadness, significant depression, pain, joy, or emotional lability. This emotional response should be recognized as a legitimate modality for a patient to communicate feelings where words may be unsatisfactory. When crying is assessed to be emotional lability, distractions or redirecting the patient's attention to a new topic may alleviate the problem temporarily. Crying elicited for other reasons may alert the clinician to the need for psychiatric evaluation of the patient. Because the speech/language pathologist inevitably is dealing in an area where disability and adjustment are paramount issues, emotional responses should be expected and responded to in an appropriate therapeutic manner.

SUMMARY

Developing the skills necessary to complete the first steps in the diagnostic process (forming hypotheses and the patient interview) is essential for any clinician who desires to contribute significantly to a medical team. The sophistication with which a speech/language pathologist interprets the historical data included on a consultation; attends to clinical observations, both behavioral and medical; and integrates all information in order to formulate diagnostic hypotheses will grow with quality experience. On one hand, the speech/language pathologist must remain focused on communication and related functions that are within the realm of expertise. On the other, he or she must be cognizant of the overall contribution that speech/language pathology can make to the medical team and the management of patients' health. The speech/language pathologist should not ignore signs and symptoms that, while not primarily associated with speech, language or swallowing problems, are related to disease processes or pathologies that may be the etiological bases for the disorders.

What has been described as a conscious, perhaps overly mechanical, diagnostic process eventually should become automatic and unconscious. Experience allows the clinician to expand knowledge, to recognize the significance of subtle clinical features, and to carry out and adjust interviews in a fluent manner. Hypotheses should become guideposts to direct the clinician through the maze of diagnostic possibilities. Reaching this point, however, requires disciplined and organized thinking, conscientious effort, and genuine concern for patients' needs.

NOTES

1. Donald O. Castell and Martin W. Donner, "Evaluation of Dysphagia: A Careful History Is Crucial," *Dysphagia* 2, no. 2 (1987): 65–71.

2. Jo Anne Robbins, Jerilyn A. Logemann, and Howard S. Kirshner, "Swallowing and Speech Production in Parkinson's Disease," *Annals of Neurology* 19, no. 3 (1986): 283–87.

3. Alvin M. Lieberman et al., "Dysphagia in Parkinson's Disease," *American Journal of Gastroenterology* 74, no. 2 (1980):157–60.

Chapter 6

The Physical Examination

INTRODUCTION

DeGowin states that patient examination is entirely dependent on the knowledge of the observer.[1] This is epitomized by the maxims: *"Was man weis, man seicht"* (Goethe), that translates to "What one knows, one sees"; and "We see what's behind the eyes" (Wintrobe). Regardless of the examination outline followed in performing a physical inspection of a patient with communication impairment, there is no substitute for the knowledge gained by experience. The tendency is to see only those findings that have personal clinical significance, and it is only with experience that the list of significant findings expands.

An examination outline that consists of components borrowed from several different medical disciplines is presented in Table 6–i. A number of the tools employed may not be taught in any traditional speech/language pathology educational program. However, these techniques are recommended particularly for the beginning clinician as a means of expanding awareness of each patient's physiologic system.

The components that make up the examination should be considered as questions that the clinician will ask regarding the patient's condition. If the clinician feels confident that he or she knows enough about the patient's condition relative to each of these components, whether by clinical observations or from the history, then that aspect of the examination can be omitted. By conscientiously applying each of these components, the examiner not only will learn to recognize subtleties of pathology, but also will have an organized approach to understanding communication disorders and related dysfunctions. The speech/language pathologist also will have a better appreciation for the medical record and will understand the significance of many of the notations contained in the record of a physical examination.

EXAMINATION PRINCIPLES

Two contrasting examples of how physical examination procedures may be modified are provided. Case 1 is a patient who arrives for an evaluation of an isolated voice disorder that has been described by an otolaryngologist as "recurrent vocal nodules." In this case one would not expect a detailed examination of the neurological system to be particularly useful. Assuming the patient was observed to ambulate into the clinic without disturbance, had no other unusual clinical signs, and spoke in a clearly articulated, well-organized manner, the examination would focus on the vocal mechanism and related structures (e.g., respiratory mechanism and speech production musculature). Case 2, however, presents similarly for a voice disorder that has been described by the otolaryngologist as a hoarse voice with a normal laryngeal examination. In this case, the speech/language pathologist observes that the patient ambulates abnormally and his speech is characterized by hypernasality in addition to the vocal hoarseness. The clinician now must determine whether or not this is an isolated voice disorder or a problem in which voice is just one of the manifestations of another, more diffuse process. The examination should include a neuromotor and sensory screening, as well as a thorough speech and voice assessment.

The speech/language pathologist should not be surprised to find referrals, such as Case 2, who frequently have a form of dysarthria that includes vocal dysfunction rather than the previously diagnosed isolated voice impairment. Sometimes it is the subtle findings on the neurologic part of the examination that lead to the correct assessment and then to the appropriate referral. The examination described in the following pages provides the speech/language pathologist with the tools necessary to confirm clinical impressions, make accurate diagnoses, and strengthen the case for making appropriate referrals.

Even the beginning clinician should attempt to give the patient the impression that the examination is being conducted by a clinician who is confident in the procedures and organized in the approach. It is important to convey a calm manner and to avoid communication of alarm or disgust when confronted with unexpected findings. The clinician should give a brief explanation of what is being examined and why. For example, when inspecting a patient's arms or hands, the clinician might remark, "In order to assess the function of your speech muscles I want to see how the other muscles in your body are working since they may behave in the same way." Experience has confirmed that a thorough examination communicates to the patient an attitude of competency on the part of the examining clinician. If treatment is indicated, this will assist the clinician in establishing needed rapport. It is not unusual to find a patient more willing to add significant facts to the case history when it is realized that the speech/language pathologist is interested in the patient as a whole person, rather than the examiner focusing on one fragmented symptom.

It is important to emphasize that the role of speech/language pathologist should be communicated to the patient. The speech/language pathologist should clearly state that he or she is not a physician. The examination, even though it includes components that are not directly linked to the speech mechanism, is nevertheless focused toward those areas that are encompassed by appropriate education and training expertise. Much of the clinical data and most of the clinical observations recorded do not need to be communicated through the medical record. Rather they are supporting bits of data that should assist the speech/language pathologist in making an assessment and diagnosis. For example, it serves no useful purpose for the speech/language pathologist to grade reflexes and report these findings in the progress notes or reports when these have no bearing on the patient's communication disorder. Conversely, there are times when reflexes or the condition of muscles in the extremities may assist the speech/language pathologist in developing a clinical picture that, when taken in its entirety, helps to support or confirm a specific speech or language assessment. The line between overstepping one's clinical and professional bounds and the utilization of all legitimate clinical data in making an assessment is not definitively established. In the final analysis, it is only good clinical judgment that will determine the appropriateness of a clinical action in any given circumstance. Examples of this approach are given in Chapter 8.

Table 6–1 outlines the areas that should be explored on a physical inventory. Whether or not each area is examined, the clinician should have some knowledge about the condition of these areas even if they are presumed to be normal.

MOTOR FUNCTION EXAMINATION

The examination begins with an assessment of motor function. The observations may not be made in the order of presentation; the sequence can be adjusted to fit the circumstances.

Handedness

Dexterity of the patient and the patient's preferred hand use should be observed. In the case of hemiparesis, asking the patient or making observations to gain knowledge about premorbid hand preference is necessary.

Gait

If the patient is ambulatory the gait should be observed closely. Disorders of gait are not always due to neurological disorders but may be related to mechanical factors, such as the ankylosis of a joint in the lower extremity, a shortened limb or tendon, or a painful lesion on the foot. Neurological gaits include those with the appearance of a broad base, as in cerebellar disease; a shuffling gait with stooped posture, sometimes accelerating, found in parkinsonism; a flopping sound suggesting foot drop, or the scraping sound of the hemiplegic patient; and the high-stepping, stamping gait of the tabetic (syphilitic) patient. Just as the speech/language pathologist differentiates among the various forms of dysarthria, so the student of gait disturbances can make a differential diagnosis based on the characteristics of the patient's ambulation. In many cases, the pathological symptoms

Table 6–1 Speech Pathology Inventory of Physical Findings and Observations

Motor Functions	*Sensory Modalities*
Handedness	Superficial tactile
Gait	Motion and position
Musculature (trunk and limbs)	Stereognosis
• Adventitious movements	Graphesthesia
• Muscle strength	Extinction phenomenon
• Tone	Eyes and vision
• Coordination	• Complaints
— Diadochokinetics	• Gaze
— Finger-to-nose	• Pupils
— Heel-to-shin	• Extraocular movements
• Reflexes	• Visual fields
— Deep tendon	• Extinction
— Pathologic	• Optokinetic nystagmus
	Ears and hearing
	• Inspection
	• Hearing tests

Head and Neck	*Oral and Laryngeal Motor Functions*
Facial muscles	Imitative movements
• Lips	• Lips
• Platysma	• Tongue
• Frontalis	Respiration
Muscles of mastication	• Vital capacity
• Masseter/temporalis	Voice
• Pterygoids	• Quality
Pathologic reflexes	• Prolongation
• Snout/rooting	• Volitional control
• Jaw jerk	Cough
• Glabellar	• Reflex
Intraoral examination	• Volitional
• Mucosa	Swallow
• Teeth and gums	• Mastication
• Velum	• Oral stage
— At rest	• Laryngeal elevation
— Phonation	• Coughing
• Oropharynx	• Airway congestion
• Tongue	• Laryngeal inspection
— At rest	Imitative speech
— Strength	• Pa-pa-pa
— Speed of movement	• Ta-ta-ta
• Laryngeal inspection	• Ka-ka-ka
— Valleculae	• E-e-e
— Epiglottis	• Pa-ta-ka
— Aryepiglottic folds	• Words
— Pyriform sinuses	• Sentences
— False folds	Speech characteristics
— True vocal folds	
• At rest	
• Inspiration/expiration	
• Phonation	

associated with disorders of ambulation also can be found in the motor production of speech.

In a spastic gait, for example, there usually is an adducted, flexed posture in the arm with the fist clenched. As illustrated in Figure 6–1, the pelvis usually is tilted to the stronger side in an attempt to clear the toe from the ground on the paretic side. The weak limb is then swung around with the toe dragging on the floor.

At least two types of ataxic gait have been described.[2] In sensory ataxia, as sometimes seen in multiple sclerosis, patients watch the ground and their feet as they try to walk. This is done in an attempt to provide visual information that serves to compensate for impaired sensory feedback from muscles and joints. Balance is maintained by widening the base. Patients tend to throw their feet forward with toes and heels slapping the ground. In cerebellar ataxia, the face may be tilted upward to the opposite side. The patient has a reeling gait with irregular swaying movements of the extremities. The ataxic patient looks like, and is often confused with, someone who is drunk. The patient will tend to veer to one side, usually stumbling to the affected side. This gait can be made obvious by having the patient

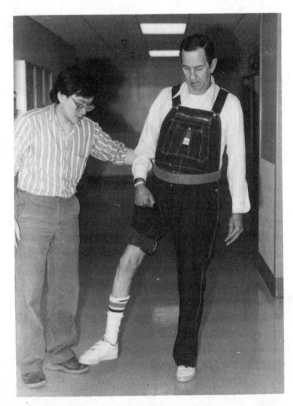

Figure 6–1 Spastic gait. Hemiparesis and increased extensor tone of the lower extremity cause the patient to flex at the hip and knees and to dorsiflex the ankle on the impaired side. The pelvis is tilted to clear the toes. The affected arm is held close to the body and in a flexed position.

attempt to walk heel-to-toe. Such irregular movements also may affect the coordination of the processes of respiration and phonation.

Muscle Inspection

Conditions that affect the movement, coordination, strength, and tone of skeletal muscles also can interfere with speech and swallowing by causing similar dysfunction in the muscles responsible for these processes. Because the skeletal muscles are easier to see and palpate, observation and examination of these muscles allows the examiner to make certain inferences regarding the characteristics of the muscles used in speech production and swallowing.

On general inspection of the muscles, particularly in the extremities, the examiner should note symmetry, atrophy, hypertrophy, and adventitious movements. Much of the neurologic examination and muscle inspection used to detect pathology compares symmetry of movement, size, strength, and reflexes. Observations should be made to detect any asymmetry with regard to muscle size. In the case of atrophy one muscle or a group of muscles may be wasted and thus diminished in size. In hypertrophy a particular muscle or muscle group may be enlarged, often because of adaptation or compensation. Asymmetries in the extremities may be more obvious than in the speech musculature and may assist in providing important clues in explaining the patient's communication deficits.

Adventitious Movements

Adventitious movements may be particularly revealing with regard to localization of disease and type of pathology. Scheinberg described adventitious movements, including fasciculations, spasms, myoclonus, tremors, chorea, athetosis and other tonic movements, spasmodic torticollis, hemiballismus, and habit spasms.[3] The observation of any of these adventitious movements should be considered significant and noted for further consideration, because some of them impact negatively on speech production.

Fasciculations. Small local contractions of muscles that are visible through the skin are called fasciculations. They represent a spontaneous discharge of muscle fibers innervated from a single motor unit. Fasciculations may give the appearance of fine crawling twitches under the skin or mucous membranes. In true pathologic conditions, fasciculations suggest lower motor neuron disease. When they occur without atrophy or muscle weakness they may be considered to be benign myokymia (muscle quivering).[4]

Spasms. Spasms are signs of upper motor neuron disease and are characterized by episodic extensor rigidity. They are found most commonly in patients with progressive spinal cord disease.

Myoclonus. Myoclonus is the jerking of a limb or muscle group, usually characterized by rapid, synchronous up-and-down movements. Myoclonus can be seen in a number of lesions and with a number of anatomic locations. It is not unusual to find this condition in cases of severe metabolic encephalopathy and in other conditions that result in spasticity.

Tremors. A great deal of attention has been paid to tremors and their differentiation. Resting tremors are seen characteristically in parkinsonism and are described as fine, rhythmic, pill-rolling movements of the fingers. In familial or hereditary essential tremor, the patient shows no signs of the rigidity or akinesia associated with parkinsonism, and the tremors are aggravated during voluntary movements. The cerebellar or intention tremor is more a form of dysmetria brought about by the inability to coordinate agonist and antagonist muscle groups so that the extremities overcorrect directional movements. Other tremors also are evident in disorders of the endocrine system and in drug toxicity.

Chorea. A quick, inappropriate movement of the extremities, head, neck, or trunk is characteristic of chorea. In many cases these sudden movements are constant; initially they may appear as movement peculiarities or fidgety behavior. Two of the most common types of choreatic movements are those seen in Sydenham's chorea, a childhood disorder, and Huntington's disease, a disorder of adults. Both of these appear to be linked genetically. Lesions usually are found in the putamen and caudate nuclei of the basal ganglia.

Dystonia. Athetosis and other tonic movements involve abnormal posturing and writhing in various body parts. This class of adventitious movement includes the various forms of dystonia, some of which eventually can produce severe deformities. Dystonic movements are not uncommon following drug intoxication, particularly with phenothiazines like Thorazine (chlorpromazine) that are used to treat many psychiatric disorders. When dystonic movements are isolated in the mouth or tongue they are referred to as orofacial or buccolingual dyskinesia. The term "tardive dyskinesia" is applied to movement disorders that are late occurring, sometimes appearing years after taking the drug.

Spasmodic torticollis. A dystonia in which the patient's head and neck are twisted to one side is referred to as spasmodic torticollis. The anatomic basis for this condition is not known.

Hemiballismus. Hemiballismus is a rare disorder caused by a lesion in the subthalamic nucleus. It results in violent spontaneous throwing movements of the extremities of one side.

Tics. Habit spasms, sometimes called tics, generally are not associated with any organic lesion. They are usually thought of as compulsive movements of the face that may involve the eyes, frontalis muscles, or mouth.

Muscle Strength

The flexion and extension movements of the major joints are evaluated initially without resistance and then with the examiner offering resistance. The examination compares corresponding muscles on each side of the body. When muscle weakness is evident, it may suggest a disturbance in the pyramidal pathway that courses from the cerebrum, through the brainstem and spinal cord (see Figure 6–2); in its peripheral nerve extensions; at the neuromuscular junction; or in the muscle itself. In cases where there is obvious hemiplegia or hemiparesis there may be little reason to examine for the strength of the limbs. However, the speech/language pathologist should be aware of the methods used to evaluate more subtle weakness. One method is pronator drift, illustrated in Figure 6–3, in which the patient, with the eyes closed, attempts to hold his or her arms out with the fingers and thumbs extended and the palms up. In the case of mild weakness there will be a downward drift and pronation of the weak extremity. Weakness of a lower extremity usually will show itself in a gait disturbance. Muscle strength, when reported in the medi-

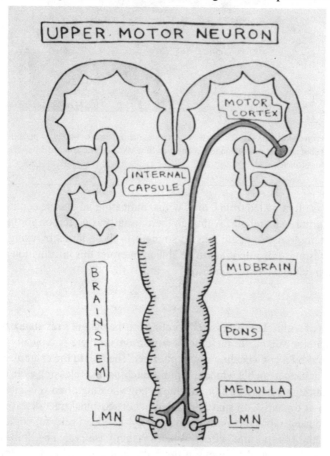

Figure 6–2 Corticospinal tracts originate in the motor cortex and course through the internal capsule and into the brainstem on their way to the spinal cord. They are referred to as pyramidal tracts, because they pass through the medullary pyramids where 80 to 90 percent of them cross to the opposite side in the pyramidal decussation. *Source:* Reprinted with permission of George Zito, M.D.

Figure 6–3 Pronator drift, a test for subtle weakness in the upper extremities, is performed with the patient's eyes shut and the arms extended, palms up. In weakness, one arm drifts down and the hand turns inward, or pronates.

cal record, is often scaled from 0 to 5, with 0 indicating no muscle contraction and 5 indicating normal strength. Although there usually is no reason for the speech/language pathologist to grade muscle strength in these terms by using selective resistance testing, it is important to be able to interpret this information and relate it to the individual patient's condition.

Tone

The tone of a muscle is assessed by feeling for the patient's resistance to rapidly repeated passive stretch. In the case of parkinsonism there is typically a rigidity characterized by a cogwheeling of the muscles. The feel to the examiner is somewhat analogous to a ratchet wrench, rapidly catching and releasing as an extremity is moved through a range of motion. Subtle cogwheeling often is elicited by passive stretch at the wrist. In spasticity, seen in corticospinal tract disease, there is resistance during rapid movement followed by a sudden release, sometimes referred to as the "clasp-knife" effect. When spasticity is severe and limbs have not been routinely exercised by moving them through a complete range of motion (ROM), contractures such as those illustrated in Figure 6–4 can develop. Hypotonia may be found in cerebellar disease and flaccidity. It can occur in peripheral nerve damage, intranuclear damage, or in some instances of hemispheric lesions.

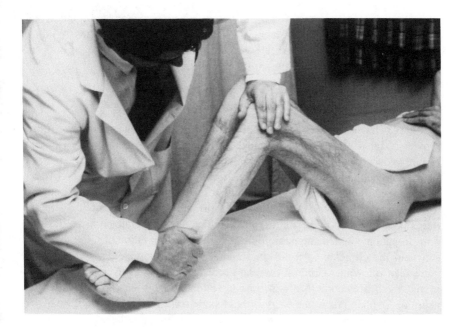

Figure 6–4 Contracture. Contractures fix the limbs into a flexed position with high resistance to passive stretch. Untreated contractures may interfere with hygiene and other nursing care, limit mobility, and cause pain.

Hypotonia is characterized by diminished tone and flail muscles. In some cases patients with diffuse brain disease or bilateral frontal lobe lesions exhibit increased resistance that corresponds to the increasing efforts of the examiner to flex or extend the extremity. This is referred to as *gegenhalten* or paratonia.

Coordination

The coordination, accuracy, and precision of movements are primarily cerebellar functions. When weakness has been detected in an extremity it is extremely difficult to assess coordination accurately. If cerebellar disease is suspected, however, the two sides of the body can be compared for rapidity, smoothness, and rhythmic cadence of movement. Rapid alternating movements (RAM), or diadochokinesis, can be assessed through several maneuvers. Two tests commonly used are rapid finger tapping, whereby a patient alternates touching the forefinger to the thumb; and hand slapping, in which the patient alternately slaps the palm and dorsum of one hand against the thigh. Another useful test to assess upper extremity coordination is the finger-to-nose task. In this test the patient alternately reaches out to touch the examiner's finger held at arm's length and returns to touch the tip of his or her own nose. This should be performed repeatedly and the patient observed for differences in posturing, accuracy of movement, and smoothness. Abnormalities include overshooting the target with overcorrection and tremor. Heel-to-shin testing can bring out dyscoordination in the lower extremities. With the patient in a supine or sitting position the heel of one foot is brought to the opposite knee and slowly moved along the shin toward the foot. The two sides are compared for smoothness and accuracy.

Reflexes

Reflex behavior is an important tool for the speech/language pathologist. It can provide insights into the condition of the patient's nervous system and provide confirmative data to support a final assessment. In some cases the reflex behavior assists the speech/language pathologist in forming a differential diagnosis between bulbar (flaccid) dysarthria and pseudobulbar (spastic) dysarthria. In other cases it may provide additional data to help in the formation of a prognosis, because the reflex behavior may suggest either localized or more generalized brain dysfunction. In patients with acute neurologic conditions, observation of reflex behavior can help the clinician to follow the course of the disorder. For example, immediately following a cerebral vascular lesion an examining physician may record in the medical record that a patient's tendon reflexes are absent. After the neurologic shock phase has passed, these same reflexes may return or be hyperactive. The speech/language pathologist familiar with reflex behavior can assess the status of the patient during the stages of neurologic recovery.[5] In another case, a finding of abnormal reflexes may confirm or support a diagnosis of organic neurologic language dysfunction and help to differentiate patients with specific neurologic lesions from those with psychiatric disorders.

A number of classification systems have been used to describe reflexes, for example, muscle stretch (deep tendon), superficial, autonomic, and pathologic. Muscle stretch and pathologic reflexes are discussed in this chapter.

Muscle stretch reflexes. The muscle stretch or deep tendon reflex is a simple segmental reflex in which the afferent impulse is conducted to the spinal cord or brainstem by sensory fibers of the peripheral nervous system. After passing across one or more synapses within the central nervous system, these impulses connect with the primary motor cells. When activated, motor impulses emerge from the same segments as those in which the afferent impulses entered. This final common pathway begins at the inferior horn cells within the spinal cord and exits as peripheral nerves to reach the reacting muscles.

In the absence of any lesion affecting the components of this reflex arc, the final muscle stretch reflex represents a balance between the inhibitory and excitatory impulses that influence the lower motor neurons. Because the pyramidal tracts have an inhibitory effect on reflexes, a lesion in these long tracts creates a loss of this suppressor influence that results in hyperreflexia. Conversely, impairment of the excitatory centers can result in diminished activity, or hyporeflexia. Muscle stretch reflexes are elicited by tapping briskly on a tendon or bony prominence and feeling for the sudden stretch of corresponding muscles. The examiner will grade a reflex from 0 to 4 plus on a very subjective scale. Pathology is not suggested in the final grading of a single reflex (as a 4+ is better or worse than a 2+), but rather in comparing corresponding reflexes from each side of the body. For example, the patient with classic spastic hemiparesis will show hyperreflexia on the impaired side when compared to reflexes on the unimpaired side of the body. It should be emphasized that muscle stretch behavior provides the speech/language pathologist with confirmatory data that must be correlated with other observations and medical history before they can be used to aid in the assessment of the patient. In a given instance this final bit of supportive data may give the speech/language pathologist confidence in a diagnosis or prognosis.

Pathologic reflexes. Reflexes that cannot be elicited in normal individuals but show up in patients with neurological disease are referred to as pathologic reflexes. These reflexes tend to be more complex than the simple segmental reflexes. However, when present, they represent a disturbance in the balance of impulses reaching the effector organs. One of the most commonly reported pathologic reflexes is the Babinski reflex. It is seen in the pathologic condition as an extension of the great toe and fanning of the other toes in response to the upward stroking along the lateral margin of the foot using a semisharp object such as a key. This pathologic response is seen in conditions that result from pyramidal tract disease. It often is found on the side opposite a cerebral vascular lesion, but it may be observed bilaterally during the acute stages until cerebral edema resolves.

Several other pathologic reflexes have been described as "cortical release signs," because they usually appear in patients with bilateral hemispheric disease. One of these reflexes, the *snout,* shown in Figure 6–5, is elicited by using a reflex hammer to gently tap over the patient's upper lip; a puckering movement represents a pathologic response. The sucking or *rooting* reflex may be elicited by lightly brushing the corners of the patient's mouth with a tongue blade and watching for a sucking or pulling movement of the lips in the direction of the stimulus. A positive *jaw jerk* can be seen in patients with corticobulbar disease. It is elicited by tapping with a reflex hammer on the examiner's finger which is placed against the patient's chin in an effort to stretch the masseter muscles. When pathologic, the downward stretch elicits a vigorous jaw-closing response. The assessment of the jaw jerk is very subjective, and therefore, more difficult to interpret. The *glabellar* reflex is seen as an uninhibited rhythmical blinking of the eyes in response to tapping above the bridge of the nose. The name is derived from the smooth area on the frontal bone between the eyebrows, the glabella. The presence of this uninhibited eye blink response is associated with parkinsonism or other basal ganglia disease.[6] The *grasp* reflex is an exaggeration of a normal palmar reflex. It is said to be pathologic when the examiner places two or more fingers on the patient's palm or strokes the palm and observes an involuntary grasp by the patient. The pathologic grasp reflex also is evident when a patient grasps an object but is unable to release the hold. The grasp reflex usually is found in patients with frontal lobe disturbance.

Because many of these pathologic reflexes indicate bilateral involvement, they can be very important tools in making a prognosis when used appropriately and with good judgment. It must be recognized that these reflex behaviors are inte-

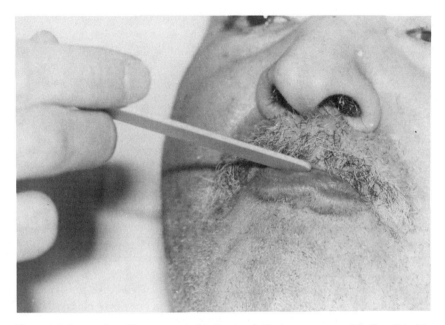

Figure 6–5 Snout reflex. The snout or suck reflex is a puckering movement of the lips elicited by tapping above the upper lip or touching the lips. It is a pathologic reflex usually associated with bilateral cortical disease.

---

grated with other clinical observations and all available examination data in order to make a final assessment. A given pathologic reflex may not be significant unless the patient exhibits other related signs of pathology.

SENSORY FUNCTION EXAMINATION

Testing sensory function integrity depends upon the patient's perception and interpretation of stimuli received. Under the best of circumstances sensory tests are difficult to evaluate and are dependent upon the cooperation, comprehension, and, to some extent, the patient's preconceived notions concerning sensory stimuli. Most tests of the sensory system require the patient to make judgments of the presence or absence of a specific stimulus and then to compare it with the same stimulus on the opposite side of the body. Most are tested with the patient's eyes closed. The primary forms of sensation include superficial tactile, superficial pain, sensitivity to temperature, vibration sense, deep pressure pain, and motion/position sense. In addition there are a number of forms of sensation that require cortical discrimination and interpretation. These sensations, usually evaluated by a neurologist, include two-point discrimination, stimulus localization, texture discrimination, stereognostic function, graphesthesia, and extinction phenomena.

In most cases a speech/language pathologist would have little need to perform a complete sensory examination. Because most speech/language pathology patients are either unreliable informants or cannot be understood in their responses due to their communication deficits, sensory tests are even more difficult to evaluate. While it can be assumed that certain peripheral sensory inputs play an important role in speech and swallow, there is little evidence to guide one in the clinical evaluation and interpretation of the data. Nevertheless, it is helpful to understand some basic sensory examination techniques.

Superficial Tactile Sensation

In order to evaluate a patient's ability to perceive light touch, the patient may be touched with a wisp of cotton to compare sensitivity on one side of the body with that of the corresponding area on the opposite side. The face, hands, forearms, upper arms, trunk, thighs, lower legs, and feet are evaluated. In a complete neurological examination for peripheral neuropathies, the physician also compares sensitivity of the proximal part of each extremity to the distal portion.

Motion and Position

With the patient's eyes closed, the fingers and toes may be moved passively and the patient asked to indicate the direction of movement and the final position of the digit. The examiner should grasp the patient's digit laterally with the thumb and index finger to avoid giving a clue to the direction of movement. An abnormal response on this test will be indicative of a disturbance anywhere along the pathway extending from the receptors in the skin, muscles, joints, and tendons to the sensory cortex of the cerebrum.

Stereognosis and Graphesthesia

Sometimes it is useful to evaluate stereognostic function by placing a small familiar object in the patient's hand. The patient is asked to identify the object, and the examiner compares performance on the two sides. In evaluating graphesthesia the examiner asks the patient to recognize letters or numbers that are written on the palms of the hands or on other parts of the body with a blunt-tipped instrument. Once again, performance on corresponding sides is compared.

Extinction Phenomenon

A patient can be evaluated for extinction after it has been determined that the patient is able to perceive touch on each side of the body. With the patient's eyes closed, the examiner simultaneously touches two corresponding points on opposite sides of the body. The patient is asked to identify the areas that were touched. When the primary sensory modalities are intact, a disturbance in this cortical sensory modality is indicative of parietal lobe involvement. This phenomenon is frequently present in patients with unilateral neglect. It has strong negative implications regarding prognosis for independent self-care when extinction to double simultaneous stimulation persists.[7,8]

Eye Examination

Speech/language pathologists do not receive training with regard to the anatomy and physiology of the eye. However, a screening examination of the eye performed by a speech/language pathologist is justified on the basis that vision is a primary modality for communication. Further, this organ is rich in clinical signs that relate directly to the diagnosis of disorders associated with communication impairment and to the prognosis of these disorders. For example, eye findings may support or confirm a differentiation of upper motor neuron from lower motor neuron disease or differentiate a patient with homonymous hemianopia from one with neglect. The intent of this section is not to make experts of speech/language pathologists in diagnosing disorders of the eye, but rather to assist them in recognizing common features that show up as eye findings and can be related to communication disorders.

Complaints

If patients are able to give a history and describe problems, they should be asked about their vision. Particular attention should be paid to complaints suggesting blind spots or scotomas, visual field cuts such as homonymous hemianopia, double or blurred vision, or a perceived inability to see or read as the patient did previously. The speech/language pathologist can play an important role in interpreting communicatively impaired patients' complaints to the appropriate disciplines.

Gaze

The general appearance of a patient's eyes can yield significant clues to various disorders. For example, the position of the eyelids may suggest a specific impairment. The position of the lids is governed by the tone of the lid muscles and the degree of protrusion of the eyeball. When there is weakness of the levator palpebrae, ptosis or drooping of the upper eyelid will be evident. Ptosis may be due to paralysis of the levator muscle and a sign of third cranial nerve impairment or paralysis of smooth muscle resulting from a sympathetic lesion. Ptosis also is evident in cases of myasthenia gravis (pictured in Figure 6–6) or in ocular myopathies.

The antagonist to the levator palpebrae is the orbicularis oculi, the sphincter muscle of the eyelid. This muscle is innervated by cranial nerve 7, and its impairment results in an inability to close the eye.

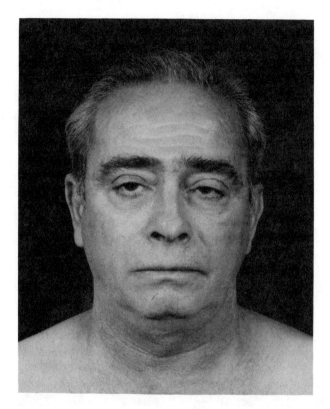

Figure 6–6 Patient with myasthenia gravis demonstrating ocular muscle fatigue. Note ptosis of both eyelids. *Source:* Reproduced with permission from Michael Groher (Ed.), *Dysphagia: Diagnosis and Management*, Butterworth Publishers, Stoneham, MA, © 1984.

Lid retraction implies some form of spasm of the upper lids and is sometimes seen in cases of multiple sclerosis, parkinsonism, and other upper midbrain lesions. Retraction of both upper and lower lids long has been recognized as a principal sign of Graves' disease, associated with hyperthyroidism.[9] This feature takes on the appearance of bulging eyeballs and is referred to as exophthalmos.

A lesion affecting cranial nerves 3, 4, and 6 that control eye movement results in an imbalance in the muscle contractions and in impaired gaze. Any deviation of the eyes that the patient cannot overcome, referred to as strabismus, should be noted.

The appearance of the eyes also is significant as they contribute to the picture of a "masked" face. This is associated with parkinsonism. In this condition the eyes appear to stare straight ahead, and there is loss of spontaneous movements. This feature also may be seen in patients with frontal lobe and diffuse brain disease, particularly those with traumatic injuries to the brain. Figure 6–7 illustrates a patient with staring eyes and fixed facial posture.

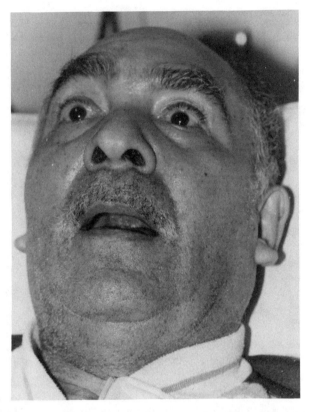

Figure 6–7 Loss of spontaneous facial expression and retraction of the eyelids result in an immobile yet anxious appearance. This appearance may be found in parkinsonism, frontal lobe disease, and diffuse brain disease.

Another feature that may be recognized when observing the patient's gaze is nystagmus. This is an involuntary rhythmic movement or oscillation of the eyeball that may be unilateral or bilateral; fine or coarse; rapid or slow; horizontal, vertical, or rotary; and transient or constant. Each form has its own particular diagnostic significance. Some forms of nystagmus are congenital in nature, while others are acquired and thus associated with a particular disorder. Nystagmus has been classified as physiological, sensory deprivation, or motor imbalance type. Physiological nystagmus is found in normal subjects. It includes end-point nystagmus, occurring when the eyes are moved to an extreme gaze position; optokinetic nystagmus, the to-and-fro jerking of the eyes in response to tracking visual stimuli across the visual field; and vestibular nystagmus, elicited by altering the input from the vestibular nuclei as in caloric stimulation (water stimulation of the labyrinth). Sensory deprivation nystagmus generally is found when there is central visual loss occurring congenitally. Motor imbalance nystagmus can be found in patients with disease of the brainstem or cerebellum, usually in multiple sclerosis or tumor, and in some patients with drug intoxication.

Pupils

The shape, size, and symmetry of the pupils should be observed. The size of the pupils is controlled by the muscles of the iris and include circular fibers innervated by cranial nerve 3 to constrict the pupils and radial fibers innervated by cervical sympathetic nerves to dilate the pupils. The normal pupil is generally about 4 mm in diameter and is never completely at rest. The size of the pupil at any given moment is dependent on the amount of light reaching it and upon the degree of convergence accommodation (adjustment of the eye for near and far vision).

When examining the pupils, the pupillary light reflex should be observed. There is both a direct and a consensual reaction to light. With a light shining on one pupil, both pupils should constrict symmetrically. If neither pupil constricts, a lesion in the afferent system must be present. This lesion could exist in the retina, optic nerve, or at the optic chiasm. In this case when the lesion is unilateral, the consensual reaction will be present when the normal side is stimulated. With a lesion in cranial nerve 3, or an efferent lesion, the affected pupil will not constrict regardless of the side stimulated.

Pupillary constriction also can be seen during convergence. When the patient focuses normally from a distant point to a near target, the pupils will constrict. If this accommodation reflex of the pupil is lost while light reflex is preserved, the lesion is presumed to be in the midbrain.

Other anomalies of the pupil that may interest the speech/language pathologist include the *Argyll Robertson* pupil, which is almost pathognomonic of neurosyphilis, and *Horner's syndrome*. Argyll Robertson pupils generally are small and frequently irregular in shape and may be asymmetrical in appearance. There usually is no reaction to light, but there is a brisk response when adjusting to near focus. Conditions such as diabetes mellitus can produce pupillary changes similar to those of the Argyll Robertson pupil. Misshapen or oval pupils also may be caused by cerebral vascular disease or be a transient feature during recovery from brainstem lesions.

Horner's syndrome includes findings of one pupil being smaller with a narrowing of the palpebral fissure on the same side. The palpebral fissure is the distance between the inferior portion of the upper lid and the superior portion of the lower lid. In Horner's syndrome the narrowing of the palpebral fissure is due to ptosis or drooping of the upper lid and an elevation of the lower lid. Two additional, but less constant, features in Horner's syndrome include diminished sweating on the ipsilateral portion of the face and vasodilation on the same side. Horner's syndrome may be due to disease in the central nervous system with signs localizing it to the brainstem or upper spinal cord. In this case it is usually associated with vertigo and sensory deficits. The sympathetic pathways also may be interrupted in their peripheral course by tumors, thoracotomy, or injuries to the neck or brachial plexus.

There are a myriad of other findings that may be noted in observing the eyes and the pupils. Some of these findings may be only curiosities, and others are rare and somewhat exotic. One common observation, particularly evident in the elderly patient, is the white ring appearing around the peripheral cornea. This ring is referred to as arcus senilis and is a characteristic of aging resulting from a normal deposition of lipids.[10] In younger patients it can represent a metabolic disorder. A relatively rare condition called the *Kayser-Fleischer ring*, found in Wilson's disease (hepatolenticular degeneration), is characterized by a zone of golden-brown granules around each pupil. These rings are caused by the widespread deposition of copper in tissues of the eye. The disease itself may be characterized by a flapping tremor of the extremities, mental status changes, spasticity, dysarthria, and dysphagia.

Extraocular Movements

Eye movements are controlled by three cranial nerves. The oculomotor nerve (cranial nerve 3) allows each eye to be moved up, down, and medially. As described previously, when this nerve is affected there will be ptosis of the lid and dilatation of the pupil. The trochlear nerve (cranial nerve 4) provides for some downward movement and lateral gaze. The abducens nerve (cranial nerve 6) also contributes to lateral eye movement. With involvement of any of these cranial nerves, the patient usually complains of double vision (diplopia). Lesions may be due to involvement of the nerves themselves or to their nuclei located in the midbrain and pons.

An examination of extraocular movements can be carried out by asking the patient to follow the examiner's finger as it is moved in all directions of gaze. During this examination the examiner should observe closely for the presence of nystagmus and movements that are dysconjugate (not working in unison).

Visual Fields

The speech/language pathologist should have some knowledge of the visual tracts (see Figure 6–8) and be able to perform basic visual field testing. Although it is not the responsibility of the speech/language pathologist to describe precisely the visual impairment of patients, it is important to describe in general terms the vision of patients with communication impairments or to refer those with suspected impairments after screening. In order to conduct visual field testing, a patient should have one eye covered and look at the examiner's nose with the uncovered eye. Starting at the periphery of each quadrant of vision, the examiner will move a finger or cotton-tipped applicator toward the patient's center of vision. The patient is asked to indicate the instant the target comes into view. When this test is performed for each eye, gross visual field defects can be appreciated. If precise information is needed, standard perimetric tests should be recommended.

When it has been determined that a patient's visual fields are intact, visual extinction should be tested. This examination is performed in much the same way as

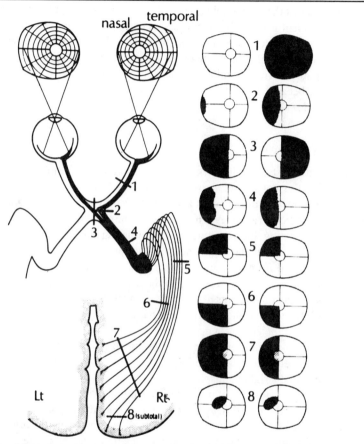

Visual fields that accompany damage to the visual pathways. 1. Optic nerve: Unilateral amaurosis. 2. Lateral optic chiasm: Grossly incongruous, incomplete (contralateral) homonymous hemianopia. 3. Central optic chiasm: Bitemporal hemianopia. 4. Optic tract: Incongruous, incomplete homonymous hemianopia. 5. Temporal (Meyer's) loop of optic radiation: Congruous partial or complete (contralateral) homonymous superior quadrantanopia. 6. Parietal (superior) projection of the optic radiation: Congruous partial or complete homonymous inferior quadrantanopia. 7. Complete parieto-occipital interruption of optic radiation. Complete congruous homonymous hemianopia with psychophysical shift of foveal point often sparing central vision, giving "macular sparing." 8. Incomplete damage to visual cortex: Congruous homonymous scotomas, usually encroaching at least acutely on central vision.

Figure 6–8 Visual fields that accompany damage to the visual pathways. *Source:* Reprinted from *Cecil Essentials of Medicine* by C.J. Carpenter, F. Plum, and L.H. Smith with permission of W.B. Saunders Company, © 1986.

the tactual extinction test. In this case the fingers are moved simultaneously on opposite sides of the visual fields. The patient is asked to identify the side or sides where movement is seen. In most cases of extinction testing, even the impaired patient sometimes correctly observes movement in both fields simultaneously. Even inconsistent unilateral extinction is a significant finding. It may suggest that the patient suffers from a unilateral neglect that eventually will impact on communication, because the patient may fail to respond to input that comes from the neglected side.

Optokinetic Nystagmus

Optokinetic nystagmus is a jerky nystagmus induced in normal subjects by moving a series of visual stimuli across the visual field. The slow, or pursuit, phase is in the same direction as the target and is followed by a fast, or saccadic, phase in the opposite direction as the eyes refixate on the next target. Optokinetics are tested with either a rotating drum designed with alternating black and white stripes, or an optokinetic tape consisting of 3/4-inch black stripes on a white background. As the targets are moved from the patient's right to left, the left parieto-occipital region controls the slow pursuit movements to the left, and the left frontal lobe controls the rapid saccadic movements to the right. Conversely, when a tape is moved from the patient's left to the right, it is the right parieto-occipital region and right frontal lobe that control the complete optokinetic nystagmus reflex. The optokinetic nystagmus reflex may be absent when stimulating horizontally right to left if there is damage to the left hemisphere, and it may be absent when stimulating left to right with damage to the right hemisphere.

The presence or absence of optokinetic nystagmus does not necessarily indicate the condition of the visual fields. Patients with true homonymous hemianopia retain the optokinetic nystagmus reflex in both directions when the targets enter the intact visual fields. The absence of the optokinetic nystagmus reflex from one direction strongly suggests the presence of a unilateral neglect on the impaired side. The absence of this reflex also has been implicated as a negative prognostic sign for the learning that is necessary to achieve many rehabilitation goals, particularly those that are dependent on learning generalization and that require the patient to be independent with self-initiated performance.[11,12]

Experience suggests that the absence of this reflex does have serious implications with regard to prognosis of treatment benefits. In some instances the reflex is absent during the acute phase following brain damage, but may return as the patient shows physiological recovery. The return of the reflex often corresponds to the patient's improved attention span and learning generalization. When the reflex is persistently absent from one side, only insignificant therapy gains have been observed. As with all singular signs and symptoms, no one reflex or finding should be used as a sole indicator of prognosis or extent of damage. Optokinetic nystagmus is important only when used as part of a comprehensive battery to assess brain-damaged patients.

Ears and Hearing

Inspection of the ear with an otoscope may be included in an examination battery used by the speech/language pathologist. Although this examination is not likely to yield significant diagnostic clues, the ear is a primary communication organ that deserves attention. It often is overlooked in the routine physical evaluation performed by the patient's physician. Speech/language pathologists who did not receive training in the use of an otoscope can work with experienced examiners (such as colleagues in audiology or otolaryngology) in order to learn appropriate examination technique; landmark recognition in the external auditory canal, tympanic membrane, and middle ear; and recognition of the existence of pathology that is appropriate for medical referral.

The speech/language pathologist usually is familiar with standard audiometric testing procedures. It is essential that the audiometric test results are interpreted in the context of the patient's overall speech and language assessment.

HEAD AND NECK EXAMINATION

After the examiner has some feel for the patient's gross motor function and the condition of the major sensory modalities, the examination should focus on the head and neck region with particular attention to those muscles involved in speaking and swallowing.

Facial Muscles

Observations of the muscles of facial expression should be conducted while the muscles are at rest and during active movement. As in most of the other motor examinations, the two sides of the face are compared for symmetry. The widening of a palpebral fissure, flattening of a nasolabial fold, or drooping of one corner of the mouth are all suggestive of unilateral facial weakness. When facial weakness involves the entire face, including the muscles of the forehead, the lesion is generally thought to be peripheral in nature and involve the seventh cranial nerve itself or the nucleus in the brainstem. When weakness involves only the lower two-thirds of the face, it is generally due to a central or upper motor neuron lesion. Usually, weakness attributed to an upper motor neuron lesion is less severe than that caused by peripheral nerve impairment. Patients with upper motor neuron facial weakness usually have good movement of the muscles of facial expression during emotional responses.

To evaluate the muscles of facial expression during active movement, the patient should be asked to make grimacing and puckering movements while the examiner observes the lips. When possible, the muscles should be palpated during the movements. The examiner should watch for the patient's ability to seal the lips by having the patient puff out the cheeks and hold air in the mouth while manual pressure is applied to the cheeks. During grimacing movement, the contractions of the platysma muscles on each side are compared. The patient also should be asked to close the eyes as tight as possible and wrinkle the brow by lifting the eyebrows and deep frowning. During this activity, the contractions on the two sides of the upper face are compared.

Muscles of Mastication

The two major muscles of biting are the masseter and temporalis. The muscles should be palpated, as illustrated in Figure 6–9, while the patient attempts to bite and chew. Only gentle resistance should be placed on the mandible to assess the strength of these muscles. Excessive resistance could result in either dislocation of the temporomandibular joint or fracture of a decalcified mandible, particularly in aged persons.

Figure 6–9 Assessment of the major muscles of biting and chewing, the masseter and temporalis muscles, can be performed by palpation as the patient bites. The examiner will feel for symmetry of contractions.

The other major muscles of chewing are the pterygoids, external and internal pairs. The action of these muscles is to move the mandible from side to side in a rotary fashion. To appreciate their strength, gentle resistance can be applied to the side of the jaw as the patient attempts to move the mandible laterally, as illustrated in Figure 6–10.

Intraoral Examination

The speech/language pathologist, like all health professionals involved in the inspection of the oral cavity, should be alert to the presence of any lesion in the head and neck region. The speech/language pathologist's responsibility is not to diagnose the pathology, but to recognize abnormalities and to refer the patient to the appropriate medical discipline for definitive diagnosis and treatment.

Mucosa

The intraoral examination begins with an assessment of the mucosa. When a patient is wearing dentures, they generally should be removed prior to this exami-

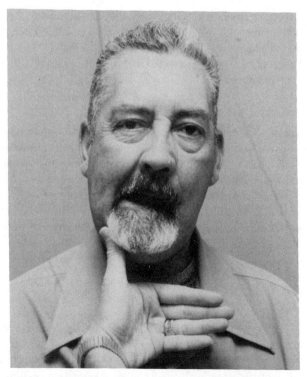

Figure 6–10 Assessment of the pterygoids, the muscles of mastication that allow the jaw to grind food, can be performed by gently resisting the patient's lateral jaw movements.

nation. The presence of any lesions should be noted and proper referral procedures followed. During the inspection of the mucosa, the speech/language pathologist should look at the tongue, lining of the cheeks or buccal mucosa, the condition of the gums, and floor of the mouth, particularly under the tongue in the anterior region. The area of the faucial pillars and tonsillar fossa should be inspected. Particular attention should be paid to the presence or absence of moisture in the oral cavity. Extreme dryness (xerostomia) can virtually prevent an effective swallow, while thick tenacious secretions can inhibit the swallow reflex. The presence of food or other oral debris pooled on one side of the mouth also is significant and may be suggestive of either sensory loss or some form of neglect.

Any suspicious lesion of the oral mucosa should be called to the attention of the responsible physician. Discoloration, particularly a whitish lesion or erythematous (reddened) area, is important to note. Irregular surface areas such as exophytic (raised) or ulcerative lesions are potentially significant. It takes a great deal of experience to differentiate pathology from variations of normal, such as thick white mucus from leukoplakia. Clinicians should refer to an appropriate medical discipline whenever there is a question.

Teeth and Gums

A notation should be made regarding the condition of the patient's teeth and presence of dentures, either full or partial. When disease is noted or the patient complains of pain, dental consultation should be considered. Discomfort resulting from poor dentition or ill-fitting dentures can impact negatively on both speech and swallow performance.

Palate

While inspecting the mucosa of the hard and soft palate, the examiner should note the shape and configuration. Patients with high, vaulted, narrow palates or evidence of cleft repair may have other congenital abnormalities that are reflected in their communication disorders. The shape of the velum at rest and during phonation also can give clues regarding the strength of these bulbar innervated muscles. Generally a velum with unilateral weakness will be pulled to the stronger side, giving the palatal drape an asymmetric appearance. Having the patient phonate while the palate is observed offers some clues regarding the competence of palatopharyngeal closure.

Oropharynx

The examiner should note the posterior pharyngeal wall during rest and active contraction. The palatopharyngeal musculature should be evaluated as a unit during reflexive action. Tactual stimulation, either at the base of the tongue or on the pharyngeal wall, will likely elicit a gag reflex. The speech/language pathologist should attempt to elicit this reflex by using a tongue depressor to stroke the tongue with progressively more posterior stimulation or a cotton-tipped applicator to touch the posterior pharyngeal wall. When contractions are visualized in the palate and pharynx, the examiner must judge the symmetry of movement. A unilaterally absent gag is significant, suggesting the presence of a unilateral lower motor neuron lesion (see Figure 6–11). However, the gag reflex is highly variable among healthy persons, and judgments regarding a finding of hypoactive or hyperactive reflexes are difficult. Decisions about the significance of this reflex in a given patient are made only after considering other related findings. For example, a bilaterally diminished reflex is considered to be significant only when found in patients who have evidence of other cranial nerve impairments. Rarely is the absence of this reflex alone predictive of pathology.

Tongue

The lingual muscles also are examined for appearance and strength. Palpation of the tongue to detect subtle lesions beneath the surface should be attempted only in very cooperative or totally edentulous patients. Visual inspection should note the presence of lingual atrophy, fasciculations, or abnormal movements. By having the patient protrude the tongue, the examiner can assess any deviation from the midline that occurs toward the side of weakness. Tongue strength should be as-

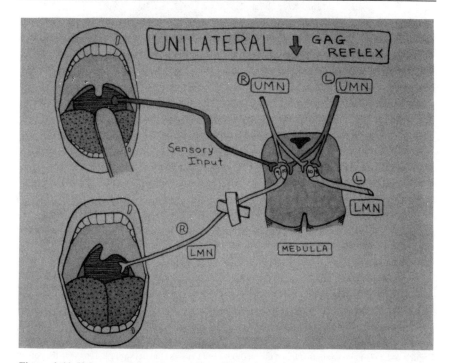

Figure 6–11 If the gag reflex is absent unilaterally, the lesion is located in the lower motor neuron.
Source: Reprinted with permission of George Zito, M.D.

sessed further by having the patient push the tongue firmly against the inner cheek while the examiner uses finger pressure to resist movement on each side. This technique is demonstrated in Figure 6–12. A patient who cannot move the tongue laterally past the incisors is suspect for weakness. In addition to strength, speed of tongue movement should be assessed by having the patient move the tongue laterally from side to side. Tongue function, as it relates more directly to speech, is assessed as the examiner proceeds with the motor function examination during diadochokinetic activities.

Laryngoscopy

Mirror examination of the larynx or inspection with a fiberoptic laryngoscope may not be part of speech/language pathologists' training. This is unfortunate, be-

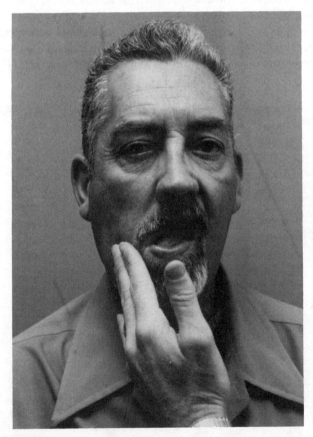

Figure 6–12 Tongue strength. One of the methods used to assess lingual strength is to have the patient push the tongue into each cheek as the examiner resists the movement. Force to each side is compared for symmetry.

cause a screening of laryngeal function is appropriate. Speech/language pathologists have been warned against performing these examinations because of the necessity of using "medical tools" during the procedure. It should be noted that while there is some risk to this examination (elicitation of emesis, vagal stimulation, or local tissue irritation), it is as benign as the elicitation of a gag reflex. Another criticism of this examination being performed by speech/language pathologists relates to their lack of training in the identification of laryngeal pathology. However, as long as clinicians refer any suspicious lesions and other conditions to the otolaryngology section, this appears to be a moot point. In order to learn appropriate procedure and technique and become familiar with the various landmarks in the hypopharyngeal region and the larynx itself, it is recommended that beginning examiners work with experienced clinicians to compare observations. Most otolaryngologists are willing to provide this initial training and welcome the speech/language pathologist's laryngeal examinations as a means of identifying some patients with laryngeal disease that otherwise would go undetected.

A complete examination of the larynx should include an inspection of the base of tongue, valleculae, epiglottis, pyriform sinuses, false and true vocal folds, and the infraglottic area. The landmarks of the larynx are illustrated in Figure 6–13. Particular attention should be paid to the presence of any pooling in the valleculae or pyriform sinuses. This is frequently an indication that a swallow reflex has been

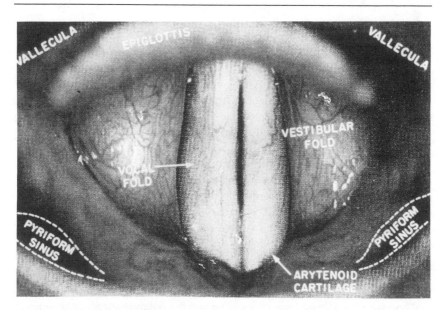

Figure 6–13 Structures visualized on mirror or fiberoptic examination of the larynx. *Source:* Reproduced with permission from Michael Groher (Ed.), *Dysphagia: Diagnosis and Management,* Butterworth Publishers, Stoneham, MA, © 1984.

either incomplete or not elicited. If pooling is observed in the aditus (entrance) of the larynx, there is a high probability for tracheal aspiration.

The vocal folds also should be evaluated for function. Symmetry of movement should be observed during quiet breathing, forced inhalation, and phonation.

ORAL AND LARYNGEAL MOTOR EXAMINATION

The examiner now should be familiar with a structural examination of the head and neck musculature associated with the speech mechanism. It is important to observe these same structures during movement. Active movement may be assessed under three conditions: spontaneous, reflexive, and voluntary.

Imitative Movements

The patient should be asked to move the lips and tongue in imitation of the examiner. The examiner should observe for differences between the voluntary actions of the patient and involuntary movements observed throughout the examination. A patient who has lost the ability to voluntarily imitate movements in the absence of weakness, paralysis, or the inability to comprehend the task may have some degree of oral dyspraxia.

Respiration

The patient's quiet breathing should be observed as well as respiratory functions during phonation and speech. Asking the patient about breathing difficulties should be a part of this assessment. Whenever possible, vital capacity should be measured. A hand-held respirometer may be used to obtain fairly accurate readings of the patient's respiratory capacity. These measures are particularly important for patients with swallowing difficulties or with progressive pulmonary or neurologic diseases. Serial measurements of respiratory function are useful in documenting the extension of progressive disease and planning for management interventions. For example, in amyotrophic lateral sclerosis (ALS) measures of vital capacity assist clinicians in documenting the severity of the disease and determining the appropriate time to offer augmentative communication systems and feeding tubes.[13]

Voice

The patient's quality of voice should be described during speech functions and as the patient attempts to prolong a vowel. The duration of vowel prolongation and the ability to volitionally change pitch should be assessed.

Cough

The patient should be asked to turn his or her head away from the examiner and produce a strong, voluntary cough. This gives the speech/language pathologist some clue as to the patient's protective cough function. It should be noted, however, that there is a distinct difference between a patient's ability to cough volitionally and the reflexive cough. In one condition, the volitional cough may be ineffective, whereas the reflexive cough may be strong and productive. In another instance, the patient may not be able to organize and coordinate the muscular sequences necessary to produce a volitional cough due to dyspraxia. In such cases the patient will maintain a reflexive cough. It is very rare to find a patient who has lost the reflexive cough but can produce a strong and productive voluntary cough. The final assessment of cough is made by combining information obtained from the assessments of oropharyngeal sensation, gag reflexes, movement of the vocal cords, respiratory function, and voice quality.

Swallow

Any patient with a speech, voice, or language impairment should be asked about swallowing problems. Often patients will not complain of this disorder, and the examiner must rely on the history or reports from the family or nurse. The physical examination and history as described in this chapter should be included in a complete swallowing examination.[14] If there is no swallowing complaint, only a cursory examination of swallowing may be needed. Sometimes, normal function can be inferred from the history and from notations that the patient is taking a regular diet without difficulty. A cursory examination may involve only palpating the laryngeal structures and the hyoid bone as a patient produces a volitional swallow. The examiner should feel for the superior-anterior excursion of the larynx as it closes the airway during the swallow reflex. Auscultation at the side of the larynx also can be used to detect swallow. If there is either complaint or dysfunction in swallowing, the examination may be extended to include test swallows with repeat laryngoscopy, test swallows using a variety of textures and consistencies, or radiographic studies when indicated.

Imitative Speech

Similar to diadochokinetic tasks using the fingers and hands, the patient is asked to perform rapid alternating movements with the lips, tongue, and phonatory mechanism. While the patient performs the bilabial pa-pa-pa, the lingual-alveolar ta-ta-ta, the lingual-palatal ka-ka-ka, and the vowel e-e-e, the examiner judges the speed, precision, and rhythm control for the respiratory, phonatory, and articulatory structures involved. Sequencing the syllables into pa-ta-ka and having the patient imitate words and sentences give the examiner an introduction into what eventually will be a description of the patient's speech characteristics as they manifest themselves in connected speech.

SUMMARY

The examination presented in this chapter is not meant to be a thorough neurological or head and neck evaluation. It does not obviate the need for any of these or other medical specialty examinations. Rather, the use of the tools described strengthens a case for making referrals to other specialists and assists in communicating with other medical disciplines. The speech/language pathologist who employs these examination techniques has a better understanding of medical tests and the interpretations made by specialists in allied areas.

The complete examination battery as described is rarely administered in its entirety. The elements have been presented as tools that can be used when the clinical situation dictates. It allows the speech/language pathologist's examination to be more versatile and explorative given the heterogenous nature of patients with communication impairments. New techniques and tools, such as the videorecording of swallow and the assessment of laryngeal function via fiberoptic endoscopy, or the use of standard medical tools, such as the stethoscope for auscultation of the lungs and the ophthalmoscope for visualization of the retina, can be added for further expansion of the armamentarium.

Rarely do physicians react negatively to the speech/language pathologist's use of this examination protocol. More often they are impressed by its use, because it shares a certain familiarity with their own procedures. Most physicians are supportive to the extent of assisting clinicians by sharing observations and teaching examination techniques. The speech/language pathologist should be equally willing to share techniques and procedures in an effort to assist the physician who desires to know more about the examination of patients with communication and swallowing impairments.

NOTES

1. Richard L. DeGowin, "Methods in the Physical Examination." In *Bedside Diagnostic Examination*, eds. Elmer L. DeGowin and Richard L. DeGowin (New York: Macmillan Publishing Company, 1987), 37.

2. John D. Spillane, *An Atlas of Clinical Neurology* (London: Oxford University Press, 1968), 309.

3. Peritz Scheinberg, *An Introduction to Diagnosis and Management of Common Neurologic Disorders* (New York: Raven Press, 1968), 17–18.

4. Raymond D. Adams and Maurice Victor, *Principles of Neurology*, 3rd ed. (New York: McGraw-Hill Book Co., 1985), 1029.

5. Houston H. Merritt, *A Textbook of Neurology* (Philadelphia: Lea & Febiger, 1973), 175.

6. John N. Walton, *Essentials of Neurology* (Philadelphia: J.P. Lippincott Co., 1960), 207.

7. Karen M. Stanton et al., "Language-Oriented Training Program to Teach Compensation of Left Side Neglect (Abstract)," *Archives of Physical Medicine and Rehabilitation* 60 (1979):540.

8. Brian J. Dudgeon, Joel A. DeLisa, and Robert M. Miller, "Optokinetic Nystagmus and Upper Extremity Dressing Independence after Stroke," *Archives of Physical Medicine and Rehabilitation* 66 (1985):164–67.

9. Jack J. Kanski, *The Eye in Systemic Disease* (London and Stoneham, Mass.: Butterworth Publishers, 1986), 2–9.

10. F.I. Caird and John Williamson, eds., *The Eye and Its Disorders in the Elderly* (Bristol, England: John Wright and Sons Ltd., 1986), 12.

11. Stanton et al., "Language-Oriented Training Program," 540.

12. Dudgeon, DeLisa, and Miller, "Optokinetic Nystagmus," 164–67.

13. Allen D. Hillel and Robert M. Miller, "Bulbar Amyotrophic Lateral Sclerosis: Patterns of Progression and Clinical Management," *Head and Neck Surgery* 11, no. 1 (January, February 1989):51–59.

14. Robert M. Miller, "Evaluation of Swallowing Disorders." In *Dysphagia: Diagnosis and Management*, ed. Michael E. Groher (Stoneham, Mass.: Butterworth Publishers, 1984), 85–110.

Chapter 7

The Mental Status Examination

INTRODUCTION

The final component necessary for the development of a clinical picture for patients referred to the speech/language pathologist for evaluation is the mental status examination. Everything that has come before—the review of the medical records, the interview, clinical observations, and the physical examination—provides a foundation upon which to build a description and explanation of the patient's behavior. The perspective is that of a clinician with expertise in the entire human communication process. In order to assess accurately any communication or related problem, the clinician must be able and willing to describe the patient's mental status. This is true whether the problem presents as an impairment of voice, motor speech, fluency, language, or swallowing. In each case the clinician should consider and screen for mental status problems as either the primary basis for the disorder or as a secondary complication. In many cases this is accomplished during the course of the interview, and no formal testing procedure is required. However, when considering the hospitalized and outpatient population of most medical centers, there will be a high percentage of patients presenting with specific speech and voice problems who have concomitant mental status impairments. The speech/language pathologist must be equipped with the tools necessary to assess mental status in a systematic manner.

MENTAL STATUS

The boundaries between medical and allied health disciplines with regard to mental status assessments are not clearly delineated. Every comprehensive neurologic evaluation includes a mental status assessment. Psychiatric examinations include mental status assessments. Most internists and physiatrists include at least a screening of mental status in their examinations. Psychologists, particularly neuropsychologists, formally assess patients' mental status. Occupational and physical therapists, vocational rehabilitation specialists, and other members of the rehabilitation team make judgments about patients' mental status and sometimes administer specific tests to evaluate particular facets of cognitive behavior. It would seem that with all of these disciplines concerned with a patient's mental state that there would be adequate description and explanation of the brain-damaged patient's behavior included in the medical record. Since communication skills are a part of that assessment, one also might expect similar documentation regarding these functions. However, this is almost never the case.

Speech/language pathologists are in a unique position to evaluate mental status, particularly in patients with a communication impairment. Because most disciplines are dependent upon effective communication in order to assess mental status adequately or their judgments about a patient's mental status are made on the basis of the patient's verbal behavior, many of their standard tools are inadequate to describe and explain accurately the behaviors of the brain-damaged patient.

The speech/language pathologist performs a full mental status evaluation in order to

- determine whether or not a communication problem exists
- differentiate among patients with specific speech and language impairments and those with more generalized cognitive deficits, such as aphasia from dementia
- make accurate prognostic statements regarding the recovery potential of communication-impaired patients and develop appropriate treatment programs
- assess learning functions for their potential as treatment modalities for brain-damaged patients in rehabilitation programs
- describe the communication behaviors of any brain-damaged patient, for example, demented, confused, or right brain-impaired

Aphasia is considered a specific impairment in the mental status of patients and is characterized by impairments in all language modalities. Specifically these include verbal comprehension, auditory-verbal memory, reading, verbal expression, writing, and gesturing. Assessment tools abound that allow one to describe the language impairment of patients who have a diagnosis of aphasia. However, for the most part these aphasia test batteries are not adequate for the differential diagnosis of aphasia, that is, a patient who does not use language in a normal manner would meet the test criteria for aphasia. The aphasic patient's language certainly can be described and defined by these tools, but the patient with dementia, confusion, or some psychiatric disorder also may appear to be aphasic when utilizing traditional aphasia test batteries. Indeed, when the characteristics of aphasic language dysfunction, such as paraphasia, perseveration, jargon, anomia, and impaired auditory memory, are considered separately, it is obvious that they are not only symptoms of aphasia but are also symptoms of brain damage.

In order to differentiate the specific disorder of aphasia from more generalized dysfunctions such as states of confusion and dementia, the speech/language pathologist must evaluate language in the context of other mental processes. For purposes of discussion these mental processes are defined as learning modalities. When aphasia is considered in this context, it is recognized that a patient has true aphasia only when essentially free from dysfunction in the other learning modalities. That is, the patient with isolated aphasia has no evidence of visual-motor-perceptual dysfunction, visual memory impairment, or problems in higher cognitive processes that do not require language. An operational definition that identifies true aphasia then might be: a patient with specific language dysfunction who can learn from demonstration and other nonlanguage modalities. Using this qualifier, aphasic patients are considered to be good rehabilitation candidates with regard to learning independent living skills and learning compensations for any motor impairments or hemiparesis that may exist. Given this context, isolated aphasia is a relatively rare disorder.

Prognosis for recovery from brain damage is a complex issue. Patients who have specific dysfunction (focal brain disease) are generally regarded as more apt to develop compensations during a rehabilitation program than those who have more generalized or diffuse impairments. By evaluating the range of learning modalities, the speech/language pathologist should be able to develop a more accurate prognostic statement and formulate appropriate treatment plans. Patients with generalized learning modality impairments perform more poorly than those whose impairments are limited to one or two learning modalities. The modalities that remain intact and are identified can be used by all clinicians concerned with a patient's rehabilitation for teaching purposes and for development of individualized treatment programs. Without a full evaluation of all learning modalities, however, the speech/language pathologist, along with other rehabilitation specialists, is at a disadvantage.

To a great extent, rehabilitation requires the patient to learn compensations and to use available mental processes to accomplish many of the functions that were once maintained by a fully integrated brain. One of the most important modalities used by rehabilitation specialists is language. The speech/language pathologist must accept a broader view of language assessments in order to understand language processing as a potential modality of treatment. Patients with right brain damage, for example, generally are able to comprehend and express language in a manner that, on the surface, appears to be well within normal limits. However, on close examination of many of these patients, the clinician finds that in spite of the fact that they comprehend and even retain verbal directions, they are unable to modify their behavior. For example, such a patient may learn the instructions of an occupational therapist that would allow the patient to dress while compensating for a left hemiparesis. The patient may even repeat these directions to the therapist. However, the patient cannot apply the instructions effectively in sequence to accomplish the task at hand.

The speech/language pathologist who evaluates more than the traditional language functions, including the relationship between the language modalities and other mental processes, contributes to the rehabilitation team's understanding of these patients' deficits and to the development of effective comprehensive rehabilitation plans. In a given case, the speech/language pathologist may describe for other rehabilitation specialists how teaching instructions can be modified to maximize the opportunity for a patient to learn. For example, written cues can assist one patient to perform a sequential motor task, while verbal self-cueing can help another. In another instance, an explanation may be provided to the rehabilitation team regarding why a particular patient repeats directions but fails to perform correctly. These contributions to a rehabilitation team are valued, because they direct everyone's energies toward providing the necessary compensations for a patient to learn new tasks.

If clinicians use only standard tools, such as aphasia tests, to evaluate mental status, they will fail to define the impairments of nonaphasic brain-damaged patients who evidence more subtle communication deficits. Standard tools may not be sensitive to states of confusion with confabulation, and problems associated with emotionally intoned language and abstract interpretations may go unrecognized. The medically oriented speech/language pathologist who regards language in a broad sense and utilizes tools to evaluate all facets of mental status will make a greater contribution in the medical setting.

EVALUATION GUIDELINES

The evaluation of mental status is much like the physical examination. It should begin with a screening of the general aspects and move toward more specifics as dictated by the patient's responses. Each modality evaluated should be assessed by starting with simple tasks and moving to more complex, abstract functions. In most instances when related modalities are being evaluated, for example, verbal comprehension and verbal expression, the input modalities should be assessed before those of output. If possible, only one modality at a time should be assessed. Tasks must be developed that require the patient to process through only one channel and respond in a manner that does not stress a potentially impaired output mode. For example, comprehension cannot be accurately assessed by requiring the patient to answer questions when all expressive modalities also are impaired.

Reinforcement should be avoided, although the clinician should be encouraging and supportive of the patient's attempts to respond at each level. Both positive and negative reinforcement can modify a patient's subsequent responses and prevent objective evaluations. The examiner must remain an objective observer by designing situations in which various behaviors can be elicited freely with a minimum of external modification. The behavior of the clinician as a diagnostitian is different from the same individual's behavior in the role of therapist, and this must be recognized. In testing it is necessary to allow the patient to fail if necessary. In treatment tasks are designed so that the patient can succeed if at all possible. Much of the encouragement and reinforcement behavior used by the clinician in remediation are not appropriate during the diagnostic evaluation, because in the diagnostic situation the clinician is seeking data free from the effects of any verbal support. It is the patient's responses to the "normal" testing routine that the examiner seeks to describe.

As do all clinicians who evaluate mental status, the speech/language pathologist must have a variety of tools to assess each learning modality. Many of these tools should be adaptable for use in the administration of bedside examinations. The clinician should be flexible enough to employ these tools in less than ideal circumstances and be prepared for situations that call for impromptu assessments, such as during bedside rounds or in the admitting area. The clinician also should be prepared for unusual cases that require the modification of assessment tools and approach. Patients with blindness, deafness, or quadriplegia present challenges that can be successfully handled with forethought. In some cases patients will require a complete battery of tests that allow for a detailed description of all learning modalities. A complete mental status assessment gives the examiner the necessary data to make an initial description of a patient's behavior and to determine the need for additional specific behavioral tests, (e.g., aphasia battery, memory assessment, referral for neuropsychological batteries, and personality inventories). This protocol allows the speech/language pathologist to develop a broad clinical picture of the patient's mental status that can lead toward the most appropriate intervention.

The tools discussed in this chapter allow the examiner to describe the behaviors of each patient in all learning modalities. Examples of clinical descriptions following evaluation are provided in Chapter 8. The tools are not intended to provide scores that can be compared to any standard group of patients, although some of the subtests can be extracted from test batteries for which standard scores exist. The differentiation of normal from abnormal function is made on the basis of clinical interpretation and is dependent on the examiner's experience and clinical judgment. The tools described do not obviate the need for standard published tests, but rather direct the speech/language pathologist to a more judicious application of these tests.

MENTAL PROCESSES: LEARNING MODALITIES

The tools described below can be incorporated into a complete battery or adapted for screening purposes. The important point is that all learning modalities must be considered in every assessment. A clinician may choose to employ other equally reliable tools, but each test should be scrutinized to ensure that it assesses the intended modality.

Attention and Vigilance

Impairments of attention and vigilance are common in most medical settings. Problems in these areas are caused by diffuse brain dysfunction; the most common etiologies are metabolic disturbances, including drug intoxication, postsurgical states, systemic infections, cerebral atrophy, multiple infarcts, encephalitis, and traumatic brain injury. Behaviors associated with disorders of attention and vigilance can take a number of forms. The disorders that affect levels of consciousness and result in somnolence and disturbances in the sleep/wake cycle are common examples of inattention. *Coma* refers to a relative state of impaired consciousness that interferes with a patient's ability to attend and respond to the environment. Observations for a given patient can be objectified in order to measure the depth of coma by using a tool such as the Glasgow Coma Scale.[1] Exhibit 7–1 demonstrates a recording method for the Glasgow Coma Scale that allows observers to monitor patients for changes in the levels of consciousness. In other instances, inattention will take the appearance of indifference or apathy toward the environment. This is typically seen in patients with bilateral lesions of the frontal lobes or impairments involving the limbic system, such as Korsakoff's syndrome (an impairment of memory and learning usually secondary to alcohol abuse).

The speech/language pathologist also must be alert to the fact that patients with severe depression often are misdiagnosed as having dementia because of their apparent apathy and disinterest in the environment. This disorder, which has been described as "pseudodementia," may be detected only after extensive mental

---

Exhibit 7–1 Recording Method for the Glasgow Coma Scale

Patient Name: _____ Date of Trauma: _____

Days/Hours Post Onset:
Date:
Time:

| I. | Eye opening | Spontaneous (3) To speech or touch (2) To pain (1) None (0) |

| II. | Best verbal response | Oriented (4) Confused (3) Inappropriate (2) Incomprehensible (1) None (0) Tracheostomy Tube: |

| III. | Best motor response | Obeying (4) Localizing (3) Flexing (2) Extending (2) None (0) |

Total Score:

status evaluation and psychiatric assessment. In other cases, inattention will be characterized by agitation and distractability. Patients become "stimulus bound" and are not able to differentiate between significant and irrelevant stimuli. Behaviors described as psychomotor agitation, in which patients constantly pick at themselves, their clothing, or other items in their immediate environment are common in severe frontal lobe disease, diffuse brain damage, and posttraumatic brain injury. Because of their attention to verbal behaviors, speech/language pathologists should be alert to the behaviors of logorrhea (excessive talkativeness), hallucination, and confabulation (verbal statements without regard to truth). Patients with disorders of unilateral neglect, common in right brain lesions, suffer from a special type of spatial inattention. These disorders can range from relatively minor neglect to total denial of space on the affected side. Most are associated with parietal lobe dysfunction.

The evaluation of attention and vigilance generally begins with an assessment of the patient's level of consciousness. As described in the section on clinical observations in Chapter 5, this can range from normally alert to comatose. The additional assessment of a patient's orientation, including person, place, time, and circumstance, also reflects the individual's level of attention and vigilance. Most often the assessment of attention is dependent upon behavioral observations and description. When the clinician suspects underlying processes may be responsible for a patient's inattention, probing questions and other techniques can be employed. For example, if depression is suspected, the clinician should ask the patient if he or she feels blue, sad, or depressed. The clinician should determine the presence of other neurovegetative symptoms associated with depression, such as loss of appetite, change in sleep habits, lack of interest in usual activities, gastrointestinal disturbances, and recent impairment of or change in concentration.

Behaviors such as hallucination and confabulation sometimes can be made evident by specific techniques. In the case where hallucination is suspected, the clinician can pretend to hold a piece of thread between the fingers of each hand and ask the patient to describe its color. In some cases the patient will reach out and take the "thread" for closer inspection. Asking ridiculous questions such as, "Can you explain why helicopters eat their young?" may elicit confabulation in the patient prone to such confused verbal behavior. The more specific disorders of vigilance, such as unilateral neglect or impaired auditory attention span, can be detected as the examination proceeds through spatial-perceptual and auditory memory tasks. The optokinetic nystagmus reflex, described in Chapter 6 under sensory function examination, is an excellent tool for beginning the assessment of spatial attention.

Language Comprehension

Language comprehension is the modality through which most directions are given for tests used to assess mental status. It should be one of the first modalities formally evaluated. Language comprehension is not assessed by having the patient verbally respond to questions, but rather by the examiner choosing directions that require motor responses within the patient's repertoire of ability. If a patient is right hemiparetic, performance may be required with the left hand. If the patient has quadriplegia but mobile facial muscles, instructions can be given to involve oral, facial, or eye movements in responses. In the severely impaired brain-injured patient, it is sometimes difficult to find any motor response over which the patient has control. This makes the assessment of language comprehension difficult or impossible. The comprehension of a patient with "locked-in syndrome" may be assessed by judging the reliability of eyeblinks as yes/no signals in response to questions. A patient in a catatonic state is equally difficult to evaluate because of the patient's inability or unwillingness to demonstrate comprehension of spoken directions.

To some degree the examiner should have developed hypotheses regarding the patient's language comprehension based upon responses made during the physical examination. Furthermore, the examiner will have an idea of the patient's ability to repeat words and phrases based on the oral-motor assessment. To confirm hypotheses and describe the degree of any dysfunction, further examination is required.

Language comprehension includes two input modalities, verbal and written. The examination, as outlined in Table 7–1, should begin with a verbal task requir-

Table 7–1 Selected Tasks Used To Assess Language Comprehension

	Bedside Examination	Clinic Examination
Auditory Comprehension		
Single word associations	Point to the light door floor ceiling pillow	coin comb pencil key paper
Serial pointing	Point to the light and floor ceiling and door pillow, light, door floor, door, ceiling	pencil and key coin and paper key, pencil, comb pencil coin, key
Following directions	Hold up two fingers. Make a fist. Form a circle with your thumb and index fingers and wave your hand side to side.	Turn over the coin. Move the key to the other side of the pencil. Pick up the pencil after you point to the coin.
Reading Comprehension		
Following directions	Slap the pillow. Draw a circle in the air. Pretend to drink a cup of coffee.	Pick up the comb. Place the key on the paper. Which of these do you write on?

ing a patient to follow a simple command. The examiner may begin by having the patient point to objects located within the room and articles collected by the examiner. Body parts can be used for these tasks; however, the examiner must recognize that a patient with parietal lobe damage and resultant disorders of space and body orientation will fail to perform accurately for reasons other than language comprehension deficits. At bedside the patient may be asked to point to the light, the door, the floor, the ceiling, or the pillow. Common objects, such as a coin, comb, pencil, key, paper, or watch, allow for the administration of simple comprehension tests. Patients who consistently point to the correct object as it is named should then be required to point to a series of objects, up to the point where the patient consistently fails or succeeds with four or more. Directions then should be given to the patient that require the manipulation of objects. Examples of such commands include: "turn over the coin," "move the key to the other side of the pencil," and "pick up the pencil after you point to the coin." Other simple commands can be given requiring manipulation of body parts. Patients may be asked to "hold up two fingers," "make a fist," "form a circle with your thumb and index finger," or "spread your fingers and wave your hand side to side." Directions should be given with increasingly complex language. As the examiner relates each spoken command, all extraverbal cues must be eliminated. This includes attention to tone of voice, inflectional emphasis, and visual cues like facial expression and gesture.

Many examiners use questions requiring yes/no responses as a measure of comprehension. In most situations this evaluative technique is not recommended as the test method of choice. First, the patient has a 50 percent chance of producing a correct response. Second, many brain-damaged patients confuse the two terms and respond in the affirmative when in fact they intend the opposite. Answers to yes/no questions that appear on many standardized test batteries are sometimes ambiguous depending upon the wording and interpretation of the questions. The level of abstraction in the wording of a yes/no question actually may determine the accuracy of the patient's response. Most tests of yes/no responses are not graded in levels of abstraction. Finally, when given a two-word choice, some brain-damaged patients perseverate with a single-word response that again may not reflect their comprehension.

Reading comprehension usually parallels the comprehension of the spoken word. However, there are some important differences between reading and auditory comprehension. Reading comprehension is usually learned as a secondary feature to auditory verbal comprehension. Auditory verbal comprehension is the primary modality through which most symbolic associations are developed. The visual transmission of language provides a constant stimulus for reprocessing (re-reading), whereas auditory input is transitory and the ability to reprocess is dependent upon the patient's immediate auditory recall. The assessment of reading should begin by having the patient match printed words to the appropriate objects using the same articles previously applied in the auditory comprehension tasks. Successful performance on this test would allow the examiner to provide printed directions, such as "point to the floor," "draw a circle in the air," or, with added complexity, "pretend to drink a cup of coffee."

For the most part, the assessment of abstract language comprehension requires the response mode to be verbal or written. For this reason this aspect of language comprehension is postponed until the adequacy of the expressive modalities can be assessed. It also should be recognized that understanding abstract language requires more mental processes than just the association of a symbol to its learned concept. The assessment of abstract language is discussed under higher cognitive functions.

Language Expression

Any verbal response on the part of the patient, whether repetitive language, automatic greetings, or formulated expressions should have been noted. The examiner should have a clear understanding of the patient's oral-motor capabilities. Disorders of dysarthria and apraxia should have been recognized and differentiated from any existing language dysfunction.

The evaluation of language expression, as outlined in Table 7–2, begins with an assessment of speech as the output mode. The patient is asked to name common items, again beginning with objects in the room, body parts, clothing, or articles collected by the examiner. The patient who is successful in naming objects may be asked to provide one-word responses for the various qualities associated with the item, for example, the object's color, the material from which it was made, or the shape. The examiner should move from very simple concepts to more abstract and eventually ask the patient to name parts of objects, such as a watch crystal, stem, band, or buckle. To assess performance beyond the single word, the patient may be asked to describe objects such as a key, pencil, or coin. The examiner may say, "Tell me everything you can about this." Definitions provided by the patient for such words as "bark," "island," and "history" allow the examiner to assess the patient's syntax and word finding and begin to reflect on the patient's higher cognitive processes.

An excellent subtest that can be used for the assessment of word finding, as well as for the patient's ability to shift from concept to concept, is a word fluency task similar to the one used in the animal-naming section of *The Assessment of Aphasia and Related Disorders*.[2] The patient is asked to list all animals, cars, trees, or other category of related nouns that can be recalled in one minute. Once again the examiner is allowed to assess not only verbal expression, but some of the patient's higher cognitive processes such as recall by category.

Performance on writing tasks is affected by the patient's ability to use visual-motor-perceptual skills as well as the language modalities. All responses must be interpreted with this in mind. The assessment of written expression begins by having the patient write his or her name. It should be recognized that this task is highly automatic and may be preserved even in the presence of severe dysgraphia. How-

Table 7–2 Selected Tasks Used To Assess Language Expression

Language	Item or Task
Spoken	
Naming	Common objects (key, pencil, and coin).
	Articles of clothing (tie, belt, and button).
	Body parts (eye, ear, and thumb).
Object description	What color is this (paper and comb)?
	What is this made of (key and coin)?
	What shape is this (coin and paper)?
Name object parts	Watch crystal.
	Watch stem.
	Watch band.
	Watch buckle.
Descriptive language	Tell me everything you can about this (key, pencil, and coin).
	Tell me the definition of these words (bark, island, and history).
Written	
Automatic	Write your name.
Words to dictation	Write: (has, spoon, time, and business).
Sentence to dictation	Write: (We have a new car.)
	(The weather becomes cold in winter.)
Descriptive paragraph	Describe this picture (use an action picture).
	Judge: syntax, spelling, number of ideas, and organization of thoughts.

ever, the task does allow the examiner to develop some insight into the patient's fine motor skill and the ability to use tools. The patient should then be asked to write words to dictation and, if successful, a series of sentences increasing in length and difficulty. In a full examination, the patient also should be asked to write a descriptive paragraph that can be assessed for syntax, spelling, development of relevant ideas, and language organization. The patient's education must be considered in the interpretation of any written errors.

Auditory Memory

The assessment of auditory memory almost always involves other input and processing modalities. For example, the examiner traditionally assesses auditory memory by the use of language input that requires comprehension. Since this has been previously assessed, the examiner will have some hypotheses regarding a patient's ability to retain auditory stimuli. Patients who are unable to comprehend one- and two-step tasks already have defined the limits of their memory. The other modality frequently utilized during the assessment of auditory memory is verbal expression. Again, the patient who is unable to express simple concepts will be unable to perform on subtests requiring expressive output. Therefore, auditory memory tests will have to be manipulated to require another output modality, such as serial pointing or a sequence of commands requiring gross motor execution.

In general, memory is divided into at least three basic types, differentiated by the time span between the stimulus presentation or memory recording and the recall event. Immediate, recent, and remote memory are the three terms most commonly used. However, the time span for each of these is vague and, in practical terms, they do not necessarily refer to three separate neurologic processes for the recall of memory traces. Immediate memory refers to recall of stimuli with an interval of only a few seconds. The repetition of digits, repeating sentences, following multistage commands, and recall of facts from auditorily presented stories of paragraph length are all tasks that require immediate memory. Table 7–3 provides examples of items that can be used to assess immediate auditory memory.

When the interval between stimulus presentation and recall is a matter of minutes, hours, or days it is referred to as recent memory. Clinically, this intermediate stage of recall is assessed by administering "paired associate learning" tasks (see the example in Exhibit 7–2) or delayed word recall. In the delayed recall task, Strub and Black[3] suggest using the words "brown," "honesty," "tulip," and "eyedropper" because of their semantic and phonemic diversity. In this examination the patient is told to remember the four words that will be tested in a few minutes. To ensure that the patient has heard the words, he or she should repeat them once immediately after the presentation. The examiner then continues with other aspects of the evaluation and after a 5-minute delay asks the patient to recall the four

---

Table 7–3 Selected Tasks Used To Assess Immediate Auditory Memory

Repetition of	7-4	3-9
digits	6-1-8	9-7-4
	3-1-7-8	5-2-8-3
	2-1-4-6-3	6-8-4-3-1
	4-1-9-8-7-2	1-6-3-5-8-4
	8-6-1-9-5-3-7	7-2-9-6-1-8-5
Repetition of	Will you call me later?	
sentences	She walks up five flights of stairs.	
	Let's get ready so we can catch the first bus.	
	I would like to order a roast beef sandwich	
	with fries and a soft drink.	
Multistage commands	See language comprehension tasks	
Recall of facts	A.R. Dull / an 87 year old / farmer / from King	
from a story	County / Georgia / bought an old, used tractor / at	
	the annual auction / last winter. / The first time he	
	used it / the brakes didn't work / and he ran into a	
	tree / down by the pond. / His son, / Craig, / found	
	him dazed / sitting in the field. / He loaded him / into	
	his pickup truck / and drove him nine miles / to	
	Riverton Hospital / where the doctor said he had a	
	concussion. Five days later / he was fully recovered /	
	and had returned to plowing the field, / but this time	
	with a new rig.	

Exhibit 7–2 Selected Tasks Used To Assess Auditory Associate Learning

Instructions: Explain that the subject is to remember the word pairs, some easy and some difficult. Read the presentation list at a rate of one word per second, pause for 5 seconds, and present the recall list. If a subject's response is incorrect, the subject cannot recall the paired word, or the subject gives no response for 10 seconds, the examiner supplies the correct response.

Presentation Lists

1	2	3
Spring - Closet	Plane - Signal	Left - Right
Left - Right	Tree - Limb	Plane - Signal
Plane - Signal	Spring - Closet	Tree - Limb
Tree - Limb	Left - Right	Spring - Closet

Recall List

1	2	3
Plane _____	Left _____	Tree _____
Left _____	Plane _____	Spring _____
Spring _____	Tree _____	Plane _____
Tree _____	Spring _____	Left _____

Score: Easy paired associates recalled _____
Difficult paired associates recalled _____

words. In some cases the patient may be tested again at delay intervals of 10 and 30 minutes.

Remote memory traditionally refers to the recollection of facts and memory traces from previous months and years. Again, the exact span of memory is vague. To some degree remote memory is assessed during the orientation evaluation. It should be recognized, however, that to remain oriented a patient must not only recall historical information but also relate the facts to more recent recall. Some examiners use questions such as, "Who is the president?" "Who was the last president?" "When was World War II?" or "Name four presidents during the 1900s," to assess remote memory.[4]

Visual-Motor-Perception

A mistake frequently made by speech/language pathologists is to form a diagnostic impression based upon a mental status examination that has not included nonlanguage modalities. Aphasia, as previously described, is not just a language impairment but a specific language disorder that occurs in patients who do not have signs of dementia or generalized cognitive dysfunction. In part it is the necessity to rule out nonaphasic disabilities with accompanying disorders of communication that provides the greatest justification for proceeding with a complete mental status examination. Even for the patient who has been accurately diagnosed as having aphasia, the speech/language pathologist is obliged to determine the patient's potential for learning through nonlanguage modalities (e.g., demonstration, motor exploration, and physical manipulation) because communication should include how the patient relates to the environment through every sensory and motor system.

Visual-motor-perception is the mental process that allows an individual to construct. It involves the integration of a number of nonverbal cognitive functions that require a patient to receive information visually, make perceptual judgments based on that information, and plan and execute motor performance based on current and past experience with that information. Neurologically, the process involves integration of the occipital, parietal, and frontal lobes. Because it requires diffuse cortical areas functioning together to perform constructional tasks, visual-motor-perceptual abilities can be disrupted in mild forms of brain damage.[5] Table 7–4 outlines tasks that can be used to assess visual-motor-perceptual function.

The evaluation of visual-motor-perception (constructional praxis) may begin with paper and pencil tasks that require the patient to reproduce simple line drawings after the examiner's model. A circle, diamond, cross, and daisy are examples of two-dimensional drawings that can be used to begin this assessment. When these are successfully reproduced the examination can proceed to the reproduction of three-dimensional shapes such as a cube, house, and pipe. The free drawing of a Christmas tree or clock face, complete with numbers, also is useful and may help to detect or confirm the presence of unilateral neglect. Two-dimensional block designs, such as those included on the *Wechsler Intelligence Scale for Children*[6] or the *Wechsler Adult Intelligence Scale*[7] are useful in eliciting evidence of constructional impairment. Three-dimensional block constructions also should be included in a complete battery of tests to confirm disturbances in constructional praxis and to quantify abilities.

Table 7–4 Selected Tasks Used To Assess Visual-Motor-Perception

Skill Evaluated	Example
2 dimensional line drawings	circle diamond cross daisy
3 dimensional line drawings	cube house pipe
Free Drawings	Christmas tree clock face
2 dimensional colored block designs	WISC WAIS
3 dimensional block construction	Hiskey-Nebraska

Visual-Motor-Memory

Visual memory modalities, like auditory memory, can be broken down into immediate, recent, and remote recall. Just as auditory memory is largely dependent on language comprehension, so visual-motor-memory is dependent on visual-motor-perception. Evaluation of this important modality (outlined in Table 7–5) may begin by having the patient reproduce simple line drawings of increasing complexity and detail from memory. The examiner provides the patient with a stimulus card using drawings such as those included in the Wechsler Memory Scale.[8] The patient is allowed to study the card for five seconds and then after a five-second delay is asked to reproduce the drawing. Other tests include demonstrated sequential motor tasks, such as the Knox's Cube Test.[9] In this test the examiner taps an increasingly complex series of up to four blocks in a variable sequence that the patient must imitate. Visual attention span also can be measured by a picture recall test such as that used in the Hiskey-Nebraska battery.[10] In this test the patient is shown a series of pictured items, increasing in number, for a set exposure time of three seconds per picture, and asked to recall and select the same pictures from an array of similar stimuli.

Ideation/Higher Cognitive Functions

At this point the examination has included the major input and output modalities of attention, language, construction, and memory. Acting together, these processes allow an individual to communicate and perform basic functions in relating to the environment. The examination is incomplete, however, unless the clinician assesses the patient's ability to manipulate these basic learning modalities in order to demonstrate abstract thinking and problem-solving ability. Examples of these higher cognitive functions are provided in Table 7–6.

Abstract thinking can be evaluated by having the patient interpret proverbs. Examples include "Don't judge a book by its cover," "The mouse that has but one hole is easily taken," "Let sleeping dogs lie," or "People who live in glass houses shouldn't throw stones." In each case the examiner assesses the patient's response

---

Table 7–5 Selected Tasks Used To Assess Visual-Motor-Memory

Skill Evaluated	Example
Drawing from Memory	Wechsler Memory Scale[8]
Sequential Motor Memory	Knox's Cube Test[9]
Picture Recall	Hiskey-Nebraska[10]

Table 7–6 Selected Tasks Used To Assess Higher Cognitive Functions

Skill Evaluated	Example
Abstract thinking	Proverbs (Don't judge a book by its cover) (The mouse that has but one hole is easily taken) (Let sleeping dogs lie) (People who live in glass houses shouldn't throw stones)
Problem solving	Picture associations (Hiskey-Nebraska) Picture analogies (Hiskey-Nebraska)
Calculations	13 + 5 = 7 + 36 = 14 − 5 = 13 − 8 = 6 × 9 = 3 × 8 = 56 ÷ 8 = 42 ÷ 7 =
Spatial reasoning	Raven Coloured Progressive Matrices
Fund of information	1. How many hours in a day? 2. What does the heart do? 3. Name six presidents. 4. Where is Denmark? 5. How far is it from New York to Seattle? 6. Why do we wear light colored clothes in the summer? 7. What is the capital of Venezuela? 8. What is fog? 9. Who wrote Hamlet? 10. What is the Vatican?

regarding the ability of the patient to think beyond the concrete meaning of each item. Typical concrete responses include the patient paraphrasing the proverbs or statements such as, "Yes, books do have covers," or "Dogs might bite if you wake them." Although some examiners have attempted to quantify responses, in the final assessment the examiner must make a subjective assessment of the patient's response. More objective tests, such as the Pictorial Associations and Pictorial Analogies subtests from the Hiskey-Nebraska battery, are excellent tools. They require no verbal instructions and can be administered easily to the language-impaired patient.[11]

Problem-solving tasks, such as simple calculations evaluating addition, subtraction, multiplication, and division, should be included in any complete battery. Raven's *Coloured Progressive Matrices* is a good tool when used to evaluate spatial reasoning ability.[12]

Some examiners include "fund of information" in their assessment of higher cognitive functions. Such questions are helpful in certain cases where more information is needed about general intelligence, education, and social exposure.

SUMMARY

The diagnostic workup of mental status is an exciting process and requires as much art as it does science. A patient's failure on any given subtest should lead the examiner to ask why. In fact, the entire diagnostic process is a series of questions that allows the clinician to focus on an explanation for the patient's disabilities.

When medically oriented speech/language pathologists have completed examinations that include all of the facets of mental status described in this chapter, they will be able to make statements regarding the nature of patients' communication impairments, whether they stem from motor involvement or language dysfunction. They will be able to specify whether impairments are specific to the language modalities or just single components of generalized cognitive dysfunctions. They should be in a position to make statements regarding prognoses for the learning potential of language-impaired patients in a comprehensive rehabilitation program. They can describe communication behaviors of other brain-damaged patients and recommend the learning modalities that are most likely to be effective in remediation. Clinicians who approach examinations with this orientation become valuable members of a team and contribute to the rehabilitation process in the most complete sense.

In the final analysis, the results of the mental status assessment are combined with the data from the review of the medical record, the interview and history obtained from significant others, pertinent clinical observations, and the physical examination. No single component of the assessment process should define the diagnosis of a patient. Rather, the sum of all available data should lead the speech/language pathologist to a summary assessment.

NOTES

1. Graham Teasdale and Bryan Jennett, "Assessment of Coma and Impaired Consciousness," *Lancet* 12 (July 13, 1974):81–84.

2. Harold Goodglass and Edith Kaplan, *The Assessment of Aphasia and Related Disorders* (Philadelphia: Lea & Febiger, 1983).

3. Richard L. Strub and William F. Black, *The Mental Status Examination in Neurology* (Philadelphia: F.A. Davis Co., 1977):68–69.

4. Ibid., 85.

5. Ibid., 108–09.

6. David Wechsler, *Wechsler Intelligence Scale for Children* (New York: The Psychological Corporation, 1949).

7. David Wechsler, *Wechsler Adult Intelligence Scale* (New York: The Psychological Corporation, 1955).

8. David Wechsler, "A Standardized Scale for Clinical Use," *Journal of Psychology* 19 (1945): 87–95.

9. Mark H. Stone and Benjamin D. Wright, *Knox's Cube Test* (Chicago: Stoelting Company, 1987).

10. Marshall S. Hiskey, *Hiskey-Nebraska Test of Learning Aptitude* (Lincoln, Nebr.: College View Printers, 1955).

11. Ibid.

12. J.C. Raven, *Coloured Progressive Matrices* (London: H.K. Lewis and Company Ltd., 1962).

Part III

Managing Clinical Problems

Chapter 8

Reporting the Findings

INTRODUCTION

The speech/language pathologist must think in a consistently logical, orderly fashion in order to reach a valid diagnostic conclusion, regardless of the specific consult request or the communication problem encountered. The preliminary data must be gathered by reviewing the medical record and conducting all interviews that are appropriate. The examination must proceed with attention to clinical observations, physical findings, and a mental status assessment. With experience, the speech/language pathologist will develop flexibility that allows the diagnostic workup to proceed even when one or more of the elements are unavoidably eliminated. In the day-to-day world of a medical center, misplaced medical records, misinformation in interviews and medical charts, and uncooperative patient behavior should not prevent the speech/language pathologist from accumulating and integrating the available information to reach at least a tentative diagnostic conclusion.

The speech/language pathologist's report, whether verbal or written, should reflect systematic diagnostic thinking. The best type of report will paint a verbal picture of a clinical case and lead the reader or listener through the collection of pertinent data to a logical diagnostic conclusion. Some beginning clinicians have difficulty gathering enough meaningful data to form complete clinical impressions. Others, when learning the methodology required for a complete diagnostic workup, tend to report too much data and force the reader or listener to lose focus on the pertinent findings. For example, the speech/language pathologist may obscure a clinical description of a brain-damaged patient's communication disorder by reporting the details of reflex testing and sensory examination. In most cases it would suffice to report that the examination was consistent with the patient's known neurologic impairment. With experience, the speech/language pathologist can learn to distinguish between the pertinent diagnostic information that should be used in a logical presentation and the irrelevant information. Even experienced clinicians occasionally err at the other extreme by reporting too few

243

facts and assuming incorrectly that the reader or listener will be able to close information gaps and reach the same logical diagnostic conclusion. The goal of reporting is to maintain a balance between reporting essential data and keeping reporting standards at a high level.

A well-organized, logical speech/language pathology report does more than merely list the observations and examination data, state a diagnostic conclusion, and describe a plan of action. The best report teaches readers or listeners about the specialty and orients them to the services that are provided. Some speech/language pathologists, by virtue of their reporting styles, generate in other health professionals an interest and enthusiasm for understanding communication disorders. For those working in teaching hospitals this aspect of reporting is invaluable. For those dependent on the respect of medical colleagues, this style of report writing can enhance the value of the service and increase the consultation rate.

The diagnostic process is not a simple procedure. It is more than assigning a label to an impairment; it includes the determination of a prognosis and the preliminary outline of treatment plans and recommendations. In many cases the process of attaching a diagnostic label to a set of symptoms is a straightforward matter that does not require creative thought. The clinical facts in these cases lead the clinician to a definitive, inescapable diagnostic impression (e.g., the patient suffered a left brain stroke, is minimally hemiplegic, has poor comprehension, is fluent with paraphasic errors, has no evidence of perceptual or other cognitive impairments: Wernicke's aphasia). Other clinical cases are challenging and tax the creative problem-solving skills of the clinician (e.g., the patient had a sudden loss of speech, no evidence of stroke, understands complex commands).

It would be surprising to find experienced clinicians who have not faced situations in which the facts failed to support a definitive diagnosis. While many find the diagnostic process to be an exciting and stimulating aspect of their clinical work, it is also the time when clinicians are most vulnerable. In a sense, one's professional reputation is dependent on accurate diagnoses. However, the threat of being wrong should not inhibit the right to provide an opinion. Even the most experienced clinicians sometimes are inaccurate in their diagnoses. If the clinician's thinking is clear and supported by known facts, the logical line of thought can be followed by other professionals. When a diagnostic conclusion remains elusive, the clinician should not be defensive, but rather offer several alternatives or be willing to state that no conclusion is possible with the amount or quality of data at hand. A plan for obtaining more data usually can be reported.

Even if the speech/language pathologist cannot provide a definitive diagnosis, in virtually every case an opinion or impression can be rendered. Statements such as "the patient cannot be evaluated" should be avoided. Some patients may not be capable or willing to respond to directions, commands, and other test requirements, but the speech/language pathologist can state an opinion based on the evaluation of historical data combined with observations of the patient's behavioral and physical characteristics. Even observations regarding the patient's lack of response to testing are important diagnostic clues. The assessment rendered may confirm an altered state of consciousness or some behavioral peculiarity. Confirming assessments are valued in the medical setting, and their importance should not go unrecognized.

The purpose of a report is to inform others of findings, conclusions, and plans. Consideration should be given to the person who will receive the report. For instance, greater detail in the assessment regarding the speech and language characteristics of a patient with Broca's aphasia and apraxia would be appropriate in a consult from a rheumatologist who probably is unfamiliar with this disorder, whereas the mention of Broca's aphasia and apraxia would suffice in response to most neurologists. The language used by the speech/language pathologist should not conflict with the vocabulary of the receiver. For example, when terms are applied that are not in general use by the receiving health professional, they should be defined within the context of the report. Because most speech/language pathologists are trained in programs outside of health sciences, their professional jargon may not be universally understood. This is evident in the use of acronyms for testing instruments, such as the ALPS, PICA, and WAB, and in combining terms like "pragmatics of language."

Each report should be concerned with what the receiver needs to know. If the consult was sent from a diagnostic service seeking an explanation for communication abnormalities, the report should emphasize the diagnosis. If the consulting service is concerned with rehabilitation, the report must address a plan of action and attempt to provide information that would allow a team of rehabilitation specialists to coordinate their efforts toward a common goal. If a medical service seeks the expertise of the speech/language pathologist to recommend a course of management, for example, the most appropriate method of nutritional management for a patient with swallowing dysfunction, the report should focus on a clear statement defining the patient's risk for oral intake and listing measures to minimize the chances for failure of the plan.

VERBAL CASE REPORTS

Verbal case reports can be given in a number of hospital circumstances. These may include formal team meetings, during rounds at the patient's bedside, an in-depth case conference presentation within or outside the department, and informal discussions with colleagues. In most situations, verbal reports should be no longer than three minutes. Therefore, the presenter must concentrate only on the most relevant information. Ideally the presentation should be done extemporaneously with reliance on only a few brief notes.

In general, a verbal report is a concise account of the patient's workup. The first element of the report is identifying information that may include the patient's name, age, sex, and other relevant social, economic, occupational, racial, ethnic, or religious facts. Name, age, and sex are obviously pertinent and should be listed at the outset in most verbal reports. The other data may or may not be pertinent in a given case. Social information as to whether a patient is married or unmarried, a hermit or living in a collective is important when the patient has a communicable disease, is unable to provide a history, or if discharge issues are relevant. Economic and occupational facts are equally relevant in some medical centers when considering discharge, occupationally related diseases, or the effect of a disability on the patient's future. Although race, religion, and ethnic background may be pertinent in a given case, such as with a dysphagic patient in determining food preference, these facts are not necessary in most verbal summary reports.

The second element of the verbal summary report is the patient's chief complaint (CC) and the circumstances of the patient's presentation for admission or examination. This usually is stated as the reason for referral by the speech/language pathologist. In problem-oriented medical records (see Chapter 4), the complaint is stated under "subjective" data. The complaint may be stated in the patient's own words or as a restatement of the consult information. The complaint should not be a definitive diagnosis, although it may be a restatement of the referral source's diagnostic impression. Most often it is a description of the problem and is not labeled.

The third essential element is the patient's medical history. There should be little attempt to be all-inclusive in a verbal summary report, but rather to give pertinent history that relates to the hospital admission and the current problem. If there is no pertinent history, it should be so stated (e.g., "the medical history is unremarkable," or "the patient was in his usual state of health"). When the clinician is unsure about the relevance of a historical fact, it is best left unstated. However, it should not be ignored. The clinician should maintain a list of all potentially relevant historical data, some of which will become significant after more examination data is available. The medical history also may include a report of any medications, allergies, surgeries, or other conditions that are potentially relevant to the current problem or complaint.

The fourth element in verbal reports is the objective data. Examination data should be presented in the same order that it was obtained. When an examiner has established a pattern of evaluation, it becomes easy to review the case orally in the same format. Pertinent clinical observations include the patient's orientation, if relevant; significant physical findings; and deficits in any sphere of mental status. The observations should be documented and presented verbally in a manner that allows the listener to form a mental image of the patient. Descriptors such as cachectic, emaciated, or disheveled allow the listener to develop a vivid mental impression of a sickly, malnourished patient. By describing orientation, the examiner allows the listener to recognize immediately conditions that have affected the patient's mental status and influenced behavior. Only those physical findings that are relevant to the complaint and have contributed to the eventual diagnosis should be reported. Interesting but irrelevant findings can be presented in another context. When mental status deficits are evident, the reporter should briefly outline and describe behaviors associated with the impaired learning modalities. This may be presented as a general statement regarding the patient's attention span; the ability to comprehend verbal expressions; expressive language functions, particularly spoken language; visual-spatial performance on copy-drawing tasks; and the ability to recall a fund of previously learned information. Elaboration of mental status findings may not be possible until a complete battery of tests can be administered and scored. Detailed mental status reports tend to be long and tedious and usually are not necessary when reporting to other health professionals. A preliminary report can be highlighted and made more meaningful by giving brief examples of the patient's language behaviors that are abnormal and by showing distorted drawings consistent with perceptual impairment when relevant.

The fifth element of the report, the examiner's diagnostic impression, should be supported by the objective data and lead the listener to understand the logic of the conclusion. Even in preliminary reports, alternative diagnoses can be offered when a definitive label is not possible. If this is the case, the plan that follows should indicate how a specific differential diagnosis will be made. In some cases the diagnostic impression is stated as a single word, for example, aphasia, dementia, dysarthria, or apraxia; in other cases the diagnostic impression may serve to describe behaviors without using a specific label. Even when a specific label is applicable, descriptive qualifiers may be used to specify the degree of severity or the unique characteristics. In some cases of aphasia, disorders may be characterized relative to the degree of fluency. Dysarthric speech may be specifically defined relative to its neuromuscular type, for example, spastic, flaccid, hypokinetic, hyperkinetic, ataxic, or combinations (spastic-flaccid or spastic-ataxic), and even finer distinctions (fast or slow hyperkinetic) may be indicated.

The sixth and final element in the verbal summary report is the plan or recommendations. Preliminary reports may state an intention to examine further, or to administer specific subtests or standard test batteries. If the diagnostic workup is complete and the conclusion definitive, a treatment plan may be specified. In some cases, the plan may include further specific psychometric or laboratory tests to be completed by the speech/language pathologist to verify or establish a diagnosis. In most cases, whether the problem can be treated or not, a management plan can be formulated and reported. This may include recommendations or suggestions given to other health professionals that will facilitate their interactions with the patient. It may be a management plan offered to the care providers for a patient with communication or swallowing impairments in order to help them prevent complications, such as a catastrophic reaction due to communication frustration or aspiration secondary to dysphagia.

A plan may include recommendations to the referral source suggesting further consultation with other specialists or disciplines. It is not appropriate for a speech/language pathologist or any consultant to refer a patient to another service without first having the approval of the original consulting service. Proper protocol is to recommend additional consultations to the referring physician, thereby making these consultations the responsibility of that physician. In some cases, the referring physician may not agree with the speech/language pathologist's recommendations. One service must maintain primary responsibility for a patient's care and coordinate all referrals to ensure that conflicting treatments and procedures are avoided.

The speech/language pathologist can consult with other services when the patient is not being followed by any physician-controlled service or when no service has primary responsibility.

A verbal report should be tailored to fit the circumstances in which it is presented. For instance, if time is a factor, the report obviously must be brief. If the report is a part of teaching rounds, it may need to be more didactic and detailed. The amount of detail and the length of the report are variables, but the organization should remain constant. Even verbal patient presentations that occur in spontaneous discussions should follow essentially the same format.

Comprehensive Verbal Report

The sample presentation that follows is based on an initial preliminary examination. It is intended for a rehabilitation team panel that meets to consider new admissions for a rehabilitation unit. In addition to a speech/language pathologist, the team includes an attending and resident physician in rehabilitation medicine, a nurse, an occupational therapist, a physical therapist, a psychologist, a social worker, and a vocational rehabilitation specialist. Any team member may present a patient for consideration of admission to the unit.

The profile of the learning modalities testing for the patient described below is illustrated in Figure 8–1.

T.C. is a 69-year-old retired, self-employed printer who was described as being in excellent health until 2 weeks prior to admission when he experienced intermittent incoordination of the right upper extremity. On the morning of admission he had an onset of right hemiplegia and inability to speak. Although his neurologic workup is continuing, his provisional diagnosis is a left MCA thrombosis. Speech/language pathology was initially consulted by Neurology to evaluate his swallowing and speech functions. The examination was completed yesterday and we are recommending him for transfer to the Rehabilitation Unit.

We found him to be alert and cooperative, and judged him to be oriented to time and place by his yes/no gestural responses. He continues to have a right hemiplegia that includes a mild central facial weakness on the right. He has adequate strength in the tongue, palate, pharynx, and larynx to support both speech and swallowing. He is having no difficulty with his swallow and is maintaining his weight. He has a left prosthetic eye, but for purposes of testing vision this was not a problem. There was no evidence of a field cut. Optokinetic nystagmus reflexes were elicited from both directions, and he did not show extinction with double simultaneous stimulation visually or tactually.

His major loss is expressive language. He had no automatic speech during the examination, and he was unable to imitate syllables or sounds. Voice on command was effortful and had a short duration. Accompanying his total loss of verbal expression was an inability to organize gestures to demonstrate the use of common objects. Writing was limited to printing his name and refusal to attempt other words. In comprehension tasks he was able to perform up to two-step serial pointing tasks using common objects, and he could read printed words and match them with the correct object. He does not comprehend directions beyond this one- and two-word level.

His performance on nonlanguage tasks was in dramatic contrast to his language impairment. He copied two- and three-dimensional drawings accurately, even when reproducing them from memory. His free drawings were well executed considering his use of the nondominant hand. He followed demonstrated sequential motor acts up to four steps.

Our assessment suggests that Mr. C's findings are consistent with his diagnosis of left CVA leaving him with a residual aphasia. During this acute phase he has profound deficits in all expressive modalities and severe deficits in language comprehension. It is

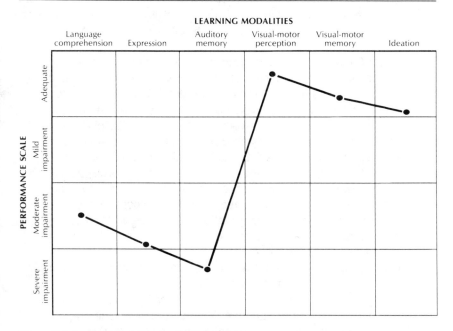

Figure 8–1 Learning Modalities Profile (Patient T.C.).

significant that the patient has retained good judgment and visual-motor-perceptual skills. He has shown that he can learn by observing a demonstration of motor acts.

We recommend Mr. C to the Rehabilitation Unit as a good candidate to learn compensatory motor skills and to benefit from language treatment. We recommend that initial attempts at training motor skills emphasize the use of demonstration as the method of choice for teaching. During this acute phase, verbal instructions should be minimized and those that must be provided should be limited to one or two words accompanied by demonstration or physical prompting. To prevent his frustration at not being able to speak, his needs should be anticipated and met as part of a routine schedule. Our service plans to provide counseling and family education for his wife. He is scheduled for further testing using standard language tests in order to document baseline functions, and we will initiate intensive language treatment for Mr. C.

Verbal Consultation

The following sample presentation is intended as a verbal consultation with senior otolaryngology residents to request their examination of a patient who is currently being seen in the speech/language pathology clinic. The original consult was sent by a medical clinic; therefore, the referring physician's permission was obtained prior to initiating the consultation with otolaryngology.

T.M. is a 55-year-old male referred to speech/language pathology from the outpatient admitting clinic to provide examination and recommendations related to swallowing difficulties. He presented to the admitting clinic claiming that he had a stroke about one month ago that led to a 10-lb weight loss. He attributes his loss of weight to swallowing difficulty and specifically describes food sticking in his throat. He has COPD that limits his ambulation distance, a 40-year smoking history, and a high intake of ETOH. His specific complaint is for dysphagia of solids greater than liquids, a sensation of intermittent obstruction at the level of the cervical esophagus, and occasional oral regurgitation of undigested food occurring within an hour after a meal. These complaints are unusual for dysphagia related to a stroke.

Our physical examination was completely unremarkable, with no signs of weakness or incoordination of his facial, oral, pharyngeal, or laryngeal muscles. His speech was clearly articulated and his voice unremarkable. He had a motion radiographic swallow study prior to his examination in our clinic. We reviewed this with the radiology resident, and we both agreed that the initiation of his oral and pharyngeal swallow was delayed and he had mild esophageal dysmotility. However, these findings were insufficient to account for this degree of weight loss and his specific complaints. It also was observed on this study that the apex of his left pyriform sinus, when compared to the right side, was blunted. Considering Mr. M's complaints, his weight loss, the lack of evidence to support a neurologic etiology for his difficulty, and the asymmetry in his pyriform sinuses, we would appreciate your evaluation.

Verbal Management Plan

The following sample presentation is intended for a nursing care unit team regarding a patient being transferred from an acute care ward. The team is composed of a nursing supervisor, a nurse specialist in geriatrics, and a social worker. The purpose of the presentation is to prepare the care providers in the unit for this individual patient's needs.

W.S. is a 66-year-old Asian male who is being transferred from the Neurology Service. He was brought into the hospital 3 weeks ago by his family who reported increased confusion and agitation. The patient has a prior diagnosis of hypertensive encephalopathy and has been previously determined to have dementia. According to his son, the patient is not compliant with his antihypertensive medications.

Speech/language pathology was consulted by Neurology to evaluate his swallowing because he was refusing to eat. Our examination found him to be cachectic and disheveled, disoriented, and verbally uncooperative. Physically he has adequate strength in all muscles necessary for chewing, swallowing, and airway protection. His speech is clear in spite of his confused language. He was able to drink juice without difficulty, but became uncooperative when offered food from the tray. He initially was placed on a liquid formula diet that he drank, and he began to gain weight. We encouraged his son to bring him traditional ethnic food from home and the patient ate this willingly and without difficulty. However, when he is interrupted during a meal by distractions he stops eating and does not resume. Because of his demonstrated judgment and motor planning difficulties, the patient does tend to overload his mouth and choke, then discontinues the meal.

It is recommended that he receive standby supervision during meals in order to avoid problems related to his judgment. The dietitian should speak with the patient's family and plan a diet that will be most appealing and nutritionally appropriate. Conversation, television, and patient care activities should be avoided during meals to prevent the distractions that interfere with his function. To help him get started with eating and other motor acts, give him simple verbal instructions in a stepwise fashion. We believe he will function well with the routine and supervised activities provided in the Nursing Care Unit.

WRITTEN CONSULTATION REPORTS

Written speech/language pathology reports serve at least three functions: (1) they become a part of the patient's permanent medical-legal record, (2) they communicate to the referral source the result of a consultation, and (3) they teach other health professionals about speech/language pathology.

The speech/language pathologist, like all health professionals who make entries into the medical record, must remain cognizant of the fact that these reports become part of a permanent medical-legal document. Every entry into the medical record potentially can be subpoenaed for presentation in a court of law. The clinicians who enter data, impressions, and plans must be accountable for their content and validity.

It is important to the continuity of patient care that the reply to a written consult request be made within 48 hours. Speech/language pathologists may argue that they cannot finish an evaluation in that period of time, but they need to streamline their procedures and approaches. Verbal consultation requests often require at least a preliminary report the same day. Prompt responses that assist the physician in the patient's care help to build strong relationships.

The format of written consultation reports will vary depending on the nature of the setting and the policies of the local medical center or service. However, the essential elements of identifying information, presenting complaint, objective data from the examination, clinical impression, and recommendations should be included in every case. Ideally, the presentation should illustrate to the reader the logical diagnostic sequence that allowed the clinician to develop diagnostic hypotheses, gather the necessary objective data, reach the appropriate clinical impression, and state recommendations. When organized in this fashion, reports will achieve their third function of educating the reader.

Consultation reports can strengthen ties between speech/language pathologists and their medical colleagues. When appropriate, the clinician should compliment other health professionals by commenting on the thoroughness of a workup or the quality of care a patient has received. Such remarks will build strong relationships. Speech/language pathologists who have experienced a note of appreciation for one of their reports recognize the value of a compliment, particularly one from a respected physician.

The recommendations in the consultation report should include those that the reader needs to know. These are management care suggestions that should be communicated to the care providers, recommendations made for further consultations or procedures, and the general plans of the speech/language pathologist. In most instances, consultation reports do not need to detail the plan for speech/language pathology treatment, but should indicate the major goals, frequency of planned treatment sessions, and the anticipated length of treatment if known.

Perhaps the greatest obstacle in preparing good written reports is deciding how much detail is necessary to present the facts in a logical but concise manner. Experience suggests that busy physicians rarely read a lengthy report, especially if the writer chooses to detail the result of test scores. Usually, physicians focus on the clinical impression (assessment) and on the plan. Therefore, it is necessary to be particularly thorough and concise in these two sections. As with so many aspects of clinical practice, the preparation of written consultation reports requires appropriate clinical judgment and the knowledge that is gained by experience. The examples that follow represent several reporting styles, but the basic organization remains constant.

Reports Describing Language and Cognitive Disorders

The first example is a response to a rehabilitation medicine consult regarding a new inpatient. Figure 8–2 summarizes the learning modalities profile of this pa-

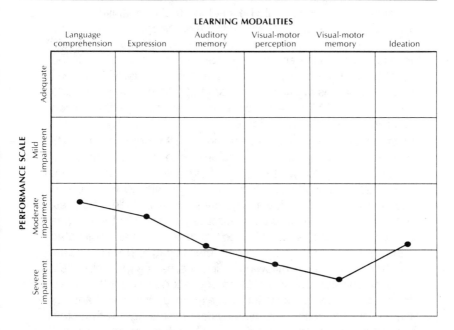

Figure 8–2 Learning Modalities Profile (Patient with Generalized Cognitive Dysfunction Including Severe Language Impairments).

tient, showing generalized cognitive dysfunction that includes severe language impairments. The patient does not fit the specific diagnosis of aphasia using its operational definition described previously (impairment of all language modalities but preservation of the ability to learn through nonlanguage modalities). The report communicates a picture of a patient (1) who is unable to use any language modality for the expression of basic needs, (2) who cannot reliably comprehend the language of others, and (3) who is not likely to benefit from a therapist's demonstration of motor actions in order to learn compensatory motor skills. The report also answers a question posed by the consult (is he speaking a foreign language?) by explaining the significance of the patient's verbal behavior.

Consult: 59-year-old white male 3 months S/P left CVA with right hemiparesis and aphasia. Is professional singer and has had previous "music therapy" to help speech. Family claims he has reverted to speaking a foreign language, possibly Scandinavian. Please explain.

Provisional Diagnosis: Aphasia

Data Base: Age: 59. Address: Willapa, WA. Social resources: Lives with wife, has five grown children and five residing in home. Socioeconomic factors: Patient teaches voice in community college; wife employed as a preschool teacher. Health history: Patient transferred from community hospital for stroke rehabilitation. He was in his usual state of health until 3 months ago when he had a sudden onset of right hemiplegia and dense aphasia. His current hospital course has been complicated by thrombophlebitis of the right LE, and he is being treated with anticoagulants. His previous medical history is significant for osteoarthritis of both knees and hypertension. CAT scan shows a large left frontoparietal lesion consistent with MCA occlusion.

Examination: The patient was examined on this day in the speech/language pathology clinic. He was unable to relate any history or respond reliably to questions requiring yes/no responses. The family has been unavailable to provide further history. He was alert and cooperative. Significant physical findings included the presence of a suck reflex and a hyperactive jaw jerk. His tongue was strong to resistance and midline on protrusion. His palate elevated in the midline and his pharynx contracted to gag bilaterally. The patient had no obvious swallowing difficulties, having good laryngeal elevation on reflex swallow. He had a questionable right visual field defect and showed extinction visually on double simultaneous stimulation. Extinction also was evident on the right with tactual stimulation to both lower extremities. Optokinetic nystagmus was elicited from his left, but was absent coming from his right side.

On learning modality tests the patient maintained good attention to all tasks. He showed an inability to respond reliably on single-stage commands of pointing to common objects. He was unable to follow spoken commands involving the identification of body parts or to point to items in the room. He was unable to read printed words in order to match the word with its corresponding object. The patient's verbal responses were characterized by jargonlike expressions that had no association with the intended symbol. He tended to connect his jargon utterances with lilting intonational patterns that gave the impression of a Scandinavian language. However, there was no consistency or structure to these vocalizations, and they were without meaning. The patient produced this same jargon when presented with common objects. He did have some intelligible, clearly articulated automatic expressions consisting of social greetings, counting, and swearing. The patient was able to repeat words to imitation, but not whole phrases. The patient was not able to write his name, but perseverated with the letter "t" on all attempts. On nonverbal tasks the patient was unable to copy simple geometric forms, producing only incomplete distortions. He had marked visual-perceptual impairment including problems of spatial judgment noted on block building and design tasks. He could not stack three blocks when given a picture example. The patient was unable to follow even two-step demonstrated motor acts with any degree of consistency. Due to a lack of comprehension of the task, the patient was unable to perform any simple pictorial associations and could not do simple calculations.

Impression: The patient has generalized cognitive deficits that include severe language impairments crossing all modalities of expression and reception. The patient's examination is most consistent with diffuse, rather than focal, deficits. Combined with the initial severity and large lesion, the patient's prognosis for communication recovery is poor.

Plans and Recommendations: (1) Speech/language pathology will follow the patient on a regular basis and report any changes in his learning or communication functions. He will be seen daily for short (15-minute) individual sessions and included in a language treatment group. (2) The patient's family will be counseled regarding the extent of his deficits and management recommendations. His wife will attend spouse group to help her adjust to the changes occurring in their home. (3) At this time, the patient's needs should be anticipated and met on a routine and unchanging schedule. His responses to questions requiring yes/no answers should be considered unreliable. Demonstration and physical manipulation are recommended as methods of directing him in motor tasks. When he responds correctly, immediate positive reinforcement should be provided through facial expression, tone of voice, and touch.

When a rehabilitation team becomes accustomed to the learning modalities and communication evaluation available from speech/language pathologists, their input may be sought to describe behaviors and recommend management for patients with other neurological dysfunctions. The right brain-impaired patient, for example, is difficult for many rehabilitation specialists to treat. The speech/language pathologist's evaluation may help to explain the dysfunction and suggest methods of using available language modalities for teaching new skills or managing the patient's behavior in spite of chronic impairments. In the following report a patient with a right brain cerebral vascular accident was evaluated and described to the consulting rehabilitation medicine physician. The patient's learning modalities profile is illustrated in Figure 8–3.

Consult: 60-year-old S/P right CVA and left hemiplegia. Left visual field cut and perceptual problems interfere with self-care. Please recommend best methods for training. Looks like excellent candidate for return to independent living.

Provisional Diagnosis: Right CVA, left homonymous hemianopia.

Data Base: Age: 60. Address: Chuckanut Bay, WA. Social resources: Divorced, living alone. Socioeconomic factors: Social security disability retirement, taking classes at community college in literature. Health history: Patient disabled due to industrial accident resulting in a back injury. According to the patient's neighbor, he had been functioning independently until 6 weeks ago when he had a sudden onset of left hemiplegia. The neighbor brought him to the medical center where he was found to be in atrial fibrillation. He was successfully cardioverted, but was believed to have thrown emboli resulting in a completed right brain CVA. He has AODM controlled by diet. His hospital course was uneventful and he was transferred to the Rehabilitation Medicine unit.

Examination: The patient was evaluated over the last 2 days in the speech/language clinic. He was alert, cooperative, and completely oriented to person, place, time, and the circumstances of his hospitalization. His affect was flat, and he appeared unconcerned about his hemiplegia, stating that his left side "just got lost in the confusion." He was noted to have food covering the front of his robe and on the left side of his face. He denied any problems related to performing activities of daily living. Physical findings were consistent with his diagnosed right CVA. He had minor weakness in the muscles of speech and swallowing on the left side, but no impairment in these functions. There were no pathologic re-

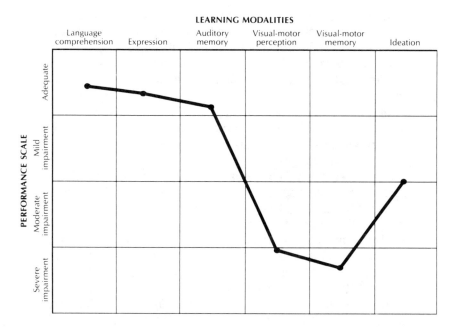

Figure 8–3 Learning Modalities Profile (Patient with Right Brain Cerebral Vascular Accident).

flexes observed. Optokinetic nystagmus reflexes, which are not affected by a homonymous hemianopia, were absent from his left side and present from his right. He showed extinction to double simultaneous stimulation on the left for both visual and tactual stimuli.

He followed multistage spoken commands correctly except when they required him to attend to stimuli placed in his left visual field. He was able to read single words, but failed to follow written directions because he neglected words printed on the left half of stimulus cards. His use of spoken language was entirely within normal limits and he used a sophisticated vocabulary. On a word fluency task he recited 26 animals in 1 minute. His intonational patterns were flat and monotonous. His writing was accurate in spelling, syntax, and idea formulation; however, consistent with his left neglect he wrote only on the right side of the page and failed to complete some letters. He demonstrated excellent auditory memory for recall of facts from stories and learned paired associate words after two trials. In nonlanguage visual-motor-perceptual tasks the patient's performance was grossly impaired. He could not copy the simplest drawings, consistently neglecting the left side. On a free drawing of a clock face he drew an incomplete circle and placed numbers on the right side only. He could not imitate demonstrated motor acts such as block tapping. He had a good fund of knowledge, could solve verbal analogies, and could do mental calculations. His interpretation of proverbs was concrete, and he could not explain common idioms, for example, "face the music."

Assessment: Severe visual-motor-perceptual disorder consistent with right brain pathology. All motor performance affected by left neglect. Affective communication impairment. Speech production is 100 percent intelligible.

This patient's excellent verbal abilities are misleading with regard to his ability to carry out motor tasks. He is able to recall and recite previously taught verbal instructions, but he cannot carry out the plan. For example, he can describe step by step how to make a safe transfer, but does not follow these same steps. His left neglect makes him unsafe. For example, he "lost" his left arm and it became entangled in the spokes of his wheelchair. Although he expressed pain he could not find the source.

Plan/Suggestions: (1) He requires verbal directions each time he is expected to perform a motor act in order to assist him in initiating the task and continuing in a safe manner. (2) At this time he will require supervision of all potentially dangerous functions (e.g., smoking, shaving, using hot water, and taking medications). He has numerous burns on his robe giving evidence to his neglect, yet he tried to convince the examiner that he was safe to smoke alone. Discharge planning must take into account his need for a closely supervised living environment. (3) With his present left neglect he will not benefit from written cues to help him organize motor functions. (4) While he remains an inpatient, the speech/language pathologist will check the patient on a twice-weekly basis to assess any change in his ability to integrate sensory input from his left side. (5) Information provided to the patient should be stated in concrete terms, avoiding idioms, facetiousness, and other subtleties of language. (6) Until, and unless, there are changes in his neurologic status, his needs should be anticipated and his schedule should remain regimented.

Reports Describing a Differential Diagnosis

Some consults will be requests to specify a diagnosis for the speech, language, or swallow impairment. Defining the specific pathology from the speech/language pathologist's perspective may contribute to the patient's overall medical diagnosis. In the example that follows the speech diagnosis is one of the factors that will be considered before the patient and his family are informed about the specific nature of his condition.

Consult: Patient with a history of CVA's x 3 with dysarthria and dysphagia. EMG suggestive of motor neuron disease. Question of speech pattern compatible with stroke or ALS?

Provisional Diagnosis: Multiple CVA's, R/O ALS.

Data Base: Age: 78. Address: Port Ludlow, WA. Social resources: Lives with his wife in a retirement center. Socioeconomic factors: Retired lawyer with excellent pension. Health history: The patient and his wife describe a series of at least three CVA's affecting both the right and left side of his body occurring about 7 years ago. His speech was initially lost, but came back to the present state within 6 months after the last CVA. He describes a minor problem when swallowing pills, but it is unchanged. He has well-controlled hypertension and AODM. He was referred to RMS for ambulation problems that are increasing.

Examination: Patient was alert, oriented, and had good language organization. He answered questions slowly, but accurately. Screening of mental functions showed the ability to spell words forward and backward, abstractly interpret proverbs, count by 7's, recall 3 of 3 words after 3 minutes, recall the last eight presidents, and copy a cross and cube without distortion. His speech was highly intelligible, but somewhat slow in articulation with imprecision of consonants and mild nasal resonance quality. His voice is slightly strained, and he was slow in all articulation and voicing diadochokinetic activities.

In addition to his previously described spastic quadraparesis, physical findings included a minimal right central facial droop. Positive pathologic suck and jaw jerk reflexes were elicited. His tongue was strong to resistance, midline on protrusion, and no fasciculations were seen. Lateral movements of the tongue were performed slowly and lacked smoothness. His palate and pharynx contracted bilaterally and equally to gag. His vocal cords were mobile, and minor pooling was noted in his valleculae and pyriform sinuses (also reported on otolaryngology consult 5 years ago). His larynx elevated briskly on swallowing.

Assessment: Spastic dysarthria. Although this pattern of speech is sometimes found in patients with progressive motor neuron disease, like ALS, it usually is combined with flaccid components. This patient's speech is slow and imprecise, but the muscles themselves are strong to resistance and no atrophy was evident clinically. Spastic dysarthria such as this is due to bilateral UMN impairment, and bilateral strokes are a common etiology for this. Since language and mentation were not impaired and there were no cranial nerve findings, his speech and language findings are consistent with disease in the subcortex or midbrain. Although motor neuron disease cannot be ruled out, his dysarthria and all physical findings can be attributed to his documented cerebral vascular accidents.

Plan: (1) Recommend a re-examination by speech/language pathology in 6 weeks in order to determine whether there is any progression of symptoms. Objective baseline measures, including a speech recording, intelligibility measure, vital capacity, prolonged phonation time, and diadochokinetic rates, will be maintained for comparison. (2) Suggestions were provided for both the patient and his wife to help him swallow pills. By placing the pills on his posterior tongue and keeping his neck flexed while swallowing, he was able to swallow successfully all medications currently prescribed.

In the second example of a report written to describe a differential diagnosis, the patient was referred for evaluation and treatment of a specific problem, voice. During the course of the evaluation, the findings suggested an alternative diagnosis that was then communicated to the referring otolaryngologist together with associated recommendations. The written consultation report should not obviate the need for a verbal interchange between the consultant and referring service, particularly when the findings have potentially serious consequences or recommendations must be acted upon with some urgency.

Consult: 49-year-old male S/P TVC stripping and laser. Voice only a whisper. Please evaluate and treat.

Provisional Diagnosis: Voice disorder.

Data Base: Age: 49. Address: Enumclaw, WA. Social resources: Lives with invalid wife. Socioeconomic factors: Employed manager of supermarket. Health history: Patient has a diagnosis of carcinoma in situ treated for 4 years. He underwent laryngofissure and right cordectomy excision of anterior third of TVC's 4 years ago with good result. This was followed by 6480 rads to larynx. He has had multiple laryngoscopies and biopsies for laryngeal polyps, but has had no diagnosis of CA. Four months ago he underwent laser excision of fibrous tissue masses on the TVC's and he continues to have glottal stenosis. Other medical information includes a partial gastrectomy 6 years ago, and a smoking history of 30 pack years, quitting × 5 years.

Examination: Patient was alert, cooperative, and completely oriented. He had no evidence of any mental status deficits. His speech intelligibility was moderately impaired and his speech was characterized by low volume; strangled voice quality; hypernasal resonance; poor breath support and decreased phrase length; and slow, imprecise articulation. Physical findings of significance and previously unreported were normal ambulation, but slight weakness in the right upper extremity. Fasciculations were observed in both biceps. He had some wasting of the intraosseous muscles of his right hand. His facial muscles appeared symmetrically strong, but his tongue was weak to resistance and had some apparent atrophy and fasciculations. Gag reflexes were equally active. The palate and pharynx were unremarkable, but laryngeal examination showed poor abduction of the vocal cords. He had pooling of secretions throughout his hypopharynx and in the aditus of his larynx. On a test swallow, his larynx elevated briskly and he showed no evidence of aspiration. Repeat laryngeal examination showed no further pooling. His volitional cough was strong, but he had a measured pulmonary vital capacity of only 2.1 liters using a hand-held respirometer.

Assessment: Spastic-flaccid dysarthria and partial dysphagia related to neurologic impairments. His worsening voice appears to be related to a progressive dysarthria. The characteristics of his dysarthria suggest the possibility of a motor neuron disease such as ALS.

Recommendations and Plan: (1) Recommend consultation with Neurology. (2) During the course of his examination, the patient stated that he was concerned about the possibility of a neurologic disease. When the suggestion of a neurology evaluation was made, he stated that his sister had died of Lou Gehrig's disease and his mother may have had the same thing. For this reason, genetic counseling also is recommended if a MND is diagnosed. (3) The patient will be followed in dysphagia clinic and monitored for swallowing and communication management. No definitive treatment plan will be established until neurologic disease is either diagnosed or ruled out. (4) The patient needs a great deal of psychological support even while he is being evaluated; therefore, a referral to the outpatient mental health clinic is recommended.

Reports Describing Prognosis

A medical or surgical service's familiarity with the speech/language pathologist's expertise in the areas of motor speech, swallowing, language, cognitive functions, and behavioral rehabilitation techniques often leads to consultation regarding a patient's prognosis relative to a planned treatment. Knowledge of medical and surgical procedures and the rehabilitation required for each allows the speech/

language pathologist to contribute to the medical treatment plan. In the following example, a surgeon is soliciting the professional opinion of the speech/language pathologist in helping to determine the best course of treatment for a patient with laryngeal cancer.

Consult: L false VC CA, L hemiplegia. Probable supraglottic. Please evaluate and advise.

Provisional Diagnosis: Supraglottic CA.

Data Base: Age: 65. Address: Moses Lake, WA. Social resources: Lives alone without identifiable support. Socioeconomic factors: Retired itinerant farmer. Health history: Admitted for evaluation of left neck mass and laryngeal lesion of the aryepiglottic fold and left false cord, staged as T2 N2 M0. Earlier surgery plans were interrupted when patient sustained a right brain CVA with left UE weakness. Significant medical history includes long-term vascular disease and a right brain CVA 2 years ago.

Examination: Patient was evaluated by speech/language pathology on this date. He was alert and completely oriented. Patient presented with a left-side weakness with LE strength greater than UE, and marked tremor of the right UE and head. Speech was characterized by mild slurring and distortion of consonants. Diadochokinetic rates were mildly reduced and he had difficulty performing imitative movements of the articulators. His initiation of a swallow was delayed and he could not volitionally cough, although his reflex cough was present. Voice was WNL. Learning modality testing revealed adequate language comprehension and expression abilities. The patient was able to follow multistage instructions presented auditorily and in written form. On verbal expressive tasks the patient was able to describe the function of objects, define words, and respond appropriately to questions and statements presented by the examiner. Graphic expression was minimally impaired as shown by spelling errors, but he could relate his thoughts legibly. On auditory memory tasks the patient showed an ability to repeat sentences, recall details of short stories that were read to him, and learn word pairs on an associative learning task following three repeated presentations. On visual-motor-perceptual tasks the patient showed severe deficits. Simple figures were reproduced with distortion and only the simplest block building tasks were completed accurately. On block design tasks, the patient was able to duplicate only the two simplest designs. Visual memory was limited to recall of two pictures. Ideational tasks were completed with only fair accuracy. The patient completed only half of the simple calculations and was concrete in his interpretation of proverbs. He could not solve pictured analogy problems because of poor attention to the visual stimuli.

Assessment: Visual-motor-perception, visual-attention, and motor-planning deficits. He has slight weakness of his oral musculature and poor voluntary motor control of these muscles. This combination of impairments makes him a poor candidate for rehabilitation after a supraglottic laryngectomy.

Recommendations and Plans: (1) Our experience suggests that patients undergoing a partial laryngectomy, particularly a supraglottic laryngectomy, must learn compensatory swallowing techniques to minimize their aspiration. Because this involves learning a sequence of motor actions, this patient is likely to have difficulty learning and executing the necessary motor plan. (2) The patient can be instructed best by verbally talking him through tasks rather than by demonstration or other visual modalities. (3) Caution should be used so as not to mistake the patient's apparent verbal strengths as an indication of his learning potential. He must be made to demonstrate safe performance of an activity before he is allowed to act independently without supervision.

Comprehensive Consultation Reports

Both written and verbal reports can take different forms of emphasis utilizing the same format. In some cases an extensive history may be necessary to confirm or refute old facts. In other circumstances the report is designed to stress the treatment approach, the prognosis, or the diagnosis. Some consultation replies will be brief, while others are designed specifically to educate. In this chapter each of these elements is highlighted by an example. It is important to understand that all of these elements can be contained within one consult reply as in the following example of a consult sent to the speech/language pathology service from vascular surgery.

Consult: 59-year-old Hispanic male recently underwent CABG x2. On 2nd postop day he developed aphasia and oral apraxia. Seems to understand most of what is said but can't talk.

Provisional Diagnosis: S/P CVA.

Data Base: Age: 59. Address: New York, NY. Social resources: Divorced and lives alone in a three story walkup. Socioeconomic factors: Employed full time as a claims clerk. Health history: Patient is 10 days post-CVA. He has a past history of angina × 10 years that is relieved with medication. He has a 20-year history of hypertension with diabetes. In the past he has been evaluated by GI to rule out reflux disease as a source for his angina. On endoscopy 4 years ago the patient was found to have a stricture that was successfully dilated. The patient does not smoke and drinks two or three beers a day. During the present admission he was seen by Rehabilitation Medicine who felt he was too medically unstable for rehabilitation; they prepared a resting splint for the patient's right arm. A CAT scan performed 2 days post-CVA revealed a large temporoparietal infarct in the left brain, with right cortical atrophy.

Subjective Data: The nurses report that the patient is cooperative, understands, but is unable to make his needs known. The patient is scheduled for a barium swallow because he choked on water the day before.

Objective Data: The patient was alert and responded to the examiner's presence. A nasogastric tube was in place. A halter monitor was on his chest. The patient expressed by facial expression and a gesture that he was concerned that he could not talk. When asked to perform some movements with his articulators and to follow simple one-step commands, he repeated the same gesture and the repetitive phrase "I need." At no time during the examination could the patient follow an auditory command, but could imitate movements after the examiner, with delay, such as hand raising and mouth opening. The patient evidenced right facial and tongue weakness. Oral secretions were normal, and he appeared to be swallowing them without difficulty. Dentition was poor. Monilia was noted on the posterior tongue. The palate was symmetrical, and bilateral gag reflexes were elicited. There was no pooling of secretions in the airway or in the pharynx. The patient was unable to swallow or cough to command; however, a swallow reflex was observed during the evaluation. Perioral reflexes were positive.

The patient could not imitate words or use automatic speech. He was unable to recognize single words and could not copy sample geometric figures. He could write his name. He did not understand, even after demonstration, how to do simple block-building tasks, expressing frustration by shrugging his shoulders and repeating "I need." When he does speak, the utterance is intelligible, but hypernasal. Optokinetic nystagmus could not be elicited from the patient's right.

Assessment: This patient presents with severe deficits in both communication and perception suggestive of diffuse pathology. Due to the initial severity of the disease and the suspected diffuse pathology, the prognosis for marked changes in communication is poor. The patient cannot benefit from a communication board due to his poor communication and motor planning skills. There is little evidence that the patient understands language, but responds appropriately to environmental situations and to basic language combined with gesture. While his shoulder-shrugging and nodding appear appropriate, as well as his attempts in expression, they are both perseverative and undifferentiated. Apraxia cannot be ruled out since the patient's comprehension is poor. However, his automatic utterances are free of any articulator groping or struggle. His speech and physical examination are consistent with pseudobulbar dysarthria that may complicate his swallow, especially on fluids.

Plan: (1) Suggest that you include a modified barium swallow before the standard barium swallow to evaluate oropharyngeal competency since the patient may aspirate barium in a recumbent position secondary to pseudobulbar dysphagia. If studies are normal, order an aspiration reduction diet and thick liquids. Page us (115) before feeding the patient so we can monitor feeding and follow for dysphagia management. (2) Recommend consult to dietetics for calorie counts. Patient also needs to be weighed twice weekly. (3) This patient can benefit from a structured hospital routine to enhance his ability to respond to the environment. All needs will have to be met as the patient is unable to communicate them. Patient's refusals to cooperate probably do not represent unwillingness but a failure to understand what is desired. A short explanation with demonstration that is repeated two or three times will facilitate cooperation. (4) Patient is not a candidate for speech and language remediation at this time. Suggest reconsultation to Rehabilitation Medicine when patient is stable medically. (5) Suggest a dental consult. (6) Suggest aggressive oral hygiene to control the Monilia.

PROGRESS NOTES

Progress notes are composed to document additional subjective data, objective facts obtained from further examinations or laboratory evaluations, treatments administered, and quality changes in the assessment. A number of formats could be used to present this information. The following example illustrates the SOAP style of the problem-oriented medical record. The note begins with a title (the problem), describes both subjective and objective observations, reassesses the patient's condition relative to the problem, and outlines new recommendations based on the objective data.

Date:
Time:
Problem: Dysphagia

S– Patient received an aspiration reduction diet with thickened fluids as ordered, but was apprehensive about trying his first meal. O– Patient was positioned upright. Attempts to feed the patient were rejected by the patient as he wanted to self-feed. The patient fed himself about 1/2 of the tray before he fatigued. Swallow was delayed, but no airway penetration was noted to auscultation. There were no oral residuals. The patient took appropriate bite sizes and fed himself at an appropriate rate. A– The patient demonstrated safe oral feeding for both solids and thick liquids. He was unable to finish the entire tray, perhaps because he was not hungry since his tube feeding was finished only 1 hour before his tray. P– (1) Continue present diet and d/c NGT. (2) Calorie counts should continue throughout the week. If patient has 4 days of adequate intake, p.o. diet can be advanced to regular tray. (3) Maintain I&O chart to assure adequate hydration. (4) Monitor vital signs closely.

DISCHARGE SUMMARIES

An effective format for a final summary should include most of the following nine elements:

1. list of problems identified and addressed in treatment by the speech/language pathologist
2. etiology for each problem
3. date of initial evaluation
4. initial assessment (severity, extent, and prognosis) for each problem listed
5. treatment or management provided for each problem
6. treatment goals and objective measures relative to each goal
7. final assessment for each problem
8. recommendations for further treatment or management
9. disposition of the patient

In some cases, a patient may have only one problem that requires summation, while others may have multiple problems. Some patients should have their problems summarized under a single heading (e.g., aphasia with apraxia of speech), while for others the elements should be addressed separately (e.g., comprehension deficits, anomia, and apraxia of speech). The specific manner in which a discharge summary is prepared depends on how the patient was treated, what needs to be recorded for the medical-legal document, and what should be communicated to the physician, other speech/language pathologists, and other health professionals involved in the patient's care. If the patient is being discharged to an extended care facility, a copy of the discharge report should be sent to that facility (after obtaining the patient's or family's permission) under separate cover, because the physician's final discharge note will lack the specificity needed to manage the patient's communication or swallowing disorder.

The following examples summarize the essential elements for three problems encountered by speech/language pathologists:

Aphasia: Patient suffered a L CVA with resulting right hemiparesis and aphasia 3 weeks before evaluation at this medical center by speech/language pathology. On initial examination he was alert, cooperative, and fully attentive. Learning tests showed he followed only one-step spoken commands and inconsistently matched printed words to the correct objects. Expression was limited by word-finding difficulty; he named only 3 of 10 objects correctly. He was treated through a combination of daily individual and group sessions for 4 weeks on an inpatient basis. Goals were established to improve his consistency on verbal expressive tasks, and to help him control the rate at which he receives spoken language to facilitate comprehension. At this time of discharge to his residence 200 miles from this medical center, he is able to follow multistage spoken commands. He recognizes instances in which he is overloaded, and he will request that the speaker slow down, repeat, or write down the information. Expressively, he names approximately 9 of 10 common objects, but continues to have hesitancies in his conversation. He has made good adjustment to his disabilities and recognizes that, while he is continuing to recover from the acute disabilities, he will probably have chronic difficulties with abstract or complex language. The patient's family has been counseled regarding his impairments, progress, and prognosis. Further speech/language remediation is recommended at a facility near his home, and several possible referrals have been provided. All reports and treatment notes will be forwarded to the speech/language pathology clinic when the patient initiates contact.

Ataxic Dysarthria: Patient initially evaluated by speech/language pathology 1 week following a basilar artery CVA. At that time he was fully alert and attentive. There was no evidence of cognitive impairments on a screening examination. His speech was characterized by poor coordination of respiratory cycles with phonation resulting in voice breaks of pitch and intensity variations. He had inconsistent articulatory contact points and inappropriate syllabic stress patterns. Initial intelligibility measures were 40 percent for words and 62 percent for sentences. Treatment focused on increasing intelligibility by having him slow his rate and pace himself by tapping out each syllable of a written stimulus, progressed to self-cueing by tapping his finger for each word, and ended with the use of pacing techniques for unintelligible utterances in conversation (less than 2 percent). After 6 weeks of treatment, the final 2 on outpatient basis, the patient's intelligibility measures were 84 percent for words and 96 percent for sentences. In view of the patient's excellent self-monitoring skills, no further speech treatment is recommended at this time. He is scheduled to return to this clinic for a recheck in 6 weeks.

Paralytic Dysphagia: Patient was referred to speech/language pathology 2 days post-brainstem CVA for evaluation of swallowing. Initial examination showed the patient to have impairments of cranial nerves 5, 7, 9, 10, 11, and 12. He was drowsy and could not maintain a state of arousal. Functionally, he could not close his jaw effectively, and lip closure was incomplete due to facial muscle paralysis greater on the right side. He had no gag reflex and could not identify touch on the pharyngeal wall. He pooled secretions in the oropharynx, valleculae, pyriform sinuses, and aditus of the larynx. His vocal cords failed to fully abduct during inspiration and bowed on attempts to phonate. His tongue was unable to move against resistance and could cross the alveolar ridge only at midline. He was completely anarthric. The patient underwent a tracheostomy on his second day of hospitalization with placement of a cuffed trach tube. Initial recommendations were made to support the patient with NGT feedings during the acute phase and a PEG was recommended at 1 month postonset due to a poor prognosis for early recovery of swallow function. The patient was followed daily by bedside examinations for his 6-week hospital stay and examined weekly during 6 months of nursing home care. During this time his degree of alertness improved considerably, but his cranial nerve weakness persisted. He did not demonstrate that he could manage his own secretions without an inflated trach tube, and he required frequent tracheal suctioning. He had five bouts of aspiration pneumonia. Because his persistent bulbar muscle weakness precluded the use of these muscles to support swallow or speech, a recommendation was made to refer the patient to head and neck surgery to consider an aspiration procedure. The patient underwent total laryngectomy 12 months post-CVA. His postoperative recovery was uneventful, and 10 days postop he began taking liquids p.o. Weakness in muscles of mastication, face, and tongue have not allowed him to progress to soft foods, but he is now maintaining his weight by taking all nutrition by mouth. Due to quadriplegia, liquids are given by syringe and injected onto the posterior tongue to prevent anterior leakage. At this time the patient is being discharged to his home where his care will be provided by full-time attendants.

In each of the above examples, the discharge summary might include a summation of other problems. For example, the final patient with paralytic dysphagia would need a summary regarding his communication problem. In this case, there would be no need to repeat all of the physical findings, but a discussion of remediation techniques for communication would be appropriate.

SUMMARY

To a great extent, the professional value of a clinical service is judged on the basis of its oral and written reports. Both verbal and written speech/language pathology reports must reflect a logical diagnostic thought process and carefully formulated plans and recommendations. The exact format used for written reports, progress notes, and discharge summaries will vary from one institution to another depending on local policies and requirements. In most instances details must be added to justify continued treatment funding or to document the need for additional tests. Whatever the circumstances, however, the organization of the data and the inclusion of the essential elements should remain constant.

This chapter focuses on how to report diagnostic information in both verbal and written formats. Additionally, examples are presented to show how the diagnostic impression should help to dictate the treatment plan. Any results from follow-up testing or interventions stated in the plan will be documented in the patient's progress notes using objective measures. If the patient is not a candidate for communication or swallowing remediation, the speech/language pathologist's responsibility with that patient ends after the consult reply is completed. If the patient is to be followed at bedside or receive active remediation, a final discharge report should be prepared at the end of the hospitalization or when the patient has achieved maximum benefit from interventions.

Chapter 9

Principles of Treatment and Management

INTRODUCTION

This chapter presents a discussion of management and treatment principles as they relate to medical speech/language pathology. An emphasis on the need for medically based clinicians to integrate their clinical practices into the mainstream of health delivery is found throughout this book. In order to accomplish this goal it is necessary to understand the medical model and those components of the model that relate directly and indirectly to speech/language pathology. Some speech/language pathologists may need to adjust their diagnostic protocols to fit with procedures accepted in general medical practice. At the same time they must maintain their sense of professional identity. Clinicians must recognize their unique contributions to the health delivery system, contributions that bridge gaps in expertise and knowledge and provide genuine comfort to patients with disabilities and impairments in communication and swallowing.

Experience suggests that speech/language pathologists may err in one of two directions. Some maintain a provincial attitude and fail to integrate their skills into the health care system. Instead, they prefer to maintain a professional identity that is distinctly separate, or even aloof, from other health care specialists. For them, the physician may even be an adversary. Others underestimate their potential contributions within the medical setting and also fail to apply their skills in the most beneficial way. At a minimum, speech/language pathologists possess knowledge and expertise in the following four areas:

1. an understanding of the anatomy and physiology of the head and neck structures, including the respiratory system
2. an understanding of principles involved in the neurological organization of speech and language
3. an understanding of diagnostic testing administration, scoring, and interpretation
4. an understanding of learning theory, reinforcement, and specific techniques used in remediation

The manner in which these skills are employed with regard to patient treatment and management determine to a great extent the value of each clinician to the institution and the population he or she serves. This chapter does not present recipes for speech, language, voice, and swallow therapies. There is no attempt to describe programs that have been created for the remediation of these functions. Sufficient resources exist to assist a speech/language pathologist in formulating specific treatment plans for all forms of communication and swallowing disorders. The diversity of disorders and the abundance of potential interventions make any discussion of specific therapy inadequate in this context. Rather, the following discussion is concerned with a philosophical approach to treatment and management that is applicable to the clinician working in a medical environment.

INTERVENTION STRATEGIES

An intervention plan should be a logical extension of the examination. The diagnostic process is described in this book, beginning with the initial consultation in Chapter 4 and concluding with the mental status evaluation in Chapter 7. It is designed to identify all potential areas of deficit, as well as those abilities that can serve as channels for new learning and adjustment. An adequate examination must attempt to identify all areas of impairment, suggest a prognosis for each problem, and expose modalities that are potentially available for intervention. If, in a given patient, a subtle communication deficit is not identified, an intervention plan cannot be devised. The clinician can make no attempt to modify the impaired behavior, the patient and family do not receive an explanation regarding the impairment and how its impact can be minimized, and no adjustment is made to compensate for its presence. An examination that has identified and described all of the patient's impairments serves as a springboard from which an intervention plan can be developed.

It is also important to consider the perspective from which the speech/language pathologist views an identified impairment. Some clinicians err in their reports by minimizing the effects of a specific disability. For example, in reporting on an aphasic patient's comprehension skills, a clinician may glibly state that "the patient can follow commands and only makes mistakes when things get too complex." As a consequence of this report, other health professionals, whose care plans are dependent upon the speech and language evaluation, would assume incorrectly that the patient will be able to follow reliably their verbal directions. It would have been better had the speech/language pathologist defined the point at which the patient's comprehension skills decompensate by stating "the patient cannot follow two-stage spoken commands," and specified for others involved in the patient's care the best methods for providing instructions, (e.g., "use short, single-step spoken commands accompanied by demonstration," or "use one- and two-word commands for each step accompanied by the written word").

The medical model encompasses two forms of intervention. One form is variously referred to as *treatment, remediation,* or *therapy;* the other is thought of as *management.* The two are not mutually exclusive, but may overlap for a single case or even for a single problem. Treatment, remediation, or therapy implies that intervention is offered to those patients who demonstrate on examination that they are capable of modifying impaired functions (speech, language, or swallowing) by either eliminating the disabilities, improving the quality or efficiency of associated behaviors, or developing compensations to minimize the effects of the impairments. Patients in treatment must have demonstrated their potential for change on the basis of either their physical findings (e.g., muscle range, strength, or coordination that can be improved) or their learning potentials.

A patient who fails to demonstrate an ability to learn or to overcome physically a disability in communication or swallowing should not be rejected immediately as a candidate for intervention. The speech/language pathologist has a great deal to offer this patient, the family, and the medical community regarding the management of the impairment. Management refers to an intervention that is intended to provide support for a patient with an impairment that is chronic, intractable, or has an undetermined prognosis. Patient and family education, recommendations for a nursing care plan, and evaluative management (diagnostic therapy) are some of the essential contributions that the speech/language pathologist can make to support management intervention.

PRINCIPLES OF TREATMENT

Treatment by speech/language pathologists usually is not intended to eliminate a disability or bring about a cure. Indeed, there are few examples whereby the interventions of a speech/language pathologist result in complete recovery of function. As a profession guided by the principles of rehabilitation, speech/language pathology seeks to assist patients in reaching their maximum physical, psychologic, social, vocational, and avocational potentials consistent with their physiologic and environmental limitations.

The guiding principles of all rehabilitation services require that clinicians work toward improving the quality and efficiency of behaviors and functions, assist patients in developing compensations to overcome disabilities, and prevent physical and psychological complications that might interfere with or block recoveries.

Improving Quality and Efficiency

Improving the quality and efficiency of a patient's communication or swallowing deficits implies that there is potential for change. The patient may have demonstrated on learning modality tests that certain positive abilities have been unrecognized by the patient and health care providers. For example, an aphasic patient may be able to improve comprehension and retention of linguistic information when it is presented in written form. By repeatedly combining written language with the spoken symbol, the clinician may qualitatively improve the patient's ability to comprehend verbal material. In patients with dysarthria, intelligibility may be enhanced by teaching the patient to emphasize certain phonemes and to include more frequent pauses during an utterance. The efficiency of a swallow may be enhanced by strengthening exercises and increased concentration. All of these techniques can improve the quality and efficiency of specific functions, but some degree of disability will remain.

In order to improve the quality and efficiency of a behavior, the speech/language pathologist may design a treatment program to help patients more consistently utilize responses that are within their capacity. For example, a clinician often can work to improve consistency of a successful language response that an aphasic patient has intermittently demonstrated during an examination or evaluative session. This requires the speech/language pathologist to analyze the patient's behavior and the circumstances in which the response was successfully elicited so that factors contributing to its success can be determined (e.g., latency, amount of distraction, and degree of abstraction). When the clinician has determined that a response is reproducible, the variables may be manipulated to recreate a situation that allows for the elicitation of similar successful responses. A patient who successfully points to a named object on four of eight trials might achieve greater consistency in comprehension if required to take more time for each response, to print the first letter of each auditory stimulus, or to repeat the stimulus and use it in a phrase. The specific requirements for a patient must be determined individually and should be based on the examination data.

Another method of improving the quality and efficiency of a behavior is to reduce maladaptive behaviors. These behaviors are plentiful in the brain-damaged population. Impulsive verbal responses, vague gestural communication, perseverations, and inattention are a few examples. For the dysarthric speaker, the clinician can attempt to control an inappropriate rate of speech to effect better intelligibility. A laryngectomee learning to use an electrolarynx can be trained to increase the maladapted slow rate of speech in order to approach a more natural speech pattern.

To a great extent, treatment intended to improve the quality of a response requires the speech/language pathologist to create situations in which patients can successfully perform. When expected behaviors are elicited, immediate positive reinforcement must be provided. This allows patients to recognize their capability of producing successful responses, defines for them the clinician's expectations, and gives them opportunities to refine their behaviors qualitatively. For patients with aphasia, immediate reinforcement is necessary for them to modify their language behaviors successfully. Positive reinforcement for patients' successful responses to each step of a multistage command, for example, may help the patients learn that they can process language input effectively if they modify the manner in which it is given, such as requesting the speaker to give directions one step at a time. Patients with dysarthria will be dependent on the speech/language pathologist to provide reinforcement that allows them to modify their functions to approach more acceptable performances.

Promoting Compensations

Some treatments are designed to assist a patient in the development of compensations that are needed to maintain the integrity of a behavior. As in the case of improving the quality and efficiency of function, the development of compensations implies that the patient is capable of changing a behavior by either learning new techniques or applying retained abilities to substitute for lost function. Training the laryngectomee to use esophageal voice may be viewed as a form of compensation. The aphasic patient may learn to use gesture to augment verbal communication or to use written lists as substitutes for verbal instructions when auditory memory is the limiting factor. The ability of a dysarthric speaker to communicate intelligibly can be enhanced by the use of visual cues to the listener, such as pointing to the first letter of each spoken word. These and many other forms of compensatory therapies serve to facilitate function while recognizing the chronic nature of the impairment.

Preventing Complications

The third focus of treatment involves the prevention of complications. Perhaps the most obvious example is the dysphagic patient. Treatment used to facilitate recovery focuses on minimizing the risk for aspiration by manipulation of diet consistency, provision of tube feeding, or even use of monitoring intake to prevent malnourishment and dehydration. Clinicians must recognize that there is a potential for psychological complications in almost all forms of communication disorders. Discouragement, loss of motivation, depression, and the development of maladaptive behaviors can serve to decompensate the patient's function. These complications usually are the result of setting communication goals at unrealistic levels, poor communication between the family and medical staff, and unrealistic expectations for improvement. They often interact to put the patient at risk for maladaptive behaviors. By anticipating these complications, the clinician may be able to buffer their effects.

Defining Treatment Goals

No matter what form treatment takes, whether to improve the quality and efficiency of the behavior, develop compensations, or prevent complications, the program should be goal directed and the goals realistic and attainable. Goals can be stated using the terminology described above, that is, "to improve the efficiency of this patient's demonstrated ability," "to develop this demonstrated ability as a compensation to substitute for this impairment," or "to prevent this specific complication that may occur as a result of this impairment." Specific terms should be substituted within the structure of these general goal statements to make them meaningful for each patient. Goals serve to demystify the process of language therapy and, in turn, help the speech/language pathologist to foster more professional credibility by objectively measuring progress.

Speech/language pathologists will encounter some medical professionals who view their treatment procedures with skepticism. Skepticism may exist because speech/language pathologists attempt to provide intensive treatment to patients with little potential for recovery or strive to return patients' functions to premorbid levels in light of insurmountable odds. Clinicians who tend to develop unrealistic goals for their patients serve to perpetuate the skepticism of other professionals. Speech/language pathologists would do well to communicate to other health professionals that their treatment goals are not intended to restore the patients' physiologic abilities to previous states, but rather to maximize the patients' use of remaining abilities. In treatment, this may translate into programs that are designed to utilize clinicians' observations of remaining communication abilities and to incorporate patients' increasing capabilities as they return during natural recovery.

The goals of treatment should be functionally based. If the goals are realistic and attainable (which they should be unless there are medical complications or setbacks), then reaching the goals should make a difference in a patient's life. This difference may be recognized as improvement in the patient's care, the quality of life, or the ability to adjust and respond to the patient's surroundings. For example, a patient's care may be improved following treatment of a swallowing problem by decreasing the amount of nursing time required to provide feedings. Facilitation of communication invariably enhances patient care. An effort should be made to identify those disabilities that impair quality of life for each individual patient. Remediation of these problems will be meaningful for the patient. Clinicians should attempt to assess the patient's living situation in order to anticipate factors that will impair the patient's ability to adjust to his or her surroundings. For example, it might be important for a patient to learn to use a telephone for emergency situations in order to remain alone for short periods of time. In this instance, treatment goals may focus on dialing the emergency numbers and relating identifying information within communication limits.

When goals are not functionally based, but merely designed as mental exercises, they simply emphasize the patient's deficits without promoting adjustment or compensation. In language treatment, for instance, speech/language pathologists should recognize that the essence of human communication lies in its capacity for dynamic creativity; the variety of symbolic associations that can serve any conceivable situation is endless. In most cases, it serves little purpose to rehearse with an aphasic patient a limited vocabulary, unless this will result in some immediate positive change in the patient's daily interactions. If, on the other hand, the patient can improve the manner in which all available vocabulary is retrieved, gains can be functionally realized. In other words, the clinician must design a treatment program in which the goal for the patient is to develop a strategy or to generalize learning that will serve the patient at the moment a situation demands.

Treatment should be customized for the individual patient. All patients differ with regard to premorbid abilities, impairment characteristics, disability reactions, and recovery courses. Although specific therapeutic techniques can be applied repeatedly, individual patient goals and the criteria for meeting these goals must be individually established.

Treatment Strategies

Treatment must be perceived as important. When the clinician approaches treatment with a manner that suggests it is important, the patient is more likely to recognize this and respond positively. The patient perceives the value of the plan when the clinician demonstrates preparation for each session. The patient should be made aware of the goals and the techniques that are being used to accomplish them. With the language-impaired, these statements need to be made frequently.

When activities are provided for the patient to accomplish between sessions, procedures should be precisely stated. This may involve specifying for the patient the length of time to perform an exercise, the exact times to perform it, and the point at which to discontinue it. When treatments are provided with specific requirements, they are more likely to be performed conscientiously and be considered similar to medication requirements. For example, in an effort to encourage practice but prevent complications of excessive effort, the clinician may give a patient beginning esophageal speech training specific directions to practice vowels and consonant-vowel combinations one hour before and after meals, for ten minutes each session, for a total of six sessions per day. Specificity in directions communicates the intended message that the patient must take responsibility for improvements in function, that practice is necessary to reach the goals, that excessive practice may result in a setback or complication, and that the clinician is experienced and knowledgeable in this area.

Unlike testing, treatment should use and emphasize reinforcement. Skilled clinicians design tasks that allow patients to successfully move through progressively more complex stages in order to reach their goals. There should be no ambiguity in the clinician's response to a patient's performance. Particularly with brain-damaged patients, reinforcement should occur through all available modalities. That is, the patient should be able to hear, see, and feel the clinician's positive reaction to successful performance. Facial expression and tone of voice to express emotion, and touch, when appropriate, to emphasize acceptance are all available. Group treatment can be particularly valuable in this regard, because the reinforcement can come from patients with similar disabilities as well as the clinician.

Treatment can carry a potential risk. Many health professionals think of risk only in terms of potential physiologic damage. In this regard, speech and language therapy only rarely incur risk. The exceptions may involve strengthening exercises provided to patients with progressive diseases, such as amyotrophic lateral sclerosis, or with other neurologic conditions that respond negatively to exercise, such as myasthenia gravis. Treatment of patients with dysphagia almost always carries a risk for complications from aspiration.

The risk that is overlooked most often, however, is related to the potential for psychological damage. Patients, their family members, and some clinicians may want to initiate or continue treatment programs when realistic goals have not been established. Prolonging treatment beyond a reasonable point serves only to delay adjustment and prevent the patient from making the best use of existing capabilities. Clinicians who encourage ongoing treatment are communicating to the patient that they expect positive gains. Families who insist on treatment beyond a reasonable point may give the patient the unintended message that they are unacceptable to their loved ones because of the remaining handicaps. In either case, prolonged therapy may convey unrealistic expectations that abilities will be restored "if we only work long enough or hard enough." In all cases, whether improvement is expected or not, clinicians must weigh the risk versus the benefit of the treatment offered. As health professionals, speech/language pathologists should recognize that treatment is not benign and that the attitude "it won't do any harm to try" often does not apply.

The specific techniques employed in treatment are dictated by the patient's medical condition and individual needs. For example, because of fatigue some patients are better treated in the morning than the afternoon. In patients with disorders like Parkinson's disease or myasthenia gravis, treatment should be scheduled when the patient is receiving maximum benefit from medications. Patients receiving renal dialysis may respond better before dialysis because of postdialysis fatigue. Consideration should be given to the relative importance of other rehabilitation therapies and scheduled medical procedures.

In a given case, a patient may perceive communication impairment as relatively minor when compared to loss of ambulation function. For this patient the communication treatment may be de-emphasized relative to the physical therapy. Other patients with the same degree of impairment may perceive their deficits in the opposite way. Therefore, treatment emphasis should be appropriately adjusted. For some conditions, treatment is best provided in a traditional one-hour session. Other patients, such as those who are uncooperative or who have short attention spans, may require only a 5-minute contact once a day or perhaps four 15-minute sessions per day. There is no formula for reaching these treatment decisions. Rather, they are based upon individual assessment data, clinical judgment, and experience with a variety of medically related disorders.

In some settings, speech/language pathologists find that treatment decisions are prescribed by other health professionals, such as physiatrists, otolaryngologists, and neurologists. Speech/language pathologists must recognize that by virtue of their own education and experience, they are the experts and specialists in communication disorders. Final decisions regarding treatment, whether deciding to treat or not, determining and applying specific treatment techniques, and establishing the treatment schedule should remain the clinical privilege of the speech/language pathologist.

One of the most difficult issues that a speech/language pathologist must face concerns decisions to discharge patients from treatment or not to offer treatment. In many of these cases, the clinician will receive pressure from a patient, the family, and other health professionals to make an attempt. While it is tempting to avoid this pressure by providing the desired treatment in spite of the clinical facts that suggest it is not warranted, the clinician must stand by his or her professional judgment to maintain self-esteem and credibility. The determination of treatment efficacy will not be clearly defined in every case. In some instances, a patient's treatment might be deferred while the clinician evaluates the condition over a period of time (evaluative management). A patient can be discharged from active treatment, re-evaluated at periodic intervals to determine the stability of previous gains, and re-enrolled in treatment if this is indicated. Whenever a no-treatment decision is reached, the issues of management become paramount.

PRINCIPLES OF MANAGEMENT

Not all patients with communication or swallowing disorders are candidates for treatment; however, they all are candidates for management. A patient who is engaged in a treatment program in which there is an attempt to remediate an impairment is also in need of the clinician's attention to the management of the disability. Management may relate to the need for recommendations to a nursing care plan, patient and family education about the disorder and its prognosis, and reporting of strengths and weaknesses to a rehabilitation team. The speech/language pathologist also represents a source for support, encouragement, and reassurance for the patient that can be provided only by a knowledgeable professional familiar with the patient's special problems.

One of the most effective ways that speech/language pathologists can integrate themselves into the medical setting is through their participation in the development of patient management plans. Clinicians must recognize that they are part of a health delivery team. Most often communication and swallowing disorders do not occur in isolation, but rather they are symptoms in a complex of symptoms that taken together result in the patient's disability. The speech/language pathologist, like all members of the health care team and particularly those concerned with rehabilitation, must be concerned with the total care and recovery process of the patient. Rehabilitation specialists must not be content to focus solely on the remediation of problems related to their own areas of expertise. The speech/language pathologist's contributions to the team should always remain in this context. For example, patients should be evaluated from the perspective that communication is (1) a possible area of deficit that requires remediation, (2) a potentially impaired function that can impede the provision of care and rehabilitation efforts of other health professionals, (3) a potentially useful channel through which rehabilitation specialists can provide patient education, and (4) a teaching modality to be used for the remediation of other disabilities.

Management Care Plans

Management begins by communicating the evaluation findings to the consulting service and others involved in a patient's care. This reporting process (described in Chapter 8) serves the purpose of alerting all health professionals involved in a patient's care to the problems identified by the speech/language pathologist. As stated previously, the problems should be well-defined and accurately described. For each significant impairment recommendations should be made to the care providers so they can deal more effectively with the patient and minimize the effects of the disorder on the provision of care. For example, for a patient with aphasia, the speech/language pathologist should describe the degree of impairment present in all communication modalities. If the patient is not able to follow spoken instructions, the recommendations must state this fact and offer the nurses, physicians, and other rehabilitation specialists an alternative means of providing directions. In this case, one might recommend the use of demonstration and physical prompting in order to provide the patient with input that can be understood.

Patients with severe comprehension impairments also may become confused and even agitated when staff engages them in what they perceive as demanding verbal directives. In order to avoid catastrophic reactions of patients, staff can be instructed to give them reassurances that they are performing as expected or that their conditions are stable by communicating their messages through a reassuring touch, nondemanding tone of voice, and pleasant facial expression. If aphasic patients are not able to verbalize adequately to express biologic needs, all of those involved in their care should be made aware of this fact. The speech/language pathologist should recommend that the patients' needs be anticipated and met on unchanging schedules. In this way a great deal of patient and staff frustration can be avoided. Allowing patients' biologic systems to adjust to a routine can obviate their anxieties about not being able to formulate requests verbally.

At times, specific information derived from the evaluation of an aphasic patient can make a difference in the patient's care and in medical decisions. If the speech/language pathologist reports that the patient's reliability in responding to yes/no questions is inadequate and, therefore, medical and nursing care decisions should not be based on the patient's response to questions, errors in medical and nursing care can be avoided. For example, a patient may be asked about the presence of pain and respond affirmatively. If the patient's inability to respond appropriately is not known or if it is ignored, sedating pain medications may be given that will decompensate the patient's fragile learning ability.

Anticipating Management Problems

Provision of care often is dependent upon finding explanations for patients' aberrant behaviors. This is particularly evident for patients who have suffered neurologic disability. Whether providing treatment or devising a care plan, all health professionals seek to understand why their patients behave in certain ways. The speech/language pathologist may be in a position to provide explanations to other health professionals for behaviors related to communication and cognitive impairments. The explanations should be based upon what is already known to be true (the clinical and diagnostic facts), rather than on speculation and contrived supposition.

Particularly with brain-damaged patients, there will be recurring problems associated with certain types of lesions. The speech/language pathologist should be able to anticipate some of these problems and explain an expected behavior before it is mislabeled and mismanaged. A classic example of this can be found in patients with right brain damage and resulting motor planning problems. These patients have difficulty initiating activities that require them to plan, organize, and execute motor actions or sequences. Additionally, they may be unable to express emotions by using appropriate inflectional patterns in their speech; their monotonous vocal tones sound emotionally flat. A health professional involved in such a patient's care may seek to explain why the patient does not join in social activities with others on the ward, appears isolated and withdrawn, and wants to stay in bed. The easy explanation would be to ascribe to the patient a new diagnosis of depression, supported by observations of social withdrawal and flat affect. Others may attribute the patient's behavior to what they assume to be pre-existing personality traits, such as stubbornness, laziness, or an unmotivated state.

A speech/language pathologist familiar with the deficits of right brain-damaged patients may be able to offer an alternative explanation based upon known clinical facts. Specifically, the patient has had brain damage in the right hemisphere that has led to motor-planning difficulties and an inability to intone language emotionally. This has resulted in the patient's inability to execute a motor plan and in a flat, monotonous speech pattern. A patient care team that is satisfied with the first explanation of depression might proceed to develop an intervention plan for this problem that could include psychiatric consultation, psychotropic medications, and counseling. The result of these interventions could lead to an exacerbation of existing problems by taking valuable time away from productive treatment. The secondary effects from the medication may precipitate drowsiness and increase difficulties with motor planning. Explanations like stubbornness, laziness, and lack of motivation are only excuses and do not assist health care professionals to formulate plans to correct a problem or to modify a behavior. By focusing on an explanation that is based on clinical facts, a more effective management plan can be devised. Specifically, necessary verbal cues and motor assistance can be provided to help the patient engage in social activities. Those involved in the care of the patient should be aware of the reason for the monotonous speech and other communication deficits, such as concretism and failure to appreciate humor. By using this plan and appropriately reinforcing and rewarding the patient for successful function, the health care staff may obviate the need for any psychiatric or medical intervention and avoid complications that may unnecessarily extend the patient's length of hospitalization.

Managing Brain-Damaged Patients

Speech/language pathologists have potential roles in management planning for all patients with brain damage affecting cognitive and motor systems that influence communication and swallowing. This category includes patients with aphasia, perceptual deficits, dementia, dysarthria, apraxia, and dysphagia of neurologic origin. It is incumbent on speech/language pathologists to recognize their expertise in these areas. Also, they should not assume that health professionals in general know enough about the behavior of these patients to formulate independently valid care plans.

The management plans developed for brain-damaged patients should be based on each patient's individual assessment. The principles involved in the management of these patients in some instances are universal, but the manner in which they are applied and modified for each patient may differ. For example, in the care of a patient with left brain damage and aphasia, the clinician should constantly strive to help the nursing staff recognize the level of language impairment and establish the best methods to facilitate communication with the patient throughout the recovery process and during the chronic phase.

Many patients who are unable to speak will be regarded by those who assist in providing their care as being more disabled than they really are. Most people, whether they intend to or not, judge intelligence on the basis of a person's verbal skills. For this reason, patients with aphasia who cannot speak for themselves and may fail to comprehend the spoken message of others may be regarded as unintelligent. Some health care personnel may isolate the patient by failing to attempt communication through any modality.

Speech/language pathologists recognize that patients with aphasia, which is not part of a generalized intellectual impairment, understand a great deal of the nonverbal interaction that occurs around them. They may be able to comprehend the emotional component a speaker communicates by interpreting the tone of voice. They observe and often learn to interpret gestures and facial expressions of the speaker. Some patients become so adept at understanding these nonverbal communication cues that other people overestimate their ability to comprehend and overload them with spoken information. Overestimations of patients' abilities can be just as damaging, because when the patients fail to respond as expected they are often labeled as being stubborn, confused, or depressed.

Patients with aphasia tend to respond best when instructions are provided through pantomime or demonstration. They should not be treated as if they were hard of hearing. Rather, care providers should use simplified messages and emphasize the nonverbal aspects of communication. These patients will need clear and frequent reinforcement that they are performing tasks correctly. The best forms of reinforcement are provided nonverbally by a pat on the back, a nod of the head, and a smile. Patients with aphasia, like all patients with brain damage, respond best in a regimented environment. A schedule that is predictable, and one in which basic needs are met within a routine, will be perceived as "safe" and often provides the impetus for communication exchanges. Speech/language pathologists who can promote such an environment will have created an atmosphere in which any possible recovery will be facilitated.

The right hemisphere functions to mediate learning behaviors that require voluntary initiation, planning, and spatial-perceptual judgment. Typically, the patient with right brain damage demonstrates visual-motor-perceptual impairments, visual memory deficits, and occasionally left-sided neglect. Most of these patients retain articulate speech and language functions. For this reason they may be mistakenly judged to have retained their full cognitive capacity. Their true cognitive deficits may be detected only through specific testing of all learning modalities (see Chapter 7).

The functional significance of visual-motor-perceptual deficits is most obvious when a patient attempts to perform self-care activities. An observer may be struck by the patient's impulsiveness, failure to recognize his or her deficits, bad judgment, and failure to meet the organizational requirements of a motor plan. Specifically, the patient may bump into a wall when moving through a doorway, attempt to stand when it is not safe to do so, attempt to put on a shirt with the sleeves inside out, lose the place on the page when attempting to read, or shave only one side of the face but include the hair above the ear.

It is significant for the speech/language pathologist to note that right brain-damaged patients' abilities are overestimated because of their relative strength in communication. These patients may be able to retain and recite the steps that they have been taught in order to perform a safe transfer, but fail to execute these steps properly when required to perform. Because of their impulsivity they may attempt to perform tasks beyond their capabilities. The picture is further complicated because the patients' perceptual impairments extend to lack of insight into their own disabilities.

Unilateral neglect is far more frequent in patients with right brain damage than those with damage to the left. Unlike the partial blindness of a visual field cut, neglect is an integrative, sensory impairment that results in inattention to one half of space. It may be most obvious in the visual modality, but it also extends to the senses of touch, proprioception, and hearing. Patients who have visual-motor-perceptual disorders that include neglect are at greater risk for self-injury.

The speech/language pathologist's role in the preparation of a management plan for the patient with right brain damage must begin with a careful examination and analysis of the data. Initially, the findings must be communicated to those who provide acute care. It is essential that they understand the deficits, because the superficial impression, based on the patient's obvious communication skills, may be misleading and dangerous. Second, a management plan based on the evaluation results should be communicated to the patient and the family. When the patient is unable to develop insight into the impairment, it is essential that those who provide care are well-informed. Third, the ultimate disposition frequently depends on the degree of residual impairment and the patient's ability to compensate for it. The speech/language pathologist may be able to add critical information necessary to plan for an appropriate disposition.

Among the elements to be considered in a management plan for patients with right brain damage is a carefully formulated, detailed schedule for daily events. The patient and all care providers should recognize the importance of a regimented environment. The schedule should include times for grooming, dressing, appointments, meals, rest periods, visitors, and social activities. Patients should be instructed verbally in specific terms to initiate each activity that they have failed to begin. In some cases, a single activity must be broken down into its elemental steps and the patient talked through the task step by step. The amount of detail required in the verbal cueing will vary according to individual needs as demonstrated by testing and observations of progress. Some patients may move toward independence by cueing themselves as they perform a motor task. Therapists may encourage patients to talk themselves through the tasks. In some cases, printed lists are useful to assist patients in self-cueing.

In those cases in which there is a persistent motor planning impairment, particularly in the presence of left neglect, independence is precluded for many functional acts. Bedfast patients with neglect need to be faced and approached from the strongest side. Even in cases where neglect is relatively mild, such activities as driving or operating machinery are hazardous and inadvisable. The speech/language pathologist must recognize these permanent disabilities and help the staff, patient, and family to adjust their expectations with regard to recovery. While the management plan should be practical and have immediate application, it should remain flexible enough to accommodate changes in a patient's condition.

Evaluative Management

When it has been determined that treatment is inappropriate or that realistic, attainable goals cannot be established for a patient, evaluative management can be valuable. Some speech/language pathologists refer to this concept as diagnostic therapy. However, the term evaluative management is preferred, because it does not suggest that the applied procedures and techniques are intended to lead to a functional change. The purposes of evaluative management sessions may be

- to administer informal diagnostic tests designed by the clinician in order to evaluate functions that were not adequately measured by the standard test used for the initial assessment
- to assess the patient's performance and response to a limited, but highly structured, teaching program designed by the clinician to determine the patient's ability to generalize new learning

- to monitor during the acute phase of impairment the patient for whom there is a reasonable basis for a favorable prognosis in order to detect changes in abilities or functions by the use of repeated measures

The clinician who has engaged a patient in evaluative management must recognize the difference between these sessions and scheduled treatment sessions. It is vital that the clinician communicate the nature of these sessions to the family and all others involved in the patient's care so that expectations will remain realistic. In treatment there should be a realistic expectation that the patient will change in a positive direction. In evaluative management there is no expectation for change as a result of the session, but there should be constant vigilance on the part of the clinician to detect positive changes that can be potentially utilized for treatment.

A clinician who maintains evaluative management sessions with a patient who is engaged in other rehabilitation therapies must maintain credibility with other specialists as they communicate their new findings, patient progress, and management recommendations. A clinician who has engaged a patient in only a limited number of diagnostic sessions and does not actively follow the patient will not maintain enough credibility throughout the course of the rehabilitation program to impact on the patient's care. Changes detected in a patient's function through evaluative management can be readily communicated to a team, and management recommendations can be adjusted in a timely manner when appropriate.

For some patients in the acute phases of impairment, evaluative management may consist of periodic, even daily, bedside screenings. Some clinicians choose to engage in daily bedside rounds in which they briefly review each inpatient on their current patient roster. This brief examination might include an assessment for major medical status changes (see the section on clinical observations in Chapter 5); a screening for changes in physical status, for example return of optokinetic nystagmus reflex, change in swallow reflex, or acoustic speech change; and a screening for mental status changes (see Chapter 7). The thoroughness of the examination will be dictated by the nature of the disability and the patient's relative medical stability. The bedside reviews also should include a chart update to read new progress notes and other pertinent entries in the medical record (see Chapter 4). A progress note should be entered at the time of the bedside screening to document changes in findings, stability of findings, and additions to or changes in the plans or recommendations. Five minutes a day spent with each patient and his or her medical chart can be invaluable. This form of evaluative management allows the speech/language pathologist to maintain visibility with other health professionals and to interact with the staff that provides the day-to-day care for patients with communication and swallowing difficulties. It is an excellent method to promote new consultations by demonstrating the value of the specialty. Furthermore, these informal, daily interactions communicate to the ward personnel that the speech/language pathologist recognizes their importance and is willing to exchange information in an effort to improve patient care.

DISCHARGE PLANNING

Because discharge planning is thought of as an event occurring at the end of a treatment program, many of the pertinent issues are not addressed in a timely fashion. Discharge planning should begin at the same time that treatment and management plans are determined. At the time of evaluation and diagnosis, information should be gathered regarding the patient's social resources and socioeconomic factors that may influence the process of recovery and the patient's eventual disposition. Medically based speech/language pathologists, like all health professionals, should recognize that part of their job is to move patients away from the health delivery system by facilitating recovery from impairments and adjustment to residual, chronic disabilities.

The majority of patients seen by the speech/language pathologist in the medical setting will not recover all of their communication and swallowing functions to the premorbid level. It is imperative that the speech/language pathologist help patients to prepare for some degree of chronic disability. The exact amount of the impact that an impairment has on a patient's life may not be determined until a course of treatment has been completed and the natural recovery processes terminated. Nevertheless, patients are required to cope with each stage of a disability. In the early stages of a severe dysfunction, the speech/language pathologist, through management planning, can assist patients to survive without important communication or swallowing abilities. Later, with some degree of recovery, patients may need assistance to adjust to incomplete or slow return of function. When maximum recovery has occurred, the speech/language pathologist should assist patients to identify ways in which they can utilize remaining abilities to bring about the greatest amount of quality in their lives.

The speech/language pathologist should encourage patients with chronic disabilities to participate in daily activities to the greatest extent possible within their limitations. The activities chosen should emphasize the utilization of remaining skills and abilities, minimize the impact of the disabling functions, and bring about the most satisfying rewards. The speech/language pathologist may recognize the greatest successes with those patients who state they are "too busy" or "have no time" to continue a prolonged outpatient treatment program.

One method that can be used to assist a patient in accepting, and perhaps welcoming, discharge from treatment is to predetermine the length of a segmented treatment program. A clinician can recommend that the patient engage in a series of sessions for a specified number of treatments, followed by re-examination. Each re-evaluation determines whether the patient should receive a recommendation for another series of treatment sessions, a revised treatment program with a new focus, a prescribed break in treatment with a scheduled re-examination, a change from individual to group sessions, or discharge from treatment.

In many cases it is important for a patient and his or her significant others to maintain contact with a specialist dealing with the area of impairment. Periodic re-evaluations may continue for a long time after discharge and can be useful to assess the stability of learned compensations and to detect the presence of any maladaptive behaviors. The emphasis of these periodic re-evaluations should be on patient and family adjustment.

When a patient is discharged to a long-term care facility, such as a nursing home or domiciliary, management recommendations should be forwarded to the supervisor of the primary care staff. Management recommendations that proved to be beneficial during the patient's acute recovery phase are likely to be of great assistance to the staff of the long-term care facility. This form of communication also serves to promote speech/language pathology services and may result in more frequent consultation from individuals who become familiar with the specialty.

The speech/language pathologist should recognize that treatment and management must focus not only on the patient, but on the patient's family and significant others. Discharge planning can be facilitated when those responsible for providing direct care, as well as those who interact most frequently with the patient, are well-trained regarding the patient's management needs. A speech/language pathologist who trains family members how to elicit information from a language-impaired patient by manipulating the timing of questions, the wording, the cueing, and the reinforcement helps the patient and family to accomplish their goals with regard to adjustment. Experience suggests that the treatment emphasis in many cases should be as much on training the significant other as it is on teaching the patient.

FAMILY ADJUSTMENT

The speech/language pathologist will utilize counseling sessions or a series of family intervention sessions for many and varied reasons. Often they are conducted to inform someone significant to the patient about the disorder and the projected course of treatment; this may be thought of as health education. The speech/language pathologist has a role in teaching significant others about the patient's communication or swallowing deficits, the expected course of recovery or deterioration, the overall prognosis for return of function, and the methods that can be used to promote recovery and to facilitate care. An example of this educational role occurs when a speech/language pathologist provides preoperative counseling for the spouse of a patient who will undergo a total laryngectomy. For the most part, the speech/language pathologist's information in this example is more positive than the surgeon's, in that the issues revolve more around recovery and rehabilitation than cancer and surgical risk. Health education also might be included as one facet of an intervention program provided to individuals who are involved in the care of patients with severe and disabling impairments.

Because patients who have suffered brain damage due to stroke, traumatic brain injury, or other neurologic diseases often have disabilities that are severe enough to disrupt their family dynamics, the requirements for family intervention are frequently complex. The following discussion focuses on these more involved cases. It should be recognized that family counseling may be provided to more than one individual, for example, the patient's entire family, or it may occur as part of a team meeting with a significant other. However, the model described in this section applies more to individual counseling.

In this context, counseling refers to the assistance given by a clinician to an individual (counselee) in order to modify that person's attitude, way of thinking, and manner of dealing with problems related to a patient's disabilities. In essence, this is the process used to promote adjustment to a loved one's disabilities. The speech/language pathologist provides counseling in the form of health education pertaining to the following:

- nature of the condition
- prognosis for recovery
- demonstration of facilitating techniques for communication and swallowing to improve the provision of care
- advice to the counselee regarding management techniques intended to maintain a healthy relationship between the patient and the counselee

Unlike mental health counselors, the speech/language pathologist does not intervene for the specific purpose of improving mental health; however, the clinician's efforts may serve to prevent the development of psychological problems related to stress and anxiety.

The clinician should approach family intervention sessions with pre-established goals. To some extent knowledge of the patient's condition allows the clinician to anticipate questions from the counselee and to formulate answers expressed in a manner that will move the counselee toward the direction of the goals. The speech/language pathologist should not limit family intervention to one session. In most cases, goals can be best met through a series of sessions in which the intended outcome is approached systematically. Intervention with a family member should be approached with the same care as patient intervention. Counselees differ from each other as much as patients and their infinite variety of deficits. Therefore, just as with the patient, intervention planning must begin with an assessment of the counselee. In most cases, this requires the speech/language pathologist to make a rapid assessment of the counselee's knowledge, education, attitude, willingness to accept information, resistance to change, relative degree of concern, expectations, emotionality, and other factors that could negatively or positively influence the intervention.

It is important for the clinician conducting the session to establish his or her authority. Because of the debilitating nature of communication disorders, the information provided to the counselee often is less than optimistic. For this reason, resistance is a common obstacle to be overcome. Unless the clinician can impart an aura of authority, there is little chance for success.

As in patient treatment and diagnosis, a relationship of trust between the clinician and the counselee must be established. Whenever possible, the clinician should begin by finding and stating points of agreement. This requires insight on the part of the clinician to judge the counselee's attitude and assess, to some extent, preconceived ideas about the patient's disabilities and recovery. After points of agreement have been established, it is much easier for the clinician to introduce new information gradually that may contradict some of the counselee's preconceptions.

It is essential for the speech/language pathologist to communicate empathy and concern that are appropriate to the patient's condition and prognosis. The clinician also must show respect for the counselee's knowledge and perceptions of the patient. It is the interpretations of the counselee's observations that may need to be modified. Whenever possible, the family's suggestions for solving a problem should be reinforced. Even when the solution is incomplete, the clinician can gradually modify a point of view or methodology in order to achieve the intended result. The clinician must maintain objectivity and not become overwhelmed with the emotional reactions of the family. While empathizing with what may be a devastating change to the family structure, the clinician must remain objective in an effort to assist the counselee in adjusting to the crisis. Presenting too much information or information that is too overwhelming in one session should be avoided. This requires the clinician to observe the counselee closely in order to recognize signs of emotional overload.

Speech/language pathologists are specialists in disorders of communication and related functions. They are not social workers who are required to intervene in financial issues; they are not psychologists or psychotherapists who intervene directly in helping the family to develop coping strategies to deal with stress and anxiety brought about by the patient's illness and in diagnosing or treating mental illness; they are not physicians who are responsible for describing the basic disease process and informing the family about the overall treatment plan and prognosis. However, in those cases in which communication disorders are the primary handicapping disability, the speech/language pathologist should not avoid the responsibility of assisting significant others in their adjustment to expected changes in the family relationships and dynamics. Referrals to other resources should be made when situations warrant.

The clinician can expect a family to be slow in accepting the full impact of a devastating situation. Most often family members continue to express some hope even when the clinician sees little reason for optimism. It is not appropriate for the clinician to dispel the counselee's hope, but rather to assist the counselee to develop a realistic point of view in making the necessary adjustments for the benefit of the patient and the family. In some cases this requires the counselee to adjust to the way things are in the present, without expectation for change. If change later occurs in a positive direction, readjustment to the improved condition is relatively easy, whereas postponement of adjustment may exacerbate problems related to the patient's disability.

The speech/language pathologist must demonstrate patience by working toward goals in small steps. An open-door policy that allows family members to return frequently to discuss or reflect upon their observations and experiences can be most beneficial. Guiding their observations with assignments aimed at documenting communicative interactions can help by giving them a feeling of participation in the patient's care. When a patient moves from inpatient to outpatient status, it is important for all rehabilitation clinicians to maintain close contact with the family as they experience the full impact of the disability. Counseling sessions can be very productive to the family immediately following the patient's first weekend pass after experiencing an impairment. The problems encountered will be fresh in the counselee's mind, and he or she may be most receptive to the clinician's recommendations. When possible, the speech/language pathologist should make a home visit to assess the patient/family interactions and note any barriers to optimal function. If the speech/language pathologist judges that home placement is not in the patient's or the family's best interest due to the severity of the disability or the degree of care required, alternative recommendations should be made. The speech/language pathologist has a role in helping the family to deal with the guilt that is so often associated with discharge to a nursing home. When a recommendation for nursing home placement is verbalized by health care professionals, the family is relieved of some of the responsibility for making this decision and the guilt associated with it.

Many times family members will ask if they can provide direct remediation in the home. In many instances, this is contraindicated, because family members lack sufficient training in the application of treatment techniques and often cannot display the objectivity needed to tolerate patient errors. When a spouse becomes a surrogate clinician, there often is a concomitant change in the spousal relationship that can perpetuate the patient's dependence. It is important to explain to the family that the strategies of communication or swallowing facilitation that were demonstrated as part of the counseling on the patient's disability are, in fact, an integral part of the treatment program and that consistency in their application is necessary for the patient's management.

SUMMARY

Decisions regarding the interventions that speech/language pathologists provide for patients with communication and swallowing disorders are dictated by the diagnostic examinations. The medical model encompasses two forms of intervention—treatment and management. Treatment is guided by the principles of rehabilitation that require clinicians to assist patients to reach their maximum physical, psychologic, social, vocational, and avocational potentials consistent with their physiologic and environmental limitations. For the speech/language pathologist this means treatment is directed not toward cure, but toward improving the quality and efficiency of the impaired function (e.g., speech, voice, language, or swallowing), assisting in the development of compensations to substitute for lost abilities, and preventing or eliminating maladaptive behaviors and other complications that can impede recovery.

Treatment is provided to those patients who have the ability to modify function. Goals should be established that are realistically attainable. The established goals, when met, should be meaningful for the patient; the change should make a difference in the patient's function and quality of life. Treatment should not be viewed as a benign gesture. Remediation goals that are not realistic or functionally based will emphasize the patient's deficits without promoting appropriate compensations or adjustment. Prolonged, nonproductive treatment may communicate to patients that they are not acceptable to others because of their impairments.

The clinician's approach to treatment must convey to the patient that participation is important. The clinician's manner of conducting and preparing for each session helps to give the patient confidence in the treatment plan. Successful treatment emphasizes the use of unambiguous reinforcement techniques to help promote positive gains. When improvement ceases to be measurable, management and discharge issues must be addressed.

Management, as contrasted with treatment, requires the clinician to focus on the issues of adjusting to disability and communicating to caregivers the techniques that will facilitate function in spite of the disabilities. All patients, whether engaged in treatment programs or not, are candidates for management. Recommendations given to nursing personnel and forwarded to long-term care facilities at discharge help to improve the care provided for patients with communication and swallowing deficits. Daily personal contact with ward personnel related to the management of these patients also facilitates the provision of care and helps to demonstrate the value of speech/language pathology services. When treatment goals cannot be well-defined due to the acute nature of a disorder or insufficient examination data, the clinician can design evaluative management sessions that may provide necessary information for valid treatment and management decisions.

Preparation for discharge should begin at the time initial treatment and management plans are formulated. Speech/language pathologists should recognize that their roles for most patients and their families include helping them to adjust their lives to accommodate some degree of chronic disability. The process of adjustment is a dynamic one that requires patients to cope with their impairments through all stages of recovery, from the acute phase to the point where they recognize that return of function is incomplete. By promoting self-acceptance and emphasizing participation in activities that utilize remaining skills, speech/language pathologists help to minimize the impact of disabilities on the quality of life of their patients.

Part IV

Program Development

Chapter 10

Program Accountability

INTRODUCTION

In the decade of the seventies there was increasing alarm among health care financiers and providers that health care costs were spiraling at a rate that the economy could not withstand. Many felt that the consequences of this escalation would make health care services available only to those who could afford them. And even for those who could afford them, catastrophic illness would soon deplete their savings. These conclusions resulted in a move toward tighter controls on the health care industry in resource allocation. The response from health care providers was "It's not me who spends too much, take a look at the other guy." But how does one know that a particular health care organization is doing a better job than another? And how does one go about measuring those differences? These were the questions that had to be answered by congressional leaders and members of the health care community. In the early eighties there was a definite shift among accrediting bodies away from evaluating the structure and services of the medical setting to stricter monitoring of the quality of care that the patient was receiving. While this was more satisfactory than previous monitoring of the hospital's ability to provide adequate care, Congress still had not found a way to curtail health care costs. In short, they had not been able to provide any incentives to hospitals to use their resources in the most efficient manner, while at the same time providing quality care to their patients.

With the implementation of the Prospective Payment System in the 1980s, a system was developed that put hospitals into the position of competing for reimbursements based on their performance in patient care. Efficiency of performance could be measured through comparisons with other medical centers of similar size and scope. The rewards in reimbursements for care were based on predetermined diagnosis-related groups (DRGs). By disease category, by each procedure, and by concurrent complication, each inpatient admission was assigned a specific length-of-stay criterion. To receive maximum reimbursement for its efforts, the hospital would have to stay within, or shorten, the expected hospitalization period. For better or for worse, hospitals had to conform to these new standards or actually lose resources. For those who met the discharge criteria on a regular basis, increased resource allocations were the reward.

The immediate and lasting effect was to put medical centers into direct competition. Congress reasoned that this competition would not only hold the line on health care spending, but also should improve the quality of patient care. In the changeover to the Prospective Payment System, there was a momentary loss of focus on the quality of patient care. Quality was confused with meeting predetermined time commitments, and time commitments did not address the issue of what happened to the patient during hospitalization. The last half of the eighties has sought to combine the two major considerations in health care that will continue into the next decade: (1) curtailing costs by providing incentives for good performance and (2) doing it without sacrificing the patient's right to the best medical care system in the world. Program accountability in every medical center today has sensitized each department, section, and health care worker into trying to provide the best medical care at the lowest possible cost. Whereas the reimbursements that medical centers receive now are based on this paradigm, in the next decades so will individual performance incentives and future employment opportunity.

QUALITY MANAGEMENT

Terminology differs among medical institutions regarding the designation of their plans for monitoring the quality of patient care and the cost of that care. Indeed, part of the confusion has come from the accrediting bodies themselves. In a short period of time, the influx of new information and terminology to replace more dated rules and regulations has left information gaps as health care providers attempt to "catch up." *Quality management* as used here could be substituted for "Health Systems Review Organization" or "Patient Care and Cost Appropriation Program" in other medical centers. However, there is agreement among institutions as to elements within a structure that constitute a quality management program. In part, this is because of congressional mandates via the major hospital accrediting body, the Joint Commission on Accreditation of Healthcare Organizations (Joint Commission). This commission discharges groups of health care professionals to hospitals on a regular basis in an effort to monitor the quality of care provided by each institution. Deficiencies in care are noted, and they must be reevaluated for compliance on the next accreditation visit.

Program Objectives

The objectives of a medical center's quality management plan may include, but are not limited to:

- compliance with standards of practice as set forth by the Joint Commission and other accrediting bodies, including third-party payers
- establishment of accountability and standards of conduct for professional and administrative staffs by clearly delineating responsibilities
- the development of ongoing, hospital-wide, and service-specific programs for monitoring and evaluating the quality and appropriateness of patient care
- development of objective criteria and standards of practice that focus on structure, process, and outcomes of patient care
- implementation of corrective actions to resolve identified problems and pursue opportunities to improve patient care
- maintenance of strict patient confidentiality in all evaluations of the patients' health care.[1]

The methods of meeting these objectives can be accomplished through a number of mechanisms that vary among institutions. The recording of data to accomplish these goals and the channels through which the information flows also differ among institutions. It is the responsibility of the hospital's governing board, in conjunction with the designated quality assurance coordinator, to establish the necessary structure for appropriate interactions.

The documentation of the quality of patient care services (quality assurance), and the cost of those services (utilization review) usually are viewed as the two major components of a medical center's efforts to provide quality management. Quality assurance focuses on the nature and type of care a patient receives (Did the treatment fit the condition? Were there unnecessary complications? Did the patient obtain the maximum benefits from the services offered?). Utilization review focuses on related and sometimes overlapping issues such as the actual need and use of services, the patient's length of stay (LOS), the necessity for the admission and discharge, and the need for continued stay. Both quality assurance and utilization review look at all levels of care: admissions, intermediate care, intensive care units, ambulatory care (outpatient), hospital-based home care, and staff education.

It is now recognized that these two major areas of concern, patient care and its costs, can be evaluated concurrently if the controls for analysis are planned carefully. By the hospital-wide practices of *risk management* (identifying factors that put patients, staff, and family at risk) and *occurrence screening* (measuring specific risk factors) objective data can be gathered at each level of care. The data are used to study patient care through quality assurance processes and to delineate cost through utilization review. The organizational chart presented in Figure 10–1 is representative of a hospital's quality management program that incorporates aspects of quality assurance and utilization review. Organization of the quality management program revolves around the principle that all specialized committees and section-level departments will achieve their quality management goals through the mechanisms of risk management and occurrence screening. Additionally, all de-

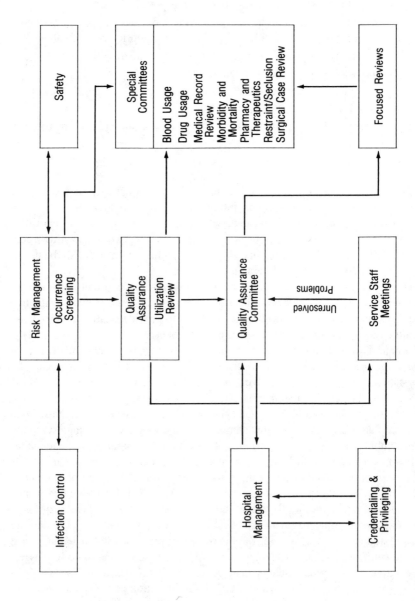

Figure 10–1 Components and Information Flow of a Quality Management Program.

partments will monitor infection control, safety, and credentialing/privileging as part of the hospital's efforts to provide the best care at the lowest possible cost.

Risk Management and Occurrence Screening

Risk management is a concept that allows a hospital to identify the activities of employees and visitors that may put the patient at risk.[2] It focuses on the reduction of the frequency of adverse occurrences through early identification and prevention. There are a myriad of hospital circumstances, including all medical procedures, patient transport, poor employee performance, and environmental hazards that potentially put a patient at risk. Each department is responsible for identifying aspects of the care they provide that may put a patient at risk for injury and create unnecessary liability for the medical center. Through occurrence screening, measuring the actual number of times a patient is put at risk with and without consequence, each hospital section attempts to identify problems and solve them before a major adverse incident occurs.

By utilizing the mechanisms of risk management and occurrence screening at each level of care and by each hospital section, the medical center is able to gather necessary data for an internal evaluation that reflects the quality of patient care and an analysis of its cost. Each hospital section analyzes its data for both favorable and unfavorable trends. The analysis that suggests a poor standard of care or care that is not cost-effective helps to pinpoint areas in need of improvement. If the improvement can be accomplished within the department, the appropriate changes are made and the occurrences remeasured to see if the changes that were instituted had a favorable impact. The entire process is documented for review by the quality management committee. If, in the opinion of the department head, the changes needed can be effected only with the assistance of other departments, this will be reported to the quality assurance manager who will design an occurrence screening measure that encompasses the same risk factors but with a larger number of occurrence screens.

Ideally, occurrence screening as part of the risk management process can be effective in answering a number of questions that relate to quality care and utilization review by using the records of a single patient. For instance, perhaps the department of surgery identified the risk factor of infection following open heart surgery. The occurrence screening within the department can be focused prospectively on the number of patients in a period of time who developed infection following open heart surgery. Additionally, the hospital's quality management coordinator may have chosen to evaluate the risk of patients to blood transfusion (that the open heart patient may have received), adverse effects from a new cardiac medication, complications from open heart surgery, and the length of stay for open heart patients, as well as review the necessity for the procedure. The occurrence of all of these factors could be documented on one patient at different points in time and provide indexes of both the quality of the care and the appropriate utilization (cost) of that care.

This same procedure is practiced by the speech/language pathologist. For instance, a speech/language pathologist can identify the risk of infection for patients receiving tracheoesophageal puncture after a number of trial fittings. An occurrence screen is developed. If a significant number of patients develop infection, then the possible reasons need to be documented and studied. The studies may include further screenings of patient selection, the surgical procedure, the fitting process, or prosthesis cleaning and maintenance.

Problems identified at departmental level through occurrence screening of high risk procedures can be the impetus for the hospital's quality assurance manager to begin focused reviews on topics that may not have otherwise come to the attention of management. Because there usually are more problems that need study than the quality assurance manager's department can manage, special committees or individuals with particular expertise in an area under question can be dispatched to review that specific problem. This is part of the hospital's internal review process and is completed through the mechanism of *peer review*.

Peer review is a system of monitoring in which a colleague (within the department or outside of the department) reviews an occurrence screening and the trends from that screening. Not all peer review is internal to the setting. For some problems, the medical center director may request peer review from a person or committee not connected with the medical center but with a special expertise in the area that the review demands. Peer review also is accomplished by standing committees (see Figure 10–1), such as committees that constantly review infection control or the morbidity and mortality associated with patient care. In most instances, peer review is not begun unless the reviewer has prearranged responsibilities. These include precise knowledge of the activity to be monitored, the length of monitoring time, knowledge of the criteria for occurrence, how the data are to be gathered, how the report is to be documented, and whether or not the reviewer is responsible for any follow-up action that may be necessary. In most cases, the peer reviewer is sent into a situation for which a known and accepted standard of practice has been established. Deviation from this standard is the risk factor. The reviewer's responsibility is to identify any occurrences that may vary from the established standard. All personnel should be included in the development of standards for their departments, assuring an awareness of the criteria for each standard.

Quality Assurance

The quality assurance process plays a major part in objectifying the success of a hospital department in meeting the standards of care established by the Joint Commission. In the past few years, there has been increasing emphasis on this activity by the Joint Commission. While the quality assurance process is practiced at all organizational levels, the backbone of the data comes from the individual services. These data may be used by the quality assurance manager to solve hospital-wide problems or to suggest to a specific service that it perform or become a part of additional focused reviews. By utilizing risk management and occurrence screening, quality assurance measures and patient care standards are established. The following are four key features of a quality assurance program.

1. It is planned in advance.
2. It is ongoing.
3. It is patient-oriented.
4. The process and results are documented, preferably in minutes from departmental staff meetings or in reports sent directly to the quality assurance coordinator.

To begin the quality assurance process, the personnel of each department identify aspects of patient care that contribute to the quality of the care. Decisions in these areas are suggested by the Joint Commission's requirements for practice in a hospital. These guidelines are summarized later in this chapter. One way to approach the problem of deciding what factors are important in ensuring quality patient care is to focus on the flow of that care, from receiving the request for services through the evaluation, the treatment/no treatment phase, and the discharge. During this process, the clinician may make errors in two general categories that can put the patient at risk. Both categories can be measured and analyzed for trends in care: (1) the number of occurrences in which the clinician should have performed an activity that was not performed and (2) the number of occurrences in which the clinician did something that should not have been done. In essence, these errors of omission and commission put the patient at risk from receiving optimal care and may cost the hospital unnecessary dollars. Additional areas of risk that require quality assurance monitoring include: (1) not practicing or implementing stated rules of safety, (2) not following effective infection control procedures, (3) not requesting assistance or additional consultation when necessary, and (4) not adequately recording clinical activities.

After each department decides on the areas of patient care to be monitored, a quality assurance plan is developed by the department and submitted for approval to the quality assurance coordinator. The plan normally is submitted on an annual basis. It is expected, however, that each department will modify its plan to meet the needs of the service as they arise, rather than utilizing the same monitors for the entire reporting period. The plan is designed as a problem-solving tool, and quality assurance is a dynamic process. For instance, it may be determined by peer review that the department's progress notes, scheduled for review as part of the original plan, were not in the proper format in the medical record. Therefore, the quality assurance plan may shift its focus to discover the reasons for improper formatting. After the reasons are identified, the medical record will be reviewed again for compliance in format.

When the quality assurance topics have been approved, individuals within each department are assigned as peer reviewers to measure the department's performance in the areas chosen for occurrence screening. Criteria for acceptable levels of performance in any targeted area usually are based on current knowledge and clinical practice as agreed upon by the staff consensus. If the levels of performance are set too low, patient care may suffer. If they are set unrealistically high, patient care may not be necessarily better; however, staff morale may be affected by trying to conform to unobtainable standards. Criteria and goals involving patient care activities should be set by deciding on a continuum of normalcy, that is, what is normal for any given group of patients receiving treatment and how far a patient may digress before treatment is reinstated. In treatment activities, common monitoring devices include whether or not (1) there are short- and long-range goals, (2) these goals are appropriate to the diagnosis, (3) the treatment activities selected are directly aimed at achieving the goals, (4) appropriate changes are made at the appropriate time to achieve the long-range goals, and (5) the patient is able to achieve the goals. If the patient achieves the goals before or after the stated time frames, the reasons should be documented and adjusted appropriately for the next patient.

There must be a stated method of data collection for each area targeted for review that includes the source (e.g., patient report, laboratory evaluation, and medical record), what is being counted, how the data are sampled, the frequency of the collection, and the frequency of the report. Results at the end of the reporting period are analyzed. If the criteria for acceptable performance are met the department head may choose to drop certain topics from the plan or continue to monitor them to ensure uniform adherence throughout the entire reporting period because of the important nature of their function. If the criteria are not met, the department must develop a set of action plans to correct its performance. The action plans themselves can serve as part of the quality assurance process. Because of failure to meet a set standard, for example, the staff may decide on another course of action to correct the deficiency that perhaps will set new standards and measure new occurrences. If new data are gathered the problem may be solved.

The impact of any new corrective action must be measured and documented. The entire quality assurance process also must be documented within the department for Joint Commission review and reports of the process forwarded to the quality assurance coordinator. The steps involved in establishing an effective monitoring and evaluation process are summarized in Exhibit 10–1.

The quality assurance process is a departmental endeavor. In *step 1* the department director assigns responsibility for providing the necessary quality assurance data. In *step 2* staff members review the scope of care provided in the service, the types of patients served, the types of treatments performed, and guidelines on how long each patient should be treated. The specific important aspects of care are identified in *step 3*. They should include elements in the scope of care that appear to be most crucial in their impact on the majority of patients. Unless these aspects of care are present, patients will be at greater risk for failure.

In *step 4* measurable variables (indicators) that impact on the most crucial aspects of care are identified. In some cases supplies, equipment, or numbers of qualified staff may impact on patient care. In other cases the variables may focus on the process of diagnosis and treatment or on identified desirable or undesirable

Exhibit 10–1 The Ten Steps in Completing Quality Assurance Monitors

Monitoring and Evaluation Process
1. Assign responsibility.
2. Delineate scope of care.
3. Identify important aspects of care.
4. Identify indicators related to these aspects of care.
5. Establish thresholds for evaluation related to the indicators.
6. Collect and organize data.
7. Evaluate care when thresholds are reached.
8. Take action to improve care.
9. Assess effectiveness of action.
10. Document improvement and report to quality assurance coordinator.

outcomes in treatment. Since the final product of treatment (outcome) depends on a large number of clinical issues preceding it (correct diagnosis, correct selection of candidate for remediation, and correct treatment approaches), many providers of clinical services have begun to focus in recent years on issues of outcome in their quality assurance endeavors.[3] By focusing on outcomes, the speech/language pathologist must determine the desirable outcome for any given set of patients with similar problems. For instance it may be decided that a desirable outcome for laryngectomees who cannot learn esophageal voice is the effective use of the electrolarynx in all speaking situations. How successful the staff is in achieving this goal, and in what length of time, would constitute the variable that is monitored. Barriers to that goal can be identified if the outcome is less than expected, and corrective actions then taken. In this example, optimal care standards can be defined and comparisons made between future attempts at treatment with another group of similar patients and the original sample of patient performances.

Another outcome study in aphasia treatment illustrating *step 4* may relate to Broca's aphasics and their ability to make their needs known by some means of communication before the end of 6 months. When the measurable indicators have been identified, the number of times an indicator should or should not be present is established (*step 5*). These thresholds for evaluation usually are expressed in terms of an event exceeding an expected level of occurrence. Further evaluation of that indicator is then needed. These criteria are based on current standards of professional practice as dictated by a hospital or accrediting body, by staff-generated standards based on past practice, or by comparisons between standards of similar institutions. *Step 6* requires the identification of the data sources, the individual collecting the data, the sampling process (e.g., every case or every 15 cases), the frequency of collection, and the frequency of reporting. After the data are collected, the reviewer must decide if a problem exists and, if so, propose possible reasons for its existence (*step 7*).

In *step 8,* action should be taken either to correct the problem or to decide that no problem exists. If a problem does exist, those variables that were found to impact negatively on the outcome must be delineated. When the needed correction is possible within the department's authority, the parameters for change have to be identified and the indicator remeasured utilizing the same process (*step 9*). Proposed changes that exceed the department's authority should be reported to the quality assurance coordinator who may choose to involve more than one department in a focused study to solve the problem. At the end of the year, a quality assurance summary (*step 10*), such as the sample presented in Appendix 10–A, is prepared.

An example of a quality assurance plan pertinent to a department of audiology and speech/language pathology is presented in Table 10–1. It should be noted that in this example nine areas of critical care are identified in the first column. The remainder of the table indicates the threshold for evaluation, monitoring methodology, reviewer's name, the sample size, frequency of collection, and the frequency of reporting for each area of care. For instance, the first indicator monitors whether or not the progress note reflects the status of the patient's care. The threshold of occurrence is set at 5 percent. In other words, a progress note that does *not* reflect the patient's current status should not occur in more than 5 percent of the patients reviewed. The review is performed by employee EE who randomly chooses 10 inpatient or oupatient charts on a quarterly basis to look for the desired indicators.

To help gather the data and to delineate the specific indicators that are necessary to decide whether or not the patient care status was documented, worksheets can be utilized. For instance, in the sample worksheet shown in Table 10–2, the criterion for the first monitor of patient care status is a progress note that includes the treatment goal, the patient's progress toward that goal, and the plan of treatment. If any of these elements are missing from the chart review, the patient did not meet the criterion. Similarly, the complications associated with videofluoroscopy that are monitored include aspiration during the study to cause termination of the study, development of an aspiration pneumonia within three days of the study, and constipation. The worksheet forms can be submitted to the quality assurance coordinator along with the yearly quality assurance plan.

Utilization Review

The second component of quality management is utilization review. This component also uses risk management technique and occurrence screening, but it focuses on utilization of health care facilities in the most cost-effective manner without sacrificing the quality of patient care. It is a measure of the demand for and use of hospital services. The goal of a utilization review program is to maximize the efficient use of patient resources by focusing on the appropriateness of the level of care as it relates to the hospital's resources.[4] For instance, a departmental utilization review program may focus on the following five areas:

1. necessity and appropriateness of patient care and support services, utilizing predetermined criteria

Table 10–1 Sample of an Annual Quality Management Plan for a Department of Audiology and Speech/Language Pathology

Indicator	Threshold for Evaluation	Monitoring Methodology	Reviewer	Sample Size	Collection Frequency	Reporting Frequency
1. Progress note reflects patient care status, including goals and discharge plan	5%	Review of in- and outpatient records	EE	20 randomly selected	Quarterly	Quarterly
2. Complications during videofluoroscopy	5%	Documentation at study and 24 hours after study	MG	Successive referrals	Monthly	Monthly
3. Dysphagia evaluation changes patient's care	30%	Bedside measurements	MG	Successive referrals	Monthly	Biannually
4. Intern accurately presents history, diagnosis, treatment, prognosis at case conference	10%	Weekly conferences	EE	All interns	Weekly	Quarterly
5. Utilization of hearing aid appointment slots	10%	Weekly review of records	AM/ JW	All records	Monthly	Monthly
6. Utilization of compensation and pension appointment slots	20%	Review of daily schedule	CC	All compensation/pension appointment slots	Daily	Monthly
7. Need for hearing aid repairs	30%	Aids brought in by patients for repairs	RB	All aids brought in	Daily	Quarterly
8. Hearing aid inventory is accurate	5%	Inventory from prosthetics	CC	All hearing aids issued	Biannually and quarterly	Biannually and quarterly
9. Appropriateness of diagnostic tests utilized on compensation, hearing aid fitting, and other examinations	10%	Review of completed audiologic evaluations	AH	10 of each type of dx examination a) 10 compensation/pension b) 10 hearing aid evaluation c) 10 other	Quarterly	Quarterly

Table 10–2 Sample of a Quality Assurance Reporting Worksheet

Criteria	Data source	Collecting frequency	Collector	Reporting frequency
1. • Progress note states treatment goal • Progress note states how close patient is to goal • Progress note reflects a plan	10 inpatient and 10 outpatient records	Monthly	EEE	Monthly
2. • Aspiration occurs so study is terminated • Patient develops aspiration pneumonia within 3 days • Patient becomes constipated • Patient in cardio-pulmonary distress	Radiologist Patient record	Monthly	MEG	Quarterly
3. Intervention for swallow brings: • Definitive source for dysphagia • Positive diet change • No respiratory complications	Patient evalua-tion Medical record	Monthly	MEG	Quarterly
4. At case conference intern reviews: • History • Diagnosis • Prognosis • Treatment plan	Weekly staffing	Weekly	EEE	Monthly

2. identification of areas in which services have been over- or underutilized
3. identification of inefficient resource scheduling
4. establishment of priorities for resolution of identified utilization problems
5. assistance to the clinical and administrative staffs in controlling use of resources and services

Hospital-wide utilization review programs focus their audits on preadmission reviews (e.g., the necessity for elective surgery), rejected applications for admission (whether a patient who was denied admission should be admitted or vice versa), appropriateness of admissions, the need for continued stay, and discharge planning and disposition.[5] An additional area of concern in utilization review is the monitoring of the level of patient care. Were patients admitted to the proper level of care? Were they transferred to another level of care properly and at the appropriate time? Was their care complicated by poor assignment? Was the level of care plan documented on admission?

All of these questions are also applicable at the departmental level. For instance, in speech/language pathology, utilization review can be practiced by asking similar questions that require monitoring. They often are a part of the quality assurance program. The department can develop monitors to assess whether a patient admitted for communication services during the reporting period actually met the criteria for acceptance. The length of stay (time spent receiving services), based on the type of disorder, can be measured against data from other departments similar in size and scope. If the length of stay was too long, were there complicating factors? If treated, did the patient reach maximum benefit within a stated period of time, and was the patient discharged promptly after reaching maximum benefit? Many of these questions can be answered if the department begins to build its own data base reflecting the information that utilization review encompasses. The establishment of normative data for future comparisons of resource utilization can be a strong tool in maintaining current resources and asking for additional funding.

DEPARTMENTAL GUIDELINES

While quality management activities have assumed a major role in monitoring the provision of speech/language pathology and audiological services within the medical setting, adherence to other policies and procedures as part of Joint Commission guidelines also requires attention. When the medical center prepares for an evaluation by the Joint Commission it asks each department to adhere to the quality management process and to other basic criteria that reflect how well a department achieves its stated function.

Criteria and Indicators

The Joint Commission's guidelines for practice in audiology and speech/language pathology are published and distributed to medical centers on a biannual schedule.[6] While the standards do not change in their entirety, certain criteria receive a different emphasis depending on congressional mandates and changes in the standards for practice in any given medical specialty. For instance, quality assurance and utilization review monitors used as problem-solving tools to improve patient care have gone through a number of revisions. In addition to standards requiring services to be involved in quality management, the Joint Commission delineates other expected performance standards that are expressed as individual criteria, followed by brief summaries of the behavioral aspects of performance that must be present to meet that criteria (indicators).

The following information represents a summary of selected areas of performance, in addition to those particular to the aspects of quality management, that should be adhered to by audiology and speech/language departments of medical centers. These are not verbatim standards, but are designed to give the clinician a sense of the documentation required to keep a program in speech/language and hearing viable. Indicators required for compliance follow each criterion statement. A brief narrative comment based on experience with the documentation required by the indicators is included for most items.

Criterion 1

Service policies are consistent with the medical center's mission.

Indicator 1. There is a statement that reflects the service's goals and responsibilities. *Comment:* The department of speech/language and hearing should develop a statement that describes its function in the hospital, the scope of its practice (types of patients treated by diagnostic category), whether it serves both inpatients and outpatients, and a description of the general emphasis in service provision, such as its roles in diagnostics and treatment. For instance, acute care settings may want to focus only on diagnostics due to the short length of time that the patient is hospitalized.

Indicator 2. There is an approved organizational chart. *Comment:* An organizational chart is a graphic summary statement approved by the administration that shows the chain of command through which information flows and decisions are made. In some cases a chart indicates that the director of speech/language pathology reports to the director of rehabilitation medicine who, in turn, reports to the chief medical director. In other cases, the director of speech/language pathology reports directly to the chief of medical services. The chart usually includes a listing of all employees in the service with their salaries and basic responsibilities by title, including the levels of supervision within the service.

Indicator 3. There is a policy and procedure manual that must include, but is not limited to, the following:

- A procedure for referral to the service. *Comment:* This includes a description of how a health professional requests services, where the requests are sent, and special procedures for requesting services that are not in writing.
- A procedure for assignment of patients. *Comment:* Are more difficult patients assigned to particular clinicians? Are specific diagnoses assigned to specific clinicians? Are consults assigned consecutively? Who makes the patient care assignments?
- A procedure that indicates how a patient's progress is documented, including content, frequency, and format. *Comment:* This may include the style of the progress note, what it should contain, and how it should be signed. Also in-

cluded may be how often a full diagnostic evaluation is required during extended treatment and how it is documented.

- A procedure for discharge and referral of patients. *Comment:* This delineates when discharge planning is to begin, criteria for discharge, how soon the discharge report must be completed after discharge, and what elements of care the discharge report should reflect. For instance, one requirement may be submission of the discharge report directly to the extended care facility if that is the patient's final disposition.

- A procedure for patient follow-up to include community interface. *Comment:* A service may provide regular re-evaluation and follow-up of patients by telephone or through clinic visits. If a patient receiving additional therapeutic treatments is not able to travel to the hospital, a procedure for providing services in a community close to the patient's home should be developed.

- A procedure for infection control. *Comment:* This delineates the service's policy in the practice of infection control as it pertains to the evaluation of the oral cavity and the sterilization of instruments used in evaluation. In most cases, a statement indicates that the service's infection control program adheres to the medical center's program. The medical center's statement has specific guidelines for practices involving contact with bodily fluids.

- A policy and procedure for supervisory levels of coverage. *Comment:* A statement should indicate who is in charge in another's absence, who is responsible for supervision of various activities within the service, and who contacts whom by telephone in the event of a disaster or emergency during nonduty hours.

Criterion 2

Budget, space, equipment, and staff allocated to the service reflect effective utilization review and monitoring.

Indicator 1. The service has sufficient space to carry out its function. *Comment:* The Veterans Administration has published guidelines that indicate the amount of space deemed necessary to provide speech/language and hearing services in a hospital setting. Other guidelines published by a medical center's space or engineering committee also may serve as references. Comparisons are made between recommended and actual space to be used for facility planning. Space shortages that interfere with the functioning of the service should be documented.

Indicator 2. Any appropriate service needs are reflected in short- and long-range plans. *Comment:* Budget, space, and equipment requests require documentation to ensure that the service's needs are viewed as part of the hospital's total management planning program. Short-range allocations are usually for the forthcoming year, whereas long-range planning covers five years. Both plans are updated on an annual basis and revised as appropriate.

Indicator 3. Calibration, equipment repair, and preventive maintenance procedures are routinely managed. *Comment:* Each item needs to be documented in a logbook along with the name of the person performing the work and the date completed. Both formal and informal (biological) calibration checks should be documented. Records of equipment repair and maintenance performed should be kept in a separate folder. A routine maintenance plan should be stated in a departmental policy memorandum.

Indicator 4. A yearly staff/utilization review study is completed and documented. *Comment:* The numbers and types of patients seen during a one-year period should be analyzed to determine if each department staff member is working at full or expected capacity. Periods of patient or staff inactivity and periods of greater activity should receive further analysis. For instance, if there are periods during a day or month when the staff is not busy treating patients or when it is especially busy, with a possible reduction in the quality of care, an analysis focused on the explanation for these trends can be initiated. Utilization of staff-to-patient ratio is an important index of productivity that will reflect on future staffing and funding patterns.

Criterion 3

The staff is competent and qualified to provide services essential to the medical center's stated goals.

Indicator 1. Written performance requirements are established for each staff position and used as part of the annual supervisory evaluation.

Indicator 2. A delineation of clinical privileges is current for each staff member and consultant and is reviewed annually.

Indicator 3. Consultants are appropriately balanced with program needs. *Comment:* Each of these three indicators is discussed in the next section of this chapter under staff accountability. Privileging and credentialing have become increasingly important issues in the quality management process and require more detailed comment.

Criterion 4

Consultations provided by the service are satisfactory.

Indicator 1. There is evidence of a systematic evaluation assessment process. *Comment:* Evidence of a systematic evaluation process can be demonstrated either by a regular internal or external review of consultation replies or by a policy statement, acknowledged by all staff members, that outlines the service's evaluation procedure by patient type. For instance, the procedure in evaluation of a laryngectomized patient may include the following:

- to counsel the patient preoperatively on the postoperative complication to communication (and related issues)
- to assess the patient's learning skills and report them to the surgeon
- to evaluate the oral peripheral speech mechanism
- to include the significant family in the counseling process
- to review all options for postoperative communication, including a preoperative session with a laryngectomized visitor if the patient desires

Policies of this nature should be kept general without specific mention of the types of tests performed. For instance, it is better to indicate that each aphasic will receive a full evaluation of communicative ability, rather than test x, y, or z.

Indicator 2. Routine consultations are provided in a timely manner consistent with local service policy. *Comment:* There should be a written departmental policy stating the acceptable time period allowed between receiving the request for services and completing the consultation in a formal report. Forty-eight hours is a normal standard. Measuring the staff's adherence to response times to consultation requests is a valuable quality assurance topic.

Indicator 3. Referral sources are satisfied with the services they receive. *Comment:* If a service wants to explore the value of its contribution to other services requesting its assistance, a survey can be developed and administered by the quality assurance coordinator, who will avoid bias in recording and reporting the results.

Criterion 5

The service provides appropriate and timely outpatient services. *Comment:* The service should outline a procedure indicating the service staff member to contact for an appointment if the patient requires further treatment after leaving the hospital. Criteria should be delineated regarding acceptable waiting periods for appointments. The policy should reflect how outpatients are identified for future outpatient treatments (usually via the inpatient progress notes) and the need to document this in the medical records. If the medical center's policy states that an outpatient requiring a hearing aid at the time of discharge must receive the hearing aid within one month of discharge, the department policy should reflect this fact.

Criterion 6

Progress notes provide sufficient information to reflect accurately the patients' communicative abilities, responses to treatment, and future plans. *Comment:* Quality assurance audits in the past focused heavily on chart reviews dealing with documentation of patients' treatment plans, responses to treatment, and future plans. With more recent emphasis on the quality assurance process as a problem identification and problem-solving tool, the review of progress notes pertinent to the stated criterion has focused more on the documentation of the outcome of treatment.

Indicator 1. Progress notes should be frequent and address the evaluation results, treatment response, and goals established in the initial evaluation. *Comment:* The frequency of progress notes often is expressed in hospital policy, or it may be left to the individual service. It is good policy to place a note in the patient's chart after each contact. However, this is not always possible due to unforeseen circumstances when the medical record is not available.

Indicator 2. Progress notes indicate a patient's functional communication status, prognosis, family and community adjustment, and new review date. *Comment:* The date of re-evaluation of communicative status needs to be documented in the progress notes, together with the result of the evaluation. This usually is done on a monthly basis.

Indicator 3. Each patient has a documented discharge plan that includes a continuous treatment plan if indicated, the name and address of a referral source if needed, and an indication that the family has been notified of the reasons for the disposition.

Criterion 7

There is a service systematic internal review program. *Comment:* This encompasses the service's quality assurance and utilization review processes.

Criterion 8

The service provides staff continuing education programs that promote improvement of patient care.

Indicator 1. Findings of quality assurance/utilization reviews are translated into educational objectives. *Comment:* Internal and external quality assurance or utilization reviews may indicate that the quality or cost of a particular activity could be improved if the involved staff members receive additional training that will either update their technical knowledge or increase the speed of providing the service. After identifying this training need, the department director submits a request for a particular individual to receive special training. Because continuing education funds are limited in most medical centers, it is important that the request for training funds estimate the financial benefit of the training to the medical center. For instance, a staff member may be able to accomplish a diagnostic evaluation in a shorter time period with improved quality by attending a conference about new technology on instrumentation that results in faster and more accurate diagnoses. The department director can argue that more patients will be seen in less time if this training is provided. Estimates of the dollars saved or added to the medical center's budget can be part of the justification for training.

Indicator 2. The staff should participate in multidisciplinary conferences. *Comment:* The role of the speech/language pathologist as a member of multidisciplinary health care teams in rehabilitation medicine, gerontology, otolaryngology, neurology, and swallowing disorders is discussed in Chapter 2. It is important for the person attending these meetings to document the proceedings in a consecutive log of activities that includes the name of the patient, diagnosis, treatment goals and plans, progress, and plans for discharge. Notes are usually made on a weekly basis.

Indicator 3. There is evidence of advanced planning in educational needs assessment. *Comment:* Based on the results obtained from quality assurance monitors that may have identified areas of needed training, the department director should submit a training plan to the education coordinator so that funding can be obtained. The plan should be documented, as well as its results. For instance, how well were the training needs met, and what areas of identified need still require attention?

Indicator 4. There is evaluation of continuing education impact on patient care services. *Comment:* After completing a continuing education course, a staff member should present the information to the rest of the staff. After the staff has mastered the new skill or technique, a quality assurance monitor should be established to measure the impact of the training on the health care delivery provided. Whether or not the training experience met the intended need should be documented in the service's staff meeting minutes and in its annual continuing education report.

Criterion 9

The service should be actively involved with committees concerned with delivery, monitoring, and evaluation of audiology and speech/language pathology services.

Indicator 1. Committee minutes reflect active and ongoing participation of the service on health care evaluation, accreditation, patient care education, and other appropriate committees. *Comment:* As mentioned in Chapter 1, the speech/language pathologist may be selected to participate on hospital committees. It is necessary to keep a departmental record of the minutes of these meetings for review by any accrediting body as evidence that the department was represented and its views presented. Summaries of meetings attended by the director of the service should be documented in the monthly staff minutes as an indicator that the director has shared pertinent information with the staff.

Criterion 10

The training program is of high quality and adequately documented.

Indicator 1. There are signed training agreements between the teaching hospital and the university. *Comment:* Training agreements generally are broad in scope, but they outline basic responsibilities and assumptions of liability on the part of both parties. There should be a regular review of each training agreement, changes made if necessary, and signatures obtained to the effect that the document was reviewed by both parties.

Indicator 2. The training objectives are documented and reviewed annually. *Comment:* The training program and affiliate institution should decide on basic objectives to be accomplished as part of the clinical experience. Often these may differ, depending on the level and experience of the clinician. The criteria for evaluation and the method of evaluation should be established. Methods may include demonstration, written performance, verbal report, or a combination of any of these. Provision should be made for discussing the evaluation with the student, allowing for rebuttal, and signing documentation that the review of performance was held.

STAFF ACCOUNTABILITY

A major portion of the medical center's quality management program relates to ensuring that patients and the medical center are not put at unnecessary risk due to the hiring or retention of staff members who are not qualified to perform their assigned and expected job responsibilities. It is also the medical center's responsibility to ensure that each qualified staff member maintains a level of excellence compatible with accepted practice and within the medical center's guidelines. Any errors in judgment or incompetencies in staff performance impacting on patient care can be monitored and hopefully reduced or eliminated by three mechanisms:

1. ensuring that each staff member actually possesses the proper training for the position for which he or she was hired
2. ensuring that each staff member continues to improve or maintain excellence in the required skills
3. ensuring that each staff member is subject to peer review of his or her performance as a method of measuring ongoing clinical practices

Credentialing

Medical centers have the right to require their employees to hold licenses or certificates from accrediting bodies signifying that they have completed a course of training and are qualified to practice based on that training. To ensure that both new and present employees can meet accreditation standards set forth by their respective professions, the professional should be required to prove that he or she holds the proper credentials to practice legally in that jurisdiction. This can be done by two methods: (1) a requirement that the professional present signed original documents verifying accreditation and licensure and (2) a verification of any prior appointments that pertain to the professional's employment status. For instance, prior employers should be checked routinely for any professional improprieties that interfered with the performance of the professional's duties.

Any previous denials of licensure or certification should be explored by checking prior work assignments. If these were ever denied, the circumstances should be discussed with the employee and with the institution that denied or terminated employment because of improper credentials. Institutions can maintain high standards of care by utilizing the credentialing process to review an individual's credentials at regular (usually annual) intervals and verifying that the individual has remained in good standing with the relevant professional accrediting or licensing bodies.

Clinical Privileging

Another mechanism of quality assurance that relates to staff performance is the clinical privileging process. Clinical privileging is a process in which the professional must apply for, and have approved, the privilege to perform certain aspects of patient care based on the individual's education, previous record, and years of experience. As a method of monitoring competencies in each of the areas for which application is made, the specialist must demonstrate satisfactory completion of a prescribed number of procedures without incidence in order to be reappointed for another year. An example of an application for clinical privileges for a speech/language pathologist is presented in Exhibit 10–2. As demonstrated in the exhibit, the individual can apply for generalized, specialized, and, if appropriate, research privileges.

Generalized privileges are those that the applicant is expected to possess as qualifications for the job and as part of licensure. Specialized privileges usually encompass procedures or duties that come under the purview of the professional's scope of practice but are not necessary to obtain or maintain a license. An example is the speech/language pathologist's role in the evaluation of patients with swallowing disorders. For each specialized clinical privilege, the applicant is required to complete a prearranged number of procedures within the reporting period in order to reapply for that privilege in the following year. The minimal number of events needed to achieve reapplication rights for each privilege is listed under specialized clinical privileges in Exhibit 10–2. For instance, to retain privileges in fitting tracheoesophageal puncture prostheses, the applicant must have completed or assisted with eight fittings. In research, the applicant must have been involved in two research projects. Space on the application is reserved for indicating the midyear totals and the actual number of procedures accomplished. Failure to meet the set standards can jeopardize reappointment and may be worthy of investigation as a quality assurance topic. For example, a review of the reasons why an individual does not complete privileging requirements may demonstrate poor case selection, failure to perform a procedure when it should have been performed, or failure to

Exhibit 10–2 Sample Cover Sheet Requesting Clinical Privileges

REQUEST FOR PRIVILEGES

I request the following privileges for the position of Speech/Language Pathologist in the Audiology/Speech Pathology Services in the Medical Center.

Name _____   Date _____

	Apply for	# Needed	Mid-year	# Done
I. General Clinical Privileges	( )			
II. Specialized Clinical Privileges	( )			
1. Specialized Tests				
a. Administration of Porch Index of Communicative Ability	( )	(6)	( )	( )
b. Dysphagia evaluation and treatment	( )	(40)	( )	( )
c. EMG-Biofeedback	( )	(5)	( )	( )
d. TEP fitting	( )	(8)	( )	( )
e. Use of laryngoscope	( )	(12)	( )	( )
f. Use of otoscope	( )	(8)	( )	( )
g. Assists in videofluorography	( )	(16)	( )	( )
h. Indirect mirror laryngoscopy	( )	(8)	( )	( )
i. Pure tone audiometry screening	( )	(8)	( )	( )
j. Student supervision	( )	(4)	( )	( )
III. Research Privileges	( )	(2)	( )	( )

complete a procedure due to poor training or incompetence. An example of the entire clinical privileging document is presented in Appendix 10–B.

Peer Review

Peer review, if properly structured and implemented, may be the strongest ongoing mechanism to ensure that each professional is adhering to quality standards of practice. By implication, this reflects on the quality of care that the patient receives. If a large number of adverse occurrences are attributed to one individual in studies focusing on risk screening and quality assurance, the department head may recommend disqualification of that individual from practicing in a given area of specialization. The complaint first must be registered with the hospital director and then with the state licensure board.

Reviewing an employee's ability to provide quality patient care is a logical extension of, and should be directly tied to, the employee's annual performance evaluation. For instance, in order to receive a superior performance rating, an employee may have a performance standard indicating there should be no more than three adverse occurrences attributed to patients in their care for one calendar year. Standards more specific to a particular task assignment also may be targeted, such as "When assisting in the videofluoroscopic evaluation of patients with swallowing impairment, there will be no more than three adverse occurrences associated with the procedure in the reporting period." A director of a service may have broader performance standards that also could be peer reviewed to reflect the quality of care patients receive in that service. For instance, a standard may state, "The service will have fewer than five justified registered patient complaints against the care that the service provides in the calendar year," or "On no more than three occasions during the calendar year will the monthly quality assurance report not be timely."

Continuing Education

Ensuring staff accountability also is linked to the continuing education process. A staff that remains current in its practices is better prepared to meet the needs of its patients. New technology often is a continuing source for improving the quality of care, either by reducing the morbidity and mortality rates or by reducing the cost of procedures. Sometimes a quality assurance review discovers that certain risks occurred because state-of-the-art technology or equipment was not available, or that no staff member had received adequate training in the use of the equipment. In the latter case it is prudent for the medical center to provide the necessary training to reduce the risk occurrence associated with the lack of education.

Some professionals need to demonstrate that they have participated in a required number of certified training experiences in a given time period in order to maintain their licenses to practice. Some employees work toward continuing education credits so they will have more opportunities for job promotions. In some cases, participation in continuing education programs is tied to the employees' performance standards. For instance, in order to receive superior ratings, employees may be required to attend three postgraduate courses relating directly to their job responsibilities within the reporting period. When possible, institutions make an effort to provide financial support for continuing education. The current trend is to have the employee pay a portion of the cost and the institution fund the balance.

Performance Evaluation

A method of evaluating part of an employee's clinical preparation is to tie together the processes of competency, privileging, and continuing education as measures of performance. An example of a form used to document an employee's performance as it relates to demonstrations of the ability to maintain and improve clinical skills is presented in Exhibit 10–3. In this example, eight major areas of performance are used to judge an employee's previous and current educational and clinical expertise:

1. audit results/peer review
2. credentials
3. clinical privileges
4. continuing education record
5. publications
6. lectures
7. university courses taught
8. university courses taken

Exhibit 10–3 Data Collection Form Tying Evaluation to Competency and Privileges

---

1. Audit Results/Peer Review

  a. **Item:** Response to consults
    Result: 2 percent not punctual
    Correction: None needed

  b. **Item:** Documented goals
    Result: 100 percent of the time
    Correction: None needed

  c. **Item:** Clear discharge plan
    Result: 10 percent not clear
    Correction: 1 percent not clear

2. Credentials

  License: New York
  Certification: Certificate of Clinical Competence/Speech Pathology (CCC/SP)
  Copies on file: Yes

3. Clinical Privileges

  Applied for: 12
  Met: 12

4. Education, Continuing

  a. Aphasia Workshop, Indiana
  b. Head Trauma, Virginia
  c. Dysphagia, New York
  d. Diagnostic Related Groups (DRGs), New York
  e. Supervising Skills, Connecticut
    Continuing Education Units (CEUs): 12

5. Publications in Journals

(copies on file)

  a. Archives of Otolaryngology
  b. Dysphagia
  c. Neurology

6. Meeting Presentations

  a. Dysarthria, state meeting
  b. Dysphagia, downstate hospital
  c. Clinical Evaluations of Aphasia, American Speech-Language-Hearing Association (ASHA)

7. University Courses Taught

  a. Dysphagia, summer
  b. Neuroanatomy, fall

8. University Classes Taken

  a. 6 credits in public health
  b. 6 credits toward Ph.D.

Ideally, preestablished goals for the year are set by mutual agreement between the employee and the supervisor against which the employee's performance in each area of responsibility is judged. The value of this evaluation relates to ensuring and documenting that the employee is capable of performing the required duties with a high level of expertise and that the employee's approach to patients represents the most current techniques and provides the patients with a high standard of care. Attendance at accredited courses and conferences and participation in teaching also demonstrate that the employee is committed to application of the most recent scientific innovations in providing services for communication-impaired patients.

AUDIT PREPARATION

Periodic peer reviews by outside agencies, such as the Joint Commission's audit of the speech/language and hearing department's performance in the medical setting, are necessary and mandatory if the medical center wants to obtain accreditation and maintain its teaching affiliations. Even though an audit is scheduled for the entire hospital, it does not mean that a reviewer will visit the speech/language and hearing department. However, the medical center director usually will know the schedule after meeting on the first day with the individuals who will perform the audit. Sometimes the speech/language and hearing department is scheduled for a visit, but due to time constraints or scheduling difficulty the audit is not conducted. However, it is paramount that the necessary preparations for the visit are accomplished before the audit team arrives.

Most external reviewers have knowledge of a hospital's organization, structure, and processes and have had experience in the audit process. A reviewer assigned to the speech pathology section often is not a speech/language pathologist. However, the reviewer's background should include contact with speech/language pathologists through clinical experience. Representatives from the specialties of neurology, otolaryngology, or rehabilitation are appropriate reviewers. As auditors, they may be familiar with the duties and responsibilities of a speech/language pathologist although, as pointed out in Chapter 1, discrepancies and misconceptions of this role do exist. However, the reviewer's duties are guided by the outline of factors presented earlier in this chapter under departmental guidelines. The reviewer also will assess the service's quality assurance and utilization review program in four major areas:

1. The goals of the program, developed and approved, are consistent with the medical center's policy and objectives.
2. The department's program demonstrates an ongoing, active process of problem identification and solution by utilizing the mechanisms of risk management and occurrence screening.
3. The program measures how problem-solving activities impact on the provision and cost of services.

4. The program has summarized the department's activities in reports to the quality assurance coordinator.

The preparation for review of the quality management aspects of departmental function is less consequential when the department has remained active in its quality management activities. To ensure that each staff member participates in data collection and analysis, these activities should be included as a part of the staff member's annual performance evaluation. Attempting to play catch-up in quality assurance and utilization reviews only defeats the purpose of the activities and places undue pressure on the staff in preparing for audits. If the department's quality management program is used as a legitimate problem-solving tool and program documentation is current, the department always should be prepared for an unannounced audit of its services.

The auditor may find it necessary to review the medical records of either preselected or randomly selected patients who recently received speech/language or hearing services. It is important to remember that an auditor is unable to determine if a department is performing a necessary function unless there is documentation of that function. It is not sufficient, for instance, for the director to indicate orally to the reviewer that there is an active, ongoing continuing education program within the department if there is no written evidence that the program exists. Documentation of continuing education activities includes a written record of the department's plan for continuing education, the topics that have been covered, who was in attendance, the date of the training, and its impact on service function.

The visit of an external peer reviewer should not be confrontational but should be welcomed in the spirit of a mutual effort to improve patient care. A cardinal rule is to be as cooperative as possible, offer only information that is requested, and confine remarks to the functions of the service.

Policy and Procedures

Review of each criterion of performance and the indicators of that performance is accomplished in large part by the auditor's review of the department's policy and procedures manual. The task is facilitated if the manual has an index and is readily available. There should be a signature page in the manual verifying that each staff member is familiar with the contents. These signatures should be obtained on an annual basis. Suggested policies and procedures to be documented should include:

- complaints (how they are managed)
- credentialing/privileging
- disaster and fire plans
- discharges (criteria and procedures)
- health and infection control

- community referrals (how they are made)
- patient injury (prevention and maintenance)
- patient visits (tabulation of workload)
- processing consultations
- procedures in evaluation by disorder (including dysphagia)
- safety
- supply and equipment procurement
- employee time and leave schedules
- videofluorographic evaluation technique

The department also should have documentation of its continuing education program. This could include a logbook of all training activities in which the staff has participated. All inservice training, both within and outside the department, requires documentation as evidence that the training is ongoing and that the department is active in its efforts to educate others about the role of the speech/language pathologist in a medical center.

If the department supervises and trains clinical interns, there should be an outline of the training objectives, criteria for the selection of interns, how the interns are evaluated, and how the intern evaluates the training and supervision.

In general, if a department has remained active in its quality management activities, an external peer review will be favorable. Both favorable and unfavorable findings can help to strengthen the department's function. Favorable results confirm that the program meets the standards of the scope of practice and imply that the department should continue in the same direction. Unfavorable findings must be corrected before the next peer review visit and should become topics for quality assurance and utilization review in the intervening period. In most cases, the subsequent review will document whether or not deficiencies in performance have been corrected. Sometimes the external peer reviewer will not note deficiencies specific to the department but may make recommendations concerning the department's structure or organization. For instance, the reviewer may feel that the space and equipment allocated to the department are insufficient to carry out its function or that its function could be enhanced if it were reorganized within another service or as a freestanding service. These recommendations can assist a department in acquiring additional resources, but it is not mandatory for the medical center director to approve such a plan.

SUMMARY

It has become increasingly necessary for each department in the medical center to monitor the quality and cost of patient care. By the use of ongoing, systematic internal and external peer reviews and the utilization of risk management and occurrence screening mechanisms, hospitals have developed quality assurance and utilization review processes. These processes are aimed at problem identification: problems in hospital care that put patients at risk and problems associated with the cost of the services provided, such as staff and space utilization. Proposed solutions are then tested and the results documented. If change is implemented, the impact is measured and documented.

In addition to quality assurance and utilization review processes, departments of speech/language and hearing must adhere to structural and organizational guidelines that are provided by the Joint Commission on Accreditation of Healthcare Organizations (Joint Commission). Most of the guidelines relate to policies and procedures that are consistent with the professional's scope of practice, documentation of standards of care, continuing education programs for the staff, and clear objectives and measures of evaluation for the intern training program. External peer review, such as that performed by the Joint Commission, documents the strengths and weaknesses of a department's program. Preparations for an audit consist of a complete policy and procedures manual; ongoing, timely, and appropriate documentation of intervention in patients' medical records; and demonstration of active quality assurance and risk management programs.

The quality of care patients receive is further enhanced by the processes of credential verification and clinical privileging. Speech/language pathologists must make formal requests to perform specific procedures not always common to their scope of practice. To retain their privileges to practice these procedures, they must demonstrate expertise in their performance. This usually is accomplished by a prearranged number of demonstrations of the procedures performed under supervision.

NOTES

1. Nancy Graham, *Quality Assurance in Hospitals: Strategies for Assessment and Implementation* (Rockville, Md.: Aspen Publishers, Inc., 1982), 82–108.

2. American College of Surgeons, *Patient Safety Manual,* 2nd ed. (Rockville, Md.: Bader and Associates, Inc., 1987), 100–04.

3. Patricia Larkins, "Outcome Assessment," *Quality Assurance Digest* (Rockville, Md.: American Speech-Language-Hearing Association, 1986), 1–4.

4. Patricia Larkins, "Quality Assurance and Utilization Review," *Quality Assurance Digest* (Rockville, Md.: American Speech-Language-Hearing Association, 1986), 1–4.

5. Albert W. Knox, *Quality Assurance Manual* (Kansas City, Mo.: Veterans Administration Medical Center, 1985), 1–75.

6. Joint Commission on Accreditation of Hospitals, *Accreditation Manual of Hospitals* (Chicago: 1986), 22–44.

Quality Assurance Summary: Audiology and Speech Pathology

1. Evaluation of Goals and Objectives

The staff feels that the goals and objectives were appropriate and improved patient care. Inasmuch as each staff member was responsible for a quality management (QM) topic, each felt "involved" in the process of quality management. Our indicators were specific and measurable for the most part, although we felt that some of them were too time-consuming and should be modified. Most of our indicators (Nos. 1, 2, 3, 8, and 11) were ongoing monitors and deemed essential to ensuring that we provided quality care through utilization review. Other indicators (Nos. 5, 6, and 10) focused on ensuring that our paperwork was timely. While these indicators may appear to be merely bookkeeping, the special circumstances of how Audiology maintains stock levels of hearing aids means that timeliness of paperwork impacts directly on patient care.

2. Evidence of Problem Identification and Resolution

Indicator No. 6, utilization of compensation and pension appointment slots, kept us acutely conscious of the demand for compensation and pension appointment slots. Early in the fiscal year we had a sudden influx of requests and were asked to increase the number of appointment slots. Because we knew exactly what the status of used and unused appointment slots had been in the previous month we were able to ascertain immediately how many additional slots were needed. As the year progressed the compensation and pension requests dwindled. In spite of reluctance to reduce the number of appointment slots available, we were able to provide solid documentation of the decline and to insist on using the appointment slots for other types of patient visits. Monitoring intern case conferences helped us develop an outline for our interns to follow to ensure that appropriate points were highlighted and patient information and data extracted and presented. The students themselves expressed appreciation for the clarity of the new outline.

Indicator Nos. 2 and 3 (complications during videofluorography and effects of dysphagia evaluation) produced no negative data. This indicated to us that our procedures were excellent, and that we provided the best possible care. We have used our reviews to illustrate our "un"complication rates in encouraging other medical centers to adopt our practices.

3. Evaluation of Focused Studies Conducted during Fiscal Year

Two focused studies were completed. One study, "Ear Mold Satisfaction," grew out of staff and patient discontent with an ear mold laboratory. The quality and fit had declined significantly. We invited other laboratories to speak to us. We evaluated the molds they said they would make for us, and then we selected a new laboratory. The old laboratory complained and tried to convince us to switch back to them. The focused study involved timeliness and patient satisfaction. Without exception, the hearing aid users who had had experience with both laboratories preferred the new one.

The second focused study, "Nature and Frequency of Hearing Aid Repairs," indicated that the most frequent repairs were to aids most frequently prescribed. This was not very enlightening information. We knew that in-the-ear aids presented special problems and our data confirmed that. Certain aids seemed to be causing us particular difficulty, and we were able to provide solid information to Central Office concerning those aids.

4. Sustained Improvements in Patient Care Activities as Outgrowth of QM Activities

The indicators that have had the most direct impact on patient care have been No. 10, hearing aid appointment slots, and No. 5, utilization of hearing aid appointment slots, where paperwork went into Denver promptly. This meant that we received new hearing aids immediately and had an adequate stock of hearing aids so that patients could leave the clinic wearing the aids they were tested with instead of having to wait months for replacement aids to arrive. Monitoring indicator No. 1, complications during videofluorography, and indicator No. 3, effects of dysphagia evaluations, ensured ongoing quality patient care in areas that can directly impact on a patient's physical well-being. Indicator No. 11, adequacy of diagnostic procedures, is a review process that helped to ensure that as many diagnostic procedures as appropriate had been used on our Audiology patients.

5. Evaluation of Adequacy of Monitors and Criteria

It is our opinion that indicator No. 11, resolution of special problems, is superfluous, because all problems are "special," and Audiology spent a lot of extra time tracking down these problems. Indicator No. 1, progress note reflects patient care status, proved much too difficult and time-consuming and should be more narrowly focused. Otherwise, we feel that all of our indicators were well-chosen and should be continued.

6. Evidence of Integration of Information with Hospital-wide QM Program

The videofluorography procedures (No. 2) impact on Radiology's QM programs, and the dysphagia evaluation (No. 3) on Dietetics' programs.

7. Goals and Objectives of QM Plan for Next Fiscal Year

Our goals and objectives for the next fiscal year will be the same except that we shall eliminate indicator No. 8, resolution of special problems, and reduce No. 1 to quarterly reporting of a sample of 10 cases chosen from each supervisor's caseload in Speech Pathology.

Clinical Privileges for Speech/Language Pathologists

I. Introduction

All speech/language pathologists at the time of appointment will be required to qualify for general privileges, and either at the time of employment or subsequently may apply for one or more specialized privileges and/or research privileges. Privileges will be granted initially on the basis of the speech/language pathologist's education, training, experience, references, and clinical certification status with the American Speech-Language and Hearing Association or state licensure as reviewed by the Service Chief.

Speech/language pathologists are considered to have provisional or limited privileges until satisfactorily completing the requirement for the Certificate of Clinical Competence in Speech Pathology (see Exhibit 10–B–1) granted by the American Speech-Language and Hearing Association or state licensure. Any clinical fellowship-year personnel or student who has not completed the requirements for the Certificate of Clinical Competence in Speech/Language Pathology or a state license at the time of appointment will be given provisional general privileges. This means that the individual will be allowed to perform general privileges *only* under direct supervision of a staff speech/language pathologist who has been granted full clinical privileges.

Maintenance of privileges at all levels will be based upon exercising them satisfactorily in accordance with continuing proficiency standards. The Service Chief may review them at any time. If, following appropriate disciplinary action, there is continued evidence that the speech/language pathologist's performance fails to meet these standards, the Service Chief may recommend that any one or all clinical privileges be revoked or suspended. All privileges will be reviewed at least annually by the Service Chief as part of the employee's annual performance evaluation. A recommendation will be forwarded to the Clinical Executive Board certifying the continuance of privileges for each employee. Requests for additional privileges may be submitted any time the employee can produce qualification evidence.

Exhibit 10–B–1 Sample Privileges Certification

Certification of Mental and Physical Competency

I am mentally and physically capable of performing the privileges herein requested. I have read and agree to abide by the By-Laws of this Medical Center.

Name: _____

Date: _____   Signature: _____

The above speech pathologist is granted the full privileges requested with the following exceptions and/or limitations. (If none, so state.)

_____

_____

_____

_____

Approved: _____   Date: _____
　　　　　Chief, Speech Pathology Service

Approved: _____   Date: _____
　　　　　Chairman, Professional Standards
　　　　　Committee

Approved: _____   Date: _____

Date Practitioner Notified: _____

These privileges are granted for a one-year period. Should your qualifications change, you may request that your privileges be changed accordingly.

All patients referred for evaluation and treatment of a communication disorder will be referred through a Medical Center physician. The following clinical privileges will be coordinated with the referring physician who has the primary responsibility for the patient's medical care.

II. General Privileges

A. Requirements:

The speech/language pathologist has earned a master's or doctoral degree in speech pathology from an accredited university. The speech/language pathologist must be able to treat a minimum of five cases per day in order to retain general privileges.

B. Inclusions:

1. Reviewing the medical record to assess the presence of variables relating to the cause and/or maintenance of a communication disorder.

2. Interviewing the patient and/or the patient's informant to obtain a complete case history to evaluate causal and/or maintaining factors for the communication disorder.

3. Requesting records through Medical Administration or from other institutions where the patient has received treatment to evaluate the na-

ture and extent of this treatment and its effect on the patient's communicative ability.

4. Examining a patient to determine whether a communication disorder exists, the type of disorder, the causal and/or maintaining factors, and the severity of the disorder.

5. Employing appropriate standardized tests to evaluate the nature and extent of the communication disorder.

6. Employing nonstandardized test procedures and observations to obtain a subjective impression of the type and extent of the disorder.

7. Determining whether there is some organic basis for the communication disorder through examination of the oral peripheral speech mechanism that includes inspecting the interior of the mouth and posterior pharynx. In some cases the external neck and chest muscles may be felt.

8. Employing standard electronic equipment, such as audio- and videotape recorders in the evaluation and treatment of the patient with the patient's written permission and knowledge, as well as other electronic equipment, such as computers and assistive devices.

9. Attempting to alter various aspects of the patient's communication behavior to determine whether the patient can change it in response to verbal directions, manipulation of body posture, or manipulation of parts of the oral anatomy relating to speech production.

10. Referring the patient to a senior-level speech/language pathologist or other services for evaluation of factors related to the communication disorder (i.e., Audiology, Psychology, Psychiatry, ENT, Neurology, or Otolaryngology).

11. Evaluating prognosis for improvement of communication skills based on case history, test results, observations, patient's response to attempts to alter behavior, and patient's desire and motivation.

12. Determining whether a patient could benefit from nonmedical treatment of the communication disorder or that such treatment is contraindicated.

13. Writing impressions of the type and severity of the disorder, prognosis, and recommendations on the consultation sheet for the medical record.

14. Determining frequency and type of treatment appropriate (individual or group), modality or modalities to be treated, and traditional methods of treatment to be used.

15. Designing and carrying out a treatment program appropriate to facilitate the communication needs of the patient.

16. Keeping data and impressions of the patient's performance in treatment, evaluating performance, and documenting this information in the medical record.

17. Communicating with other medical and surgical services (including nursing) concerning the patient's progress to provide a unified, coordinated, goal-directed treatment program.
18. Providing counseling to the patient and the family or other health professionals concerning the communication disorder and ways to manage it. This includes teaching family members techniques to use at home to help the patient improve communication skills and documenting the teaching in the medical record. In some cases information may be provided to employers or special activity centers.
19. Terminating treatment of a communication disorder because of maximum benefit, lack of progress, lack of interest or motivation, failure to keep appointments, or other complicating factors that preclude successful treatment, or because medical treatment for the disorder has reached maximum benefit.
20. Evaluating the appropriateness of communication aids, ordering the aids, and training the patient and family in their use.

III. Specialized Privileges
   A. Requirements:
   The speech/language pathologist must have met the requirements for and obtained the general clinical privileges before applying for specialized privileges. Any of the specialized clinical privileges may be requested individually.
   The speech/language pathologist must provide evidence of the completion of the clinical fellowship year, a state license in speech/language pathology, or certification from the American Speech-Language-Hearing Association to be eligible to apply for specialized privileges. In addition, training or regular use of these skills should have been maintained within a three-year period prior to requesting the privileges. Competency of these privileges will be evaluated biannually by the clinical supervisor.
   B. Inclusions:
   1. Administration of the Porch Index of Communicative Ability.
   2. Dysphagia evaluation and therapy.
   3. Electromyography (EMG)—biofeedback, therapy, and equipment.
   4. Tracheo-esophageal (T-E) shunt voice acquisition fitting and therapy.
   5. Use of laryngoscope.
   6. Use of the otoscope.
   7. Assistance with videofluoroscopy procedure.
   8. Indirect mirror laryngoscopy.
   9. Conducting pure-tone audiometry.
   10. Supervising students.

IV. Research Privileges
   A. Requirements:
   Quality care and improved evaluation/treatment procedures for the com-

municatively handicapped are the product of continuous scientific research in speech/language pathology. Due to the complexity of human behavioral research, these privileges require the highest degree of academic training and experience.

In all cases the speech/language pathologist with this privilege has the responsibility to develop the research question and design and propose a procedure for each study. The speech/language pathologist must present a prospectus for peer review by professional colleagues with approval of the Service Chief. All research with human subjects must be further approved by the Human Studies Subcommittee and the Research Committee before it is implemented.

These privileges are reserved for staff speech/language pathologists who hold the doctoral degree in speech/language pathology from an accredited university or members holding the master's degree who demonstrate adequate research skill through the design, implementation, and completion of two research projects under staff or consultant supervision.

B. Inclusion:
1. The design and implementation of research concerning normal and/or abnormal aspects of communication.
2. The design and implementation of research to evaluate, compare, and contrast the effects of various experimental behavioral treatment procedures.
3. Utilization of various electronic devices and programming equipment to measure changes in human communication behavior.
4. Collaboration with staff physicians in studying the effects of certain surgical procedures, prostheses, or medications on communication behavior.
5. Collaboration with other behavioral scientists in the study of communication disorders and psychological and/or emotional correlates.
6. Publication of the results of these research findings in appropriate journals or publications and/or presenting these results verbally in the form of lectures, seminars, or workshops.

Chapter 11

Education

INTRODUCTION

One of the important rationales for developing this book is to help fill a perceived void that exists in the preparation received by a speech/language pathologist before entering a medical environment. The void continues to exist in spite of the shift in the employment demographics of speech/language pathologists and audiologists from educational settings to hospitals, clinics, universities, long-term care facilities, and private practice. These facilities all have the potential for significant interaction between speech/language pathologists and the medical community. Of professional persons hired into medical settings during the period 1982–1984, speech/language pathologists and audiologists held the second highest percentage.[1] While this trend may have stabilized for all professional categories, a more recent manpower development report suggests that in order to meet the needs of the communicatively-impaired, speech/language pathologists and audiologists must expand their services into adult day care, nursing homes, long-term care, acute care, home health care, and physicians' offices.[2] All of these settings have primary ties with medicine and, by implication, with the physician as the leader of the health care team.

Even though the data suggest an increased need for the direct involvement of speech/language pathologists in medical settings, there continues to be a lack of emphasis in training these professionals to compete as equals in the provision of health care. Aronson presents one reason for the lack of preparation by suggesting that the profession as a whole has not been forthright in its acknowledgment of an increasing relevance to the physician and a commitment to the concept that the communication sciences should play an important part in the provision of health care.[3] A second reason is that universities have been unable to educate adequately the speech/language pathologist who may choose to enter a medical setting. Part of their difficulty to meet this need stems from prearranged standards and requirements that limit students to courses that will not prepare them for specialization in a medical setting. Additionally, there are a lack of training sites that offer clinical experience and too few professors in speech and language pathology with a background in the medical sciences. Universities may enjoy the freedom to offer courses of increased specialization with preparation for the medical setting when new guidelines for the minimal requirements of certification are implemented.

This chapter presents a suggested format for training speech pathologists who will enter a medical setting. It is based on an understanding of the requirements needed to compete successfully with other health care disciplines and on an appreciation for the tutorial style consistent with the medical model.

UNIVERSITY PREPARATION

Preparation for the speech/language pathologist entering the medical setting should begin at the undergraduate level. In particular, emphasis should be placed on the basic sciences, including biology, chemistry, physiology, and basic anatomy. Additional, desirable coursework should include neuroanatomy, general psychology, and introductory courses to the health sciences. These courses will enable the beginning student to become familiar with how organs and systems function normally and how they interrelate to perform specific activities. The goal of this preparation should be teaching the student to have an appreciation of the impact that an insult to any system can have on communication. An appreciation of the difference between normalcy and deviation from the normal should be the main focus of the graduate experience. As discussed in Chapters 1 and 2, most speech/language pathologists entering the medical setting fail to understand the ramifications of how disease and disease processes impact on communication. Rather, they have an understanding only of the types of diseases that may result in communication disorders, but not the more useful knowledge of the mechanisms of the illnesses that impact on each disorder.

Outside the classroom, undergraduates should be encouraged to participate in activities in a medical setting, either as a volunteer, as a member of a planned set of university- or hospital-sponsored observations, or as a paid employee in some capacity. This opportunity, no matter what the role, cannot be underestimated in preparation for entering the medical environment as a speech/language pathologist. Becoming familiar with the sights, sounds, and smells of a hospital environment can be an important step in the orientation and adjustment to the daily routine of providing services for patients. These first sensations are overwhelming for some individuals, and it is not unusual for beginning clinicians to experience lightheadedness or fainting spells in certain situations, particularly those at the patient's bedside. Usually, this is only a transitory experience. For some clinicians, however, the sensations remain overwhelming, and they are constantly uncomfortable in the medical environment. Supervisors should be sensitive to this condition and lead these students away from medically oriented speech/language pathology early in their training. The sensations of the medical center are factors to be recognized and dealt with at a conscious level. Failure to deal with all of these factors that impinge upon the students in approaching patients will serve only to cloud their judgment. This impairs the effectiveness of interactions that are necessary for medical speech/language pathologists to succeed in their relationships with other medical personnel.

Undergraduates who are able to observe evaluations and treatment of patients in a medical setting should be required to record their observations for discussion in practicum classes. At this level, most practicum site supervisors are willing to sponsor observations, because they do not have to be concerned with the type of disorder scheduled that day, the need for extensive question and answer periods, or a didactic presentation. The goal of directed observations should be for exposure only. The focus should not be on the disorder itself (e.g., characteristics of a Broca's aphasic), but on what the students observed during the period of time they were present and what they noticed about the patient's behavior and physical abilities, the patient's ability to learn and cooperate, and the approach in remediation.

To be avoided at the undergraduate level is a separation of the diagnostic categories (e.g., courses in articulation, aphasia, or voice) from the processes that are used in their identification, differentiation, and treatment. For instance, traditionally a student in speech/language pathology learns how to perform a voice evaluation for a patient with a known vocal disorder or how to evaluate a dysarthric, as if the two evaluations are distinct because the two disorders are not alike. It is more productive for the student who wants to enter a medical setting to learn the fundamentals of a good physical and psychometric examination of a patient with *any* communication disorder. The learning outcome should be focused on giving students the ability to place particular emphasis on any one area of the examination as the need arises. Similarly, students should not be taught how to do an acoustic analysis on the voice of a cleft palate speaker, but should learn the indication for, and value of, the technique for any patient for whom the analysis may improve the specificity of the diagnosis or treatment.

An undergraduate enrolled in courses that emphasize basic science should be able to continue to graduate school for training as a medical speech/language pathologist with as much knowledge about the kidneys or anatomy of the foot as a specialist in head and neck disorders learns in undergraduate education. Ideally, part of the undergraduate training in health sciences should include familiarity with basic medical terminology and evaluation tools, such as an otoscope, stethoscope, reflex hammer, and ophthalmoscope, not in preparation for the medical profession, but so students can become familiar with physiological assessment as it applies to examination for communication and swallowing disorders. This familiarity also allows students to be comfortable with use of tools, such as the stethoscope in assessment of respiration and swallow, and the reflex hammer in assessment of perioral reflexes, that add additional depth and substance to the peripheral examination of the speech mechanism.

In general, the university setting is equipped to provide a solid foundation in the basic sciences. Undergraduates who seek a graduate experience in speech/language pathology should take advantage of courses offered outside of that department in order to receive the necessary preparation for the medical setting. Such an arrangement has the potential to create problems in scheduling and curriculum development; however, the sharing of resources for a common goal through inter-departmental cooperation may prove to be both fiscally and academically advantageous. Programs that provide training in specialty areas, such as speech/language pathology, will attract students by offering curricula that are creative in their design. Access to cross-departmental training in the health sciences provides the necessary incentives to attract and retain those students who choose to enter a medical setting.

As the student begins graduate training in speech/language pathology, emphasis should be shifted from knowledge of processes of normal anatomy and physiology to an understanding of the consequences on communication when these systems fail. Focus should be on diseases and disease processes that can affect communication, such as those discussed in Chapter 3. The clinician must obtain a thorough understanding of the signs and symptoms of each disease; the course, consequences, and complications of the disease; the available medical and surgical treatments; and the expected prognosis and outcomes. Graduate students specializing in medical speech/language pathology should make strong efforts during the first year to begin comparing the normal and the pathologic through their own observations and the observations of their supervisors, by direct examinations, and through lectures and demonstrations. In most medical settings, the ideal situation would be assignment of a permanent university faculty member to provide lectures and demonstrations on a regular basis at the medical center and draw on the wealth of both normal and abnormal conditions available for instruction purposes.

THE PRACTICUM EXPERIENCE

When the clinicians enter the medical setting and begin regular patient contact, they often are forced to evaluate and question their own feelings and fears about issues such as aging, illness, disease, and death in transference from their patients. Pushing these feelings into the back of their minds may work temporarily, but eventually they take their toll by either subtly altering interactions with patients or interfering with the psychological or physical health of the clinicians. In addition to these fears, there can be feelings of inadequacy or protectiveness or a need to dominate, feel important, and maintain a sense of power and authority. Other clinicians are shy, proceed cautiously, and accept responsibility tentatively. To be a successful clinician does not mean changing one's whole persona, but recognizing those factors that influence all professional interactions.

A practicum supervisor who criticizes a student clinician for either shyness or aggressiveness could be performing a disservice to that student. The shy individual attempting to be assertive, or the aggressive individual attempting to be demure, usually only succeeds in looking socially awkward. A supervisor would do well to point out to students their qualities that may affect clinician-patient interactions, and the way these qualities can be used to their advantage, rather than attempt to change the nature of the individual. Evaluation and discussion of clinicians' feelings and their reactions to the hospital setting should be done early in the practicum experience to deal with fears and attitudes that later can interfere with performance.

Teaching Hospitals

Students would be wise to select a medical setting for their practicum experience that has a known commitment to training medical professionals. Teaching hospitals usually are affiliated with large medical schools and reward their medical staffs for their teaching and research efforts in addition to the clinical services they provide. Teaching hospitals encourage student involvement in all aspects of hospital life, both inside and outside their chosen specialties, by sponsoring open lectures and multidisciplinary conferences, by publishing their training schedules, and by inviting students to participate in bedside rounds.

Built into this setting is the attitude of the senior staff members who do not expect their students to enter fully prepared to complete all aspects of patient care without any time for interaction between students and supervisors. Since students are not expected to generate revenue for the teaching hospital, they can feel more comfortable in profiting by their mistakes. Other departments with whom the students have contact are also tolerant of inexperience. It should be noted that this atmosphere is not exclusive to the organization of teaching hospitals but can be found in nonaffiliated centers. However, it is important for the students and the university to choose sites that encourage and support the training of all medical professions.

In most teaching hospitals, the patients, especially if they have had multiple admissions to that facility, are aware that they may be examined by a clinician who is in the early stages of professional development. However, they also are aware that the beginning clinician will be supervised closely and that the interaction between the novice and the certified expert actually can help to strengthen their care, because each aspect of the diagnosis and treatment has received close scrutiny by virtue of the medical teaching model.

The Medical Teaching Model

After speech/language pathologists in training spend some time in a medical setting, they become aware of the methods and processes used to educate physicians at each level of their experience. A large part of the physician training experience is accomplished through peer review; that is, the first year resident is assisted in learning by the second year resident, or chief resident, and looks to that individual for guidance. The chief resident, in turn, learns from the attending physician by presenting the facts on any patient for review and approval if a change in patient care is warranted. As residents complete their training, they are given more responsibility for the total care of patients and are expected to perform in an increasingly independent manner. This model of learning one's craft presupposes at each level of responsibility that clinicians will be constantly tested on the soundness of their own knowledge, their clinical judgments, their responses to challenges and questions, and their decisions regarding actions appropriate to their levels of expertise. As students progress in experience, they are required to assume greater clinical and teaching responsibilities.

There are several distinct advantages to this model that are worthy of consideration for use in training speech/language pathologists in all settings, but in particular for those who choose to be involved in medical environments. First, it is more consistent with how other professionals in a medical setting are trained. This eventually leads to more immediate recognition and acceptance of the role and responsibilities of the speech/language pathologist in health care. The long-term effect of this acceptance is an easier transition of the medical speech/language pathologist into partnership with the entire health care team. However, a change in the terminology currently in use to describe the training program would be helpful. Undergraduate majors would not go to practicum sites as "observers," but would be assigned *clerkships* for such participation. First-year graduate students would not be "practicum students," but *interns* in their internship year. Second-year graduate students would not be "second-year practicum students," but *residents,* with the most fully prepared assigned positions of *chief resident* as they complete their residency training program in speech/language pathology. Those completing their clinical fellowship year would be called *clinical fellows* or *fellows.* Clinicians certified by the American Speech-Language-Hearing Association are certified *attendings,* with positions on the hospital staff.

The second major advantage of adopting the medical model as it relates to training medical speech/language pathologists is the utilization of residents already in the program to teach other residents and interns. Those with more experience could provide guidance for their peers. This would expand the number of persons providing training and result in more direct supervision of activities at each level of responsibility. The ultimate authority and responsibility for the patient's total care would still rest with the attending and remain within the guidelines of ethical practice.

The third advantage of the training model is that at each level questions are asked that require answers and force the respondents to solidify their own information as they teach it to their peers. Persons who have had the opportunity to teach realize the value in having to review, organize, and understand concepts when they have to be communicated to those less familiar with the information. In oral communication or in demonstrations of patient care, it may become obvious to the teachers that they are unsure of their own information or approaches. In these circumstances they will learn to resolve the issues, either by reviewing written resources or seeking assistance from the next highest authority. This method of teaching also helps the person in higher authority judge the ability and growth of the subordinates who are asking the questions. Interns and residents who come to attendings with questions and problems that they should be able to solve without assistance demonstrate that they are not performing at independent levels. Corrective action can be immediate in these situations. In reviewing patient diagnosis and treatment issues case by case as part of normal hospital routine, the attending also tests the knowledge and teaching ability of the residents and interns by asking them to clarify or explain various aspects of patients' care. In this role, the attending also solidifies his or her knowledge, since it will be necessary to respond to the questions if the residents are unable to do so. This helps the attending to avoid professional staleness and burnout by keeping current.

It is this method of supervision that leads to the fourth strength in the medical model of instruction: students learn that they can make mistakes and profit by them without recrimination or embarrassment. In the medical model interns observe residents who may not know how to perform particular procedures, how to proceed in diagnosis, or how to manage a particularly difficult personality. Further, interns observe residents being criticized, corrected, or praised by the attending, frequently on a daily basis, for their performances in patient care. While the interns may not feel comfortable with accepting criticism in front of peers, by the end of their training experience they come to see the process as a positive interaction that improves not only their own expertise but also patient care.

Beginning students in speech/language pathology who enter the medical setting often are privy to heated discussions among physicians about patient care. The usual student reaction is one of shock and disbelief, with the impression that surely the discussants would never speak again. While this may be true on occasion, it is rare, and more friends are won than lost by such debates. Spirited discussions on issues of patient care are commonplace in the medical setting. But more important, and attributable to the training method in the medical model, is that most individuals do not take these discussions personally, even if they are proven wrong or their suggestions ignored. Rather, they come away with the feeling that they provided the best possible input, and most importantly they learned more about the relevant issues from the argument. And while they might not agree with the final decision, everyone recognized that the confrontation was in the patient's best interest.

In general, students in speech/language pathology have much to learn from the medical model in this regard. Many students feel threatened by supervision and consequently ask too few questions, are less than willing to make mistakes and profit by them, and fail to state their case for fear that it might be an unpopular viewpoint or irrational justification. And it is not their fault nor the fault of the supervisor. The fault lies with the method of training and the perceived barriers inherent in the traditional teacher/student relationship. Speech/language pathologists who survive successfully in a medical setting learn quickly that they should not take personally every discussion, recommendation, and written opinion that was rejected or neglected.

Some may say that it takes time to develop a thick skin; however, it is not time as much as the process of being constantly allowed to make mistakes consistent with the level of training. Being asked to justify approaches in diagnosis and treatment on a regular basis allows the students not to feel threatened when their ideas are neglected or rejected, either by their own perceived lack of expertise or experience or by associations with their peers. Having confidence in their abilities gives them the freedom to continue to learn and profit by mistakes and to feel unthreatened by new information or by persons with differing viewpoints. If beginning speech/language pathologists were assisted in developing this confidence, graduates of a training program would be better advocates of the profession because they could describe their skills and contributions to health care to others, both experts and nonexperts, without feeling threatened or frightened that their positions will be challenged.

THE INTERNSHIP AND RESIDENCY

Students graduating from medical schools will have spent the final two years of their experience observing and examining patients with a wide array of diagnoses and disorders. Speech/language pathologists also should spend their two graduate years observing and examining patients. A conservative estimate, however, indicates that the medical student sees in the identical period of time about 10 times as many patients as the graduating speech/language pathologist with a master's degree. Even if the fellowship year is included, the differences in patient exposure is still large. This is unfortunate, because one of the major goals of the internship, residency, and fellowship programs for the speech/language pathologist should be seeing as many patients as possible, regardless of the type and complexity of disorders or stages of diagnosis and treatment, or whether the clinician has seen similar examples in other settings.

Concentrated exposure to a large number of patients eventually will give the student a better perspective of the range and scope of problems that are presented to the medical speech/language pathologist and of the diversity of treatments offered to patients with seemingly similar problems. The student needs to leave the internship and residency programs with the feeling that no two Broca's aphasics are ever really alike; that both will present different challenges in diagnosis and treatment; and that decisions in their treatment need to be individualized, based not only on the patients' speech and language profiles but on other concerns. Factors that are relevant include medical course and response to treatment, the patient's motivation and personality, the premorbid medical and social history, the extent of the patient's family supports, and the final disposition of the case. For instance, a hospitalized patient who needs to receive further speech and language remediation but cannot travel to the hospital for outpatient treatment will require a home program. Such a program may need to be implemented by a family member who requires training, or if a family member is not available or suitable, other arrangements must be made.

Traditionally, each student is assigned to one supervisor for training and must rely on that supervisor for the number of patient exposures they receive. However, programs should be designed so that students are encouraged and required to observe other supervisors' patients in addition to their own. They also should be required to observe their peers in their interactions with patients. Increased exposure to patients should not be limited to those patients who are seen in the speech/language pathology department or to patients with communication disorders. For example, students could benefit by observing the otolaryngologist as they evaluate 20 to 30 patients in a scheduled afternoon outpatient clinic, or by observing a neurologist evaluating patients with suspected neurologic disease at different age levels who may have abnormal or normal examinations. The goal of these observations should not be for the student to observe patients with communication dysfunction, but to see how a clinic is run, what evaluation tools are used, how other clinicians takes histories, how evaluations are structured and documented, how the results of evaluations are imparted to patients, and how patients react to interventions.

It is important for students to see patients with neurologic disease without accompanying communication disorders to be able to evaluate the impact of communication impairment on patients with similar illnesses. Students should be encouraged to attend walking bedside rounds with specialists in rehabilitation medicine, neurology, and otolaryngology. While they initially may not be able to understand each case because they lack the medical background or are unfamiliar with the terminology, regular attendance supported by their supervisor will convince them of the value. Being able to observe and, in some cases, take part in the discussion of at least 20 patients in a one-hour period will result in the necessary foundation that graduate training should provide.

In short, students who train as speech/language pathologists need to be immersed in both formal and informal patient contacts as a primary goal in their clinical training. The supervisor's job should be to assist them by sorting and categorizing their observations, making corrections if necessary, answering questions, and embellishing the observations by linking them to the role of the medical speech/language pathologist.

Classroom Applications

Immersion in patient contacts does not obviate the need for more traditional exposures such as those that are necessary to help bridge classroom experience to the application of that knowledge. The two are not mutually exclusive. Students must be allowed to see an ataxic dysarthric and a Wernicke's aphasic, to state their signs and symptoms, to hear about and recite their speech and language characteristics, to be able to differentiate them from similar problems, to describe the approaches to treatment, and to describe the steps in treatment and the steps involved in evaluation of that treatment. Time with these patients also must be allowed the student to observe the entire process of speech and language interventions: from receiving the request for services, to making decisions about an evaluation approach, to the application of the evaluation tools at the bedside or in the clinic, to treatment, and to discharge. Observing the entire process is a unique experience for many students entering the medical center. Patients are followed for longer periods of time in university clinics, and students may not be included in the complete diagnostic or discharge process for the patients that they are assigned.

Being a part of the entire treatment process provides the student a framework for the necessary steps in learning within that process. These steps will include:

- how to recognize the professions most likely to request the services of a speech/language pathologist and for what reasons they require these services
- how to determine when the consult dictates the role of the speech/language pathologist in evaluation
- how to choose evaluation tools
- how to perform a differential diagnosis
- how to formulate a prognosis based on the diagnosis
- how to select a treatment candidate
- how to establish short- and long-term goals and to make modifications in these goals
- how to measure the effects of treatment
- how to determine and use discharge criteria
- how to plan a patient's discharge

Each element of this process can be taught by direct discussion and demonstration by the supervisor, by student participation with supervisory feedback, and by the student's own observation of peers and supervisors. (For various discussions of each topic, review Chapters 5 through 9).

Documentation

The student who enters a medical setting often struggles initially with the medical record because of unfamiliarity with medical shorthand and terminology (see Chapter 4 and Glossary of medical terms). Practice in becoming familiar with the contents of the medical record should be an initial goal at the training site as a primary method of orienting the student. Entering progress notes into the medical record, impromptu oral presentations of the patient's history and treatment at patient care conferences, responding to a consult in less than two days, and preparing a discharge summary are all new experiences for the beginning student. These aspects of documentation can be taught by demonstration followed by student participation. In general, the student struggles with documentation in three major areas because of lack of experience in these areas or because prior experience has been contrary to techniques used in a medical setting: (1) difficulty in selecting the important elements needed to complete the communication, (2) difficulty in completing the report or progress note within a limited time frame, and (3) the propensity not to be succinct, or recognizing when a short note is equally as valuable as one that has greater detail.

Bedside Rounds and Conferences

Interns and residents will benefit from attendance at bedside rounds and patient care conferences both within and outside of the speech/language pathology department. Exposure to other disciplines in their management and approach to patients is valuable experience for speech/language pathologists because it helps them to have clearer perspectives on how their roles fit in with those of other disciplines. Of greater importance to the definition and value of speech/language pathologists on the health care team is their perceived presence at the patient's bedside. Students who make observations and participate in bedside evaluations, develop better understanding of what patients endure during hospitalization and develop comfortable approaches to bedridden patients that will carry over into the clinic circumstance. Most other medical professionals have roles at the patient's bedside, and it is also important for medical speech/language pathologists to be visible and comfortable in this setting. This should be accomplished early in the intern and residency periods. The bedside and clinic evaluations and treatment of patients may differ, and the differences need to be highlighted for the student by the attendings.

Bedside rounds within the speech/language pathology department should be conducted weekly, with speech/language pathology residents presenting a verbal summary of each patient to their peers and attendings that includes the patient's history, diagnosis, prognosis, and treatment and discharge plan. When appropriate, attendings should ask residents to demonstrate aspects of the evaluations to confirm or deny a diagnostic or treatment viewpoint and answer questions pertaining to rationale in treatment, basis for treatment selection, or plans for discharge. Each bedside visit should be limited to a maximum of 10 minutes. The review of the patient's progress at bedside is an important aspect of the training program for three reasons: (1) it provides immediate feedback to residents and interns that in turn improves their learning, (2) it gives patients confidence in their health care providers because they can see that their illnesses are receiving close scrutiny and attention, and (3) it offers visibility of speech/language pathologists to other services and may influence them to become more receptive to the value of this service that is available to their patients.

Clinical Judgments

After the student is comfortable in recognizing the signs and symptoms of each type of communication disorder, the latter part of the internship and the entire residency and fellowship year focus on the processes of formulating sound clinical judgments. Areas of concentrated effort include the following:

- how to integrate the information from the communication and swallowing evaluation to form a diagnostic impression
- how to use the diagnostic impression in differential diagnosis (i.e., is the communication disorder consistent with the working medical diagnosis?)
- how to decide whether to treat patients, follow them for a period of time, or reevaluate them at a later date
- how to know when patients should be discharged from treatment.

Guidelines for these issues are discussed in previous chapters; however, they can be learned well only when students and supervisors are able to observe and evaluate a large number of patients with a variety of disorders at different severity levels. Ideally, the patients will come from different referral sources. In some cases, it is necessary to observe or talk to patients for whom physicians did not send consult requests. For instance, a physician may have felt that a severely demented patient could not benefit from a communication evaluation. However, it could be beneficial for the intern to observe the patient to understand the severity of the patient's disorder as it impacts on communication. Such patients can be identified by a supervisor who is a visible member of the floor on which the patient is hospitalized or who regularly attends multidisciplinary team meetings.

In the residency and fellowship year, emphasis in clinical judgment also should include how, and to whom, one makes a referral for additional services. Preparatory to this, the resident must become familiar with other services in the hospital and their purposes, functions, and expected need to interact with patients who have communication and swallowing dysfunction (see Chapters 1 and 2). Using sound clinical judgment when making a referral also is dependent on a thorough investigation of the patient's complaint, together with an understanding of the particular expertise of the service to whom the patient is referred.

An example of how to exercise good judgment in referral is apropos to a patient who complains to the speech/language pathologist of recent "falling spells." The patient is aphasic, and the clinician is aware of his past medical history. When questioned, the patient denies loss of consciousness and reports no feelings of angina, palpitations, weakness, or seizures. However, before falling, he experiences severe vertigo that he describes as a spinning sensation (not as light-headedness) with tinnitus and nausea. The origins of "falling spells" can be diverse, ranging from neurologic origin to a psychogenic or systemic basis. This case may be of cardiac origin; however, the patient does not have a past history of heart disease and denies angina and palpitations. While falling spells can result from neurogenic causative factors, the patient also denies seizures and muscular weakness. A metabolic source, such as diabetes, is unlikely because the patient does not have a history of diabetes. Since the patient describes true vertigo, either an impairment of the peripheral system for balance or a source more central in the brain stem may be suspected. Therefore, the most appropriate referral would be to the otolaryngologist.

The purpose of learning how to make an appropriate referral is not to make a medical diagnosis, but to make an intelligent decision on how best to manage the patient's medical complaint. If the intern or resident is not sure when to refer, it is helpful to call the physician of choice, present the case, and ask if a referral to that service is appropriate. Proper referral saves patient care costs and helps to maintain good relationships with other hospital services through mutual recognition of expertise in problem identification and knowledge of referral sources.

The clinical training program described in this section is time-consuming and rigorous, both for the intern and supervisor. Speech/language pathologists who wish to enter the medical setting with knowledge of their role and function need to work beyond the demands of current licensure and university requirements. Stricter requirements for practice eventually will attract quality professionals to the program and increase the demand and compensation for those who wish to enter a medical setting in the communication sciences.

CONTINUING EDUCATION

Utilizing the medical model as a training device helps to keep senior staff members current in their information because of the demands on supervision from the intern, resident, and fellow, but it does not guarantee that they will remain on the cutting edge of the technology available to the profession. That is, supervisors may be very familiar with the signs and symptoms of each aphasic and dysarthric type, but they may not be aware of the more recent thinking or research in the differential diagnosis or treatment approaches with these groups of patients. Attendings can remain current in their field either by their own participation in research activities (by literature review and planned investigations) or by attending conferences where invited experts provide new information.

It is enticing to attend conferences only in one's area of special interest (e.g., aphasia, head trauma, or swallowing disorders). However, it also is beneficial to the individual, to the medical setting, and to the field of speech/language pathology to attend conferences on issues that are less familiar but nonetheless directly applicable to the job setting and individual performance description. Specialists should occasionally attend conferences on topics that are familiar or well-known as a method of verifying that what they think they know actually is in the mainstream of current technology and that what they are doing in patient care is "on the right track." Such confirmation of knowledge also can be done among the attendings within a department or among attendings at regular meetings outside of the department. Sponsoring mini-seminars for local colleagues without cost or elaborate arrangements provides an excellent forum for continuing education activities.

SUMMARY

The availability of training programs to prepare the speech/language pathologist for the medical setting is limited. The majority of training the speech/language pathologist receives in the medical center is gained from on-the-job experience. The lack of preparation is due in part to the hesitancy of the field of communication sciences to ally itself formally with the health sciences, to the failure of university-sponsored programs to offer emphasis in medically based communication disorders, and to the lack of hospital training sites. The classroom and clinical preparation for the medical setting in speech/language pathology needs to begin at the undergraduate level with a curriculum focus in the basic sciences. Students should concentrate on the normal aspects of human anatomy and physiology. Emphasis in graduate training should be on comparisons of those normal and abnormal physiologic processes that impact on communication.

The first graduate year (internship) should require that the student master the signs and symptoms of specific diseases and disease processes that can decompensate communication and swallow. The second graduate year (residency) should focus on the application of skills in differential diagnosis and treatment, in participation at case conferences, in establishment of relationships with physicians and other health care professionals, and in the teaching of interns. In both graduate years, students should be required to observe and examine as many patients as possible, both with and without communication dysfunction. Certified medical speech/language pathologists should be required to maintain their clinical and teaching skills by attending sponsored conferences on subjects relating to their identified weaknesses and interests. Attendance at meetings should be included in staff members' annual performance evaluations.

NOTES

1. Arnold E. Aronson, "The Clinical Ph.D.: Implications for the Survival and Liberation of Communicative Disorders as a Health Care Profession," *American Speech-Language-Hearing Association* 29 (November, 1987):35–39.

2. "Committee on Personnel and Service Needs in Communicative Disorders," *American Speech-Language-Hearing Association* 30 (January, 1988):59–60.

3. Aronson, "The Clinical Ph.D.," 35–39.

Glossary

The following list of commonly used medical abbreviations and definitions will help the clinician decode medical shorthand. The list represents a compilation of recognized abbreviations taken from 13 medical centers. There is variation in the use of abbreviations among centers, particularly in punctuation and capitalization. For instance, some write "a.s." to mean "left ear," while others prefer "as." Some recognize "A-V" as arterioventricular; others use "AV." When possible, all of these variations have been reflected. Difference in usage is common within centers and among physicians. New abbreviations creep into medical records as new syndromes and terminology emerge. For example, a whole new vocabulary is associated with acquired immunodeficiency syndrome (AIDS). Therefore, the clinician should continue to update this list. Abbreviations save time, but their excessive use should be discouraged because of the wide variations in meaning. When possible, terms should be spelled out to avoid ambiguity. Decoding a medical abbreviation is easier if the clinician concentrates on the context in which the abbreviation is set. This strategy must be used when there are two identical abbreviations with different meanings.

A—(1) alert or (2) assessment (SOAP)

a—(1) before or (2) artery

Å—Angström unit

A₁—aortic first sound

A₂—aortic second sound

AA—Alcoholics Anonymous

aa—(1) amino acid or (2) equal parts of each

A-a—alveolar-arterial

A & A—aid and attendance

A & P—(1) anterior and posterior or (2) auscultation and percussion

AAA—abdominal aortic aneurysm

AAE—active assisted exercise

AAL—anterior axillary line

AAROM—active assistive range of motion

A > B—air greater than bone

AB—abortion

A.B.—Ace bandage

343

ABD—abduction

abd—abdomen, abdominal

ABE—acute bacterial endocarditis

ABG—arterial blood gas

ABN—abnormal

ABP—arterial blood pressure

ABR—auditory brainstem response

ABS—acute brain syndrome

AC—(1) anterior chamber or (2) alternating current

A/C—(1) after care or (2) anterior chamber

A.C.—(1) air conduction or (2) acromioclavicular (joint)

ac—before meals

AC > BC—air conduction greater than bone conduction

accom—accommodation

ACG—angiocardiography

acid phos.—acid phosphatase

ACTH—adrenocorticotropic hormone

AD—right ear (auris dextra)

Ad—to, up to

ad—(1) right ear or (2) to, up to

ad lib.—as desired

ADC—(1) Aid to Dependent Children or (2) AIDS dementia complex

ADCC—antibody-dependent cell-mediated cytotoxicity

ADD—adduction

ADH—antidiuretic hormone

ADJ—adjustable

ADM—admission

ADL—activities of daily living

ADTP—alcohol, drug treatment program

AE—above elbow

A/e—air entries

AF—(1) atrial fibrillation or (2) auricular fibrillation

af—auricular flutter

AFB—acid fast bacillus

AFDC—Aid to Families of Dependent Children

AFL—atrial flutter

AFO—ankle-foot orthosis

AFP—alpha-fetoprotein

A/G—albumin/globulin ratio

AGA—appropriate for gestational age

AGN—(1) acute glomerulonephritis or (2) silver nitrate

AHG—antihemophilic globulin

AI—aortic insufficiency

AIDS—acquired immunodeficiency syndrome

AJ—ankle jerk

AJCC—American Joint Committee on Cancer

AK—above knee

AKA—above-knee amputation

AKO—above-knee orthosis

AL—anterolateral

A-L—arterial line

Alb—albumin

ALC—(1) alternate level of care or (2) argon laser coagulation

alc—alcohol

Alk ph—alkaline phosphatase

ALL—acute lymphocytic leukemia

ALS—amyotrophic lateral sclerosis

ALT—(1) alternating with or (2) Alanine amino transferase

alv—alveolar

AM—(1) morning or (2) Austin Moore

AMA—against medical advice

amb—ambulation, ambulate

AMI—(1) anterior myocardial infarction or (2) acute myocardial infarction

AML—acute myeloid leukemia

AMP—(1) amputee or (2) adenosine monophosphate

amp — (1) ampere or (2) ampule

amt — amount

AN — admission note

ANA — antinuclear antibody

anes — anesthesia

ANF — antinuclear factor

Angio — angiogram

ANS — autonomic nervous system

ant — anterior

ant-ax line — anterior axillary line

ANT. C — anterior chamber

ante — before

ANUG — acute necrotizing ulcerative gingivitis

A & O — alert and oriented

AOB — alcohol on breath

AOD — admitting officer of the day

AODM — adult onset of diabetes mellitus

AOR — at own risk

aort regurg — aortic regurgitation

aort sten — aortic stenosis

AOS — aortic stenosis

AP — (1) antepartum or (2) anteroposterior

A-P — anteroposterior

A/P — antepartum

A-P Lat — anteroposterior and lateral

APB — atrial premature beat

APC — (1) atrial premature contraction or (2) aspirin, phenacetin, and caffeine

app — apparently

Appl. T — applanation tonometry

approx — approximate

appt — appointment

APTT — activated partial thromboplastin time

aq — water

aq dist — distilled water

AR — aortic regurgitation

A.R. — (1) apical radical or (2) aural rehabilitation

ARA-C — cytosine arabinoside

ARC — (1) anomalous retinal correspondence or (2) AIDS-related complex

ARD — (1) acute respiratory distress or (2) ambulatory rehabilitation division

ARDS — (1) adult respiratory distress syndrome or (2) acute respiratory distress syndrome

ARF — (1) acute respiratory failure or (2) acute renal failure

A Rh F — acute rheumatic fever

AROM — (1) active range of motion or (2) artificial rupture of membrane

ART — (1) automated reagent test or (2) accredited record technician

art. — arterial

ARU — alcohol rehabilitation unit

AS — (1) left ear (auris sinistra) or (2) aortic stenosis

as — left ear

ASA — aspirin

ASCVD — arteriosclerotic cardiovascular disease

ASD — atrial septal defect

ASHD — arteriosclerotic heart disease

ASIS — anterosuperior iliac spine

ASLO — antistreptolysin

ASMI — anteroseptal myocardial infarction

ASO — (1) arteriosclerosis obliterans or (2) antistreptolysin

ASS: — assessment

AST — (1) antibody screening test or (2) aspartate aminotransferase

astig — astigmatism

ASU — ambulatory surgery unit

A/T — atraumatic

ATC — around the clock

ATG — antithymocyte globulin

ATN—acute tubular necrosis

ATNR—asymmetrical tonic neck reflex

ATS—ambulatory transfusion service

AU—(1) both ears (aures unitas), (2) each ear (auris uterque), or (3) Angström unit

Aud—(1) auditory or (2) audiology

Aud Haluc—auditory hallucinations

audio—audiogram

aur fib—auricular fibrillation

ausc—auscultation

AV—atrioventricular

A-V—atrioventricular

AV fistula—arteriovenous fistula

AV mode—atrioventricular mode

AVB—atrioventricular block

AVCD—atrioventricular conduction defect

AVF—arteriovenous fistula

AVM—arteriovenous malformation

AVR—aortic valve replacement

AVS—arteriovenous shunt

AW—anterior wall

A & W—alive and well

AWMI—anterior wall myocardial infarction

AWOL—absent without leave

ax—axillary

AXR—abdominal x-ray

AZ—Aschheim-Zondek test

AZT—azidothymidine

B—both

B-1—Billroth I (gastrectomy)

B > A—bone greater than air

Ba—barium

BAD—bipolar affective disorder

Ba. E—barium enema

BAER—brainstem auditory-evoked response

bal—balance

bas—basophils

baso—basophils

B & B—bowel and bladder

BB—Brown-Buerger cystoscope

BBB—bundle branch block

BBT—basal body temperature

BC—Blue Cross

B. C.—bed and chair

BC > AL—bone conduction greater than air conduction

BCBS—Blue Cross and Blue Shield

BCC—basal cell carcinoma

BCE—(1) basal cell epithelioma or (2) barium colon enema

BCG—Bacillus Calmette-Guérin

BCM—below the costal margin

BCP—birth-control pill

BD—base deficit

BE—(1) below elbow or (2) barium enema

BEE—basal energy expenditure

BEH—benign essential hypertension

BEI—butonal-extractable iodine

BF—black female

B. Ex—base excess

BFP—biologic false-positive

BFU—balance forearm orthosis

BG—(1) Bender Gestalt test or (2) buccogingival

b.i.d.—twice daily

BIH—bilateral inguinal hernia

bil—bilateral

bilat—bilateral

bili—bilirubin

bin—twice a night

b.i.w.—twice a week

BJ—(1) Bence Jones protein or (2) biceps jerk

BK—below knee

BKA—below-knee amputation

Bl. cult.—blood culture

Bld. irrig.—bladder irrigation

BLE—bilateral lower extremities

Bleph—blepharoplasty

BL. T—bleeding time

BM—bowel movement

BMR—basal metabolic rate

BND—bilateral neck dissection

BNL—below normal limits

Bn M—bone marrow

BNO—bladder neck obstruction

BNR—bladder neck resection

BO. S—bowel sounds

BOT—base of tongue

BOW—bag of water

BP—blood pressure

BPD—(1) bronchopulmonary dysplasia, (2) biparietal diameter, or (3) biparietal disease

bpd—bronchopulmonary dysplasia

BPH—(1) benign prostatic hyperplasia or (2) benign prostatic hypertrophy

BPP—biophysical profile

BR—bed rest

B.R.—bathroom

BRB—bright red blood

BRBPR—bright red blood per rectum

Br M—breast milk

BRO—brother

BRP—bathroom privileges

Br.P—breech presentation

Br.S—breath sounds

br. sounds—breath sounds

BS—(1) breath sounds, (2) bowel sounds, or (3) Blue Shield

B.S.—(1) blood sugar, (2) breath sounds, or (3) bowel sounds

bs—bowel sounds

BSE—breast self-examination

BSO—bilateral salpingo-oophorectomy

BSP—bromsulphalein (excretion)

BSS—black silk sutures

BT—(1) bladder tumor or (2) brain tumor

b.t.—bedtime

BTL—bilateral tubal ligation

BTS—brain tumor suspect

BTSG—brain tumor study group

BTW—behind the wheel

BTW M—between meals

BU—burn unit

BUE—both upper extremities

BUN—blood urea nitrogen

BVL—bilateral vas ligation

BW—birth weight

Bx—biopsy

C—complaint

C.—centigrade

c̄—(1) with or (2) complete

C1, C2, etc.—cervical (in vertebral formulas)

CA—(1) catecholamine, (2) cancer, or (3) carcinoma

Ca—(1) carcinoma, (2) cancer, or (3) calcium

Ca + +—calcium

CAB—coronary artery bypass

CABG—coronary artery bypass graft

CABGx4—coronary artery bypass graft (four vessels)

CAD—coronary artery disease

CAE—complete audiometric evaluation

CAH—chronic active hepatitis

cal—calorie

CALLA—common acute lymphocytic leukemia antigen

CAN—cord around neck

caps—capsules

cardio—cardiology

CAS—cerebral arteriosclerosis

CAT—computerized axial tomography

cat—cataract

cath—catheter

caut—cauterize

CAVH—continuous arteriovenous hemofiltration

C & B—chair and bed

CBC—complete blood count

CBD—(1) common bile duct or (2) closed bladder damage

CBI—continuous bladder irrigation

CBR—complete bed rest

CBS—chronic brain syndrome

CC—(1) cardiac catheterization or (2) chief complaint

c̄C—with correction

cc—cubic centimeter

c/c—case completed

CCA—common carotid artery

CCD—Center for Communicable Diseases (former name for Centers for Disease Control [CDC])

CCF—cephalin-cholesterol flocculation

C. Ch—common chair

CCL4—carbon tetrachloride

CCMS—clean catch midstream

CCT—contrast CAT scan

CCU—coronary care unit

CD—(1) common duct, (2) closed drainage, or (3) convulsive disorder

C/D—cup/disk ratio

C & DB—cough and deep breaths

CDC—Centers for Disease Control

CDH—congenital dislocation of the hip

CEA—(1) carcinoembryonic antigen or (2) carotid endarterectomy

ceph. floc—cephalin flocculation test

CF—counting fingers

CFT—complement-fixation test

C G—contact guarding

CGD—chronic granulomatous disease

C. gl—with correction glasses

Cgm—centigram

Ch—(1) child or (2) chest

CHB—complete heart block

CHD—(1) coronary heart disease, (2) chronic heart disease, or (3) congenital heart disease

CHF—congestive heart failure

CHI—(1) closed head injury or (2) creatinine height index

CHO—carbohydrate

Chol—cholesterol

Chol est—cholesterol esters

chr—chronic

CHS—child health centers

CI—cardiac index

CICU—coronary intensive care unit

CIN—cervical intraepithelial neoplasia

CIS—carcinoma in situ

CK—creatine kinase

CKC—cold knife cone

Cl—chloride

cldy—cloudy

clk—clerk

CLL—chronic lymphocytic leukemia

cln—clinic

Cl. T.—clotting time

CM—(1) cardiomegaly or (2) costal margin

cm—centimeter

CMB—carbolic methylene blue

CMD—(1) chief medical doctor or (2) chief medical director

CMG—cystometrogram

CMG-EMG-UPP—cystometrogram with electromyography and urethral pressure profile

CMHC—community mental health center

CML—chronic myelogenous leukemia

CMV—(1) continuous mechanical ventilation or (2) cytomegalovirus

CN—cranial nerve

CNHP—contract nursing home placement

CNPS—cardiac nuclear probe scan

CO—cardiac output

c/o—complains of

c̄ OJ—with orange juice

col.—colony

col/cc—colonies per cubic centimeter

COLD—chronic obstructive lung disease

coll—collyrium

col/ml—colonies per millimeter

comm—community

COMP—compensation

Comp—compulsions

comp—(1) compound, (2) complete, or (3) complication

conc—concentration

CONG—congregated care

cont—continued

contr.—contractions

COPD—(1) chronic obstructive pulmonary disease or (2) congestive obstructive pulmonary disease

COS—chief of staff

COTA—certified occupational therapy assistant

CP—(1) cerebral palsy or (2) chronic phase

C & P—cystoscopy and panendoscopy

CPA—(1) carotid phonoangiography, (2) cerebellar-pontine angle, or (3) costophrenic angle

CPAP—continuous positive airway pressure

CPB—cardiopulmonary bypass

CPBG—cardiopulmonary bypass graft

CPD—cephalopelvic disproportion

cpd.—compound

C-peptide—connecting peptide

CPK—creatine phosphokinase

CPm—continuous passive motion

CPR—cardiopulmonary resuscitation

CPS—child protective service

C.P.T.—chest physical therapy

CR—complete response

Cr—creatinine

CRD—(1) chronic renal disease or (2) chronic respiratory disease

creat—creatinine

CRF—chronic renal failure

CRL—crown-rump length

CRP—C-reactive protein

CRT—cardio resuscitation

CRYO—cryoprecipitate

C/S—cesarean section

C & S—culture and sensitivity

C sed rate—corrected sedimentation rate

CSCU—cardiac special care unit

CSF—cerebrospinal fluid

CSMG—cystometrogram with sphincter electromyography

C Sp—cervical spine

CSR—central serous retinopathy

CSS—community support system

CT—(1) chest tube, (2) computerized tomography, or (3) clotting time

ct.—count

CT ratio—cardiothoracic ratio

CT scan—computed tomography scan

cta—catamenia

CTLSO—cervicothoracic-lumbosacral orthosis

CTM—connective tissue massage

CU—cystourethrocele

cub. cent.—cubic centimeter

CUG—cystourethrogram

CUS—chronic undifferentiated schizophrenia

CV—cardiovascular

CVA—cardiovascular accident

CVD—cardiovascular disease

CVL—central venous line

CVP—central venous pressure

CVS—(1) cardiovascular system or (2) clean-voided specimen

CVT. A—costovertebral angle

c/w—(1) consistent with or (2) chest wall

CWP—childbirth without pain

Cx—(1) convex or (2) cervix

cx—(1) cylinder axis or (2) cervix

CXR—chest x-ray

cyl—cylinder

cysto—cystoscopic examination

CZI—crystaline zinc insulin

D—(1) dose or (2) diopter

d—day

DA—dopamine

DAMA—discharged against medical advice

db—decibel

DC—discharge

D & C—dilatation and curettage

D/C—discontinued

d/c—discharged

d.c.—discontinue

DCc—double concave

DCF—domiciliary care facility

DCR—dacryocystorhinostomy

DCx—double convex

DD—(1) dry dressing or (2) disc diameter

DDS—doctor of dental surgery

DDTP—drug dependence treatment program

DDX—differential diagnosis

D & E—dilatation and evacuation

Decr—decreased

decub—decubitus

def—deformity

Deg—degree

deg—degenerative

Degen—degenerative

Del—delusions

Dem—dermatology

Derm—dermatology

desc—descending

Detox—detoxification

DF—dorsiflexion

D.F.—diabetic fractional

D.F.A.—difficulty falling asleep

DFG—direct forward gaze

D5/NS—dextrose in normal saline

D5/RL—dextrose in Ringer's lactate

D5S—5 percent dextrose in saline

DG—downward gaze

Dgm—decigram

DH—day hospital

DHEAS—dehydroepiandrosterone sulfate

DI—diabetes insipidus

Diab—diabetic

diag.—diagnosis

diam.—diameter

dias.—diastolic

DIC—disseminated intravascular coagulation

Diff.—differential

dig—digoxin

DIP—distal interphalangeal (joint)

disc.—discontinued

disch.—discharged

DISH—diffuse idiopathic skeletal hypertrophy

disp.—(1) disposition or (2) dispense

disartic.—disarticulated

DIU—death in uterus

div—divorced

DIVA—digital intravenous angiography

DJD—degenerative joint disease

DKA—diabetic ketoacidosis

DL—danger list

D.L.—(1) direct laryngoscopy or
(2) distolingual

dl—deciliter

DLE—disseminated lupus erythematosus

DM—(1) diabetes mellitus or (2) diastolic
murmur

DMFT—decayed, missing, and filled teeth

DNKA—did not keep appointment

DNR—do not resuscitate

DNS—deviated nasal septum

DO—distal occlusal filling

DO—doctor of osteopathy

DOA—dead on arrival

DOB—date of birth

DOI—date of injury

dorsi—dorsiflexion

DP—dorsalis pedis

DPH—diphenylhydantoin (Dilantin)

DPT—diphtheria, pertussis, and tetanus

DR—(1) D-related (tissue typing) or (2) delivery
room

D.R.—diabetic retinopathy

dr—dram

DRG—diagnosis-related group

DSD—dry sterile dressing

DSM—Diagnostic and Statistical Manual of
Mental Disorders

DSSAB—aid to the blind

DSSAD—aid to the disabled

DSSPA—public assistance

DST—dexamethazone suppression test

D5W—5 percent dextrose in water

D.T.—diphtheria, tetanus

DTC—day treatment center

d.t.d. no.—let such dose be given

DTN—diphtheria toxin normal

DTO—deodorized tincture of opium

DTR—deep tendon reflexes

DT's—delirium tremens

DU—duodenal ulcer

DUB—dysfunctional uterine bleeding

DUF—dry ultrafiltration

DVA—(1) digital vascular angiography or
(2) decreased visual acuity

DVD—double vessel disease

DVI—digital vascular imaging

DVR—department of vocational rehabilitation

D/W—dextrose and water

Dx—diagnosis

dyn—dynamic

E—(1) eye, (2) enema, or (3) extremity

e—epinephrine

E. coli—Escherichia coli

ea—each

EAC—external auditory canal

EAHF—eczema, asthma, hay fever

EB—elementary body

EBL—estimated blood loss

EBV—Epstein-Barr virus

EC—enteric-coated

ECA—external carotid artery

ECCE—extracapsular cataract extraction

ECF—(1) extracellular fluid or (2) extended care facility

ECG—electrocardiogram

ECHO virus—enteric human orphan virus

ECT—electroconvulsive therapy

Ed—emergency department

ed—education

EDC—estimated date of confinement

EDENT—edentulous

EDx—electrodiagnosis

EEG—electroencephalogram

EENT—eye, ear, nose, and throat

EF—ejection fraction

EFI—elongation initiation factor

EFW—estimated fetal weight

EH—(1) essential hypertension or (2) enlarged heart

EIPD—esophageal intraluminal pseudodiverticulosis

EJ—elbow jerk

EKG—electrocardiogram

EKY—electrokymogram

elec—electric

elev—elevation

Elix—elixir

ELOS—estimated length of stay

EM—(1) electron microscope or (2) evaporated milk

Em—emmetropia

EMA—early morning awakening

EMC—encephalomyocarditis

EMF—electromotive force

EMG—electromyogram

end—endurance

ENG—electronystagmography

ENT—ear, nose, and throat

EO—elbow only

E & O—examination and observation

EOM—(1) extraocular movement or (2) extraocular muscle

EOS—eosinophil count

EPI—epilepsy

Epi—epinephrine

epis—episiotomy

EPITH—epithelium

EPR—electrophrenic respiration

EPS—extrapyramidal symptoms

equil—equilibrium

ER—emergency room

ERCP—endoscopic retrograde cholangiopancreatography

ERG—electroretinogram

ESP—extrasensory perception

ESR—erythrocyte sedimentation rate

ESRD—end stage renal disease

EST—(1) electrostimulation therapy or (2) exercise stress test

ET—endotracheal tube

et—and

ET3—erythrocytic triiodothyrodinal uptake

Eth—ethmoid

ETIOL—etiology

ETOH—alcohol

ETT—(1) exercise tolerance test or (2) endotracheal tube

ET-T—endotracheal tube

EUA—examination under anesthesia

eval—evaluation

ever—eversion

EWHO—elbow wrist hand orthosis

ex—(1) exercise or (2) example

EXAM—examination

EXP—expired

EXPIR—expiratory

Ext—(1) extract, (2) extern, or (3) extremities

ext—(1) external or (2) extension

ext fld—fluid extract

ext gen—external genitalia

ext rot—external rotation

extr—extract

F—(1) female, (2) Fahrenheit, or (3) fair

F.—Fahrenheit

FA—fatty acid

F.A.—fluourescein angiography

F/A—femur-abdomen

Fa—father

FACP—Fellow of the American College of Physicians

FACS—Fellow American College of Surgeons

FAM—family

FANA—fluourescent antinuclear antibody

FAP—functional ambulation profile

FB—(1) finger breadth or (2) foreign body

F.B.—foreign body

f.b.—finger breadths

FBS—fasting blood sugar

FC—(1) Foley catheter or (2) family conference

F-cath—Foley catheter

FD—(1) focal distance or (2) fully dilated

FDP—flexor digitorum profundus

FDS—flexor digitorum superficialis

Fe—iron

Fe def—iron deficiency

FEF—forced expiratory flow

fem.—femoral

fem. pop—Femoropopliteal

FeSO₄—ferrous sulfate

Fet.—fetal

FEV—forced expiratory volume

F/F—removable full (complete denture)

FFA—free fatty acid

FH—(1) family history or (2) fetal heart

FHR—fetal heart rate

FHS—fetal heart sounds

FHT—fetal heart tone

FID2—fractional concentration of inspired oxygen

Fl—fluid

fl. dr.—fluid dram

fl. oz.—fluid ounce

flds—fluids

flex—flexion

fluoro—fluoroscopy

FM—family medicine

FN—fairly nourished

F/N—finger to nose

FO—foot orthosis

FOI—flight of ideas

FOIA—Freedom of Information Act

FOF—full of feces

FOM—floor of mouth

For body—foreign body

FOS—full of stool

FP—(1) flat plate, (2) family planning, or (3) function profile

F & R—force and rhythm (of pulse)

fr—French (catheter measurement)

FRACT DOS—in divided doses

FREE—family residences and essential enterprises

FRIM—full joint range of motion

FROA—full range of affect

FROM—full range of motion

FS—(1) frozen section or (2) fasting sugar

FSH—follicle-stimulating hormone

FSP—fibrin split product

FT—(1) feeding tube or (2) full term

Ft.—foot

FTA—fluorescent treponema antibody test

FTI—free thyroxine index

FTN—finger to nose

FTND—full-term normal delivery

FTR—failed to report

FTSG—full-thickness skin graft

FTT—failure to thrive

F/U—follow-up

FUB—functional uterine bleeding

FUD—fever of undetermined origin

Func—function

FVL—fast vital capacity

FWB—full weight-bearing

Fx—fracture

G—(1) gravida or (2) good

g—gram

g%—grams per hundred milliliters of blood serum as specified

GA—(1) general anesthesia, (2) gastric analysis, or (3) glycogenic acanthosis

GB—gallbladder

G-B—Guillain-Barré syndrome

GBM—general basic medical

GBS—(1) gallbladder series or (2) Guillain-Barré syndrome

GC—gonorrhea

GCE—general conditioning exercises

G-dl—grams/deciliter

GE—gastroenterology

gen—genetics

GER—gastroesophageal reflux

GERD—gastroesophageal reflux disease

Geront—gerontology

gest.—gestation

GFR—glomerular filtration rate

GG—gamma globulin

GGPT—gamma glutamyl transpeptidase

GGTP—gamma glutamyl transpeptidase

GH—growth hormone

GHP (s)—gated heart pool (scan)

GI—gastrointestinal

GIB—gastrointestinal bleed

G & L—gains and losses

Glu—glucose

GM—grand mal seizure

gm—gram

gm/dl—grams per deciliter

GN—glomerulonephritis

gold sol.—colloidal gold curve

GP—general practitioner

Gr.—grain

Gr. del—grandiose delusions

Gr. Fa—grandfather

Gr. Mo—grandmother

GS—general surgery

G/S—glucose in saline

g.s.—gram stain

G-6 PD—glucose-6-phosphate dehydrogenase

GSW—gunshot wound

GT—group therapy

gt.—drop

GTT—glucose tolerance test

gtt.—drops

G-tube—gastrostomy tube

GU—genitourinary

GVHD—graft vs. host disease

G & W—glycerin and water enema

GYN—gynecology

H—(1) Hispanic, (2) hydrogen, or (3) hour

h—hour

HA—(1) hyperalimentation or (2) headache

H.A.—hospital aide

H/A—(1) headache or (2) head-abdomen

HAA—hepatitis-associated antigen

HAC—hearing aid check

HAE—hearing aid evaluation

Halluc—hallucinations

Hap. Halluc1—haptic hallucinations

HASCVD—hypertensive arteriosclerotic cardiovascular disease

HB—housebound

Hb—hemoglobin

HB$_s$AG—hepatits B surface antigen

HBHC—hospital-based home care

HBP—high blood pressure

HBV—hepatitis B virus

HCC—home care coordinator

HCF—higher cortical functions

HCG—human chorionic gonadotropin

HCl—hydrochloric acid

HCO$_3$—bicarbonate

HCT—hematocrit

HCTZ—hydrochlorothiazide

HCVD—hypertensive cardiovascular disease

HD—(1) hemodialysis, (2) hearing distance, (3) hip disarticulation, or (4) Hodgkin's disease

HDL—high-density lipoprotein

He—helium

HEENT—head, eyes, ears, nose, and throat

hemi—(1) hemiplegic or (2) hemiparesis

H.F.—hemofiltration

Hg—mercury

Hgb—hemoglobin

HH—hiatal hernia

HHA—homonymous hemianopia

HHNK—hyperglycemic hyperosmolar nonketotic

HI—homicidal ideations

5-HIAA—5-hydroxyindoleacetic acid

HIF—higher integrative function

HINT—Hinton test for syphilis

HIP—health insurance plan

HIV—human immunodeficiency virus

HJR—hepatojugular reflux

HKAFO—hip-knee-ankle-foot orthosis

HL—(1) hearing loss or (2) hearing level

HLA—human leukocyte antigen

HM—hand movement

HMD—hyaline membrane disease

hMG—human menopausal gonadotropin

HN—head and neck

H.N.—head nurse

HNP—herniated nucleus pulposus (herniated disk)

HNV—has not voided

HO—heterotopic ossification

h/o—history of

HOB—head of bed

HOP—high oxygen pressure

HP—(1) hot pack, (2) hemipelvectomy, or (3) hypopharynx

H & P—history and physical

HPE—history and physical examination

HPF—per high-power field

HPI—history of present illness

HPL—high peroxidase activity

HP2—high pressure zone

HPV—human papillomavirus

HR—(1) home relief or (2) heart rate

hr—hour

HRD—hemo-renal dialysis

HRF—health-related facility

H.S.—hours of sleep

H/S—heel-to-shin

h.s.—at bedtime

HSG—hysterosalpingography

HSV—herpes simplex virus

HT—height

ht—(1) head trauma or (2) hematocrit

HTLV III—human T-cell lymphotropic virus, type III

HTN—hypertension

Hus—husband

HV—(1) Hemovac or (2) home visit

HVD—hypertensive vascular disease

HVDT—Hopper visual organization test

HVG—high-voltage galvanic stimulation

Hx—history

HY—hyperopia

hyper—hypertrophy

hyperal—hyperalimentation

Hypng. Halluc—hypnagogic hallucinations

Hypo—hypodermic

hyst—hysterectomy

Hz—hertz

I—(1) iodine, (2) independent, or (3) intermediate

I^{131}—radioactive iodine

IA—(1) intra-arterial or (2) induced abortion

IABP—intra-aortic balloon pump

IAC—internal auditory canal

IB—inclusion body

IBC—iron-binding capacity

IBD—inflammatory bowel disease

IBG—iliac bone graft

IBW—ideal body weight

IC—intermittent catheterization

ICA—internal carotid artery

ICC—interstitial cells of Cajal

ICCE—intracapsular cataract extraction

ICF—(1) intermediate care facility or (2) intracellular fluid

ICP—intracranial pressure

ICS—intercostal space

ICSH—interstitial-cell stimulating hormone

ICT—inflammation of connective tissue

ICU—intensive care unit

ID—(1) intradermal or (2) identification

I.D.—infectious disease

I & D—incision and drainage

IDDM—insulin-dependent diabetes mellitus

IDK—internal derangement of knee

IDM—infant of diabetic mother

IDRM—intradermal

IE—initial evaluation

I/e—inspiratory/expiratory ratio

IEP—immunoelectrophoresis

IF—interstitial fluid

Ig—immunoglobulin

IH—infectious hepatitis

IHSS—idiopathic hypertrophic subaortic stenosis

I & J—insight and judgment

IM—intramuscular

IMF—intermaxillary fixation

IMI—inferior myocardial infarction

IMP—impression

Imped—impedance

IMV—intermittent mandatory ventilation

In—inch

Inc—incontinent

Inc. ab—incomplete abortion

incl—include

Incr—increased

ind—independent

indiv—individual

INF—interferon

inf—inferior

ING—inguinal

INH—isoniazid

INJ—injury

Inj—injection

ins—insurance

insp—inspiration

INSPIR—inspiratory

Int—(1) internal or (2) intern

INTHC—intrathecally

inv—inversion

IO—inferior oblique

I & O—intake and output

IOL—intraocular lens

IOP—intraocular pressure

IOR—ideas of reference

IP—(1) interphalangeal or (2) intraperitoneally

IPPB—intermittent positive pressure breathing

IPPR—intermittent positive pressure respiration

IQ—intelligence quotient

IR—(1) internal resistance or (2) internal rotation

I.R.—infrared

IRBBB—incomplete right bundle branch block

irrig—irrigate

is—in situ

IS—intercostal space

ISOL—isolation

iss—One and one-half

IT—(1) inferior temporal, (2) intrathecal, or (3) inhalation therapy

ITP—idiopathic thrombocytopenic purpura

IU—international unit

IUCD—intrauterine contraceptive device

IUD—intrauterine device

IUFD—intrauterine fetal death

IUGR—intrauterine growth retardation

IUP—intrauterine pregnancy

IUTP—intrauterine term pregnancy

IV—intravenous

Iv. chol—intravenous cholangiogram

IVC—(1) inferior vena cava or (2) intravenous cholangiogram

IVCD—intraventricular conduction disorder

IV push—intravenous push

IVCT—isovolumic contraction time

IVDA—intravenous drug abuse

IVH—intraventricular hemorrhage

IVP—intravenous pyelogram

IVPB—intravenous piggyback

IVSD—intraventricular septal defect

IVU—intravenous urogram

IW—inferior wall

IWMI—inferior wall myocardial infarction

J—joule's equivalent

JARAN—junior admitting resident admission note

Jj—jaw jerk

JND—jaw-neck dissection

JODM—juvenile onset of diabetes mellitus

J.P.—Jackson Pratt (drainage tube)

JRA—juvenile rheumatoid arthritis

JROM—joint range of motion

JT—junctional tachycardia

Jt.—joint

J-tube—jejunostomy tube

JVD—jugular vein distension

K—potassium

K cal—kilocalories

KAFO—knee-ankle-foot orthosis

KB—knee-bearing

KCl—potassium chloride

KD—knee disarticulation

Kg—kilogram

KI—potassium iodide

KJ—knee jerk

KK—knee kick

KLH—keyhole-limpet hemocyanin

KO—knee only

KP—keratitic precipitate

KS—Kaposi's sarcoma

KUB—Kidney, ureter, bladder

kV—kilovolt

KVO—keep vein open

kW—kilowatt

K-W Disease—Kimmelstiel-Wilson disease

17-KGS—17-ketogenic steroids

17-KS—17-ketosteroids

L—(1) left or (2) liter

l—liter

L1, L2, etc.—first lumbar, second lumbar, etc. (spine)

LA—left atrium

L.A.—local anesthesia

L & A—light and accommodation

lab—laboratory

LAC—long arm cast

LAD—left axis deviation

LADA—left anterior descending artery

LAE—left atrial enlargement

LAH—left atrial hypertrophy

LAHB—left anterior hemiblock

LAK—lymphokine-activated killer

LAO—left anterior oblique

LAP—(1) left atrial pressure or (2) leukocyte alkaline phosphatase

lap—laparotomy

lat—lateral

lat. dol—to the painful side

LATS—long-acting thyroid stimulator

LAV—lymphadenopathy-associated virus

lax—laxative

lb.—pound

LBBB—left bundle branch block

LBD—(1) left border dullness or (2) lower body dressing

LBP—lower back pain

LBW—low birth weight

LC—laser cone

LCM—left costal margin

LCS—low constant suction

LCXA—left circumflex (coronary) artery

LD—learning disabled

L & D—labor and delivery

LDEA—left deviation of electrical axis

LDH—lactate dehydrogenase (serum enzyme)

LDL—low-density lipoprotein

LE—(1) lower extremity, (2) lupus erythematosus, or (3) left eye

LE Prep—lupus erythematosus preparation

LES—lower esophageal sphincter

LET—linear energy transfer (radiation)

LF—low flap (cesarean section)

lf—left

LFA—left frontoanterior

LFD—low forceps delivery

LFP—left frontoposterior

LFT—(1) liver function test or (2) left frontotransverse

lg—large

LGA—large for gestational age

LGV—lymphogranuloma venereum

LH—luteinizing hormone

LHF—left heart failure

LHT—left hypertrophia

LI$_2$CO$_3$—lithium carbonate

LIF—left iliac fossa

lig—ligament

LIH—left inguinal hernia

lim—limitation

Linim—liniment

liq.—liquid

LKS—liver, kidney, and spleen

LL—(1) lower lid or (2) leg length

LLB—long leg brace

LLC—long leg cast

LLD—(1) left lateral decubitus or (2) language learning disabled

LLE—left lower extremity

LLG—left lateral gaze

LLL—left lower lobe

LLQ—left lower quadrant

L/M—liters per minute

LMD—local doctor

LML—left mediolateral

LMN—lower motor neuron

LMP—last menstrual period

L.N.—lymph node

LOA—(1) looseness of associations or (2) left occipitoanterior

LOC—(1) level of consciousness or (2) loss of consciousness

loc—level of consciousness

LOH—loss of hearing

LOM—limitation of motion

LOP—left occipitoposterior

LOS—length of stay

LOT—left occipitotransverse

Lot—lotion

LP—lumbar puncture

L.P.—light projection

LPF—leukocytosis-promoting factor

LPHB—left posterior hemiblock

LPN—licensed practical nurse

L.P.N.P.—licensed practical nurse permit

LPO—left posterior oblique

LPS—liters per second

LR—lateral rectus

LRG—long-range goal

LRM—left radical mastectomy

LS—lumbosacral

L-S—lumbosacral

L/S ratio—lecithin-sphingomyelin ratio

LS sp.—lumbosacral spine

LSA—left sacroanterior

LSB—left sternal border

LSBM—loose bowel movement

LSCS—lower segment cesarean section

LSK—liver, spleen, and kidney

LSO—left salpingo-oophorectomy

LSP—(1) left sacroposterior or (2) long sitting position

L Sp—lumbar spine

LST—(1) labor-saving techniques or (2) left sacrotransverse

LT—(1) Levin tube or (2) laryngotracheal

Lt—left

LTA—lengthening of tendon Achilles

LTH—luteotropic hormone

LTL—laparoscopic tubal ligation

LTM—long-term memory

LUC—large unstained cells

LUE—left upper extremity

LUL—left upper lobe

LUQ—left upper quadrant

LV—(1) left ventricular or (2) left ventricle

LVEDP—left ventricular and diastolic pressure

LVEF—left ventricular ejection fraction

LVF—left ventricular hypertrophy

LVP—large volume parenteral

LW—lateral wall

L & W—living and well

Lx—larynx

lymphs—lymphocytes

lytes—electrolytes

M—(1) male, (2) murmur, or (3) meter

M.—meter

m—(1) murmur or (2) minim

M1, M2—mitral first, second sound

MA—medical assistance

MAC—midarm circumference

MAFO—molded ankle-foot orthosis

MAL—midaxillary line

MAMC—midarm muscle circumference

MAIO—monoamine oxidase inhibitor

MAO—monoamine oxidase

MAP—mean arterial pressure

MAR—medical assistance resident

MAT—manual arts therapy

max—maximal

MB—mix well

6 MB—six-meal bland diet

MBD—minimal brain dysfunction

MCA—middle cerebral artery

McB pt—McBurney's point

McC—McCarthey panendoscope

MCCU—medical comprehensive care unit

mcg—microgram

MCH—mean corpuscular hemoglobin

MCHC—mean corpuscular hemoglobin concentration

MCL—midclavicular line

MCP—metacarpophalangeal (joint)

MCV—mean corpuscular volume

M.D.—(1) medical doctor or (2) muscular dystrophy

M-D—manic-depressive

MDNT—midnight

M.E.D.—(1) minimal effective dose or (2) minimal erythema dose

Med.—(1) medical or (2) medicine

meds—medications

mEq/l—milliequivalent per liter

mets—metastases

MFD—midforceps delivery

MFG—manofluorography

MFT—muscle function test

Mg—magnesium

mg—milligram

mg%—milligrams per 100 milliliters of serum blood

mg/dl—milligrams per deciliter

MGF—maternal grandfather

MGM—maternal grandmother

mgmt—management

MgSO$_4$—magnesium sulfate

MH—(1) marital history or (2) mental health

MHB—maximal hospital benefit

MHC—(1) mental hygiene clinic or (2) major histocompatibility complex

MI — myocardial infarction

MIC — (1) minimal inhibitory concentration or (2) maternal and infant care

mict — micturition

MICU — medical intensive care unit

MIF — maximum inspiratory force

Mil Hx — military history

min — (1) minute or (2) minimal

mitr. I — mitral insufficiency

mix. astig. — mixed astigmatism

ml — milliliter

MLC — mixed lymphocyte culture

MLF — medial longitudinal fasciculus

MM — (1) mucous membrane or (2) major medical

M&M — morbidity and mortality

mm — millimeter

mm³ — cubic millimeter

mm Hg — millimeter of mercury

mm/l — millimeters per liter

MMPI — Minnesota Multiphasic Personality Inventory

MMR — measles, mumps, and rubella

MMS — mini-mental state

MMTP — methadone maintenance treatment program

MN — midnight

MND — motor neuron disease

MO — (1) mesial occlusal filling or (2) mineral oil

MO — male

Mo — mother

mo — months

MOD — medical officer on duty

mod. — moderate

MODY — maturity onset diabetes of youth

MOE — movement of extremities

mol wt — molecular weight

MOM — Milk of Magnesia

mono — (1) monocyte or (2) mononucleosis

MP — (1) mental patient, (2) metacarpophalangeal, or (3) menstrual period

MPA — main pulmonary artery

MPI — maximum point of impulse

MR — (1) mitral regurgitation, (2) medial rectus, (3) mentally retarded, or (4) magnetic resonance

M & R — measure and record

M & R, I & O — measure and record, intake and output

MRE — manual resistive exercise

MRFIT — multiple risk factor intervention trial

MRGT — murmur, rub, gallop, thrill

MRI — magnetic resonance imaging

MRT — medical records technician

MS — (1) multiple sclerosis, (2) mitral stenosis, (3) morphine sulfate, or (4) mental status

M.S. — morphine sulfate

M/S — mental status

MSE — mental status examination

MSH — melanocyte-stimulating hormone

MSL — midsternal line

MSQ — mental status quotient

MSR — moderate sodium restriction

MSU — midstream urine

MSW — Master of Social Work

MT — multiple trauma

MTP — medial tibial plateau

mU — milliunit

MULTIP — multiparous

multivits — multivitamins

MVA — motor vehicle accident

MVI — multivitamins

mvmt — movement

MVP—mitral valve prolapse

MWD—microwave diathermy

My—myopia

MYO I—myocardial infarction

myop.—myopia

N—(1) normal or (2) nitrogen

n—(1) night or (2) nerve

NA—not applicable

N.A.—(1) nursing assistant or (2) not applicable

N/A—no authorization

Na—sodium

NaCl—sodium chloride

NAD—(1) no acute distress or (2) nothing abnormal detected

NaHCO$_3$—sodium bicarbonate

NAI—no acute infiltration

NAPD—no active pulmonary disease

NB—newborn

NBN—newborn nursery

NC—(1) noncontributory or (2) no chance

N/C—(1) nasal cannula, (2) no charge, or (3) normocephalic

NCCT—noncontrast CAT scan

NCJ—needle catheter jejunostomy

NCP—(1) nursing care plan or (2) near point of convergence

NCS—no concentrated sweets

NCV—nerve conduction velocity

ND—(1) nasal deformity or (2) neck dissection

NDEA—no deviation of electrical axis

NDT—neural developmental training

NE—(1) norepinephrine or (2) neurologic examination

NEC—(1) not elsewhere classified or (2) necrotizing enterocolitis

neg—negative

NEMD—nonspecific esophageal motor disorder

Neur.—neurological

Neuro—neurology

NF—National Formulary

NFTD—normal full-term delivery

NFTDSD—normal full-term spontaneous delivery

NG—(1) nasogastric or (2) nanograms

NG tube—nasogastric tube

NGT—nasogastric tube

NH—nursing home

NH$_3$—ammonia

NHP—nursing home placement

NICU—neonatal intensive care unit

NIDDM—non–insulin-dependent diabetes

NIH—National Institutes of Health

NK—natural killer

NKA—no known allergies

nl—(1) normal limits or (2) normal

NLDS—neuroleptic drugs

NLP—no light perception

NMG—neuromyography

NMR—nuclear magnetic resonance

N/N—negative for sugar and acetone

N.O.—nursing office

no.—number

noct—at night

norm—normal

NOS—not otherwise specified

NP—(1) neuropsychiatric or (2) nasopharynx

NPH—(1) Neutral Protamine Hagedorn (insulin) or (2) normal pressure hydrocephalus

NPN—nonprotein nitrogen

NPO—nothing by mouth

NPOD—neuropsychiatric officer of the day

N-psychodx—neuropsychological testing

NPT—nocturnal penile tumescence

NR—do not repeat or refill

NRC—normal retinal correspondence

NREM—non-rapid eye movement

NS—(1) neurosurgery, (2) normal saline, or (3) nursing supervision

N.S.—normal saline

N/S—normal saline

NSAID—nonsteroidal anti-inflammatory drug

NSB—normal sinus bradycardia

NSC—no significant change

NSD—normal spontaneous delivery

NSE—neuron-specific enolase

Nsg—nursing

NSR—normal sinus rhythm

NST—normal sinus tachycardia

N.S.T.—nonstress test

NSVD—normal spontaneous vaginal delivery

NT—not tested

N/T—nasotracheal

N&T—nose and throat

NTD—neural tube defect

NTG—nitroglycerin

NTP—Nitropaste

NUA—nursing unit activities

NV—naked vision

N & V—nausea and vomiting

NVD—neck vein distension

NVS—neurological vital signs

NWB—non-weight bearing

Nx—nourishment

O—(1) oriented or (2) objective (SOAP)

o—oral

O₂sat—oxygen saturation

OA—osteoarthritis

OAF—osteoclast activating factor

OB—obstetrical

OB-GYN—obstetrics and gynecology

OBS—organic brain syndrome

obs—(1) obsessions, (2) obstetrics, or (3) observations

obst.—obstruction

OC—oral contraceptive

occ—occipital

Occ. Hx—occupational history

Occas—occasionally

OCG—oral cholecystogram

OC/OP—oral cavity/oropharynx

OD—(1) right eye, (2) overdose, or (3) officer of the day

O.D.—right eye

O/D—overdose

o.d.—once a day

ODM—ophthalmodynamometry

OE—otitis external

OFD—occipital frontal diameter

OG—operative gastrostomy

OHD—organic heart disease

oint.—ointment

o.j.—orange juice

OKN—optokinetic nystagmus

Olf. Halluc.—olfactory hallucinations

OM—otitis media

om—every morning

OM AD—otitis media right ear

OM AS—otitis media left ear

OM AU—otitis media both ears

OMPC—otitis media purulent chronic

OMS—organic mental syndrome

ON—optic nerve

on—every night

OOB—out of bed

OP—opening pressure (for lumbar puncture)

O/P—(1) outpatient or (2) oropharynx

O & P—ova and parasites

op—operation

OPC—outpatient clinic

OPD—outpatient department

oper.—operation

OPG—oculoplethysmography

OPH—ophthalmology

Ophth—ophthalmology

OPT—outpatient treatment

OPV—oral polio vaccine

OR—operating room

o/r—original order

ORIF—open reduction, internal fixation

orophx—oropharynx

Orthdon—orthodontic

Ortho—orthopedics

OS—left eye

O.S.—left eye

os—mouth

osteo—osteomyelitis

OT—(1) occupational therapy or (2) old tuberculin

OTD—organ tolerance dose

OTO—otolaryngology

Oto—otology

OTOL—otolaryngology

OTR—occupational therapist registered

OU—both eyes

O.U.—both eyes

OV—both eyes

OVR—office of vocational rehabilitation

OW—once a week

Oz—ounce

P—(1) pulse, (2) phosphorus, (3) poor, or (4) plan (SOAP)

P.—(1) pulse or (2) after or following

p—after

P. flex—plantar flexion

P$_2$—pulmonic second sound

PA—(1) pulmonary artery, (2) pernicious anemia, (3) posteroanterior, or (4) physician's assistant

P.A.—pulmonary artery

P & A—percussion and auscultation

P-A—posteroanterior

PA-C—physician's assistant certified

PAC—premature auricular contraction

pacer—pacemaker

PACO$_2$—partial pressure of carbon dioxide

PAD—peripheral artery disease

PAD (P)—pulmonary artery diastolic pressure

PAF—(1) paroxysmal atrial fibrillation or (2) patient aid fund

PAO$_2$—partial pressure of alveolar oxygen

PaO$_2$—partial pressure of arterial oxygen

PAP—(1) peak air pressure, (2) Papanicolaou, (3) pulmonary artery pressure, or (4) prostatic acid phosphatase

Pap—Papanicolaou smear

Pap smear—Papanicolaou smear

Pap test—Papanicolaou test

PAR—(1) postanesthesia room or (2) postanesthesia recovery

Par. Sz.—paranoid schizophrenic

para—(1) paracentesis or (2) paraplegic

paracent—paracentesis

paren.—parenterally

Part. aeq.—equal parts

PARU—postanesthesia recovery unit

PAS—(1) pulmonary artery systolic or (2) *para*-aminosalicylic acid

P.A.S.—sodium *para*-aminosalicylic acid

PAT—paroxysmal atrial tachycardia

Path—pathology

PAWP—pulmonary artery wedge pressure

PB—phenobarbital

P.B.—piggyback

Pb—lead

PBI—protein-bound iodine

PBLC—premature birth living child

pc—after meals

P.C.'s—packed cells

PCA—patient care assistant

PC-BPC—buffy coat-poor packed cells

PCN—penicillin

PCO₂—partial pressure carbon dioxide

PCP—pneumocystis carinii pneumonia

PCV—packed cell volume

PCWP—pulmonary capillary wedge pressure

PCX—portable chest x-ray

PD—(1) peritoneal dialysis, (2) pupillary distance, (3) Parkinson's disease, or (4) post-prandial (after meals)

PDA—patent ductus arteriosus

PE—(1) physical examination or (2) pulmonary embolism

PEC—patient evaluation center

Pecs—pectoralis muscle group

Ped—pediatrics

PEEP—positive end-expiratory pressure

PEFR—peak expiratory flow rate

PEG—(1) pneumoencephalogram or (2) percutaneous endoscopic gastrostomy

PEJ—percutaneous endoscopic jejunostomy

PEN—penicillin

PEP—(1) pre-ejaculation period or (2) protein electrophoresis

per—through or by

Per. del—persecutory delusions

Per. I—peripheral iridectomy

perf—perforation

PERLA—pupils equal and react to light and accommodation

PERRLA—pupils equal, round, and react to light and accommodation

PES—pharyngoesophageal segment (or sphincter)

PET—(1) positron emission tomography or (2) polyethylene tubes

PF—plantar flexion

P.F.—peak flow

P & F—prophylaxis and flouride

PFA—percutaneous femoral angiogram

PFC—persistent fetal circulation

PFFD—patient failed to keep appointment

PFKA—patient failed to keep appointment

PFM—porcelain fused to metal crown

PFS—pulmonary function study

PFT—pulmonary function test

PG—prostaglandin

PGF—paternal grandfather

PGH—pituitary growth hormone

PGM—paternal grandmother

PH—past history

Ph—(1) phosphorus or (2) phenyl

pH—hydrogen ion concentration

PHC—posthospital care

Phenobarb—phenobarbital

P.H.N.—public health nurse

PHOS—phosphorous

Physiol—physiological

PI—present illness

PICA—posterior inferior cerebellar artery

PICU—pediatric intensive care unit

PID—pelvic inflammatory disease

PIE—psychiatric intake and evaluation

PINS—person in need of supervision

PIP—(1) proximal interphalangeal or (2) peak inspiratory pressure

PIPJ—proximal interphalangeal joint

PIS—pregnancy interruption service

PIT—Pitocin

PJE—premature junctional contraction

PK—psychokinesis

PKU—phenylketonuria

PL—light perception

Pl. surg.—plastic surgery

Plac.—placenta

Placebo—to please

plant—plantar flexion

PLS—posterior leaf spring

PLSO—posterior leaf spring orthosis

Plt—platelets

PLT con—platelet concentration

PLTR—psychological test report

PLTS—platelets

PM—(1) petit mal seizure or (2) pemphigus

PMB—(1) polymorphonuclear basophil leukocytes or (2) postmenopausal bleeding

PMD—private physician

PME—polymorphonuclear eosinophil leukocytes

PMF—pupils midposition fixed

PMH—past medical history

PMI—point of maximal impulse

PML—progressive multifocal leukoencephalopathy

PMN—polymorphonuclear neutrophil leukocytes

PMP—previous menstrual period

PMR—physical medicine and rehabilitation

PMT—perceptual motor testing/training

PN—pneumonia

PNC—prenatal clinic

PND—(1) paroxysmal nocturnal dyspnea or (2) post nasal drip

pneumoc—pneumococcus

PNF—proprioceptive neuromuscular facilitation

PNS—(1) parasympathetic nervous system or (2) peripheral nervous system

PO—postoperative

P & O—prosthetics and orthotics

po—by mouth

PO$_2$—oxygen partial pressure

POD—(1) postoperative day or (2) podiatry

poly—polymorphonuclear neutrophil

polyprop—polypropylene

polys—polymorphonuclear leukocytes

POMR—problem-oriented medical record

POP—persistent occipitoposterior

pop—popliteal

poplit—popliteal

pos—positive

p.o.s.—pressure of speech

post—posterior

post ax line—postaxillary line

post-op—postoperative

POT—postoperative treatment

PP—(1) postpartum or (2) pulse pressure

P.P.—postprandial

P/P—removal partial denture, maxilla/mandible

p.p.—after meals

p.p.b.s.—postprandial blood sugar

PPD—(1) purified protein derivative of tuberculin or (2) packs (of cigarettes) per day

PPF—plasma protein fractions

PPH—postpartum hemorrhage

PPLO—pleuropneumonia-like organisms

ppm—parts per million

PPN—peripheral parenteral nutrition

PPS—postpericardiotomy syndrome

PR—(1) pityriasis rosea or (2) by rectum

P & R—pelvic and rectal

p.r.—per rectum

PRBC—packed red blood cells

PRC—packed red cells

PRE—progressive resistive exercise

pre-op—preoperative

prep—preparation

Pre-Voc—prevocational

pri—private

p.r.n.—whenever necessary

PRO—peer review organization

Pro—protein

Prob—probable

Prog—prognosis

PROM—(1) premature rupture of membranes or (2) passive range of motion

Prop—proprioception

Prophy—prophylaxis

pro time—prothrombin time

prot—protein

prox—proximal

PS—(1) pulmonary stenosis, (2) psoriasis, or (3) pyriform sinus

P & S—patch and shield

PSH—past surgical history

PSIS—posterosuperior iliac spine

PSM—peripheral speech mechanism

PSP—(1) phenolsulfonphthalein test or (2) progressive supranuclear palsy

PSRO—professional standards review organization

PSS—progressive systemic sclerosis (scleroderma)

Psych—(1) psychiatric or (2) psychology

Psycholdx—psychodiagnostic testing

PT—(1) physical therapy, (2) psychotherapy, (3) prothrombin time, or (4) posttibial

pt—patient

Pt. ed—patient education

PTA—prior to admission

P'tase—phosphatase

PTB—patellar tendon-bearing

PTB pros—patellar tendon-bearing prosthesis

PTH—parathyroid hormone

PTS—patients

PTSD—posttraumatic stress disorder

PTT—partial thromboplastin time

PTX—pneumothorax

PU—peptic ulcer

PUD—peptic ulcer disease

Pulm. A—pulmonary artery

PUO—pyrexia of unknown origin

P.V.—per vagina

PVB—premature ventricular beats

PVC—(1) premature ventricular contraction or (2) pulmonary vascular congestion

PVCO$_2$—venous carbon dioxide tension

PVD—peripheral vascular disease

PVL—periventricular leukomalacia

PVO$_2$—venous oxygen tension

PVP—peripheral venous pressure

PVR—postvoiding residual

Pvt.—private

PW—posterior wall

PWB—partial weight-bearing

PWMI—posterior wall myocardial infarction

PWP—pulmonary wedge pressure

Px—(1) prognosis or (2) physical

PZI—protamine zinc insulin

P^{32}—radioactive phosphorus

q—(1) every or each or (2) daily

qam—every morning

qc—quad cane

qd—every day

qgh—every hour

qh—every hour

q__h—every ____ hours

qhs—every bedtime

qid—four times daily

qiw—four times a week

ql—as much as desired

qn—every night

qns—quantity not sufficient

qod—every other day

qs—quantity sufficient

q/s—every shift

qt—quart

quad—(1) quadriplegic or (2) quadriparesis

quads—quadriceps

quant—quantitative, quantity

qv—as much as you please

q__w—every ____ weeks

qw—once a week

R—(1) respiration, (2) right, (3) resistant, or (4) Roentgen

RA—(1) rheumatoid arthritis, (2) right atrium, or (3) room air

Ra—radium

rad—unit measure of absorbed dose of ionizing radiation

RAE—right atrial enlargement

RAH—right atrial hypertrophy

RAI—radioactive iodine uptake

RAM—rapid alternating movements

RAN—resident's admission note

RAO—right anterior oblique

RAP—right atrial pressure

RATx—radiation therapy

RBBB—right bundle branch block

RBC—(1) red blood cell or (2) red blood count

rbc—red blood cell

RBD—right border dullness

RBE—(1) relative biological effects or (2) relative biological effectiveness

RBN—retrobulbar neuritis

RC—recheck

RCA—right coronary artery

RCM—right costal margin

RCS—reticulum cell sarcoma

RCT—root canal therapy

RD—(1) reaction of degeneration, (2) registered dietitian, or (3) retinal detachment

RDEA—right deviation of electrical axis

RDS—respiratory distress syndrome

RDU—renal dialysis unit

RE—(1) right extremities or (2) regional enteritis

REB—red blood cells

rect.—rectally

ref—referred (to)

reg—regular

rehab.—rehabilitation

Rehab. Med—rehabilitation medicine

REM—rapid eye movements

rep—repeat

repre—reprepare

rept—repeat

req.—require

RES—reticuloendothelial system

RESP—respirations

ret—return

retic—reticulocytes

RF—rheumatic fever

RFA—right frontoanterior

RFL—right frontal lobe (brain)

RFP—right frontoposterior

RFT — right frontotransverse

Rh — rhesus blood factor

Rh (−) — rhesus factor negative

Rh (+) — rhesus factor positive

RHC — right hemicolectomy

RHD — rheumatic heart disease

RHF — right heart failure

Rhm. A — rheumatoid arthritis

RH. Neg. — rhesus negative

RHT — right hypertrophia

RI — radioisotope

RIA — radioimmunoassay

RICU — respiratory intensive care unit

RIF — right iliac fossa

RIH — right inguinal hernia

rIFN — recombinant interferon

RISH — radioiodinated serum albumin

RLE — right lower extremity

RLG — right lateral gaze

RLL — right lower lobe (lung)

RLN — recurrent laryngeal nerve

RLQ — right lower quadrant

RM — rupture of membranes

RMG — reflexmyography

RML — right middle lobe (lung)

RMS — rehabilitative medicine service

RMT — retromolar trigone

Rn — radon

RNA — ribonucleic acid

RND — radical neck dissection

RNP — registered nurse permit

R/O — rule out

r/o — renewal order

ROA — right occipioanterior

ROM — range of motion

ROP — right occipitoposterior

Ror — Rorschach test

ROS — review of systems

ROT — right occipitotransverse

RP — retrograde pyelogram

R.P.A. — registered physician's assistant

RPF — renal plasma flow

RPR — rapid plasma reagin

RPS — resistance of passive stretch

RQ — respiratory quotient

RR — (1) recovery room or (2) respiratory rate

RRE — round, regular, and equal

RSA — right sacroanterior

RSO — right salpingo-oophorectomy

RSR — regular sinus rhythm

RST — right sacrotransverse

RT — (1) radiation therapy or (2) recreational therapist

Rt — right

RTA — renal tubular acidosis

RTC — (1) return to clinic or (2) residential treatment center

RTOG — radiation therapy and oncology group

RUE — right upper extremity

RUL — right upper lobe (lung)

RUQ — right upper quadrant

RV — (1) right ventricle, (2) right ventricular, or (3) rectovaginal

RVE — right ventricular enlargement

RVH — right ventricular hypertrophy

RVO — relaxed vaginal outlet

Rx — (1) treatment or (2) prescription

Rx plan — treatment plan

Rx'd — treated

S — (1) sacral, (2) subjective (SOAP), (3) sensitive, or (4) esophoria

s — without

S. gl — without corrective glasses

S1, S2, S3, — first, second, third heart sounds

SA — sinoatrial

S-A — sinoatrial (node)

S & A — sugar and acetone

SACH — solid ankle cushion heels

SAD — (1) sugar, acetone, and diacetic acid or (2) sugar acetone determination

SAH — subarachnoid hemorrhage

SAR — surgical assistant resident

SAT — Stanford-Binet test

sat — saturation

SB — (1) sinus bradycardia, (2) Stanford-Binet test, (3) still born, or (4) small bowel

S.B. — scleral buckle

SBD — straight bag drainage

SBE — subacute bacterial endocarditis

SBO — small bowel obstruction

SBS — small bowel series

SC — (1) subcutaneous or (2) supracondylar

S.C. — subcutaneous

SC disease — sickle-cell disease

SCC — squamous cell carcinoma

SCCA — squamous cell carcinoma

SCFE — slipped capital femoral epiphysis

Schiz. — schizophrenic

SCI — spinal cord injury

SCIV — subclavian intravenous

SCM — sternocleidomastoid muscle

SCP — sickle-cell preparation

SD — (1) straight drainage or (2) shoulder dislocation

SDH — subdural hematoma

SDP — single-donor plasma

sec — second (s)

sed rate — sedimentation rate

SEER — surveillance, epidemiology, and end results

SEM — systolic ejection murmur

SEMI — subendocardial myocardial infarction

SEP — (1) somatosensory-evoked potential or (2) serum electrophoresis

sep — separated

Sept — septum

SEWHO — shoulder-elbow-wrist-hand orthosis

SG — (1) specific gravity or (2) Swan-Ganz

S-G — Swan-Ganz

SGA — small for gestational age

SGOT — serum glutamic-oxaloacetic transaminase

SGPT — serum glutamate pyruvate transaminase

SH — (1) social history or (2) serum hepatitis

shold — shoulder

SHx — social history

SI — (1) suicidal ideations, (2) seriously ill, or (3) sacroiliac

si/sx — signs/symptoms

SIADH — syndrome of inappropriate antidiuretic hormone

sibs — siblings

SICU — surgical intensive care unit

SIDS — sudden infant death syndrome

SIF — sensory integrative functions

sig — label

SIL — seriously ill list

SIO — Sacroiliac orthosis

Sis — sister

SK — streptokinase

sk — skull

SL — sublingual

S.L. — serious list

S/L — (1) sublingual or (2) split lamp

sl. — (1) slightly or (2) sublingual

sl bd — sliding board

SLB — short-leg brace

SLD—serum lactic acid dehydrogenase

SLE—systemic lupus erythematosus

SLN—superior laryngeal nerve

SLO—short-leg orthosis

SLR—straight leg raising

SMA—Sequential Multiple Analyzer

SMAG—electrolytes, bun, glucose, and FBS (fasting blood sugar)

SMAS—submusculoaponeurotic system

SMBFT—small bowel follow through

SMD—senile macula degeneration

SMF—submandibular fistula

SMR—submucous resection

SN—(1) superior nasal or (2) sensorineural

S.N.—student nurse

SNF—skilled nursing facility

SNHL—sensorineural hearing loss

SNR—septonasal reconstruction

SNS—sympathetic nervous system

SNT—soft, nontender

S.O.—superior oblique

S/O—standing order

SO₄—sulfate

SOAA—signed out against advice

SOAP—subjective, objective, assessment, and plan

SOB—shortness of breath

Soc. Hx—social history

Soc. Net—social network

SOD—surgical officer of the day

sol—solution

solv—dissolve

SOM—serous otitis media

SOMA—signed out against medical advice

SONO—sonogram

SOS—only if necessary (si opus sit)

SP—(1) suicide precaution or (2) supracondylar

S/P—status post

Sp—spirits

S.P. Alb.—salt-poor albumin

Sp. fl—spinal fluid

Sp gr—specific gravity

spa—salt-poor albumin

spec—specimen

SPECT—single photon emission computed tomography

SPEP—serum protein electrophoresis

sp. quad—spastic quadriplegic

sph—spherical

SPONT—spontaneous

SPT—stand and pivot transfer

SQ—subcutaneous

sq—square

sq. cell—squamous cell

SR—(1) suture removal, (2) system review, or (3) sedimentation rate

SRN—subretinal revascularization

SRO—single room occupancy

SROM—spontaneous rupture of membrane

SRT—speech reception threshold

SS—(1) soapsuds or (2) social security

ss—one-half

SS enema—soapsuds enema

SSA—Social Security Administration

SSC—(1) sign, symptom complex or (2) stainless steel crown

SSD—Social Security disability

SSDI—Social Security disability insurance

SSE—soapsuds enema

SS lig—sacrospinal ligaments

SSEP—somatosensory-evoked potential

SSI—supplemental security income

SSKI—saturated solution potassium iodine

SSP—short sitting posture

SSS—sick sinus syndrome

sss—layer upon layer

SSV—under a poison label

ST—(1) sinus tachycardia, (2) let it stand, (3) speech therapy, or (4) esotropia distance (near)

st—stage (as a disease)

St cane—standard cane

Staph—staphylococcus

Stat—at once

STD—(1) skin test dose or (2) sexually transmitted disease

std—standard

Stereog.—stereognosis

STH—somatotropic hormone

still b.—stillborn

STM—short-term memory

STNR—symmetrical tonic neck reflex

str.—strength

strep—streptococcus

STS—serologic test for syphilis

STSG—split thickness skin graft

Subcu—subcutaneous

Sublin—sublingual

Subopt—suboptimal

Subq—subcutanous

SUI—stress urinary incontinence

sup—superior

super—supervisor

Supp—suppository

Suppos—suppository

Surf—surface

Surg—surgical

Susp—suspension

SV—stroke volume

SVC—superior vena cava

SVD—(1) single vessel disease or (2) spontaneous vaginal delivery

SVT—supraventricular tachycardia

SWD—shortwave diathermy

SX—symptoms

SX:—surgery

Sympat—sympathetic

Sympt—symptom

SYN—synergy

Syph—syphilology

Syr—syrup

Syst—systolic

Sz—schizophrenic

SzD—seizure disorder

T—(1) temperature, (2) trace, or (3) ocular tension

T1, T2, etc.—thoracic (spine)

T$_3$—triiodothyronine

T$_4$—thyroxine

T & A—tonsillectomy and adenoidectomy

T & C—blood type and cross match

T of F—tetralogy of Fallot

Tab—tablet

Tact. Halluc—tactile hallucinations

TAH—total abdominal hysterectomy

TAL—tendon Achilles lengthening

TAPPL—tonometry applanation

TAT—(1) tetanus antitoxin or (2) thematic apperception test

TB—tuberculosis

TBC—tuberculosis

TBI—(1) thyroid-bound iodine, (2) total body irrigation, or (3) traumatic brain injury

TBLC—term birth living child

TBSB—total body surface burn

TC—therapeutic community

TCN—tetracycline

TD—tardive dyskinesia

TDT—tone decay test

T.E.—tracheoesophageal

TEF—tracheoesophageal fistula

temp—temperature

temp A—temperature by axilla

temp M—temperature by mouth

temp R—temperature by rectum

TENS—transcutaneous nerve stimulation

TEP—tracheoesophageal puncture

TER—transurethral electrosection

TF—tube feeding

THA—total hip arthroplasty

Ther—therapeutic

THIO—thioglycollate blood culture bottles

THR—total hip replacement

TI—tricuspid insufficiency

TIA—transient ischemic attack

TIBC—total iron-binding capacity

tid—three times daily

tin—three times a night

tinc—tincture

tinct—tincture

TIUP—term intrauterine pregnancy

TIUV—total intrauterine volume

tiw—three times a week

TJ—triceps jerk (reflex)

TKA—(1) trochanter-knee-ankle or (2) total knee arthroplasty

TKO—to keep open

TKR—total knee replacement

TL—(1) tubal ligation or (2) total laryngectomy

TLA—translumbar aortogram

TLC—total lung capacity

TLE—temporal lobe epilepsy

TLSO—thoracic-lumbosacral orthosis

TM—tympanic membrane

TMJ—temporal mandibular joint

TN—tension

TNF—tumor necrosis factor

TNM—tumor, node, metastasis (tumor classification)

TNS—transcutaneous nerve stimulation

TNTC—too numerous to count

TO—(1) tubo-ovarian or (2) telephone order

T/O—telephone order

TOA—(1) tubo-ovarian abscess or (2) thrombangiitis obliterans

TOAA—to affected areas

TOD—tension right eye

tol—tolerated

tomo—tomography

TOP—termination of pregnancy

top—topically

TOS—tension left eye

TP—(1) total protein, (2) trigger point, or (3) term pregnancy

T & P—turn and position

TP-ALB—total protein/albumin

TPC—total proctocolectomy

TPI—(1) trigger point injection or (2) Treponema pallidum immobilization test

TPN—total parenteral nutrition

TPR—temperature, pulse, and respiration

TPUR—transperineal urethral resection

Tr—tincture

tr—therapeutic recreation

trac—tracheostomy

TRAM flap—transverse rectus abdominis musculocutaneous

trans—(1) transverse or (2) transferred

TRB—transrectal biopsy

TRH—thyrotropin releasing hormone

trich—trichomonas

trigly—triglycerides

TS—tricuspid stenosis

TSB—trypticase soy broth blood culture

TSF—triceps skinfold

TSH—thyroid-stimulating hormone

TSNA—tobacco-specific nitrosamines

TSP—thoracic spine

TSR—total shoulder replacement

TT—(1) thymol turbidity, (2) thrombin time, or (3) tilt table

TTN—transient tachypnea of newborn

TTP—thrombotic thrombocytopenic purpura

TUR—transurethral resection

TURB—transurethral resection of bladder

TURP—transurethral resection of prostate

TV—tidal volume

TVC—true vocal cords

TVD—triple volume

TVR—tricuspid valve replacement

TWE—tap water enema

Tx—(1) treatment, (2) therapy, or (3) transfusion

tx—traction

Tymp—tympanic

U—unit

UA—urinalysis

U/A—urinalysis

UAC—umbilical arterial catheter

UBD—upper body dressing

UC—(1) uterine contractions or (2) ulcerative colitis

UCD—usual childhood diseases

UCG—urinary chorionic gonadotropin

UCHD—usual childhood diseases

UD—(1) as directed or (2) urethral discharge

UE—upper extremity

UFN—until further notice

UG—upward gaze

UGI—upper gastrointestinal

UGIS—upper gastrointestinal series

U/L—upper lid

ULOS—upper limb orthosis system

Umb—umbilicus

UMN—upper motor neuron

Undiff—undifferentiated

Unemp—unemployed

ung—ointment

UNK—unknown

uo—urinary output

UP Junt—ureteropelvic junction

UPJ—ureteropelvic junction

URI—upper respiratory infection

URO—urology

urol—urological

US—ultrasound

u/s—ultrasound

USI—urinary stress incontinence

USN—ultrasonic nebulization

USO—unilateral salpingo-oophorectomy

USOH—usual state of health

USP—United States Pharmacopeia

Ut—uterus

Ut dict—as directed

UTI—urinary tract infection

UV—ultraviolet

UVC—umbilical venous

UVJ—ureterovesical junction

UVL—ultraviolet light

V—(1) vision or (2) volt

V tach—ventricular tachycardia

Va—visual acuity

VA—(1) visual acuity or (2) Veterans Administration

V-A—ventriculoatrial (shunt)

vag—vagina

VASC—vascular

VBI—vertebral basilar insufficiency

VC—(1) vital capacity, (2) verbal cues, or (3) vocal cord

vc—vital capacity

VCG—vectorcardiogram

VCT—venous clotting time

VCU—voiding cystourethrogram

VD—venereal disease

VdB—van den Bergh test

VDRL—Venereal Disease Research Laboratories

VEP—visual evoked potential

VER—visual evoked response

Vest—vestibular

VF—(1) ventricular fibrillation or (2) visual field

VH—(1) video hysteroscopy or (2) vaginal hysterectomy

VHD—ventricular heart disease

VIN—vulvar intraepithelial neoplasia

Vis—visual

Vis. Halluc.—visual hallucination

vit—vitamin

viz—namely

VLL—videolaser laparoscopy

VN—visiting nurse

VNA—Visiting Nurse Association

VNS—visiting nurse service

VO—verbal order

V/O—verbal order

Voc. Hx—vocational history

VOD—veno-occlusive disease

Vol—(1) volume or (2) voluntary

VP—venous pressure

V-P—ventriculoperitoneal (shunt)

VPB—ventricular premature beat

VPC—ventricular premature contraction

VPS—ventricular premature systole

VR—vocal resonance

VS—vital signs

vs—visited

VSD—ventricular septal defect

VSS—vital signs stable

VT—ventricular tachycardia

V & T—volume and tension

Vt—tidal volume

Vtx—vertex

VW—vessel wall

VxP—vertex presentation

W—(1) wife, (2) widowed, or (3) watt

w/—with

W.A.—ward activities

W & A—wrist and ankle

WAIS—Wechsler Adult Intelligence Test

WAIS-R—Wechsler Adult Intelligence Test Revised

WAP—wandering atrial pacemaker

Wass—Wassermann test

WB—(1) whole blood or (2) weight-bearing

W/B—weight-bearing

WBC—(1) white blood cell or (2) white blood count

wbc—white blood cell

WC—wheelchair

W/C—wheelchair

WD—(1) well-developed, (2) wet dressing, or (3) Wilson's disease

WDWN—well-developed, well-nourished

WF—white female

W.F.—welfare board

WFL—within functional limits

WHO—(1) wrist-hand orthosis or (2) World Health Organization

WISC—Wechsler Intelligence Scale for Children

WISC-R—Wechsler Intelligence Scale for Children Revised

wk—week

WL—wavelength

WM—white male

WN—well-nourished

wn—well-nourished

WNL—within normal limits

WO—wrist orthosis

w/o—without

WP—whirlpool

WPW—Wolff-Parkinson-White syndrome

WR—Wasserman reaction

WS—weight shift

wt—weight

w/u—workup

w/v—weight by volume

X—(1) times or (2) exophoria distance

XM—cross match

X-match—cross match

XO—exodontia

XP—xeroderma pigmentosum

X-R—x-ray

XRT—radiation therapy

XT—exotropia

X3—oriented to time, person, and place

XX—female sex chromosomes

XY—male sex chromosomes

Y—yttrium

YO—years old

yr—year

Z—(1) contraction or (2) impedance

ZE syndrome—Zollinger-Ellison syndrome

ZN—zinc

Z-plasty—surgical relaxation of contraction

Index

A

Abbreviations, 146, 343–376
Abscesses, *see also* specific types
  intracranial, 108
  peritonsillar, 110
Abstract language comprehension, 231
Abstract thinking, 236
Accountability
  program, 293–320
  staff, 312–317
Achalasia, 123
Acquired immunodeficiency syndrome
  (AIDS), 11, 14, 109, 110
  terminology in, 343
Activities of daily living (ADL), 18, 37
Acute anxiety, 88
Acute care services, 3, 5, *see also*
  Specific types defined, 5
Acute depression, 90
Acute encephalopathy, 106
Acute epiglottitis, 110
Acute laryngitis, 110
Acute pain, 90
Acute polymyositis, 109
Acute postinfectious polyneuropathy
  (Guillain-Barre syndrome), 91, 93, 110
ADL, *see* Activities of daily living

Adventitious movements, 195
Aerodigestive tract infection, 110
Affective disorders, 88, *see also* specific
  types
Ageusia, 91
Aging, 208, *see also* Geriatrics
  communication and, 85–86
  skeletal changes and, 116
AIDS, *see* Acquired immunodeficiency
  syndrome
AIDS related complex (ARC), 11
Alcohol, 111, 112–114
Alcoholism, 89, 90, 114, 122, 227
Allied health, 19–20, 21, 222
ALS, *see* Amyotrophic lateral sclerosis
Alzheimer's disease, 89, 97
Amyloidosis, 118
Amyotrophic lateral sclerosis, 24, 93,
  94, 218, 277
Anabolic disease, 102, *see also* specific
  types
Analgesics, 90, *see also* specific types
Anarthria, 111
Anesthesiology, 19
Aneurysms, 98
Angina, 110
Animal–naming section of *Assessment
  of Aphasia and Related Disorders*, 231

About the Authors

Robert M. Miller is Chief, Audiology and Speech Pathology Service, at the VA Medical Center, Seattle, Washington. He is consultant to the Neuromuscular Clinic for Swallowing and Speech Disorders at University of Washington Medical Center and holds clinical faculty appointments in several departments at the University of Washington and Seattle University. He is on the Editorial Advisory Board for the journal *Dysphagia*. Dr. Miller has published extensively in general medical journals and medical textbooks and has described and emphasized the role of speech/language pathology in medicine. Dr. Miller received his bachelor's and master's degrees from the University of Redlands and his Ph.D. from the University of Washington.

Michael E. Groher is the Assistant Chief of Audiology and Speech Pathology at the VA Medical Center in New York City. In this capacity his responsibilities include supervising the clinical activities in speech pathology and directing the student intern program. Dr. Groher has numerous publications in the field of neurogenic communication and swallowing disorders. He has edited a book about patients with swallowing disability, *Dysphagia: Diagnosis and Management*. Currently he is an associate editor for the journal *Dysphagia* and an editorial board member for the journal *Topics in Geriatric Rehabilitation*. Dr. Groher is a professional associate in the Department of Rehabilitation Medicine at The New York Hospital and holds adjunct teaching appointments at Adelphi University and Hunter College. Dr. Groher received his bachelor's and master's degrees from the University of Redlands in California and his Ph.D. from the University of Washington.